Borders and the Politics of Space in Late Medieval Italy

OXFORD HISTORICAL MONOGRAPHS

The *Oxford Historical Monographs* series publishes some of the best
Oxford University doctoral theses on historical topics, especially
those likely to engage the interest of a broad academic readership.

Editors

P. BETTS   F. DEVJI   P. GAUCI
K. LEBOW   J. McDOUGALL
R. REID   D. PARROTT   H. SKODA
J. SMITH   W. WHYTE

Borders and the Politics of Space in Late Medieval Italy

Milan, Venice, and their Territories

LUCA ZENOBI

Great Clarendon Street, Oxford, OX2 6DP,
United Kingdom

Oxford University Press is a department of the University of Oxford.
It furthers the University's objective of excellence in research, scholarship,
and education by publishing worldwide. Oxford is a registered trade mark of
Oxford University Press in the UK and in certain other countries

© Luca Zenobi 2023

The moral rights of the author have been asserted

All rights reserved. No part of this publication may be reproduced, stored in
a retrieval system, or transmitted, in any form or by any means, without the
prior permission in writing of Oxford University Press, or as expressly permitted
by law, by licence or under terms agreed with the appropriate reprographics
rights organization. Enquiries concerning reproduction outside the scope of the
above should be sent to the Rights Department, Oxford University Press, at the
address above

You must not circulate this work in any other form
and you must impose this same condition on any acquirer

Published in the United States of America by Oxford University Press
198 Madison Avenue, New York, NY 10016, United States of America

British Library Cataloguing in Publication Data
Data available

Library of Congress Control Number: 2023932556

ISBN 978-0-19-887686-1

DOI: 10.1093/oso/9780198876861.001.0001

Printed and bound in the UK by
Clays Ltd, Elcograf S.p.A.

Links to third party websites are provided by Oxford in good faith and
for information only. Oxford disclaims any responsibility for the materials
contained in any third party website referenced in this work.

Acknowledgements

The seeds of this project were sown in a bunker. At my alma mater, the University of Milan, that is what students affectionally call the meandering series of underground rooms housing the History Library. It is there that I laid much of the groundwork which led to this book. For that I must thank Andrea Gamberini, without whose guidance this project would never have materialized. It was also there, in that same bunker, that I met a great many colleagues and friends from whose knowledge and generosity I have benefited greatly over the years. I am especially indebted to Michele Baitieri, Fabrizio Costantini, and Stefano Locatelli.

As I developed the project, I accumulated more and more debts, which I am pleased to be able to acknowledge here. For sharing their insights on various chapters, I thank Stephen Bowd, Nadia Covini, Filippo de Vivo, Serena Ferente, Marcus Meer, Hitomi Sato, and Rosa Salzberg. For their friendship and many inspiring conversations, I thank Rachel Delman, Michael Depreter, Daniele Dibello, Parwana Fayyaz, Giacomo Giudici, Thomas Goodwin, and Pablo Gonzalez Martin. For their mentorship and countless acts of academic kindness, I thank David Abulafia, Nicholas Davidson, Isabella Lazzarini, Brian Maxson, David Parrott, Alex Walsham, and John Watts. For helping me shape the text and its images into their final form, I thank Suzie Maine and Alice Zenobi.

Still, my debts are not just academic. My parents have been a constant source of encouragement and wholehearted support. Without knowing much about academia or history writing, they offered me many words of wisdom; and without much knowledge of English, they were able to improve my prose in many unexpected ways. This book is dedicated to them, with all my gratitude.

Contents

List of Figures	ix
List of Abbreviations	xi
Note on Usage	xiii

Introduction	1
Borders	2
The Politics of Space	7
Milan, Venice, and their Territories	12

1. *Iurisdictio* in Practice: Cultures of Space, Borders, and Power	23
The Theory of Territorial Pluralism	25
Urban Communes and their *Contadi*	29
Regional States and their Dominions	32
The Rise of Intermediate Entities	38

2. War and Peace: The Establishment of a New Political Geography	45
Mediation and Jurisdiction in the Treaty of Ferrara	50
Geopolitics and Scale in the Peace of Lodi	56
Trading Territories, Shifting Borders	61

3. *Confinium Compositio*: Territorial Disputes and the Making of Borders	68
Who Broke the Treaty?	69
The Limits of Factional Allegiance	79
Mapping the Negotiations	87

4. From Macro to Micro and Back Again: Constructing Borders in the Localities	98
Collective Action and Space Appropriation	100
Empowering Interactions and Border-Making	109

5. Borders as Sites of Mobility: Crossing External Frontiers and Internal Boundaries	124
Negotiating Movement in Times of War	126
Trading across Borders in Times of Peace	139

viii CONTENTS

6. Committing Borders to Paper:
Written Memory and Record-Keeping   158

At the Centre   162
In the Peripheries   171
On the Move   176

7. Drawing the Line?
The Visual Representation of Territorial B/orders   181

From District Maps to Imagined Territories   186
The Lion, the Viper, and the Border   200

Conclusion   213

Borders   213
The Politics of Space   215
Milan, Venice, and their Territories   216

Bibliography   219
General Index   261
Index of Names   263

List of Figures

1. 'L'Italia dei comuni', as depicted in a recent publication on medieval Italy: Wickham, *Sleepwalking into a New World*, 3. Reproduced with permission from Princeton University Press   13

2. 'L'Italia degli stati territoriali', as depicted in a recent publication on Renaissance Italy: Gamberini and Lazzarini, *The Italian Renaissance State*, xiv. Reproduced with permission from Cambridge University Press   14

3. The Visconti dominion envisioned as a 'catalogue of cities' in a manuscript illumination from the mid-fourteenth century (BNFr, ms. Latin 6467, c. 1r). © Gallica.bnf.fr   39

4. List of contested localities from the Milanese Chancery (ASMi, *Carteggio* 1525, s.d.). Reproduced with permission from the Italian Ministry of Cultural Heritage   60

5. Satellite view of the disputed valleys in their wider context. © DigitalGlobe   74

6. Satellite view of the disputed valleys between Bergamo and Lecco. © DigitalGlobe   75

7. Guelph and Ghibelline communities in the Bergamasco, respectively in light and dark grey. © Provincia di Bergamo   84

8. Guelph and Ghibelline villages in the Val Taleggio, respectively in light and dark grey. © DigitalGlobe   88

9. Fifteenth-century sketch of the Val Taleggio and the surrounding valleys (ASMi, *Confini* 290). Reproduced with permission from the Italian Ministry of Cultural Heritage   91

10. Satellite view of the area and place names included in the sketch of the Val Taleggio. © DigitalGlobe   92

11. An illustration from Bertrand Boysset's fifteenth-century copy of the *Traité d'Arpentage* by Arnaud de Villeneuve (1240–1315) showing people at work by boundary markers (BICa, ms. 327, c. 157v). © Irht.cnrs.fr   110

12. The last page from the fragment of the *Liber Albus* (ASMi, *Frammenti* 1, f. 15, c. 24v), including a transcription of the duke's

X LIST OF FIGURES

own signature at the end. Reproduced with permission from the Italian Ministry of Cultural Heritage   148

13. Temporal distribution of the licences of the *Liber Albus* (July 1454–March 1455). The light-coloured bars represent the portion of licences granted to legal representatives rather than to the person nominally applying for them. © Luca Zenobi   149

14. Area covered by the *Liber Albus*, shown in Figure 15 in greater detail. © Luca Zenobi   152

15. Origins and destinations of the itineraries of the *Liber Albus*. The dotted line distinguishes the two polities' spheres of influence. © Luca Zenobi   153

16. Network of food trade in fifteenth-century Lombardy, based on data extracted from the *Liber Albus*. © Luca Zenobi   156

17. First map of the Bresciano (ASBr, *Archivio storico comunale* 434/2). Reproduced with permission from the Italian Ministry of Cultural Heritage   188

18. Second map of the Bresciano, including a detail of the city of Brescia and the motto 'Brixia magnipotens' (BEMo, *Carte geografiche* A 8). © edl.beniculturali.it   191

19. Third map of the Bresciano (BQBr, ms. H V 5). © Biblioteca Queriniana   194

20. One of the illuminations of the manuscript to which the third map of the Bresciano is attached (BQBr, ms. H V 5, c. 64v), showing the lords of the Bresciano plucking the winged lion of Venice. © Biblioteca Queriniana   195

21. The Trompia and Sabbia valleys in a fifteenth-century map of Lombardy (BNFr, *Cartes et plans* Ge C 4090). © Images.bnf.fr   198

22. Fifteenth-century map of the road system near Reggio (ASRe). Reproduced with permission from the Italian Ministry of Cultural Heritage   199

23. The so-called map of Lombardy by Giovanni Pisato, including a detail of various territorial markers (BCTv, ms. 1497). © Biblioteca comunale di Treviso   205

24. Map of Crema and the Cremasco showing the thin red line as well as localities with the Visconti viper painted on their walls (MCVe, *Cartografia* 35). © Fondazione Musei Civici di Venezia   208

25. Close-up of the sketch of the Val Taleggio and the surrounding valleys showing border stones painted on the lines marking the contours of local bodies (ASMi, Confini 290). Reproduced with permission from the Italian Ministry of Cultural Heritage   210

List of Abbreviations

ASBg	Archivio di Stato, Bergamo
ASBr	Archivio di Stato, Brescia
ASCr	Archivio di Stato, Cremona
ASMi	Archivio di Stato, Milano

Carteggio	*Archivio visconteo-sforzesco, Carteggio sforzesco*
Comuni	*Archivio diplomatico, Fondo comuni*
Confini	*Atti di governo, Confini parte antica*
Esenzioni	*Atti di governo, Esenzioni*
Frammenti	*Archivio visconteo-sforzesco, Frammenti di registri*
Missive	*Archivio visconteo-sforzesco, Registri delle missive*
Registri	*Archivio visconteo-sforzesco, Registri ducali*

ASRe	Archivio di Stato, Reggio Emilia
ASVe	Archivio di Stato, Venezia

Miscellanea	*Secreta, Miscellanea atti diplomatici e privati*

BAMi	Biblioteca Ambrosiana, Milano
BAVa	Biblioteca Apostolica Vaticana, Roma
BBMi	Biblioteca Nazionale Braidense, Milano
BCCr	Biblioteca Comunale, Crema

Annona	*Archivio storico comunale, Documenti cartacei—Annona*
Ducali	*Archivio storico comunale, Ducali dell'ufficio della città*
Finanza	*Archivio storico comunale, Documenti cartacei—Finanza*
Provisioni	*Archivio storico comunale, Provisioni e parti della comunità*

BCTv	Biblioteca Comunale, Treviso
BEMo	Biblioteca Universitaria Estense, Modena
BICa	Bibliothèque Municipale de l'Inguimbertine, Carpentras
BMBg	Biblioteca Civica Angelo Mai, Bergamo

Confini	*Archivio della camera dei confini*
Municipali	*Archivio storico comunale, Registri di ducali municipali*

BMVe	Biblioteca Nazionale Marciana, Venezia

It.	*Manoscritti italiani*

BNFr	Bibliothèque Nationale de France, Paris

xii LIST OF ABBREVIATIONS

BQBr	Biblioteca Civica Queriniana, Brescia
BSCr	Biblioteca Statale, Cremona
BTMi	Biblioteca Civica Trivulziana, Milano
MCVe	Museo Correr, Venezia

c./cc.	*carta/cartae*
col./cols.	column/columns
ed.	edited
f./fs.	folder/folders
ms.	manuscript
no./nos.	number/numbers
r.	*recto*
s.d.	*sine die*
s.v.	*sub voce*
trans.	translated
v.	*verso*
vol./vols.	volume/volumes

Note on Usage

In both the footnotes and the main body of the text, all dates have been adjusted to the modern calendar. This is especially important for records made in Venice, where the year began on 1 March; hence, 14 February 1454 *more veneto*, for example, is rendered as 14 February 1455.

All translations from primary and secondary sources are the author's. When a source is cited in English in the body of the text, a transcript in the original language is offered in the footnotes. On several occasions, a paraphrased excerpt has been provided instead of a word-for-word translation. When the precise wording is significant, this has been included between round brackets. The spelling used in the original records has generally been retained; however, punctuation and word separation have been modernized. For ease of reading, the presence of contractions in any source has not been marked.

Place names are given in their modern Italian form (e.g. Rivolta d'Adda, not Ripalta). When available, standard English translations have been adopted (e.g. Mantua, not Mantova). Similarly, personal names are presented in modern Italian spelling rather than in the original language (e.g. Giacomo, not Jacobus or Iacomo). As with place names, where anglicized translations exist, these have been adopted (e.g. pope Martin V, not Martinus V or Martino V). Where anglophone usage calls for Latin over Italian, and vice versa, this has been followed (e.g. Bartolus of Sassoferrato, not Bartolo da Sassoferrato).

Unless otherwise stated, all references are to page numbers. They are given in full in the bibliography, but only in abbreviated form in the footnotes.

Introduction

This book is about medieval borders, about the cultures and interactions by which they were shaped (the Politics of Space), and about the political communities which they bounded (Milan, Venice, and their Territories). It centres on the fifteenth century and on the making of a new frontier between two major Italian states: the Duchy of Milan and the Republic of Venice. Following decades of war, this process paved the way for a revival of economic and cultural connections across the region, and for the establishment of a political geography which was to remain virtually unchanged for over three centuries. The book looks to achieve three goals: to challenge the idea that medieval borders were necessarily porous and ill-defined, to provide a new framework to understand pre-modern modalities of territorial control, and to offer a novel interpretation of Italian states.

The topic of borders intersects with several realms of political and social life, including the development of legitimizing theories by contemporary thinkers (Chapter 1), the practice of diplomacy and conflict resolution (Chapter 2), the relations between centres of government and peripheral bodies (Chapter 3), the life and contribution of local communities (Chapter 4), the circulation of people and goods (Chapter 5), and the activities of record-keeping (Chapter 6) and map-making (Chapter 7). Since these will be addressed specifically in the various chapters, their relationship with the topic at hand will be discussed in their respective introductions. What follows is intended as a preliminary discussion of the three broader themes explored in the book: the nature of medieval borders, the study of pre-modern forms of territoriality, and the spatial fabric of the state in Italy.

Borders and the Politics of Space in Late Medieval Italy: Milan, Venice, and their Territories. Luca Zenobi, Oxford University Press. © Luca Zenobi 2023. DOI: 10.1093/oso/9780198876861.003.0001

Borders

Scholarship on medieval borders could be grouped into two strands.[1] Each has something to offer to this book, especially in terms of research questions. The first strand was sparked by the dissemination of the so-called frontier thesis by Frederick Jackson Turner. He challenged the preconception that borders must take the form of linear divisions between nation-states, to look instead at the American West as an open area of settlement and colonization. Turner's frontier was a zone of expansion, one in which Europeans were turned into Americans through their encounter with savagery and wilderness.[2] This paradigm was soon adopted by medievalists to reinterpret what they saw as equivalent developments, starting with the eastward expansion of European civilization at the height of the Middle Ages.[3] In the 1970s and 1980s, this was especially true of scholars such as Angus Mackay and Charles Bishko, whose research on medieval Spain was explicitly framed in frontier terms. Like Turner, they paid particular attention to the dynamics of settlement and to the unfolding of military and cultural clashes.[4] The same approach was then adopted to enable comparative investigation of other 'frontier societies' across Europe, such as the Anglo-Scottish and Anglo-Gaelic frontiers in the British Isles or the eastern German marches.[5]

These studies used borders as a lens to pin down the defining features of the societies under study, such as the intensity of military confrontation and their propensity for trade and negotiation. But as Nora Berend has convincingly argued, such traits were not unique to regions defined by frontier

---

[1] Alternative accounts can be found in the recent Peters, 'Omnia permixta sunt'; and Janeczek, 'Frontiers and Borderlands in Medieval Europe'.

[2] Turner, *The Frontier in American History*. Over the years, this interpretation has been variously challenged by scholars of early American history, starting with Billington, *American Frontier Thesis*. It is now more common to frame the American frontier as an area of interactions between Europeans and Native Americans, rather than as a framework for the relentless expansion of the former against the latter, as exemplified by Clayton and Teute, *Contact Points*.

[3] Thompson, 'Profitable Fields of Investigation'; Lewis, 'The Closing of the Mediaeval Frontier'.

[4] MacKay, *Spain in the Middle Ages*; Bishko, *Studies in Medieval Spanish Frontier History*. The long-term influence of this approach, as well as its drawbacks, are discussed in Torró, 'Viure del botí'; and Mantecón Movellás, 'Frontera(s) e historia(s)'.

[5] See especially the essays collected by Bartlett and MacKay, *Medieval Frontier Societies*; but examples include full-length monographs too, such as TeBrake, *Medieval Frontier: Culture and Economy in Rijnland*. Among recent publications, see especially the essay by Urban, 'The Frontier Thesis and the Baltic Crusade'; and the volume by Edwards, *Families and Frontiers*.

INTRODUCTION 3

experiences; like war, peaceful interactions were typical of the heartlands of Europe as much as of its peripheries.[6] More importantly, these studies did not investigate what frontiers themselves were actually like; they employed frontiers as a framework or focus point to study vast areas or indeed entire societies rather than as objects of inquiry in their own right.[7] This is precisely what a group of scholars, rallied in Cambridge by Berend herself in 1998, set out to do. The result was a collective volume, coedited with David Abulafia, in which scholars moved away from examining the dynamics of peace, trade, and conflict to consider instead a broader spectrum of exchanges that took place along borders.[8] The volume marked a shift from previous scholarship: it cautioned against forced comparisons and loose definitions, and brought different kind of borders, including religious and cultural frontiers, into focus.

As this first strand of research was initiated, a second strand began to emphasize an opposing perspective, that of medieval borders as linear boundaries. This was inspired by a paradigm which was just as strong and pervasive as Turner's proposition: the rise of territorial states. Having worked on charters outlining the boundaries of private properties, historians have always known that linear demarcations were already quite common in medieval Europe. Less clear, however, was—and still is—the extent to which this phenomenon applied to territorial distinctions between polities. While some framed this inquiry as a search for the antecedents of modern borders, scholars such as Bernard Guenée integrated the question of linearity into their study of the political and social structures of the time.[9] For the French kingdom, which was Guenée's frame of reference, these structures included feudal jurisdictions as much as the king's own territorial authority. He argued that as the limits of royal justice were expanded at the expense of local lordships, the boundaries of law and politics came to overlap. The establishment of linear boundaries was thus linked to administrative rights and demands, and to the transformation of

---

[6] Berend, 'Medievalists and the Notion of the Frontier'. An earlier criticism can be found in Linehan, 'Segovia: A *Frontier* Diocese'.

[7] In passing, it is worth noting that this is also the defining feature of the remarkable array of studies devoted to the frontiers of the British Isles, on which see mainly the work by Ellis, 'The English State and its Frontiers'; Ellis, 'Defending English Ground'.

[8] Berend and Abulafia, *Medieval Frontiers*.

[9] Aside from Guenée and French historiography, notable examples include the book by Karp, *Grenzen in Ostmitteleuropa*; and the essays collected by Haubrichs and Schneider, *Grenzen und Grenzregionen*.

4 BORDERS AND THE POLITICS OF SPACE IN LATE MEDIEVAL ITALY

multiple forms of power over people into a seemingly unified rulership over territories.[10] While this second strand of research has not undergone the same level of reassessment enjoyed by the frontier thesis, it has informed at least two other historiographical developments. The first is an interest in the role played by state boundaries in processes of self and group identification. Following the pioneering work of Peter Sahlins, scholars have explored the theme of borders in relation to various national histories and as a crucial factor in the interplay between local and national identities.[11] The second development is increased attention to non-European frontiers, particularly in a comparative perspective and across much larger chronological spans. Among others, a collective volume edited by Daniel Power and Naomi Standen put Eurasian frontiers firmly on the map, while also taking the time to revise some inveterate assumptions about the nature of Europe's own boundaries.[12] It is striking, however, that the scholars involved in these developments remained concerned with the same issue which already lay at the core of much of Guenée's work: to what extent were pre-modern polities able to exert control over their borders, particularly at the expense of pre-existing territorial divisions?

To this day, these two strands have largely ignored the Italian peninsula. One explanation is that Italy presented a very different scenario from that of Spain or France, a scenario to which the approaches above could not be easily extended. To start with, only some of the Italian regions could be interpreted in frontier terms. Unlike Spain, medieval Italy did not experience a formative exposure to frontier life. Although cultural exchanges and religious intermingling were very much the norm at the beginning of the Middle Ages, they became less and less integral in later centuries, when the peninsula became more and more Italian—so to speak—and more and more Christian. Exceptions remained, starting with the religious diversity of the kingdom of Sicily, not to mention the linguistic juxtapositions which

---

[10] Guenée, 'Les Limites de la France'; Guenée, 'Des limites féodales aux frontières politique'. For more on borders in medieval France, consider the early works reviewed in Schlesser, 'Frontiers in Medieval French History'; and the recent studies collected in Boissellier and Malbos, *Frontières spatiales, frontières sociales*.

[11] Sahlins, *Boundaries*. A broad but scattered inquiry into these issues was conducted more recently by different research groups within the European History Network, from which see mainly Ellis and Klusáková, *Frontiers and Identities*. Another take, combining these issues with matters of law, is offered by the highly original book by Herzog, *Frontiers of Possession*.

[12] Power and Standen, *Frontiers in Question*. Other examples include essays such as Gommans, 'The Eurasian Frontier'; and Lamouroux, 'Frontières de France, vues de Chine'.

would long underscore Adriatic frontiers.[13] Yet despite internal conflicts and ongoing tensions, much of late medieval Italy was built on the same foundations: the 'communal chromosomes', as Gian Maria Varanini famously dubbed them, that underpinned the formation of polities centred around urban centres and urban life.[14]

This is not to say that borders did not run through the peninsula, but rather that they were internal boundaries between units of the same society instead of external frontiers between two or more blocks. It follows that examining the world of borders in late medieval Italy means looking at the mechanics through which groups sharing the same set of principles and beliefs recognized forms of distinction between them. Similarly, Italy did not resemble a frontier society in the Late Middle Ages, for it did not participate as extensively as other regions of Europe in a sustained level of frontier exchanges (again, with the notable exception of Sicily and the Adriatic coast). However, that does not mean that Italian borders cannot be used as a focus point for investigating the society which shaped them. In fact, that is precisely what this work sets out to do. Drawing on the first strand of research outlined above, it seeks to answer the following questions: how were spatial distinctions envisioned, practised, and negotiated in late medieval Italy? To what extent did Italian borders reflect the distinctive features of the society to which they belonged? In short, how Italian were the borders of Italy and what can they tell us about the ways in which space was imagined, experienced, and navigated in the peninsula at this time? And finally, were Italian borders just as vast, fluid, and porous as other frontiers of the medieval world are often made out to be?

If Italian borders did not resemble Spanish frontiers, they also had little in common with those of other European contexts, starting with France. As the French monarchy asserted its claim over a large territory, the peninsula saw the establishment of a polycentric system of regional and sub-regional formations built around the expansion of either republican oligarchies or princely dynasties. The French kingdom was far from a fully integrated polity in the Late Middle Ages; forms of political organization alternative or indeed openly opposed to the monarchy existed and would continue to exist for a very long time. Yet the French king remained the only actor

---

[13] On these considerable exceptions, see at least Abulafia, *Mediterranean Encounters*; and Wolf and Herbers, *Southern Italy as Contact Area*; as well as Ivetic, *Un confine nel Mediterraneo*; and Fara, *Italia ed Europa centro-orientale*.

[14] Varanini, 'Governi principeschi e modello cittadino', 97. Along similar lines, consider also Ascheri, 'Beyond the *Comune*'; and Chittolini, '*Crisi e lunga durata*'.

6 BORDERS AND THE POLITICS OF SPACE IN LATE MEDIEVAL ITALY

capable of promoting the image—if not the actual control—of an exclusive territory. As a result, historians of France were able to frame the issue of borders around the formation of a French space, namely around the limits of France itself.[15] By contrast, scholars of Italy were presented with a very different picture. For one thing, not a single kingdom but multiple polities claimed authority over their respective territories. For another, as will be discussed at greater length in the last section of this Introduction, the degree of territoriality exhibited by these polities remains the object of much debate. Together, these issues might well explain why medievalists working on Italy have generally shied away from the topic of borders.[16]

This is not to say that scholars have failed to address the topic altogether, but rather that they have been looking at borders from perspectives other than that of statehood. One such perspective is that of the boundaries of rural society and particularly of the 'micro frontiers' between villages.[17] In this vein, borders have been studied in relation to the topography of property, the process of community formation, and the ideas of territory and possession exhibited by peasants during litigation. Unlike their French colleagues, however, scholars of Italy have largely refrained from exploring the same sort of issues on a larger scale. Little work has been devoted to studying the making of borders in relation to the topography of power, the process of polity formation, and the ideas of territory and possession exhibited by deputies during disputes. So, again, this is precisely what this work sets out to do. Building on the second strand of research into medieval borders, the book seeks to address the following issues: what did the borders of Italian states actually look like? Were polities such as the Duchy of Milan and the Republic of Venice capable of establishing the sorts of linear demarcations which supposedly bounded the kingdom of France, for example?

---

[15] In addition to the works by Guenée referenced above, consider Dauphant, *Le Royaume des Quatre Rivières*; and, for a later period, Nordman, *Frontières de France*.

[16] Partial exceptions are the short essay by Pirillo, '*Fines, termini et limites*'; and tangential treatments such as Varanini, 'Ai confini dello stato regionale'. One also ought to mention the recent volume edited by Pirillo and Tanzini, *Terre di confine tra Toscana, Romagna e Umbria*, though this is mostly a study of subjects or dynamics relevant to frontier areas (seigneurial powers, territorial disputes) and not a study of borders themselves. The gap is even more striking when compared with the literature devoted to borders and borderlands by early modernists, first as part of micro-historical investigations into peripheral communities, on which see the introduction to Chapter 4, and recently as part of a vast research project on national scale, on which see the discussions by Blanco, 'Confini e territori in età moderna'; and Raviola, 'Frontiere regionali, nazionali e storiografiche'.

[17] For the term 'micro frontier', see the short paper by Toubert, 'Frontière et frontières'. Relevant studies are discussed throughout Chapter 4. For now, see the essays collected in Guglielmotti, *Distinguere, separare, condividere*.

How precise were these demarcations and how were they controlled? And finally, to what extent did such borders overcome pre-existing territorial divisions?

The Politics of Space

Besides raising the matter of the shape and nature of borders in late medieval Italy, the section above has drawn on two research strands to formulate some fundamental questions for the book to consider: what can borders tell us about the relationships between a society and its spaces, and about the way in which people navigated the world around them? And similarly, what can we learn from borders about the polities and communities which they bounded? Although suitable lines of inquiry in their own right, these questions are also closely intertwined. What brings them together is the issue of territoriality.

Drawing on classic works of geography and political theory, territoriality could be defined as the capacity to control people, things, and relationships by controlling a delimited area. This capacity can be acquired and subsequently enhanced in many ways: by naming and classifying space, by enforcing claims of authority over it, by monitoring access to it, by (mis) representing it on maps, by establishing rights and duties in relation to it, by fostering a sense of belonging, and generally by ruling over the several domains of human activity taking place within that same arena. In essence, territoriality is a form of power; in fact, it is 'the geographical expression of power', to use Robert Sack's definition.[18] It follows that borders are but the material and symbolic markers of such power, in that they define and embody the scope of territorial control. It is in this way that borders are understood in this work: not as dividing lines or zones of contact but as instruments and expressions of human territoriality.[19] The same goes for

---

[18] Sack, *Human Territoriality*, 5; but see also the classic by Gottmann, *The Significance of Territory*. Of course, not all geographers and political theorists—let alone historians—use equivalent definitions. One notable example is Maier, *Once within Borders*, 2, who sees territoriality as an attribute not of politics but of political space: the ensemble of the ever-changing 'properties that territory entails'.

[19] Along similar lines, see the geographical as well as theoretical takes by Paasi, 'Boundaries as Social Processes'; Novak, 'The Flexible Territoriality of Borders'; and Perrier Bruslé, 'The Border as a Marker of Territoriality'.

8   BORDERS AND THE POLITICS OF SPACE IN LATE MEDIEVAL ITALY

terms such as 'boundaries' and 'frontiers', which are employed as synonyms of borders here.[20]

In addition to an exhaustive definition, geographers and political theorists have developed two key insights concerning territoriality. Together, such insights can do much to change the way in which we view the spatial fabric of pre-modern societies. The first is that territoriality is rarely the exclusive domain of the state. Over the last two decades, scholars such as John Agnew have cautioned tirelessly against the assumption that the spatiality of power can be reduced to its highest level. Agnew calls this 'the territorial trap', one set by the tendency to dismiss alternative forms of territorial organization.[21] His target is an established theory of international relations which envisions the territorial order as a jigsaw of mutually exclusive nations. In his view, this fails to recognize that 'sovereignty is neither inherently territorial nor is it exclusively organised on a state-by-state basis'.[22] Agnew's field of inquiry is the new world order, with its global flows and supranational bodies, but his words of caution should resonate just as strongly among scholars of pre-modern Europe.

The second key insight developed by geographers and political theorists is that territoriality is a historical product—a construct which reflects and at the same time determines historical conditions. On a basic level, this insight comes down to the idea that the changing modalities of territorial control can be extremely revealing about the evolving relationships between a society, its polities, and their spaces. In recent years, however, scholars have gone on to recognize that those same modalities could be linked to specific ways of thinking about such relationships. In other words, as a construct of a specific time and place, territoriality implies a specific understanding of spatial interplays, one shaped by culture as much as by practice.[23] In this

---

[20] This is not to say that linguistic variations do not exist or that they are not useful in other scholarly contexts, as discussed, among others, by Kristof, 'The Nature of Frontiers and Boundaries'; Nordman, 'Frontiere e confini'; and Krocová and Řezník, 'Boundaries and Identities'.

[21] Agnew, 'The Territorial Trap'; with a broader reappraisal in Newman, 'Territory, Compartments and Borders'. The need to move beyond the state as the principal unit of analysis was reiterated by Taylor, 'Embedded Statism'; and Brenner, 'Beyond State-Centrism?'. However, warnings against naturalizing the state and its territorial dimension go back as far as Lefebvre, as discussed by Elden, 'Henri Lefebvre on State'.

[22] Agnew, 'Sovereignty Regimes', 437. Equivalent views, albeit from different perspectives, have been expressed by Paasi, 'Bounded Spaces in a *Borderless World*'; and Sassen, 'When Territory Deborders Territoriality'.

[23] It is worth noting that while Agnew's views have been adopted by most in the social sciences, this second approach remains limited to a small squad of historically savvy geographers,

INTRODUCTION 9

sense, territoriality is a discourse of power as much as it is a specific form of it; it is conceived, represented, and talked about as much as it is exerted. What historians can take away from this is that territoriality should not be taken for granted. Like power, not only does it take many forms, but it is constantly challenged and reimagined.

To be clear, there is no question that historians are already aware of the contingent nature of territoriality. The issue is that they have generally failed to consider the full implications of that contingency. Most scholars note that the specific form of territoriality they may be studying differed from modern territorial control. But while they recognize that territoriality is not universal, they still treat it as immanent—as something already in existence, no matter what form it took. To put it another way, some specialists are undoubtedly asking what territoriality looked like in certain times and places; what they are not asking, with some exceptions, is how it was constructed.[24] The gap appears especially vast when compared with our understanding of other power structures and dynamics. No scholar would now deny that pre-modern power was distributed rather than centralized, that political change arose from below as much as from above, that pacts and compromises were the norm rather than the exception, and that images and representations were just as important as the practice of government and decision-making.[25] Yet the same cannot be said about our understanding of that particular form of power that is territoriality—in its many different historical incarnations. For most historians, territoriality remains a top-down imposition, if not a natural trait of every polity.

Among Italianists, as noted by Francesco Somaini in a recent overview, there has always been a tendency to assume that pre-modern modalities of territorial control strove towards the same outcomes as modern territoriality: internal cohesion, unbroken continuity, and mutual exclusivity.[26] To be

---

such as Ruggie, 'Territoriality and Beyond'; Anderson, 'The Shifting Stage of Politics'; and especially Elden, 'Thinking Territory Historically'.

[24] These exceptions are largely to do with francophone scholarship, starting with that informed by the acquisitions of the so-called *géographie culturelle*, on which see Pichon, 'Espace vécu, perceptions, cartes mentales'; together with the Italian perspective of Comba, 'Il territorio come spazio vissuto'. Some recent examples are the historiographical reappraisal undertaken by Cursente and Mousnier, *Les Territoires du médiéviste*; and the original studies collected by Boissellier, *De l'espace aux territoires*; Bührer, Patzold, and Schneider, *Genèse des espaces politiques*; and Fray, Gomis, and Le Bras, *Flux réels versus flux immatériels*.

[25] This understanding of late medieval politics and political cultures informs much of what follows, as several footnotes will demonstrate (though see particularly the second section of Chapter 4). For now, it should suffice to refer to Watts, *The Making of Polities*.

[26] Somaini, 'Territory, Territorialisation, Territoriality'.

10 BORDERS AND THE POLITICS OF SPACE IN LATE MEDIEVAL ITALY

sure, some scholars have long recognized that states were not the only actors that could exert some form of power over their respective spaces. Examples include the organizational structures of the *signorie territoriali* studied by Cinzio Violante, the *comitatinanza* process placed at the heart of the city's 'conquest' of the surrounding territory by Giovanni de Vergottini, and the territorial pluralism highlighted as a defining feature of the Italian version of the *Territorialstaat* by Giorgio Chittolini.[27] However, these historians' recognition that the spatiality of power was not produced by a single actor did not prevent them from falling anyway into the same trap. This is because they assumed that the power non-state actors were trying to exert could be understood in the same way as we tend to understand modern territoriality: 'homogeneous, compact, and complete in itself', as Somaini put it.[28]

In recent years, as will be discussed further in the last section of this Introduction, more and more specialists have come to terms with the idea that pre-modern forms of territoriality were fundamentally different from their present equivalents and that different modalities of territorial control could exist side by side. It is also agreed that the polities of the time exerted control over their respective spaces by means of negotiation and by allowing semi-autonomous bodies to continue to exist, creating enclaves and over-lapping jurisdictions. As a result, the presence of areas not directly con-trolled by these polities is no longer seen as some sort of resistance against the new territorial order, one in which the state strove to eliminate older competitors. Rather, these abiding competitors are seen as the defining fea-ture of that very order. But again, while scholars now recognize that pre-modern forms of territoriality were manifold and contingent, they still see them as inherent to the polities which they are studying; while they agree that territorial control is not universal, they still see it as immanent—as something which was already there and, indeed, there to stay.

Among Italian scholars, this static approach to the issue of territoriality is best exemplified by the numerous studies devoted to what is commonly referred to as 'the organization of territory' (*l'organizzazione del territorio*).[29] Over the years, these have built up a remarkable picture of how territoriality

---

[27] Violante, 'La signoria *territoriale*'; de Vergottini, 'Origini e sviluppo storico della comi-tatinanza'; Chittolini, 'La crisi delle libertà comunali e le origini dello Stato territoriale'.

[28] Somaini, 'Territory, Territorialisation, Territoriality', 29. For a broader perspective on these debates, consider Calzona and Cantarella, *Autocoscienza del territorio*; and Salvemini, *Il territorio sghembo*.

[29] Examples abound, so it is best to refer to surveys instead: Castagnetti, *L'organizzazione del territorio rurale*; Bocchi, 'La città e l'organizzazione del territorio'; Varanini, 'L'organizzazione del territorio in Italia'.

INTRODUCTION 11

was asserted: from the administration of justice to the collection of taxes, and from regulating the circulation of things and individuals to policing bridges and roads. Although seminal in Italian historiography, this approach has two limitations. The first is that it frames the assertion of territoriality as a matter of policy rather than as one of politics—as a system which a ruler or ruling group single-handedly adopts rather than as a discourse or practice to be negotiated among all those involved. The second limitation is that it tends to focus only on institutions, thus paying little attention to the cultures which shaped them; in brief, it fails to relate the way in which a society structured its territories to a contingent understanding of power over space.[30]

This work is partly an attempt to correct these tendencies and partly an effort to incorporate the interdisciplinary insights introduced above into the study of pre-modern forms of territoriality. To do so, two methodological principles are adopted. The first is that borders should not be seen as universal artefacts but as spatial constructs. Following the spatial turn in the humanities, it has become something of a commonplace to observe that space is not an empty container but rather a social construction filled with multiple meanings. Scholars have explored spaces as diverse as houses, palaces, churches, streets, and even entire cities but much less territories or borders.[31] This does not mean that the spatial turn has had little influence on political historians. It would be fairer to say that their interests have diverged towards other areas of inquiry, such as political sites (squares, monuments, memorials) and sites of politics (royal courts, town halls, rallying points).[32] Once more, we can learn much from the social sciences. Amidst his extensive treatment of the sociology of space, Georg Simmel had already framed borders as both social and spatial constructs. As he put it, more than a century ago, 'the border is not a spatial fact with sociological consequences, but a sociological fact that forms itself in space'.[33]

---

[30] As will be discussed further in Chapter 1, there is a partial exception to this rule, which is the excellent cluster of studies examining the language used to write about territories in late medieval Italy: Guglielmotti, 'Linguaggi del territorio'; Gamberini, 'Linguaggi politici e territorio'; Francesconi, 'Scrivere il contado'; Lazzarini, 'Scritture dello spazio'.

[31] The relevant historiography is both vast and varied, in quality as much as it is in scope. Overviews include Kingston, 'Mind over Matter?'; Kümin and Usborne, 'At Home and in the Workplace'; and Stock, 'History and the Uses of Space'.

[32] Two collections representative of these areas are Kümin, *Political Space*; and Boone and Howell, *The Power of Space*.

[33] Simmel, *Soziologie*. On this quotation, see the essay by Ellebrecht, 'Qualities of Bordering Spaces'; while, broadly, on the relational making of space as understood by sociologists today, see Fuller and Löw, *Spatial Sociology*. Geographical theories of borders as social constructs can

12 BORDERS AND THE POLITICS OF SPACE IN LATE MEDIEVAL ITALY

The second methodological principle is that the assertion of territoriality—and, with that, the making of borders—should not be reduced to the way in which historical territories were 'organized'. Instead, this activity should be investigated within a wider analytical framework, which this book calls the 'politics of space'.[34] That politics was not merely the strategies deployed by power holders to control their areas of influence; rather, it was the ensemble of political exchanges and social activities which underpinned and sometimes thwarted those very strategies. In essence, this means examining the development of territoriality, and of borders with it, in the same way we have learned to investigate other power structures and dynamics: namely as a practice, not simply as a fact, and as an interactive process, rather than as an authoritative imposition. Still, politics is not just about political dialogue and relationships of rule; it is also about the ideas and languages that have informed that dialogue, and about the codes of conduct and beliefs that have framed those relationships. Where there is a politics of space, to put it briefly, there is also a political and territorial culture—a contingent understanding of the way in which power relations should be negotiated and play out in space. What this book sets out to do, then, is to investigate the contingent nature of borders in late medieval Italy in relation to both the politics and culture that shaped them.

Milan, Venice, and their Territories

Save for some incursions into the fourteenth century, the book centres on the Quattrocento and on the consolidation of a new political geography in the Italian peninsula. This development makes the fifteenth century the perfect platform from which to observe how contemporaries engaged in the politics of space, while also examining how they achieved a settlement which was set to remain in place throughout early modernity. Though long-lasting, this new political geography was actually the culmination of a long-term transformation. Accounts vary, but they tend to agree on a common narrative, which could be labelled as the 'narrative of simplification': between the fourteenth and fifteenth centuries, the many principalities and

---

be found in Paasi, 'Fences and Neighbours'; and Bauder, 'Toward a Critical Geography of the Border'.

[34] Although it was largely ignored by historians, who have gravitated towards his writings on the 'production of space', this wording had already been used by Lefebvre: Elden, 'There Is a Politics of Space because Space Is Political'.

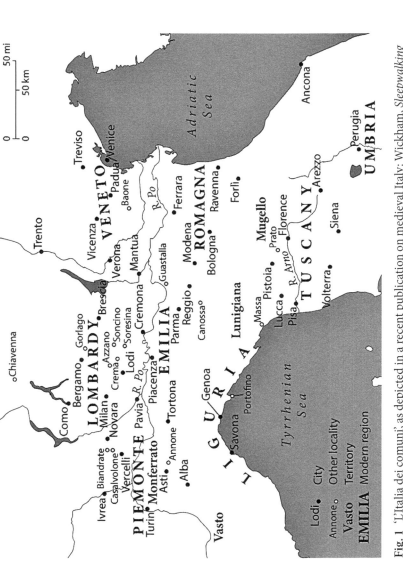

Fig. 1 'L'Italia dei comuni', as depicted in a recent publication on medieval Italy: Wickham, *Sleepwalking into a New World*, 3. Reproduced with permission from Princeton University Press

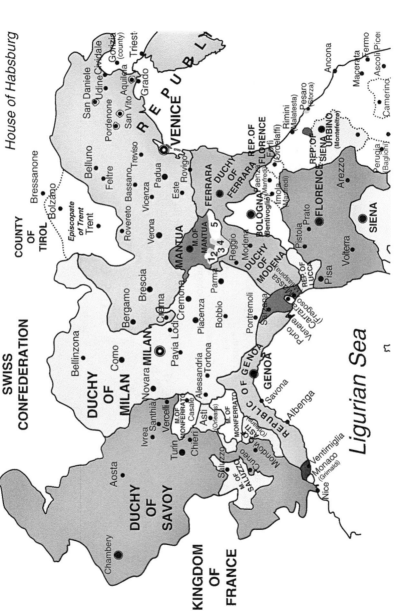

Fig. 2 'L'Italia degli stati territoriali', as depicted in a recent publication on Renaissance Italy: Gamberini and Lazzarini, *The Italian Renaissance State*, xiv. Reproduced with permission from Cambridge University Press

INTRODUCTION   15

city-republics of central and northern Italy were absorbed by a small number of large polities, such as the Duchy of Milan and the Republic of Venice.[35] As shown in Figures 1 and 2, this transformation could be exemplified by a pair of before-and-after maps. The first shows the peninsula in the twelfth century; the second presents its fifteenth-century political geography. More importantly, the first map shows an Italy of city-communes, in which dozens of identical dots are the only sign of their spatial dimension; the second presents an Italy of territorial states, in which a limited number of colour-filled areas covers most of the peninsula.

Over the years, scholars have viewed the spatial dimension of these new polities in many ways. In the 1950s, Federico Chabod made the case that what he called 'the Renaissance state' was nothing but the Italian version of the rising modern state.[36] At the time, territories were treated almost as an extension of the state itself—mere containers within which state offices and bureaucracies operated. Though long influential, this approach was slowly replaced by a new paradigm between the 1970s and 1990s, one which set aside teleological interpretations to look instead at Italian polities in their own terms. As mentioned, emphasis was placed on the intensity of political exchanges between centres and peripheries, and on the preservation of privileges and customs on the part of older bodies within the new polities. At the time of writing, the consensus is that regional polities did manage to create spaces within which their authority was seen as superior; however, this was not achieved by subduing internal competitors or by the means of modernization but by holding a formative dialogue with the political and social bodies over which they had come to rule (from townships and city-republics to fiefs and principalities).[37]

Following similar developments in other parts of Europe, these new polities were thus framed as 'composite' or 'contractual' states. In Italy, however, the term that stuck was another, that of 'regional' or 'territorial' states.[38] This was famously adopted by Giorgio Chittolini, among others, to identify the

---

[35] By way of example, the term is used in overviews, such as Gamberini, 'Processi di ricomposizione', 120–7; surveys, such as Tanzini, *Dai comuni agli stati territoriali*, 61–2; and reassessments, such as Savy, 'Gli stati italiani', 737.

[36] Chabod, 'Y a-t-il un État de la Renaissance?'; on which see now Lazzarini, 'Y a-t-il un état de la Renaissance?'.

[37] The first formulations of this approach can be traced to Fasano Guarini, 'Gli stati dell'Italia centro-settentrionale'; and Chittolini, 'Stati padani, *Stati del Rinascimento*'.

[38] Among many insightful discussions of these developments, consider Petralia, 'Stato e moderno'; and Gentile, 'Leviatano regionale o forma-stato composita?'; as well as the more recent Lazzarini, 'I nomi dei gatti'; and Ferente, 'Stato, stato regionale'.

16 BORDERS AND THE POLITICS OF SPACE IN LATE MEDIEVAL ITALY

enlarged dimension of the new polities and signal their reliance on the 'modern principle of territoriality' already asserted by the communes.[39] The many studies that followed built on these foundations. Over the years, we have learned about the state's reliance on informal networks, such as those of factions, condottieri, and family clans.[40] We have been shown the importance of the social dimension of state institutions, starting with those of chanceries and diplomacy: not mere arms of the state but arenas where people with different motives and backgrounds interacted.[41] And we have come to recognize the plurality of languages and ideas which underpinned these phenomena, together with the state's inability—and, in part, unwillingness—to develop an alternative conceptual framework to that established by the communes.[42]

Yet in the face of such a rich and nuanced picture of late medieval politics and political cultures, our understanding of the spatial dimension of Italian polities has remained largely the same. If anything, the paradigm of the territorial state has been pushed into the background, almost as a stage upon which those structures and dynamics played out. Most specialists now talk about states with a territorial 'vocation' or 'disposition', terms which were already used by Chittolini to frame the territorial accomplishments of the communes.[43] In recent years, however, some scholars have called attention to the necessity of problematizing these definitions. While highlighting the changing fortunes of the process of territorialization in the *contado* of Reggio, Andrea Gamberini argued that when it comes to late medieval Italy, territoriality is still an 'open problem'.[44] Similarly, Isabella Lazzarini, while surveying the lexicon used by contemporaries to write about territories, noted that the territorial nature of fifteenth-century Italian polities 'remains to be verified'.[45]

This uneasiness about the paradigm of the territorial state raises a number of questions. To start, what exactly makes a territorial state? Can a new

---

[39] Chittolini, 'Organizzazione territoriale', 12. The point is made more fully in Chittolini, 'Cities, *city-states*, and regional states'; and Chittolini, 'A Geography of the *Contadi*'.

[40] In this case but also in the two footnotes that follow, the relevant studies are simply too many to be referenced here. A representative selection may include Gentile, *Guelfi e ghibellini*; Ferente, *La sfortuna di Jacopo Piccinino*; and Arcangeli, *Gentiluomini di Lombardia*.

[41] Fubini, *Politica e diplomazia*; de Vivo, Guidi, and Silvestri, *Archivi e archivisti*; Lazzarini, *L'ordine delle scritture*.

[42] Varanini, 'Legittimità implicita'; Lazzarini, 'Culture politiche, governo, legittimità'; Gamberini, *La legittimità contesa*.

[43] Chittolini, 'Città e stati regionali'; Chittolini, 'Poteri urbani e poteri feudali-signorili'.

[44] Gamberini, 'La territorialità nel Basso Medioevo', 13.

[45] Lazzarini, 'Scritture dello spazio', 141.

INTRODUCTION   17

agglomeration of older territories be territorial in its own right? Or, to put it another way, was the territory of the state any different from the sum of its parts? And was its territoriality in any way superior to that exerted by preexisting bodies? In turn, these issues pose another series of questions: could different entities assert territoriality over the same space at the same time? And were there other entities capable of doing this, beyond the city and the state? If so, then our view of the spatial fabric of the peninsula might need to be questioned further. How does the presence of multiple territorial entities sit with the narrative of simplification? Did the decreased number of dominant polities on the Italian stage equate to a decreased number of territories? To what extent was the state's capacity to coordinate multiple bodies within its borders accompanied by a new spatial consciousness? In short, how territorial was Italian society and where, exactly, did territoriality lie?

* * *

To answer these questions, this book will look at the Duchy of Milan, the Republic of Venice, and their respective territories. As we have seen, between the fourteenth and fifteenth centuries, these polities absorbed most of the old principalities and city-republics of northern Italy. However, when the interstices between them finally filled up, Milan and Venice found themselves in direct competition with each other. In the first half of the Quattrocento, this rivalry led to a long series of diplomatic tensions and, eventually, open war. At the outset, thanks to its condottieri and experienced armies, Milan had the upper hand. But in the end, it was Venice that prevailed, coming to extend its dominion over areas which had long been subject to Milan: the territories of Bergamo, Brescia, and Crema. In 1454, the famous treaty of Lodi put an end to these conflicts, paving the way for nearly half a century of relative peace in Lombardy and for the creation of a novel power balance between all Italian polities. At its heart was the establishment of new state borders between Milan and Venice and a clear delineation of their respective spheres of influence in northern Italy.[46]

This brings us to the first of four preliminary remarks to be made here, concerning chronology. Although certainly not the only episode of bordermaking in late medieval Italy, the Lodi settlement was undoubtedly the most notable. As such, it offers the ideal setting in which to examine the

---

[46] These developments will be treated in full in Chapter 2. For now, see the maps in Somaini and Cengarle, '*Geografie motivazionali*'; and broadly Fasano Guarini, 'Geographies of Power'.

18   BORDERS AND THE POLITICS OF SPACE IN LATE MEDIEVAL ITALY

construction of borders in the context of the politics and cultures that shaped them. While the years surrounding the peace of Lodi will provide the focus for several sections of the book's chapters, others will expand the analysis to other crucial moments, such as the 1420s, with the Venetian expansion in eastern Lombardy, and the 1480s, with the return of war in northern Italy. In addition, all chapters highlight patterns and circumstances rooted in long-standing practices and understandings of space, often dating back to the fourteenth and thirteenth centuries. Still, the Lodi settlement produced an unusual amount of evidence, which is now scattered in various libraries and archives. Sources are particularly abundant on the Milanese side. In the 1450s, a series of upheavals and regime changes caused the loss of much of the ducal archive, but it also saw the rise of a new dynasty, one which promoted the making and conservation of written records on a whole new level.[47] The trend is especially visible in the growing body of correspondence amassed in the second half of the Quattrocento. Every week, the Milanese Chancery sent and received dozens of letters to and from Venice, most of which have survived to this day. For the 1450s alone, they number in the thousands. In addition, material regarding Milan's relationships with Venice has been found in copybooks recording outgoing correspondence, in particular that exchanged with peripheral communities and border officials, as well as in manuscripts collating minutes of negotiations and finalized treaties.

The second remark has to do with source balance. Where Milan relied extensively on the correspondence between a limited number of core offices and many peripheral officials, Venice built a far more complex institutional architecture. Alongside a myriad of different offices operating side by side in the lagoon city, Venice allowed its representatives in the peripheries to conduct affairs which in Milan would have been managed by central magistracies, if not by the duke himself and his core council. These include several areas of government touching on the issue of borders, such as the management of frontier fortifications, the regulation of economic flows, the relationships with peripheral bodies, and, at times, even territorial negotiations. For these reasons, the book employs a large number of sources from the Milanese archives and complements the relatively small number of records available in Venice for this period with material drawn from its

---

[47] These events and their archival ramifications are discussed more extensively in Chapter 6. For now, see Leverotti, 'L'archivio dei Visconti'; and Leverotti, 'La cancelleria dei Visconti e degli Sforza'.

INTRODUCTION   19

subject cities, notably Brescia, Bergamo, and Crema.[48] While the correspondence between Venice and these areas is largely lost, other sources have
survived, including collections of state ordinances, municipal statutes,
notarial records, council minutes, and even maps.

The third remark is about terminology. Venice and Milan shared many
similarities; yet their constitutional differences have made them representative of two contrasting models. Following Machiavelli, it is often said that
the polities established in the peninsula towards the end of the Middle Ages
were either republics or principalities.[49] This distinction has the advantage
of being clear and to the point, which is why it is adopted here to refer to
Venice (the Republic) and Milan (the Duchy), even at the risk of oversimplifying the complex nature of these polities and their distinctive traits. In
reality, however, Venice and Milan encompassed similar aggregates of territorial bodies, including many of the largest city-communes (Cremona and
Brescia, Verona and Padua) with which they interacted in similar ways.
Their size and population were also comparable, though Venice was wealth-
ier than Milan in relative terms. In this sense, it may be fair to say that what
distinguished the two polities the most is what had brought them together
in the first place: a republican oligarchy (Venice) and a princely dynasty
(Milan).[50] The same goes for the very terms 'Venice' and 'Milan'. The book
employs them to speak of the two polities and, at times, their leaderships.
Still, there is no question that this is at the cost of unduly personifying them
or even giving the impression that either could be equated with a homogeneous entity or interest group. What these polities truly were remains to be
established, but one thing we know for sure is that they were nothing of
the sort.

The fourth and final remark concerns the rest of the peninsula. In turn,
what 'Italy' really means for the end of the Middle Ages is open for debate.
Two things appear more certain. The first is that both foreigners and
Italians, as much literature has already shown, saw Italy as a self-contained

[48] The archival *traditio* of this material is discussed in various places throughout the book.
For now, see Viggiano, 'Le carte della Repubblica'; and de Vivo, 'Ordering the Archive'.
[49] MACHIAVELLI, *The Prince*, 5: 'all the dominions that have held sway over men have
been either republics or principalities'. The distinction was then reiterated by noting how he
had already treated republics in a separate body of work: the *Discorsi* (6).
[50] While many comparative insights can be found in the literature, the only piece devoted to
comparing Venice and Milan is now more than three decades old: Law, 'Un confronto fra due
stati'. Today, it might be more profitable to confront the essays in Dursteler, *A Companion to
Venetian History, 1400–1797*; and Gamberini, *A Companion to Late Medieval and Early
Modern Milan*.

20 BORDERS AND THE POLITICS OF SPACE IN LATE MEDIEVAL ITALY

society—as an assemblage of people with similar customs, norms, and beliefs.[51] Although the book mentions frontier events elsewhere in the peninsula (for example in Tuscany or the Adriatic), it is decisively the study of one frontier, that between the Duchy of Milan and the Republic of Venice. However, the book also seeks to uncover a shared territorial culture—a common way of doing things with space. There is no reason to think that this culture was not part of the same set of customs, norms, and beliefs shared by a large part of Italian society. The second thing is equally rooted in historiography. It is the conviction that despite significant differences, as in the case of the kingdom of Naples or even the Florentine dominion, some parts of Italy were far more alike than we once thought. Polities up and down the peninsula were dealing with similar challenges in similar ways: by establishing legitimacy through theoretical reflections as much as practical interventions, by balancing the influence of power groups, as in the case of the nobility but also urban elites, and by constantly bargaining with both internal and external actors.[52] Similarly, there is no reason to think that the politics of space was not among those challenges and that similar solutions might not have been adopted across multiple regions. The book uses the term 'Italy' with these caveats in mind. Conscious of the specificities of its case study, it seeks to build a model to explain borders and territoriality in light of the broader cultures and politics featured in much of the peninsula at this time.

* * *

The book consists of seven chapters, charting how borders were conceptualized (Chapter 1), negotiated (Chapter 2), disputed (Chapter 3), delimited (Chapter 4), crossed (Chapter 5), recorded (Chapter 6), and mapped (Chapter 7).

Chapter 1 lays the foundations for the remainder of the book. It does so by outlining the ideas which shaped people's attitudes towards territoriality,

---

[51] Webb, 'Italians and Others'; Margaroli, 'L'Italia come percezione'; Fubini, 'L'idea di Italia'; Airò, Caldelli, De Fraja, and Francesconi, 'Italia, italiae, italicae gentes'; Inglese, 'Italia come spazio politico'.

[52] On Florence and Tuscany, see the seminal Connel and Zorzi, *Florentine Tuscany*; together with Boutier, Landi, and Rouchon, *Florence et la Toscane, XIVe–XIXe siècles*. Recent scholarship on politics and political culture in the South could not be more exciting. On Naples, see at least Vitale, *Ritualità monarchica*; Vitolo, *L'Italia delle altre città*; Cappelli, Maiestas. *Politica e pensiero*; and Storti, *El buen marinero*. On Siciliy, see Corrao, *Governare un regno*; Mineo, *Nobiltà di stato*; Titone, *Governments of the Universitates*; and Silvestri, *L'amministrazione del regno*.

thus guiding the politics of space. Reading a variety of public records in the light of intellectual treatises, the chapter traces these ideas to the work of medieval jurists and highlights their underpinning of a shared territorial culture.

Chapter 2 uses the preparation of major treaties, notably those of Ferrara (1428) and Lodi (1454), to uncover the range of practices through which territories were annexed and frontiers shifted, while also contributing to the recent revival of interest in the history of peace and peace-making. Building on Chapter 1, it is especially concerned with the fundamental principles applied by state deputies during negotiations and with their ramifications for the changing geography of the peninsula.

Chapter 3 develops the inquiry begun in Chapter 2 one step further. It does so by searching for the adoption of the same principles at play during territorial negotiations in the resolution of border disputes—episodes in which treaties broke down, mistakes occurred, and new conflicts arose. The chapter pays particular attention to instances when the politics of space was driven by localized exigencies. This is to evaluate the contribution of pre-existing groups and formations in novel political landscapes.

Chapter 4 investigates the intersections between localized practices of territorial demarcation and the establishment of state borders. Drawing on constructivist and relational theories of space, the chapter locates the definition of local boundaries within the range of collective activities through which territories were created and identities forged. In addition, the chapter studies the interactions which transformed local boundaries into the new state frontiers.

Chapter 5 shifts the focus of the book from the making of borders to the way in which people encountered them, starting with their role as sites of mobility. Using network analysis and new digital tools, the chapter traces the circulation of people and objects across both internal boundaries and external frontiers, questioning their porosity and assessing the control of movement flows on behalf of the new polities.

Chapter 6 responds to the current surge of interest in the history of archives by analysing how the written memory of borders was recorded, shared, and preserved. Having considered the contribution of state chanceries alongside that of local communities, the chapter investigates their complementary knowledge of spatial arrangements in view of the necessity of dialogue between centres and peripheries over the division of space.

Chapter 7 examines how territorial orders—and borders—were visualized. It does so by focusing on regional and district maps. Building on the insights of critical cartography, the chapter examines the performative value of these maps, showing not only how they depicted the limits of Italian polities but how territoriality itself was visually constructed by them.

The conclusion discusses the importance of the chapters' findings for three broader fields: the history of medieval borders, and especially their supposed porosity and muddled nature; the study of pre-modern forms of territoriality, as seen through the framework of the politics of space; and the paradigm of the territorial state in Italy, now reappraised from the perspective of borders.

1
Iurisdictio in Practice
Cultures of Space, Borders, and Power

If we were to look for mentions of the word 'space' or 'political space' in the writings of medieval thinkers, we would not find many. That is because much—if not all—of the medieval reflection on the notions of space and power revolved around a concept which encompassed them both: the concept of *iurisdictio*. In Roman Law, *iurisdictio* was quite literally the capacity of pronouncing the law (*ius dicere*), namely the power of laying down principles which could then settle litigations; it was the authority of the magistrate, which made it attached to a person. By the end of the Middle Ages, however, *iurisdictio* did not stand for judicial power alone but for power over space. At this stage, as a much-repeated maxim famously put it, *iurisdictio cohaeret territorium*: space was seen as the medium through which judicial power was exercised. In brief, much as sovereignty would do in a later period, jurisdiction became the currency of territorial authority in the Late Middle Ages.[1]

The extent to which *iurisdictio* became the universal concept through which territoriality was envisioned becomes immediately evident from just a few examples from the time and region at the core of this study. In 1470, the governor of Bergamo framed his complaints about Milanese subjects who had crossed state borders to exploit Venetian lands not solely in terms of economic damage or as a violation of the peace of Lodi but also as a curtailment of Venetian jurisdiction ('una diminutio de la iurisdictione de la nostra illustrissima signoria').[2] Similarly, when Venetian subjects trespassed on Milanese lands a few years later, they were accused of encroaching on the duke's jurisdiction ('usurpare la iurisictione de vostra excellentia').[3] Border incidents were thus clearly seen as a matter of jurisdiction. The same

---

[1] On *iurisdictio* as the medieval currency of power, see, for now, Wurtzel, 'City Limits and State Formations', 30. Further references to this maxim as well as the relevant scholarship can be found below, in the chapter's first section.

[2] ASMi, *Carteggio* 1517bis, 13 March 1470.   [3] ASMi, *Confini* 239, 9 August 1475.

Borders and the Politics of Space in Late Medieval Italy: Milan, Venice, and their Territories. Luca Zenobi, Oxford University Press. © Luca Zenobi 2023. DOI: 10.1093/oso/9780198876861.003.0002

24   BORDERS AND THE POLITICS OF SPACE IN LATE MEDIEVAL ITALY

can be said about territorial negotiations. A good example comes from the autumn of 1428, when the doge and his council nominated the first in a long series of deputies in charge of concluding treaties with the duke of Milan. As explained in his letter of appointment, the deputy would also oversee any quarrel that might arise from matters of borders and jurisdictions ('causa et occasione confinium et iurisdictionum').[4]

But how did it come to this? How did the concept of *iurisdictio* develop from the judicial capacity held by an ancient magistrate to the territorial authority of a medieval prince or republic? In the first section of this chapter, we shall trace the intellectual development that led to this spatial turn *avant la lettre*—that made jurisdiction, to put it simply, territorial. Following an established tradition, starting with the work of Joseph Canning, we shall look for instances when medieval thinkers were guided by the need to make sense of the realities of their time.[5] Over the last two decades, this approach has allowed specialists to examine medieval political ideas alongside contingent practices of power. Until recently, however, historians of political thought have done little to explore how those same ideas intersected with the issue of space.[6] If anything, this line of inquiry has been followed by geographers and political theorists. Works such as Stuart Elden's conceptual history of 'territory' offer valuable insights into the long-term evolution of ideas about space and power.[7] However, unlike the historiography on medieval political thinking, these works are rarely concerned with relating those ideas to actual practices. In an attempt to combine these approaches, this chapter's first section will trace the intellectual journey of *iurisdictio*, before turning to assess how this notion came to frame the nature of territorial authority in late medieval Italy.

The chapter's remaining sections will move away from the writings of medieval authors to consider the widespread adoption of a jurisdictional discourse—a way of thinking and writing about power over space hinging upon the notion and lexicon of *iurisdictio*. We shall look especially for the use of a jurisdictional vocabulary in pragmatic sources, such as official

---

[4] ASVe, *Miscellanea* 35, 3 October 1428.

[5] Canning, 'Italian Juristic Thought and the Realities of Power'. On this tradition, see also the footnotes to this chapter's first section.

[6] Recent works following this approach include Costa, 'Uno spatial turn per la storia del diritto?'; Meccarelli, 'The Assumed Space'; and Brett, 'The Space of Politics'.

[7] Elden, *The Birth of Territory*. Other examples include the miscellaneous books by Larkings, *From Hierarchy to Anarchy*; and Dahlberg, *Spacing Law and Politics*.

correspondence and public records in general. This takes into account the now-classic realization that, by using a common political language, pragmatic sources were not merely describing people's actions; they were guiding them.[8] It follows that by employing the same spatial vocabulary, these sources were both transcribing territorial practices and conveying a set of ideas framing those practices. By considering the adoption of a jurisdictional discourse, it will therefore be possible to assess the extent to which a shared territorial culture, drawing on the reappraisal of *iurisdictio*, underpinned the politics of space in late medieval Italy. In so doing, this chapter will lay the foundations for the rest of the book, through which the gap between ideas and practices of space, borders, and power will be fully bridged.

The Theory of Territorial Pluralism

How was *iurisdictio* transformed from the capacity of administering justice into the primary method of conceiving power over space? At the risk of oversimplifying what was actually a complex itinerary, we could say that the concept of *iurisdictio* passed through three consecutive steps. As is often the case with Italian political thinkers, the first step was made between the twelfth and the thirteenth centuries by a highly respected jurist: Azo of Bologna. One of the most influential glossators of Roman Law, Azo adopted the concept of *iurisdictio* to frame his treatment of rulership. He believed that the ancient notion of *imperium*, which was traditionally seen as monolithic and essentially inalienable, was not flexible enough to capture the real nature of power. By contrast, *iurisdictio* was defined by its scope and could easily be transferred to any subject. According to Azo, the emperor was thus the holder of fullest jurisdiction (*plenissima iurisdictio*) while all the other magistrates could hold only a jurisdiction that was not as full (*minus plena iurisdictio*). Hence, as Daniel Lee cleverly put it, '*iurisdictio* became the genus of which *merum imperium* was but a mere species', while the concept

---

[8] Since the publication of Austin, *How to Do Things with Words*, speech act theory has been widely adopted by historians interested in political cultures, as discussed by Genet, 'L'historien et les langages'. For an Italian perspective, see the high levels of politics examined by Viroli, *From Politics to Reason of State*; together with the more pragmatic approach advocated by Gamberini, 'The Language of Politics'. A pioneering investigation into things to do with language, power, and space is Costa, Iurisdictio. *Semantica del potere*.

26 BORDERS AND THE POLITICS OF SPACE IN LATE MEDIEVAL ITALY

itself developed from the capacity to simply state the law to a synonym for exercising power legitimately.[9]

Azo's theory provided a whole school of jurists, the so-called 'commentators', with an organizing principle which they could use to rationalize the political realities of their time, with their intersections of various layers of public authorities and customary private rights. Unlike their predecessors, however, this new generation of jurists was not concerned with explaining political facts in the light of legal theory but rather with adjusting the theory to meet the facts.[10] Azo had conceptualized *iurisdictio* as extendable to virtually anyone in medieval society. The commentators took this further, using jurisdiction to define the power of different actors in the political and social hierarchy of the time: from the tiniest entities, such as lordships and rural villages, to city-republics, to the marquis or duke ruling over multiple territories, and finally to the emperor. Thus, as Paolo Costa has explained it, jurisdiction became akin to 'the position of a subject or body along a chain made up of several rings'.[11]

A second step in medieval political thinking about *iurisdictio* was taken in the mid-1300s by the most prominent scholar among the commentators: Bartolus of Sassoferrato. This brilliant jurist is perhaps best known for his effort to legitimize the independence of the Italian city-states. While he recognized that the emperor had *de iure* a supreme power over the communes, Bartolus noted that these polities had *de facto* been exercising jurisdictional prerogatives for a very long time. 'A city that does not recognize a superior', he famously stated, 'is a prince unto itself.'[12] It follows, Bartolus argued, that such a city is the real owner of its *iurisdictio*; jurisdictional rights did not necessarily derive from the emperor but could in fact be a prerogative of the legal entity who owned them.[13] Much as the emperor could exercise his power within the empire, the cities were legitimized by Bartolus to exercise their own power within their respective territories. In this way, the debate about the nature of territorial authority moved from the level of the empire

---

[9] Lee, *Popular Sovereignty*, 88. More broadly on Azo and his contribution, see Perrin, 'Azo, Roman Law'.

[10] As first argued by Sidney Woolf, *Bartolus of Sassoferrato*, 209. See now Walther, 'Die Legitimität der Herrschaftsordnung'.

[11] Costa, 'In alto e al centro', 820. Along similar lines, consider also Vallejo, 'Power Hierarchies'.

[12] DE SAXOFERRATO, *Super secunda parte Digesti Novi*, c. 208r: 'civitas, quae non recognoscit superiorem,...sibi princeps est.'

[13] On Bartolus' contention, see Ryan, 'Bartolus of Sassoferrato and Free Cities'; and Quaglioni, 'Das Publikum der Legisten'.

to the level of a legal entity capable of bearing, in its own right, a bundle of jurisdictional rights over its territory.

The legal entity Bartolus had in mind was a corporation of free people (*universitas*) capable of making their own laws and electing officers who could then exert jurisdiction over a defined space. This definition was designed to fit the model of the Italian city-states; however, Bartolus himself recognized that it applied to all self-governing communities.[14] In turn, these could be defined by the degree of jurisdiction that they held in the political and social hierarchy of late medieval Italy. While Bartolus argued that cities which refused to acknowledge a higher power were effectively independent, not all cities were able to do that; therefore, only a limited degree of jurisdiction was conceded by Bartolus to these minor cities (*civitates minores*). The same could be said about other small corporations, such as towns and rural communities (*terrae, burgi, villae*). Just as major cities could exercise their full jurisdiction within the territory of the empire, these bodies could exercise their limited jurisdictional powers within the territories of the cities. Bartolus was not the first to frame the entrenched pluralism featured by medieval society. Crucially, however, he disentangled the jurisdictional order from imperial authority, to bind it up instead with the power of different corporations.[15]

A third and final step in the medieval theorization of *iurisdictio* was made at the turn of the fourteenth and fifteenth centuries by one of Bartolus' pupils: Baldus de Ubaldis. For Bartolus, *iurisdictio* was a quality of the entity that owned it—that is, a quality of the lord or officer exerting power in the name of a *universitas*, not a quality of *territorium*. Hence, *iurisdictio cohaeret territorium* in the sense that territory defines spatially the scope within which jurisdiction is exercised.[16] While Baldus agreed that jurisdiction hovers over territory 'like mist over a swamp',[17] the pupil went on to refine his master's claim by arguing that territory itself—and not just the owner of

---

[14] DE SAXOFERRATO, 'Tractatus super Constitutionem', s.v. *Communitas*: 'Communitas est nomen generale pertinens ad universitatem civitatis, castri et villae et cuiuslibet municipii, eo quod ab ipsa hominum communitate principaliter regatur.'

[15] On 'corporation theory', consider mainly Canning, 'The Corporation in the Political Thought'. More broadly, on the notion of *universitas*, see Najemy, 'Stato, comune e *universitas*'; and Quantin, Universitas, 206–11.

[16] On this point, see the classic study by Vaccari, '*Utrum iurisdictio cohaeret territorio*'; together with its partial revision by Quaglioni, 'Giurisdizione e territorio'.

[17] DE UBALDIS, *In usus feudorum*, c. 100r: 'imaginetis etiam quod iurisdictio sit super territorium sicut nebula super paludem quae generatur per activam potentiam solis.'

28 BORDERS AND THE POLITICS OF SPACE IN LATE MEDIEVAL ITALY

it—is equipped with jurisdiction ('munitum et armatum iurisdictione').[18] In Baldus' view, territory was not just the space over which a *universitas* exercised its power but the spatial extent of the *universitas* itself. Like Bartolus, Baldus was mainly concerned with cities, but he too generalized his conclusions to include smaller corporations. When asked about transferring possession of a *castrum*, he noted that jurisdiction over its territory is a prerogative of the *castrum* itself and should, therefore, be transferred with it.[19] In so doing, Baldus brought together the three notions around which the juristic debate about territorial authority had been centred (*iurisdictio*, *universitas*, *territorium*) to describe a political and corporate body which was itself a territorial unit.

What, then, can the intellectual development of *iurisdictio* tell us about the way in which space was politically understood by contemporary Italians? The first thing it tells us is that what we may now call political spaces were actually *territoria*, namely the spaces of one or more communities. It is in this sense that the term will be used throughout the rest of this book. Unlike modern territories, which are juridically empty containers filled with bodies designed by the state to define a population's duties towards it (provinces, counties, departments), medieval territories were filled with communities of rights, namely entities capable of exercising their own prerogatives over their spaces. As the jurists knew only too well, not all communities were territorial. Cities themselves were crammed with corporations: from merchant guilds and political parties to neighbourhood associations.[20] But in juristic thought, all territories coincided with a community, no matter what form this took: from the *universitas* of Christians over which the emperor ostensibly ruled to the urban commune or any of the small villages of the countryside. In brief, the territorial landscape was not understood as a jigsaw of states but rather as an expanse of corporations of different shapes and sizes.[21]

The second thing we can take away from this intellectual journey is that while individual territories were exclusively linked to specific communities, medieval territories were not themselves seen as exclusive. Communities

---

[18] For this passage and a discussion of Baldus' contribution, see Elden, *The Birth of Territory*, 229–33; and broadly Marchetti, De iure finium, 83–95.

[19] DE UBALDIS, *In usus feudorum*, no. 7 (*De allodiis*).

[20] As explored, among many others, by Lantschner, *The Logic of Political Conflict*; and now Gentile, 'Forms of Political Representation'.

[21] For this characterization of pre-modern political spaces, see Hespanha, 'L'espace politique'; and Mannori, 'La nozione di territorio'.

1. *IURISDICTIO* IN PRACTICE 29

(*terrae, burgi, villae*) could exist within the territories of other communities (the urban communes), which in turn could exist within the territory of an even larger community (the empire). In that chain made up of several rings that represented the political and social hierarchy of the time, all could exert different degrees of power over their respective territories, while also serving as the constituent units of larger bodies. As a small corporation exercised its limited jurisdiction over its territory, so a larger corporation could simultaneously exercise its superior jurisdiction over that same territory. In this context, as the jurists frequently stated, 'limites territorii sunt limites iurisdictionis': the spatial bounds of territorial communities were also the limits of the exercisable jurisdictional rights.[22] This confirms that before being a matter of state and sovereignty, borders were framed as a matter of territories (that is, *territoria*) and jurisdiction. As such, they were linked to the distributed but also hierarchical nature of pre-modern power, to the ingrained pluralism of late medieval society, and to the corporate character of its forms of political and social organization.

Urban Communes and their *Contadi*

Before turning to the adoption of a jurisdictional discourse by fifteenth-century Italian polities, we should take a moment to consider how that same discourse was first embraced in the context of the realities to which medieval jurists sought to accommodate their theories. As is well known, the city-states were the first polities to sponsor or at least inform the search for a universal principle which could legitimize their authority. As a *universitas civium*, the city was seen as the holder of a superior bundle of jurisdictional prerogatives over its territory, particularly once its autonomy from the emperor's sphere of influence had been recognized.[23] But the city's territory was never exclusive, for other *universitates* could exist within its borders. A jurisdictional discourse was thus employed to frame the political and spatial relations between the cities and these smaller corporations.

---

[22] The equation is drawn from DEL POZZO, 'Allegatio pro Communitate', no. 24; as discussed by Marchetti, 'Spazio politico e confini', 75. However, similar propositions can be found in the writings of several other jurists, such as Giovanni d'Andrea—writings which were then adopted and reformulated by DEL MONTE, *Tractatus de finibus*.

[23] On this idea and its practical assertion, see Ascheri, 'La cité-état italienne'; and generally Jones, *The Italian City-State*, 359–400.

30   BORDERS AND THE POLITICS OF SPACE IN LATE MEDIEVAL ITALY

This is not the place to recount the lengthy, non-linear process that between the twelfth and thirteenth centuries led to the establishment of the city's territory: the *districtus* or *comitatus* (hence *contado*, in Italian).[24] Yet it is important to note that the territorial acquisitions of the city-states were always rendered as an expansion of urban jurisdiction. Territoriality was not unknown in the countryside, but there it coexisted with different ideas of power, starting with the culture of personal possession, and with different social practices, as in the case of feudal obligations. Justice, for example, was sometimes exercised over peasants bound to a lay or ecclesiastical lord; however, as urban magistrates began visiting the countryside on a regular basis, the administration of justice came to pivot around territories rather than people. This is not to say that urban communes disposed of rural lordships altogether to create from scratch new jurisdictional precincts. Rather, the lords were compelled, through pacts and arbitrations, to exercise their power over a set of territorial units (*castra, loci, communes*).[25] In so doing, the lords were forced to play by rules designed to benefit the communes; despite their continued presence in the countryside, it was the city's culture of territoriality that prevailed. This generalized the associative nature of the urban commune to the entirety of its *contado*, intended as an expanse of minor but theoretically similar sister corporations over which the jurisdiction of the city had been expanded.

In their records, the cities developed a number of techniques to inscribe their political and spatial relationships with the surrounding countryside. Some of these techniques were complex written devices, as in the case of patrimonial inquiries (surveys of lands owned directly by a city) and of the noted *libri iurium* (compilations of records sanctioning a city's jurisdictional prerogative, such as treaties with other centres or privileges granted by the emperor).[26] Typically, however, the most common technique employed by the cities to frame their authority over rural communities was simple linguistic imagery, as in the case of lists. A well-known example is the series of imperial charters concerning the city of Pavia between the twelfth and the thirteenth centuries. In these charters, the Lombard centre grounded its authority over the surrounding countryside by presenting a detailed list of all the communities over which urban jurisdiction had been

---

[24]   That place is Zenobi, 'Beyond the State', 61–5.
[25]   For these phenomena, it is still essential to refer to classic studies such as Tabacco, 'L'allodialità del potere'; and Vaccari, *La territorialità come base dell'ordinamento giuridico.*
[26]   Rao, 'Le inchieste patrimoniali'; Rovere, 'Tipologie documentali nei *libri iurium*'.

extended.[27] This 'listed *contado*' was not only an expression of the city's 'organization of territory', as is often said; it was also a reflection of its original configuration.[28] While asserting the city's independence from the emperor and its autonomous jurisdiction over its territory, these lists were bound to acknowledge that the *contado* was not a compact and exclusive space but rather a patchwork of overlapping corporations.

The relationships between a city-state and its constituent bodies were just as central to the definition of its borders. To ground the limits of their territories, the cities commissioned registers containing surveys of the boundaries of all the communities forming part of their *contadi*. These books of borders (*libri finium*) are tangible evidence of the dialectical nature of the relationships between urban communes and rural communities, for while they resulted from the intervention of the city in matters of territorial organization, they also recorded the rights of each community over its territory.[29] More importantly, books of borders are but the practical application of the legal maxim encountered earlier, 'limites territorii sunt limites iurisdictionis';[30] conversely, the limits of jurisdiction are the limits of the individual territories upon which such jurisdiction is exercised. This notion reflected what books of borders show to have been a widespread practice: as the city-states extended their power over smaller units, their overall borders came to rest on the individual boundaries of those units. Considering this principle, the fact that the frontiers of the Italian communes were understood as a sum of boundaries between rural corporations is only logical.[31]

In short, the adoption of a jurisdictional discourse on behalf of the cities allowed them not only to define their position of autonomy from the emperor but also to frame their relationships with their own territories. On the one hand, by asserting their distinct form of territoriality, cities were able to entangle feudal powers in a mesh of corporations theoretically alike but, in practice, already subject to them. On the other hand, the cities' assertion of territoriality was bound to follow the same principles already noted by the jurists. First, the territories over which their authority was extended

---

[27] On Pavia's case, see mainly Settia, 'Il distretto pavese'.
[28] The expression is borrowed from Francesconi, 'Scrivere il contado', 520. For a more expansive treatment of this device, see Varanini, 'L'organizzazione del distretto', 138–45.
[29] On *libri finium*, consider the overview in Francesconi and Salvestrini, 'La scrittura del confine'; and a more extended case study in Francesconi and Salvestrini, 'Il *Liber finium districtus Pistorii*'.
[30] DEL POZZO, 'Allegation pro Communitate', no. 24.
[31] More broadly, on the frontiers of Italian city-states in this first phase, see the initial studies by Bortolami, 'Frontiere politiche'; and Settia, 'Tra Novara e Pavia'.

32 BORDERS AND THE POLITICS OF SPACE IN LATE MEDIEVAL ITALY

were never just empty spaces; rather, they were jurisdictional units filled with communities of people. Second, the territories established by the cities (the *contadi* or *districti*) were seen as hierarchically superior to those of rural corporations but not as exclusive. Politically, the cities had considerable success in restricting rural powers, while also extending their legal as well as fiscal regimes to the countryside. Territorially, however, their *contadi* remained congeries of corporations holding a bundle of rights and responsibilities towards their respective spaces. Pre-existing territories, to put it differently, were not effaced by the creation of the *contado*; instead, they were retained as the most basic units of territorial organization. As such, they went on to shape the frontiers of all Italian city-states.

Regional States and their Dominions

In principle, at least, twelfth- and thirteenth-century Italy knew only two types of territory: the *districtus* of the city and the *territoria* of rural corporations. Feudal and ecclesiastical jurisdictions existed and would continue to exist for decades, but they were always mapped onto congeries of rural corporations (*castra*, *loci*, *communes*) rather than being recognized as territories themselves. By contrast, in the fourteenth and fifteenth centuries, the territorial hierarchy of the peninsula evolved in two opposite—yet integrated—directions. From above, regional polities resulting from the extension of dominant cities (Venice) or princely centres (Milan) extended their power over most of the old city-states and, through them, over their subject territories. From below, new territorial bodies asserted themselves as intermediate entities—often in place of the cities themselves—between rural corporations and regional powers. This was especially the case for many towns, which managed to carve out an autonomous *districtus* within the nominal *contadi* of some city-states, as well as for several federations and lay fiefs, which officially recognized as territorial units by superior powers.

Let us start by looking at regional polities and the extent to which they drew on the same territorial culture to frame their dominions. Like the cities before them, polities such as the Duchy of Milan and the Republic of Venice presented their territorial acquisitions as an expansion of *iurisdictio*. While this was straightforward enough in respect of rural communities, city-states presented a more challenging proposition. For nearly two centuries, they had been the most notable jurisdictional framework in the

1. *IURISDICTIO* IN PRACTICE   33

peninsula, having made their tradition of self-governance the defining feature of their history and civic identity. So, just as the cities had not been able—or ever truly willing—to dissolve rural corporations into their *contadi*, the new regional polities did not efface the old city-states. Instead, their submission to regional polities was framed as an act of spontaneous surrender (*deditio*) on behalf of the communes. Far from disempowering the cities, this process allowed them to negotiate their rights and duties within the wider polity, starting with what they owed to state revenues. But it also sanctioned their subordination to a superior power, one whose own jurisdiction would now be exerted over their lands.[32]

It was an effective compromise: regional polities gained recognition of their extended power, while cities retained a place at the bargaining table. It was also one in keeping with the principles outlined by the jurists. They posited that *iurisdictio* could be transferred to any one person or body in medieval society, so it only made sense that power over a city's territory could be transferred through an act of submission. Plus, appearances were saved: regional polities could use the formal agreement of the ancient *civitates* to legitimize their authority, while the cities themselves could still appear as independently minded. Needless to say, the very fact that such appearances were so important is indicative of the ways in which contemporaries made sense of the increasing tensions between the old and the new. The writings of Silvestro Lando, chancellor of the city of Verona around the mid-fifteenth century, are but one example where the impossible balance between the appearance of autonomy and actual subjection is addressed head-on. In presenting a new edition of the city's statutory laws, Lando framed the power of Verona within the Venetian dominion in terms of temperate freedom ('moderata libertas').[33] What better way to signal that despite the curtailment of Verona's own jurisdiction contemporaries still saw the *civitas* as a self-determining body?

Other writers were equally aware of the importance of keeping up these appearances, starting with those representing Venice itself. A case in point is the narrative developed by Paolo Morosini to describe how the Republic came to extend its jurisdiction over much of northern Italy. The Venetian humanist was writing to Cicco Simonetta, first secretary to duke Galeazzo

---

[32] On *deditiones*, consider Chittolini, 'Models of Government from Below'; alongside O'Connell, 'Voluntary Submission'.

[33] Avesani, *Verona nel Quattrocento*, 99–102. Other solutions are discussed in Mazzacane, 'Lo stato e il dominio nei giuristi veneti'.

34 BORDERS AND THE POLITICS OF SPACE IN LATE MEDIEVAL ITALY

Maria Sforza in the 1460s and 1470s.[34] His aim was to challenge the idea—held by much public opinion at the time—that 'my lordship [Venice] has so much ambition that not just its state but all of Italy would not be enough for her'. Accordingly, he went on to recount the Venetian expansion in eastern Lombardy not in terms of conquest or as the result of the frontier between the two polities shifting westwards but as the outcome of the resolution taken by Bergamo and Brescia to make themselves part of the Venetian jurisdiction ('farsi de la iurisdictione del principe nostro'). This narrative was in keeping with both the required appearances and the principles outlined by the jurists: it recognized the old *civitates* as distinct and autonomous, but it also sanctioned their subordination to a superior power. As had been done earlier for the cities themselves, adopting a jurisdictional discourse allowed contemporaries to frame the relationships between power holders and subject bodies.

Of course, this does not mean that regional powers relinquished the opportunity to project an image of undisputed authority over a uniform space. In this context, borders were not presented as a sum of pre-existing boundaries between older territories but rather as the unbroken limits of their idealized dominions. This emerges with particular clarity in a number of decrees issued by Gian Galeazzo Visconti. At the turn of the fifteenth century, the 'Italian despot' brought the process of state formation in Lombardy to its apex.[35] Having claimed for himself the title of imperial vicar, the then first duke of Milan started to describe his power as involving 'taking care of the people, properties, and goods' which were located in the territory that had been committed to him by the emperor. In Gian Galeazzo's view, it was wholly unacceptable that his subjects would derogate from his authority by seeking privileges and immunities from lords and cities existing 'within the borders of his jurisdiction'.[36] According to Federica Cengarle, this message was central to Gian Galeazzo's effort to define the territory within which his authority should be exclusive and represented an attempt,

---

[34] BMVe, ms. It. VII 762 (7668), 'Miscellanea', no. IV: 'la signoria mia essere di tanta ambitione che non solo del stato suo se vole et può contentare ma nianche tuta Italia gli basta'. For a discussion of the letter, see King, *Venetian Humanism*, 132–40; and now Toffolo, *Describing the City*, 198–202.

[35] The reference is to Bueno de Mesquita, *Giangaleazzo Visconti*; though, see now Gamberini, 'Gian Galeazzo Visconti'.

[36] I quote specifically from a decree in ASMi, *Panigarola* 1, cc. 40–1, 21 September 1388: 'disponere de personis, bonis et rebus...infra metas et terminos territorii nostre iurisdictioni'. For a more extended discussion, see Cengarle, 'Le arenghe dei decreti viscontei', 76.

on the part of the Visconti, to apply the culture of territoriality developed by the communes to a regional context.[37]

This regional territoriality was nonetheless more imagined than actually asserted. The cities might have been controlled by the Visconti, but the relative solidity of their *contadi* forced Gian Galeazzo to adapt his projects to the existing territorial landscape. A famous case of this unresolved tension is Gian Galeazzo's fictitious investiture as duke of Lombardy. Acquiring a feudal title from the emperor was a legal move as much as political one, for it allowed rulers to assert a jurisdiction which was seen as superior to that of the cities. In the end, however, the title granted to Gian Galeazzo by the emperor was that of duke of Milan, which only made him prince of the city and its countryside. Visconti was keen to project an image of uniform authority over the region, so his chancellors forged him a further investiture, one in which their master appeared not as duke of Milan but as *dux Lombardiae*.[38] Yet it is telling that, in forging this document, the Milanese chancellors still felt it necessary to list the single centres forming the dominion; in addition to duke of Lombardy, Gian Galeazzo was fictionally made duke of Brescia, Bergamo, Cremona, and many other Lombard communes. The Chancery's tendency to enumerate the individual *civitates* suggests that the Visconti's projection of regional territoriality was deeply unrealistic and would long remain grounded in the territorial dimension of the old city-states.

While seeking recognition from the emperor had been a recurrent trait of Milanese politics during the fourteenth and fifteenth centuries,[39] Venice had avoided the issue altogether by asserting its status as a city born out of the sea. This allowed the Venetians to frame their dominion as *res nullius*: that is, neither *terra imperii* nor *terra ecclesiae*. In 1423, when Venice started deploying its forces for the expansion in Terraferma, the doge's own title (*Dux Venetiarum*) still included no reference to mainland territories.[40] However, the timely replacement of the notion of *commune Venetiarum* with those of *dominium* and *signoria* betrays the extended degree of

---

[37] In addition to Cengarle, 'Le arenghe dei decreti visconei', 55–87; see her 'Vassalli et Subditi'.

[38] The investiture can be found in LÜNING, *Codex Italiae Diplomaticus* (vol. I), cols. 425–32. Consider also the study by Black, 'The Emergence of the Duchy of Milan'. On the masterminds behind Gian Galeazzo's projects, see Gamberini, 'Istituzioni e scritture di governo'.

[39] As discussed more broadly by Favreau-Lilie, 'Reichsherrschaft im spätmittelalterlichen Italien'.

[40] In fact, Venice might have retained this formula precisely to avoid controversies over the recent territorial acquisitions, as first suggested by Lazzarini, 'I titoli dei Dogi di Venezia'.

36 BORDERS AND THE POLITICS OF SPACE IN LATE MEDIEVAL ITALY

territorial authority now claimed by the Republic.[41] Like their Milanese counterparts, the Venetian chancellors were striving to project an image of unity and uniformity within the polity but had full knowledge that large *contadi*, such as that of Brescia, retained a key role in the organization of political spaces in eastern Lombardy.[42] For instance, when granting some valleys various shades of autonomy from the city of Bergamo, the Venetian chancellors still felt the need to identify each valley as part of both the Venetian dominion ('sub dominio venetorum') and the *contado* of Bergamo ('in districtu et episcopatu Pergomi').[43] And despite the fact that these valleys now directly bordered the Duchy of Milan, it was the Bergamasco as a whole—or rather, the city of Bergamo in union with its *contado*—that the Venetians saw as a frontier city-state ('civitas quae est ad frontieras').[44]

It follows that just as with the cities themselves, the frontiers of regional polities could be envisioned as sums of the boundaries between smaller units. A telling example comes from a letter sent to the king of Naples, only a few years later, by the duke of Milan. The letter dates from the summer of 1468, a time when Galeazzo Maria Sforza was discussing the terms of the marriage between one of his siblings and Ferrante's eldest daughter. In order to finalize the long-delayed union, the duke promised to endow his brother with the city of Tortona. While the practice of providing entire city-states as endowments was not exceptional,[45] the limited revenues offered by Tortona compelled Galeazzo Maria to explain why any other *civitas* would have been unsuited for the deal. In doing so, the duke left a pragmatic portrait of his dominion, airing a number of geopolitical concerns and offering a revealing description of its borders. He began by saying that Parma and Lodi were not an option. They were not only the real gateways to his dominion ('porta et bocha de questo stato') but also actual borderlands which were constantly craved by his neighbours, the marquis of Mantua (Parma) and the Venetians (Lodi). To the west, the cities of Novara and Alessandria were refused for the same reason. Both were located at the frontier with the territories of other major powers: the duke of Savoy (Novara) and the marquis

---

[41] As noted by both Grubb, *Firstborn of Venice*, 19–23 and Law, 'Verona and the Venetian State', 20.

[42] On Venice's conservative policies in the mainland, consider Zamperetti, 'Dalla tutela cittadina all'identità politica territoriale'; and generally Viggiano, 'Il Dominio da Terra'.

[43] A convenient collection of these privileges is in BMVe, ms. It. II 119 (4843), 'Iura iurisdictionum octo vallium bergomensium'.

[44] ASVe, *Senato Secreti (Registri)* 12, c. 18r, 3 November 1433.

[45] Nor was that of selling them off altogether, as highlighted by Martoccio, 'The Art of Mercato'.

1. *IURISDICTIO* IN PRACTICE   37

of Montferrat (Alessandria). Como, on the other hand, would also have been a dangerous gift, in light of its position on the borders with the Swiss ('alle confine et presso alli Sviceri'), whom the duke described as unruly people, always ready to take up arms. That left Piacenza, which Galeazzo Maria strongly advised against because of the animosity ('passione') of its internal factions, and Tortona, which he finally suggested as the most suitable.[46]

What is possibly most striking about this letter is that the entirety of the Visconti dominion could be comfortably disassembled by tracing the contours of former city-states, each of which could in turn be connoted by describing its location at the frontier with other polities. In the duke's own words, it was not the Duchy as a whole that bordered the Venetian Republic but the individual territories that made up his dominion (Lodi and the Lodigiano, in this case). The same was said about the people who populated those territories. In their letters, the duke and his chancellors never talked about those who dwelled at the frontier with the Republic but rather about those who lived 'on the borders with the towns and localities belonging to the dominion of Venice'.[47] Some might contend that these words betrayed mere geopolitical observations; the Lodigiano was indeed located alongside what we would now call the Venetian state. Yet it could also be argued that the duke's letter was in line with a specific understanding of territoriality, one in which pre-existing territories mattered just as much as—if not more than—the making of a new regional dominion.

At first glance, then, the territorial vocabulary of the fifteenth century described two different contexts. On the one hand, we have the reference to the regional spaces over which the Milanese prince and the Venetian lordship claimed to exercise their authority. On the other, we have the indication of smaller units, which as often as not corresponded to the *contadi* of the old city-states. If we turn our attention to the vocabulary used when writing about borders, the same two contexts can be found. The vast dossier of ducal letters concerning Venice from the early 1450s, when the first

---

[46] ASMi, *Carteggio* 217, 4 August 1468. The topos of the catalogue of cities was just as common in contemporary chronicles and other literary texts, as discussed by Lazzarini, 'La conquista di Pisa'; and, more broadly, Ricci, 'Cataloghi di città'. The topos is also found in visual representations, as demonstrated by Figure 3.

[47] ASMi, *Confini* 239, 9 August 1475: 'subditi quali sono in vicinanza et confini cum le terre et lochi della signoria de Vinetia'. Although numerous other examples could be provided, see especially ASMi, *Missive* 4, c. 132v, 11 April 1451: 'luochi, confini ac terre de Venetiani'; and ASMi, *Comuni* 17, f. 'Caravaggio', 22 April 1490: 'alle fine de Venetiani et molto vicino ad Crema, loro terra'.

38 BORDERS AND THE POLITICS OF SPACE IN LATE MEDIEVAL ITALY

Sforza duke was still struggling to come to terms with his belligerent new neighbour, provides a consistent sample of the terminology. In writing to his agents, the duke referred to state frontiers by distinguishing a *canto de qua* or *nostro canto* ('this side', 'our side') from a *canto de là* or *canto deli inimici* ('the other side', 'the enemy side'); he also identified the contents of his own dominion by using expressions such as *nel nostro terreno* ('in our land') or *de lo stato nostro* ('of our state'). At the same time, however, he mentioned several individual territories, for example when ordering the dispatch of troops to the frontiers of single city-states ('ad confina de Mediolano, Lodi et Cremona').[48]

In essence, at the end of the Middle Ages, when Venice and Milan were still adjusting to their redefined political spaces (that of the Lion expanded farther, that of the Viper considerably reduced), the reference to older bodies, as well as to their boundaries, remained pivotal. Despite some attempts at portraying the image of a uniform regional territory, power holders were well aware that their dominions were fundamentally defined by the individual units which composed them and, by extension, that state frontiers were defined by the borders of their constituent territories. As with city-states before them, the adoption of a jurisdictional discourse on the part of larger polities allowed them to frame their political and spatial relationships with pre-existing bodies; it established their jurisdictional superiority and determined the position of subject bodies within the polity. As a corporation itself, each *civitas* was equipped with its own borders, which meant that it could serve as the unit over which a superior jurisdiction was exerted. And just as the *civitas* would continue to exist as a collective subject within the polity, so its territory would continue to exist as the space over which power was exercised, regardless of the nominal holder of such power.

The Rise of Intermediate Entities

As regional polities incorporated the old city-communes into their dominions, new bodies asserted themselves as intermediate entities between the

---

[48] For the terminology, consider a dossier in BAMi, ms. Z 227 sup, f. 'Guerra co' Veneziani e col marchese di Monferrato 1452–4', together with the letters collected in ASMi, *Carteggio* 663, f. 'Milano-ducato 1453'. Several other examples can be found throughout the *Missive* registers for this period: e.g. ASMi, *Missive* 2, c. 247v, 17 September 1450; ASMi, *Missive* 6, c. 135v, 30 August 1451; ASMi, *Missive* 12, c. 46v, 26 February 1452; ASMi, *Missive* 25, c. 161r, 18 June 1455.

1. *IURISDICTIO* IN PRACTICE   39

Fig. 3 The Visconti dominion envisioned as a 'catalogue of cities' in a manuscript illumination from the mid-fourteenth century (BNFr, ms. Latin 6467, c. 1r). © Gallica.bnf.fr

40 BORDERS AND THE POLITICS OF SPACE IN LATE MEDIEVAL ITALY

dominant powers of the time and the corporations of the countryside. As mentioned above, these were typically major towns, community federations, and lay fiefs. By establishing themselves above rural corporations, below regional polities, and at the side—if not in place—of the old *contadi*, these bodies added a further level of complexity to the territorial hierarchy of late medieval Italy. Let us then briefly recount how this phenomenon came into being, before moving on to discuss the broader significance of this process for the jurisdictional order (and borders) of the peninsula.

In Lombardy at least, some intermediate bodies achieved a degree of independence from their respective *contadi* as early as the mid-fourteenth century. This was the time when the town of Crema gained autonomy from the city of Cremona, for example, and on entering the Milanese dominion received recognition of its long-standing influence over nearby villages.[49] The same could be said about Voghera and especially Vigevano, towns which the city of Pavia had long struggled to control but which the Visconti were more than happy to recognize as separate from the Pavese.[50] These bodies were subject directly to the prince, benefiting from a distinct tax regime and functioning as separate jurisdictional units within the old *contadi*. In practice, this meant that an official sent by the prince (rather than the cities) would now administer justice within the confines of their respective territories, which thus reified their jurisdictional separation.[51] In *contadi* like that of Milan, where the city had long curbed the ambitions of centres such as Monza, Lecco, Varese, and Vimercate, towns were not as populous and independent as Crema or Vigevano, but this did not stop the Visconti from redesigning the administrative geography of the area by creating a series of 'vicariates' centred around those towns.[52]

Similar policies were put in place across the Alpine foothills, which then occupied much of the Visconti dominion, intersecting with the *contadi* of Milan, Bergamo, and Brescia. Here, new jurisdictional bodies were made to fit the federal associations which already bound together the villages surrounding a lake or valley. While the individual villages remained in charge of managing common resources and distributing the tax burden among

---

[49] On Crema and its constitutional transformation during the passage from the Milanese to the Venetian dominion, see the work of Albini, 'Da castrum a città'; Albini, 'Crema tra XII e XIV'.

[50] On Vigevano and the towns of the Pavese, see the essays collected in Chittolini, *Metamorfosi di un borgo*.

[51] On the separation of small towns, consider Chittolini, 'Quasi-città. Borghi e territori in area lombarda'; and, for the Veneto, Bellavitis, 'Quasi-città e terre murate in area veneta'.

[52] On these policies, see mainly Gamberini, 'Il contado di Milano nel Trecento'.

1. *IURISDICTIO* IN PRACTICE   41

their residents, these federal associations took up functions previously exercised by the cities, such as the organization of military defences, the issuing and enforcement of statutes, and the representation of local interests before the prince.[53] Indeed, despite the complaints of the cities, the Visconti were prompt in ratifying the autonomy of federations by granting them the status of 'separate lands' (*terre separate*).[54] In the long run, by combining a tradition of self-government with the practice of administering justice within the ambit of new jurisdictions, the contours of these territories acquired a spatial significance which was largely comparable with that of the old *contadi*.[55]

In the early fifteenth century, the place of intermediate bodies in the Milanese dominion was strengthened further by one of Gian Galeazzo's sons: Filippo Maria Visconti. Confronted with the partial disintegration of his inheritance following the unexpected death of his father and the inept rule of his brother, Filippo Maria had to remake the Milanese dominion piece by piece. Many territories had proclaimed independence from the Visconti or been taken over by ambitious condottieri, such as Pandolfo Malatesta, who now controlled both Bergamo and Brescia. Crucially, however, Filippo Maria did not rebuild the dominion as it had been constructed by his ancestors—that is, city by city—but by negotiating the obedience of a large number of intermediate territories. This explicitly recognized their political autonomy and territorial identity, but it also revealed a fundamental transformation: *contadi* and rural corporations were no longer the only types of territory existing within the polity.[56]

Once his dominion had been put back together, Filippo Maria strengthened his hold over it by enfeoffing local lords, ducal courtiers, and military captains with groups of *castra*, *terrae*, and even entire valleys. While reaffirming the duke's prerogatives in the peripheries, albeit through the mediation of a vassal, this policy also had the effect of sanctioning an array of new bodies that escaped the control of the cities.[57] Located mainly at the

---

[53] On these institutions, see yet another pioneering essay by Chittolini, 'Principe e comunità alpine', together with the general model drawn by Della Misericordia, 'La comunità sovralocale'.

[54] The reference is both to actual terminology and to the field-defining study by Chittolini, 'Le terre separate'.

[55] On the administration of justice and its territorial ramifications, see the case studies in Della Misericordia, 'Essere di una giurisdizione'; and Zenobi, 'Nascita di un territorio'.

[56] On this process, see especially Gentile, 'La Lombardia complessa'. A different interpretation, arguing for the enduring importance of urban structures and solidarities, is held by Grillo, 'La fenice comunale'.

[57] The key assessment of these policies is Cengarle, *Immagini di potere e prassi di governo*, 95–134; but consider also Gentile, 'Aristocrazia signorile e costituzione del ducato'.

42 BORDERS AND THE POLITICS OF SPACE IN LATE MEDIEVAL ITALY

interstices of the old *contadi*, the enfeoffed localities numbered in the hundreds. This was particularly true of the *contadi* of Piacenza, Parma, and Reggio, where feudal pockets had never stopped hindering the territorial ambitions of the communes.[58] Yet in contrast to the cities, which, at best, had to tolerate the presence of such fiefdoms and, at worst, had to defend urban prerogatives against their growing power, Filippo Maria gave them a recognized place in the jurisdictional order of his dominion. Crucially, again, the new fiefs were never devised afresh but rather superimposed onto existing corporations or even onto series of them, ranging from individual communities to entire federations. As with the *contadi* before them, this allowed the new bodies to rely on the territorial dimension of pre-existing communities, while simultaneously establishing their jurisdictional superiority over them.

There was a time when the persistence or indeed creation of bodies which were openly alternative to the territorial organization of the cities would have been interpreted as a resistance to the formation of larger polities, if not as relics of the incomplete 'conquest of the *contado*' on the part of urban communes.[59] More recently, however, specialists have come to reappraise these bodies; it is now agreed that while city-states served as cornerstones in the making of new regional polities,[60] this construction work made equal use of other building materials, including townships, fiefs, and community federations. The Visconti relied extensively on these bodies to balance the lasting influence of the *civitates* and increase their chances of control, but in doing so they also sanctioned their discrete territorial dimension, particularly vis-à-vis the old *contadi*. This is not to say that the territories of the cities ceased to matter. If anything, the *contadi* now served as 'hollow bricks', as Andrea Gamberini has described them: established frameworks within which more compact, territorial aggregations carried out fiscal and judicial practices in almost full autonomy.[61]

As a matter of fact, the debate on the place of these new bodies in the territorial hierarchy of late medieval Italy is not purely historiographical; in fact, it was present in the fifteenth century itself. Rather like scholars today,

---

[58] Andreozzi, *Nascita di un disordine*; Gentile, *Terra e poteri*; and Gamberini, *La città assediata*.

[59] The traditional take is represented by de Vergottini, 'Origini e sviluppo storico della comitatinanza', 347–484. For the wider context, refer to Coleman, 'The Italian Communes'.

[60] As was authoritatively argued by Varanini, 'Governi principeschi e modello cittadino'; and Chittolini, 'Organizzazione territoriale e distretti urbani'.

[61] Gamberini, 'Principe, comunità e territori', 250; but consider also the slightly different reading in Somaini, 'The Collapse of City-States and the Role of Urban Centres'.

1. *IURISDICTIO* IN PRACTICE   43

contemporaries felt the need to explain their position in the jurisdictional order of the time. Jurists were considered to be the ultimate architects of an orderly society, so Filippo Maria turned to them for advice.[62] Among others, the jurist Martino Garati came up with a fascinating solution: he argued that all the bodies holding some form of *iurisdictio* over their respective territories should be given the title of 'provinces'.[63] This equalized townships, fiefs, and community federations as collective subjects of the prince, but it also raised them to a rank which hitherto had been given only to the ancient *civitates*. As with his father, Gian Galeazzo, Filippo Maria's projects for the territorial reorganization of the whole dominion were never put into practice, but Garati's solution shows that the intellectual coordinates within which both jurists and power holders were operating were essentially still the same. Like the fiefs themselves, the theorized 'provinces' of the dominion were not designed from scratch but were rather superimposed onto an expanse of multiform territories which were both autonomous political bodies and jurisdictional units over which a superior power could be exerted.[64]

* * *

In summary, this first chapter shows the extent to which a well-established territorial culture informed how the spatial fabric of the peninsula was both conceived and actually constructed, and how new intellectual paradigms were then made compatible with practices already under way. By acquiring a territorial connotation, the notion of *iurisdictio* had come to frame the way in which all contemporaries, and not just the jurists, conceived space politically. In this context, the adoption of a jurisdictional discourse reflected a contingent form of territoriality, one that lay with the part as much as with the whole and came from below as much as from above—a territoriality which was fundamentally modular, composite, and non-exclusive. In turn, this reflected the distinctive features of the polities of the time, starting with their mosaic structure and the contractual nature of their

---

[62] On the public perception of jurists in the Duchy of Milan, see Covini, La balanza drita, 19–27. On Filippo Maria's search for juristic theorizations which could legitimize his feudal policies, see Cengarle, *Immagine di potere e prassi di governo*, 61–86.

[63] On Garati and his work, see Black, 'The Limits of Ducal Authority'; and further Baumgärtner, *Martinus Garatus Laudensis*.

[64] It is striking that similar attempts would continue to frustrate leaders for much of the early modern period in much the same way as jurisdiction continued to provide the conceptual platform upon which those attempts were made. See Ross and Benton, *Legal Pluralism*; and now Pal, *Jurisdictional Accumulation*.

44 BORDERS AND THE POLITICS OF SPACE IN LATE MEDIEVAL ITALY

power base, as seen through the *deditiones* of the old city-states and through the legitimation of intermediate entities by Filippo Maria Visconti. But it also reflected the fact that multiple bodies, from cities and towns to fiefs and federations, could retain their shape and status within the territories of larger polities.

By extension, the territorial culture of the time informed the world of borders in three ways. First, it framed the coexistence of multiple bodies within the same polity, all equipped with their own boundaries. Second, it allowed those boundaries to remain in force legitimately: as an expression of their respective territories, they would continue to exist as long as the old jurisdictional order was kept in place. This suggests that the making of borders in late medieval Italy was never a mere byproduct of the process of polity formation; rather, it was the result of the composition of pre-existing units. Third, the territorial culture of the time allowed for a modular structure. As we have seen, the frontiers of Italian city-states were nothing more than a sum of boundaries between rural corporations. In the same way, the borders of regional states were built on the contours of the cities' *contadi* and, potentially, also on those of intermediate bodies. In all, this shows that much like territoriality itself, the borders of late medieval Italy were fundamentally modular, composite, and non-exclusive.

2

War and Peace

The Establishment of a New Political Geography

For much of Italy, the first half of the Quattrocento was a transformative period. Over the course of a few decades, the peninsula saw the establishment of a new political geography, one that was to remain virtually intact for over three centuries. The forces driving this change had been growing throughout the Trecento. As internal tensions became less and less manageable, several Italian cities became more and more reliant on the influence of a single oligarchy or family clan. These developments paved the way for novel concentrations of power which eventually evolved into republican or princely states. After setting aside most sources of internal tension (in one way or another), the new regimes began to expand their spheres of influence over neighbouring territories. As they did so, they fostered new relationships with these areas, forged new tools to control them, and fabricated new narratives to justify their subjugation under an increasingly centralized domain.[1] Still, it was not until the turn of the century that the political geography of the peninsula began its drastic transformation. At the time, as Garrett Mattingly put it in his classic volume on Renaissance diplomacy, 'space was becoming completely organized; political interstices were filling up; the margins and cushions were shrinking, and the states of the peninsula were being obliged by the resulting pressures to a continuous awareness of each other'.[2] In turn, this set in motion a process that some have described as one of 'Darwinian selection'.[3] As war became more expensive and the ability to drain resources from subordinate territories became ever more crucial, many smaller and less organized dominions fell under the control of their neighbours. Some remained independent but their fate was

[1] On these developments, see De Matteis and Pio, *Sperimentazioni di governo*; and broadly Jones, *The Italian City-State*.
[2] Mattingly, *Renaissance Diplomacy*, 60.   [3] Somaini, *Geografie politiche*, 55.

Borders and the Politics of Space in Late Medieval Italy: Milan, Venice, and their Territories. Luca Zenobi, Oxford University Press. © Luca Zenobi 2023. DOI: 10.1093/oso/9780198876861.003.0003

46 BORDERS AND THE POLITICS OF SPACE IN LATE MEDIEVAL ITALY

now bound to the handful of *potenze grosse* ('large powers') that had come to dominate the Italian stage.[4]

In northern Italy, these events brought the Duchy of Milan and the Republic of Venice into direct conflict. In 1402, the death of Gian Galeazzo Visconti marked a watershed for the cities and territories of the Duchy, now claiming once again their fierce independence from Milanese influence. The same could be said for those of the Veneto: as the Visconti's sphere of influence fell to pieces and the Carrara of Padua filled the resulting void, the Venetians were forced to take the field to protect their trade routes across the mainland. By the early 1420s, Filippo Maria Visconti, Gian Galeazzo's heir to the Milanese dominion, had seen the Duchy through a painstaking process of political recomposition. For its part, Venice now controlled the cities and territories once subject to the Carrara, had recently acquired the vast Patria del Friuli, and was ready to continue its expansion towards eastern Lombardy. With such developments on the horizon, the 'continuous awareness' described by Mattingly was bound to turn swiftly into open confrontation. Filippo Maria Visconti had no intention of abandoning his father's ambitions, while the new doge, Francesco Foscari, subscribed to the views of those in Venice who were less inclined to 'farm the sea and leave the land alone'.[5] War broke out and soon extended beyond Tuscany, where the Visconti tried repeatedly to penetrate the Florentine dominion, which was then allied with Venice, to the restive hills of Romagna, where local lords summoned the support of both powers to settle their feuds, and finally to Lombardy. The conflict saw Milan and Venice deploy an unprecedented array of forces, including experienced condottieri, such as the famed count of Carmagnola, and ambitious newcomers, starting with Francesco Sforza. As the campaigns unfolded, both parties called for the intervention of other powers: from the republics of Genoa and Lucca to the duchy of Savoy, and from the Aragonese in Naples to the pope in Rome.[6]

Thanks to its experienced companies and ingenious condottieri, Milan began the conflict with an advantage. But in the long run, it was Venice's new armies and abundance of resources that proved superior, allowing the Republic to extend its dominion over areas which had long been subject to the Duchy: the cities and territories of Bergamo, Brescia, and later

---

[4] Fubini, '*Potenze grosse*'.

[5] MURATORI, 'Raphayni de Caresini', cols. 467–8: 'proprium Venetorum esse mare colere, terramque postergare'.

[6] The most reliable commentary on these events remains Cozzi, 'Politica, società, istituzioni', 3–47.

2. WAR AND PEACE   47

Crema—namely most of what is now eastern Lombardy. This constituted a huge win for the Venetians. In the 1460s, it was estimated that these areas alone supplied a third of all the revenues raised in the mainland (over 100,000 ducats).[7] Such a large sum could only be raised in populous cities such as Brescia, which at this stage (with almost 40,000 residents and an economy in full bloom) could rival centres like Florence and Bologna.[8] The same can be said about the Bergamasco, where the smaller city of Bergamo functioned as a market hub for the rich shipments of wool and iron produced in the nearby valleys.[9] Ultimately, the economic advantages gained from acquiring eastern Lombardy were twofold. Precious resources could now be drawn from these territories, and some of their traffic could be directed towards Rialto. In addition, the Venetians were able to achieve the goal which had involved them in the conflict in the first place: protecting their mainland trade against foreign interference.[10] As the Republic consolidated its hold over these territories, its frontier with the Duchy of Milan was formally shifted westwards and the political geography of the region profoundly redesigned. It was the last decisive step towards the establishment of Venice's dominion in the mainland.

Over the years, the making of the Terraferma state has drawn much attention from specialists of the peninsula. Aside from economic strategies, scholars have traditionally focused on the exercise of public functions in subject territories (such as the administration of justice and the collection of taxes),[11] on the development of new magistracies (in the centre as much as in the peripheries),[12] and on the so-called politics of law (notably the reissuing of statutes and the striking of pacts and conventions with local

---

[7] BMVe, ms. It. VII 2581 (12473): 'Cronaca Veneta sino al 1457', cc. 359r–60v. Similar figures are discussed in Luzzatto, 'L'economia veneziana', 62.

[8] The figure was calculated on the basis of fiscal records by Pasero, 'Dati statistici'. We can draw a comparison with other cities thanks to the comprehensive tables compiled by Ginatempo and Sandri, *L'Italia delle città*, 78.

[9] The only available estimate for the population of fifteenth-century Bergamo is that of 10,000 people, as put forward by Beloch, *Bevölkerungsgeschichte Italiens* (vol. III), 142. However, it is reasonable to assume that even more people inhabited Bergamo at the time, especially considering that less than a century later, in 1526, a census conducted by local authorities counted almost 24,000 residents between the core of the city and the surrounding neighbourhoods: BMBg, *Municipali* 1, c. 301v, 'description de tutte le anime dela città et borgi dentro e di fora'.

[10] The advantages this gave Venice throughout early modernity are discussed in Zalin, 'Il quadro economico'; and especially Lanaro, 'Reinterpreting Venetian Economic History'.

[11] Viggiano, *Governanti e governati*; Pezzolo, *Il fisco dei veneziani*.

[12] Knapton, 'Le istituzioni centrali'; Varanini, 'Gli ufficiali veneziani'.

48 BORDERS AND THE POLITICS OF SPACE IN LATE MEDIEVAL ITALY

bodies).[13] Recently, new research has shed light on less well-known aspects behind the construction of the Terraferma state: the control of the environment and the management of food supplies,[14] the development of new written devices and archival series,[15] and even the role of symbolic narratives and cultural relations.[16] More importantly, for the scope of this chapter, scholars have come to recognize that the degree to which Venice could enforce new policies, install new institutions, appropriate lands, and generally shape people's lives on the Terraferma varied significantly across the dominion. In this respect, Gian Maria Varanini has talked about the existence of 'two Terraferme'.[17] One was composed of cities and territories closer to the lagoon, where Venice's impact had been far more substantial, namely in the Trevigiano and much of the Padovano, as well as part of Friuli and the Adriatic coast. The other was made up of areas with less immediate access, such as the Veronese and the Trentino, and by Venice's recent acquisitions in eastern Lombardy: the Bergamasco, the Bresciano, and the Cremasco.[18] Here, the construction of the mainland dominion had to rely more heavily on the mediation of local powers, including the cities themselves and their *contadi*, as well as some of their essential components, such as the factions and mountain communities of the Bergamasco, or the urban and rural aristocracies of the Bresciano.[19]

Despite this wealth of studies, the process through which Venetian expansion in the region was first negotiated remains unclear.[20] It is often said that by putting an end to the campaigns recounted above, the first treaty of Ferrara ratified the handover of eastern Lombardy to the Venetians (1428), while the peace of Lodi sanctioned it further in the eyes of the whole peninsula (1454). But what did this truly mean for the political geography of northern Italy? What did the acquisition of Bergamo, Brescia, and later Crema actually entail for the spatial dimension of the Terraferma, and how exactly did it take place? Did the takeover of an urban centre automatically

---

[13] Cozzi, 'La politica del diritto'; Povolo, 'Un sistema giuridico repubblicano'.

[14] Appuhn, 'Inventing Nature'; Faugeron, 'De la commune à la capitale'.

[15] De Vivo, 'Ordering the Archive'; Viggiano, 'Le carte della Repubblica'.

[16] Toffolo, 'Cities Dominated by Lions'; Davidson, As Much for its Culture as for its Arms.

[17] Varanini, 'La terraferma veneta del Quattrocento', 29–32.

[18] To name but two series of studies on different Terraferme: Zamperetti, *I piccoli principi*; Varanini, *Comuni cittadini e stato regionale*.

[19] On these dynamics, see, for the Bergamasco, Pederzani, *Venezia e lo Stado de Terraferma*; and for the Bresciano, Montanari, *Quelle terre di là dal Mincio*.

[20] Significantly, some of the studies touching upon these aspects are now a half- or even a whole century old: Cessi, 'Venezia alla pace di Ferrara'; Fossati, 'Francesco Sforza e la pace di Lodi'.

2. WAR AND PEACE   49

bring with it the control of all the surrounding countryside? Could any territory always be ascribed to a specific city-state in the Late Middle Ages? And if not, what does this tell us about the spatial fabric of Italian society? To answer these questions, this chapter adopts the conflicts and peace-making efforts of the first half of the Quattrocento as a vantage point from which to explore the establishment of a new political geography in northern Italy. In line with recent studies by French historians,[21] the chapter seeks to uncover the processes through which territories were annexed and frontiers moved before modernity, while also contributing to the recent revival of interest in the mechanics of medieval and Renaissance peace-making.[22] Special attention will be paid to the range of practices and ideas employed in doing so, and to the extent to which they were informed by the specificities of the areas concerned (the second Terraferma).

Throughout, an attempt will be made to consider peace treaties not as self-contained units but as systems of records: formal documents which both relied upon and gave rise to other writings, including earlier drafts and subsequent copies, as well as minutes of negotiations and diplomatic correspondence more broadly.[23] Specifically, the chapter's first section will consider the dealings that led to the treaty of Ferrara, the actors and mediators involved in its conclusion, and the criteria which ultimately guided their actions. Building on Chapter 1, we shall focus on instances in which their choices were driven by the application of general principles as much as by immediate exigencies. In so doing, we shall assess the extent to which the same territorial culture informed the agency of Milanese and Venetian deputies, while investigating how theoretical ideas informed the realm of diplomatic practice. The second section will shift focus away from the treaty of Ferrara and onto the peace of Lodi, while recounting the changing geopolitics of this tumultuous period. We shall look, in particular, for the devices and frames of reference adopted to sanction the new political geography of northern Italy. The chapter's third and final section will examine the proceedings through which treaties such as that of Lodi were implemented in the localities, so as to assess the contribution of peripheral bodies

---

[21] Berlioz and Poncet, *Se donner à la France?*; Péquignot and Savy, *Annexer?*. However, consider also a new study on the Iberian Peninsula: Schieweck, 'Iberian Frontiers Revisited'.

[22] Wolfthal, *Peace and Negotiation*; Lazzarini, *A Cultural History of Peace*. Particularly relevant is the reappraisal of the notion of spheres of influence in diplomatic treaties by Piffanelli, 'Crossing Boundaries'.

[23] As this work was finalized, a similar approach has been put forward by Piffanelli, *Politica e diplomazia*, 41–7; and Lazzarini, *L'ordine delle scritture*, 301–33.

50   BORDERS AND THE POLITICS OF SPACE IN LATE MEDIEVAL ITALY

in enacting changes driven by a centre. On the whole, by uncovering how territories were traded and frontiers shifted, the chapter hopes to show what drawing borders really meant in late medieval Italy, while also highlighting the role of non-state actors in the politics of space.

Mediation and Jurisdiction in the Treaty of Ferrara

The treaty of Ferrara was the first in a series of agreements which were employed extensively throughout the Quattrocento (and beyond) to trace the contours of the polities they concerned. By the spring of 1428, Venice had recaptured Brescia with a dramatic siege and was about to dispatch three patricians to take charge of Bergamo. Filippo Maria Visconti, on the other hand, was now keen to reach terms, especially after the defeat of Maclodio. He had already agreed to retreat from central Italy and to finalize his truce with Savoy by marrying the count's daughter.[24] By tying up these loose ends, the treaty brought a season of intense military conflict, economic disruption, and political instability to a close. Much to the chagrin of Filippo Maria Visconti, contemporaries were anticipating a period of renewed harmony between the Italian powers. These factors may well explain the great level of detail found in the treaty; it was a text designed to address a dangerously fluid situation and to prevent—with little success, as we shall see—any future confrontation.[25]

Another element denoting the distance between previous treaties and that of Ferrara is the presence of a papal legate as arbitrator. While it was not a novelty to request that the pope supply a mediator, it was far more common to call upon the head of a neighbouring state.[26] According to Isabella Lazzarini, it was the 'flexibility and openness of the whole peninsular system of powers [that] allowed third parties to intervene as mediators'.[27] Houses like the Este of Ferrara had a long tradition of intervention in foreign politics, truces, and border negotiations. It was one of several ways in

---

[24] Especially telling are some of the instructions sent by the duke to his ambassadors at the court of the soon-to-be Holy Roman Emperor. Sigismund had proved hesitant to intervene against Venice; as a result, Filippo Maria's requests for help had become ever more defeatist by the late 1420s: Osio, *Documenti diplomatici* (vol. II), 260, 335, 351, 364, 373, and 444.

[25] Dumont, *Corps universel diplomatique* (vol. II), 208–15 (19 April 1428).

[26] For the limited developments of papal diplomacy over the long fifteenth century, see Barbiche, 'Les *diplomates* pontificaux'. Thereafter, papal legates came to play a more flexible role, as discussed by Schneider, 'Types of peacemakers'.

[27] Lazzarini, *Communication and Conflict*, 119.

2. WAR AND PEACE   51

which less powerful actors preserved their influence on the political stage. In the early 1380s, for instance, the marquis Niccolò d'Este had settled a territorial dispute between Venice and the Carrara of Padua, who were then siding with Genoa in the War of Chioggia. The marquis boasted personal knowledge of the contested areas and could rely on the assistance of scholars with direct access to preceding pacts and conventions. As he put it, he accepted his designation with the goal of preserving peace and harmony between his neighbours.[28]

The papal legate appointed to mediate the treaty of Ferrara, Niccolò Albergati, proved to have a different view of the settlement, and indeed of his very role in the process. He argued that discord was an 'enemy to all mankind' and that the peace reached through his involvement would benefit the whole of Italy.[29] These claims speak to the new policy of wide-ranging intervention adopted by pope Martin V (especially in the wake of the challenges posed by conciliarism), but they also suggest that the Ferrara settlement was far from being a local and temporary affair in the eyes of contemporaries.[30] Albergati himself was a man of renowned stature, one who could boast an unrivalled experience in peace negotiations. In the early 1420s, his first appointment as papal legate had been to visit Burgundy, France, and England to act as a mediator in the aftermath of the treaty of Troyes, and later in the events following the death of Henry V.[31] By the late 1420s, few other people in Rome could match his diplomatic prowess. In recognition of his experience, pope Martin raised him to the College of Cardinals and dispatched him once again as his legate to settle the conflict between the Venetians, the Florentines, and the duke of Savoy, on the one hand, and Filippo Maria Visconti, on the other.

Although an initial agreement was reached only at the end of December 1427, Cardinal Albergati met the deputies of the four powers throughout the summer and autumn of that year.[32] On paper, this preliminary pact was framed as a series of resolutions (*arbitramenta*) adopted by a judge (the cardinal) in the presence of a series of witnesses (the deputies of Milan, Venice,

---

[28] ASVe, *Copie dei Pacta* 6, cc. 141r–144r, 16 October 1381.

[29] DUMONT, *Corps universel diplomatique* (vol. II), 203 (30 December 1427): 'inimicus humani generis'.

[30] On the vicissitudes of the Church in the 1420s and pope Martin's new policies, see Schwarz, 'Die Organisation der päpstlichen Kurie'; and broadly Partner, *The Papal State under Martin V*, 42–52.

[31] On Albergati's European missions, see Harvey, 'Martin V and the English', 60–2; and, more extensively, Bertuzzi, 'Le legazioni in Europa'.

[32] DUMONT, *Corps universel diplomatique* (vol. II), 203–7 (30 December 1427).

52   BORDERS AND THE POLITICS OF SPACE IN LATE MEDIEVAL ITALY

Florence, and Savoy). While the minutes recording what was discussed in those meetings have not survived, we know that the Venetian Senate rejected multiple drafts of the *arbitramenta*, which suggests that the path to their final approval had been far from straightforward.[33] Traditionally, scholars have paid most attention to the text of the treaty itself, dated April 1428, in which the parties seem to be playing a more active role.[34] But it is actually through the pact of December 1427 that the thorniest issues, and particularly those concerning borders and territorial arrangements, were first raised and settled.

The most pressing matter was the fate of Brescia, which was now solidly under Venetian control. The *arbitramenta* required the duke to confirm the surrender of the city and its dependent territory. To avoid any doubt, the latter was qualified as 'districtus, comitatus, episcopatus seu diocesis Brixie', and was said to comprise different sorts of settlements ('terrae, castra, loca') as well as a variety of natural elements ('aquae, valles, montes').[35] In addition, the Venetians would be given control over bodies that enjoyed fiscal and jurisdictional independence from Brescia. By discussing the fate of these bodies separately from that of the city, the text of the pact makes it clear that the area acquired by Venice did not come down to the *contado* alone; it concerned other major territories which, although they were located within the limits of the old *districtus*, benefited from some sort of autonomy from the city itself. In 1427, this was notably the case of federations such as that of the populous Val Camonica, home to at least 7,000 people by the end of the century.[36] This large Alpine valley had once been directly subject to Brescia but had long since acquired a degree of independence from the city thanks to charters granted first by the emperor and later by the lords of Milan. During the conflict between the Duchy and the Republic, this led the assembly of all the communities in the valley, headed by the most influential family in the area (the Federici), to act as an independent party and thus assert their separation from Brescia once again.[37]

In the Bergamasco, the city could not match Brescia's effective control over the settlements surrounding the urban centre (*terrae, castra, loca*).

---

[33] ASVe, *Senato Secreti* (*Registri*) 10, cc. 97v–146r (1 November 1427–7 May 1428).

[34] DUMONT, *Corps universel diplomatique* (vol. II), 208–15 (19 April 1428).

[35] DUMONT, *Corps universel diplomatique* (vol. II), 204 (30 December 1427), no. 5.

[36] Medin, 'Descrizione della città e terre bresciane', 678.

[37] On the Val Camonica, its separation from Brescia, and the role of local families in its attainment and subsequent negotiation, see Valetti Bonini, *Le comunità di valle*; and Della Misericordia, *I nodi della rete*.

2. WAR AND PEACE   53

Likewise, only a handful of Bergamasque valleys could boast the political autonomy and clear-cut territorial arrangements enjoyed by the Val Camonica.[38] As a result, in the negotiations of 1427 the Milanese deputies were able to question the very extent of the Bergamasco. They did so by raising doubts over the submission of some minor bodies to Bergamo, and thus to Venice. Territorial ambiguity had greatly increased over the previous few decades. For the most part, this was a byproduct of the fact that the Visconti had ruled over both the Bergamasco and the Milanese for a long time, something which partly blurred the boundaries between the two *contadi*. More importantly, a distinctive feature of the Visconti's policies in the Bergamasco had been the attempt to govern local bodies, such as valley federations and small towns, without resorting to the mediation of the city. In so doing, the Visconti were able to balance the relationships between the urban centre and rural bodies, while also asserting their position as a superior power. In the long run, these policies legitimized rural bodies as alternative forms of territorial organization and lessened the importance of their original affiliation to the *contadi* of Milan and Bergamo.[39]

During the negotiations that led to the *arbitramenta* of December 1427 and later when drafting the treaty itself in April 1428, two territories in particular happened to be disputed. The first was the town of Martinengo, some fifteen miles south of Bergamo; the second was the Val San Martino, a federation comprised of a dozen villages located between the foothills of the Alps and the left side of the river Adda, not far from Lecco. The agreement of 1427 required the cardinal to act as a judge in case anyone found reason to doubt the meaning of the text, particularly where this concerned the new borders between states ('occasione confinium').[40] Until that point, the deputies of Venice and Milan had found no common ground on the fate of Martinengo and the Val San Martino, so the cardinal was forced to reassemble them in May 1428, only a few weeks after the conclusion of the treaty.[41]

Although the deputies could not reach an agreement over these territories, they did agree that the criterion to be adopted for establishing which polity should control them was their original affiliation with one of the old *contadi*. On one side, the Venetians argued that both the *terra* of Martinengo

---

[38] For comparison, see Parzani, 'Il territorio di Brescia'; alongside Pagani, 'Bergamo *Terra di San Marco*'.

[39] For an overview of these developments in the Bergamasco, consider Varanini, 'Considerazioni introduttive'; together with Chittolini, 'Legislazione statutaria e autonomie'.

[40] DUMONT, *Corps universel diplomatique* (vol. II), 206 (30 December 1427, no. 19).

[41] ASVe, *Miscellanea* 35, 5 May 1428.

54 BORDERS AND THE POLITICS OF SPACE IN LATE MEDIEVAL ITALY

and the *universitas* of San Martino belonged to the Bergamasco and so should be assigned to the Republic. On the other, the deputies of Filippo Maria Visconti, whose armies still controlled both the town and the valley at this stage, contended that they had long been part of the Duchy. The Venetians' claim that Martinengo and the valley had once been directly subject to the city of Bergamo was correct. However, their counterparts could still argue that both territories belonged to the Visconti dominion by playing on the double meaning of 'duchy'. In the fifteenth century, as Jane Black has demonstrated, 'duchy' could stand for the regional space under the rule of the duke, which had comprised the territories in question for a long time, as well as for the *districtus* of the city of Milan, namely the much more limited Milanese *contado*, which had never extended as far as Martinengo or the Val San Martino.[42] In this sense, the claim that these territories were once part of the duke's dominion (the larger duchy) was true but offered no leverage to the Milanese delegation. What mattered was the original affiliation of these territories to one of the old *contadi*, which explains why they were prepared to lie about them being part of the Milanese *districtus* (the smaller duchy).

Since the two positions were irreconcilable, the last word was left to Niccolò Albergati. One way in which the cardinal could have ruled was by applying the right of conquest. This would have sanctioned the duke's control over Martinengo and the Val San Martino while confirming that the rest of the Bergamasco would remain under Venetian rule. Alternatively, one might have expected the cardinal to determine the arrangement of the new state borders in compliance with certain geographical features, starting from the river Adda. Since its course runs along the full length of the Val San Martino, this would have made both the valley and the town of Martinengo part of the Venetian Terraferma. At the time, however, other principles informed the settlement of border disputes. The first is well known among medievalists: it is the notion that instead of judging in favour of one of the parties involved, a settlement should find a compromise that was satisfactory to all of them.[43] The second was the idea that pre-existing territories and particularly the old *contadi* should be used as the first point of reference. In the text recording the outcome of this last series of negotiations, dated May 1428, one can see the extent to which the cardinal and his

---

[42] Black, 'Double duchy'.

[43] Specifically on this principle, see Martone, *Arbiter/Arbitrator*, 103–29; and Kampmann, *Arbiter und Friedensstiftung*, 26–65.

2. WAR AND PEACE 55

secretaries were guided by these principles. The ducal forces had put substantial effort into capturing and retaining the town of Martinengo, which at this point remained a Milanese stronghold within the area controlled by the Venetian armies. Yet the cardinal had no qualms about restating its original affiliation with Bergamo, which meant that Filippo Maria Visconti was expected to surrender the town to the Venetians. Conversely, the Val San Martino was said to have been united with the *contado* of Milan in the past ('tamque unita ducati Mediolani') and was thus judged to belong to the duke ('spectare et pertinere ad illustrissimum dominum ducem').[44]

In a manner similar to that of the records examined in Chapter 1, the language employed by contemporaries to describe these decisions betrays a jurisdictional discourse: a territorial body (the valley) was subject to a superior ruler (the duke) only by virtue of being part of the wider territory (the *contado*) upon which the jurisdiction of the ruler was already exercised. More broadly, the dealings surrounding the treaty of Ferrara, between December 1427 and May 1428, offer a first glimpse into the practice of territorial negotiation in late medieval Italy. They show that aside from the old *contadi*, state deputies referred to several smaller bodies to describe the territorial modifications brought about by Venice's expansion in eastern Lombardy, and thus also to locate the new borders between the two states. Instead of describing the enlarged shape of the Venetian Terraferma against the shrinking dominion of the duke of Milan, negotiators continued to refer to pre-existing territorial units. With regard to the Bresciano, where the city's *contado* could boast a certain degree of internal unity, the treaty of Ferrara only needed to mention that except for separate bodies such as the Val Camonica, all the localities immediately 'obedient to Brescia', as chronicles and scribes then put it, were now under Venetian rule.[45] By contrast, the less coherent composition of the Bergamasco forced the negotiators to shift their focus from the level of the *districtus* to that of intermediate units (the town of Martinengo and the Val San Martino). In both cases, they were applying a principle which we could define as one of jurisdictional affiliation: as long as a body's original association with a city's *contado* could be

---

[44] ASVe, *Miscellanea* 35, 5 May 1428.

[45] Consider how these developments are described in a contemporary epitome from the ducal archives: 'relassa el dicto Duca de Milano a la signoria de Venexia Bressa e lo bressano e ogni terra obediente a quella'; together with the similar expression employed by a Venetian chronicler a few decades later: 'tutti li luoghi sui utili dove dar obedientia a Bressa'. The quotations are drawn from minutes published by Osio, *Documenti diplomatici* (vol. II), 367; and from the account of the year 1428 in BMVe, ms. It. VII 1827 (7620): 'Annali di varii successi di guerre in Lombardia et Marca Trivisana cominciando l'anno 1237 per tutto agosto 1509'.

56 BORDERS AND THE POLITICS OF SPACE IN LATE MEDIEVAL ITALY

determined, its fate as a territory subject to one of the two dominions could be decided.

Geopolitics and Scale in the Peace of Lodi

The second treaty of Ferrara (1433) and especially the treaty of Cremona (1441) had a far less transformative impact on the political geography of northern Italy.[46] One must wait until the peace of Lodi (1454) for another portion of the Duchy—the town of Crema and its territory—to be annexed to the Venetian dominion, and with that, for the new state frontier to see a second and final shift. This is not to say that the 1430s and 1440s were not riddled with changes in their own right. The politics of the peninsula were reshaped by the arrival of new actors on the Italian stage; however, the spaces within which they acted remained largely the same.[47] Next to Alfonso the Magnanimous, who had conquered Naples and transferred the court of Aragon there, this was famously the case of Francesco Sforza. Over just a few decades, the low-born condottiere had risen to marry the only daughter of Filippo Maria Visconti and eventually to take possession of the Duchy itself. His success was achieved not only through marriage and military prowess but also thanks to his ability to carve out a reputation for himself as a legitimate player on the Italian chessboard. This led to him arbitrate the peace of Cremona in 1441 and, more importantly, to establish a special relationship with the Medici, something which later prevented the alliance between Florence and Venice, which had sustained so many wars in northern Italy, from forming again.[48]

In the spring of 1450, following his triumphal entry into Milan, the position of Francesco Sforza as duke was still far from stable; however, the desire for peace and order was tangible. Shortly after his accession, the condottiere dispatched three envoys to the Venetians, charged with the task of discouraging them from renewing their military efforts against the Duchy. Although their reports to Sforza are often encrypted, signalling that

---

[46] The two treaties can be found respectively in DUMONT, *Corps universel diplomatique* (vol. II), 258–65 (26 April 1433); and DUMONT, *Corps universel diplomatique* (vol. III), 108–15 (20 November 1441).

[47] Far more exhaustive interpretations of the politics of this period can be found in Chittolini, 'Tra Milano e Venezia'; and now Somaini, 'Filippo Maria e la svolta del 1435'.

[48] On Francesco Sforza and his rise to power (in Lombardy) and influence (in the whole of Italy), see Ilardi, 'The Banker-Statesman and the Condottiere-Prince'; and Peyronnet, 'Un virtuose de la guerre et de la paix au quattrocento'.

2. WAR AND PEACE   57

relations were still quite tense, they still provide us with a window into the contrasting positions held by the two leaderships at this time. Where Sforza was desperate to ensure stability and establish clear areas of influence in northern Italy, the Venetians, who were well aware of the precariousness of his position, were considering taking up arms in Lombardy once again. On the night of 22 June, in a meeting that lasted until the early hours of the morning, the Milanese envoys laid out their case very plainly: 'waging war against one's neighbours'—they argued—'spread war everywhere and up to the stars'; but this time, they reminded the Venetians, the duke would have the support of many friends and particularly of those who 'felt hatred and envy towards the lordship of Venice' (the Medici of Florence).[49] What ensued is fairly well known: the Milanese delegation failed to convince the Venetians and war resumed for another two years, from 1452 until 1454, when the peace of Lodi brought the protracted conflict between the Duchy and the Republic to a close.

At the outset, the treaty was simply a bilateral agreement between the two northern powers. Nevertheless, the degree to which the politics of the peninsula were intertwined soon brought other major actors onto the scene to ratify its terms. Each had specific reasons for doing so: the pope was hoping to have his claims over much of central Italy recognized, Alfonso was looking to be acknowledged as a peer by the peninsular powers, and the Medici in Florence were keen to cash in their bet on Francesco Sforza. While pursuing their own motives, all these actors sought to achieve the same two goals.[50] The first was confirming their status. Unlike the city-states before them, many of the regional dominions established between the fourteenth and fifteenth centuries lacked formal legitimation. Due to the number of actors involved, the peace of Lodi offered the ideal platform for mutual recognition. The second goal was preventing a single power from overcoming the others. The propaganda orchestrated by Milanese and Florentine humanists against Venice's putative dream of conquering the whole peninsula is the most striking evidence of the reality of these worries.[51] Still, given the scope of the struggle discussed earlier, it is not hard to believe that the desire for stability went well beyond political contingencies. Peace, Sforza told a confidant after the conclusion of the treaty, was the legacy he meant

---

[49] ASMi, *Carteggio* 340, 23 June 1450: 'la guerra coi vicini si tirava dietro la guerra d'ogni luogo infino alle stelle … altri che portavano odio et invidia alla loro illustrissima signoria'.
[50] The key studies here are all by Fubini, *Italia quattrocentesca*. However, see especially Fubini, 'The Italian League and the Policy of the Balance of Power'.
[51] Rubinstein, 'Italian Reactions to Terraferma Expansion'.

58   BORDERS AND THE POLITICS OF SPACE IN LATE MEDIEVAL ITALY

to leave his progeny, so that 'his children, their children, and all their descendants until the sixth generation would not see any other war in Lombardy'.[52]

To prevent further conflicts, Venice and Milan (the powers most involved in the struggles of the first half of the century) had to put an unprecedented effort into defining the limits of their respective dominions. At this stage, as Michael Mallett wrote so lucidly, 'their concern was not to annihilate their rivals, but to achieve security and predominance within clearly defined spheres of influence'.[53] In this respect, coupled with the creation of the Italian League, the peace of Lodi marked a significant break from previous treaties: it enshrined the regional dimensions of five major states (Venice, Milan, Florence, Rome, and Naples) whilst preserving the autonomy of less extended polities, which were now formally protected from further invasion and from the ambitious plans of belligerent condottieri.[54] While seeking to prevent future conflicts, the peace of Lodi was an agreement that looked consistently to the past: it approved the territorial modifications sanctioned by previous treaties—notably those of Ferrara (1428) and Cremona (1441)—and more importantly, for the theme of this chapter, it adopted the same criteria when doing so.

To start, the negotiations that led to the final draft of the treaty are a testament to the widespread use of older units to anchor new territorial modifications. For example, when it first came to negotiating the limits of his newly acquired dominion, in the early months of 1454, Francesco Sforza proved unwilling to yield strategic territories, including several transit valleys in the Alps. At the same time, he was open to surrendering other assets, such as the group of communities that went under the name of Geradadda. These rich and populous centres were traditionally attached to the *contado* of Cremona but their location just south of the Bergamasco, on the eastern bank of the river Adda, made them hard to defend from an attack. This suggests that the duke was open to the possibility of abandoning a portion of the Cremonese (the Geradadda) to retreat to the protection offered by the river. More importantly, it shows that much like the Val San Martino in 1428, an aggregation of communities such as the Geradadda served as the

---

[52] ASMi, *Carteggio* 341, 21 April 1454: 'li filioli de li filioli loro infino a sexta generatione mai ne vederano più guera in Lombardia et questa è la heredità che volgino lassare a li suoi figlioli'.

[53] Mallett, *Mercenaries and their Masters*, 2.

[54] On this system and the politics of the Lodi settlement, see Covini, 'Political and Military Bonds'; and Isaacs, 'Sui rapporti interstatali'.

next available spatial reference when a city's *contado* (the Cremonese) happened to be fractured.[55]

In the end, the final draft of the treaty ruled that the Geradadda would remain with the Duchy, together with a few other towns that were also traditionally attached to the Cremonese (Pandino, Agnadello, and Mozzanica). However, doubts remained as to who should be awarded possession of several other villages in the area.[56] As in the case of the negotiations following the treaty of Ferrara, the issue was tackled not by drawing a line across the Cremonese but by establishing the formal jurisdictional affiliation of the contested localities ('loci de debato').[57] Much like Cardinal Albergati in 1428, the negotiators gathered at Lodi were not concerned with the localities' current state of subjection to the Duchy but with whether or not they belonged to the ancient *contado* of Cremona. Similarly, localities which were found to be extraneous to the Cremonese were not simply assigned to the Republic but united with the nearest Venetian territory, that of Crema. Like the Geradadda, the Lombard town had long enjoyed jurisdictional separation from Cremona and functioned as an administrative centre for the surrounding villages. As a result, the peace of Lodi could state that these localities should be subject to Venice precisely 'because of the jurisdiction of Crema'.[58]

In essence, as illustrated by Figure 4, establishing the new frontier between the Duchy and the Republic in eastern Lombardy came down to negotiating lists of territories whose jurisdictional affiliation needed to be determined. These could vary in scale and degree of autonomy. When possible, the chancellors and deputies involved would refer to earlier urban frameworks. According to the treaty, Francesco Sforza was expected to return to their previous owners all the towns and villages he controlled in the Bergamasco and the Bresciano, thus restoring the original extension of the two *contadi*; conversely, Venice had its hold over the Cremasco recognized. In addition to adopting the limits of large urban districts, the peace of Lodi made use of smaller territories to fix the shifting frontier between

---

[55] The episode is discussed in full by Margaroli, *Diplomazia e stati rinascimentali*, 120. While this chapter uses almost exclusively Milanese evidence, a Venetian perspective on the negotiations can be found in the old treatment by Antonini, 'La pace di Lodi e i segreti maneggi che la preparano'.

[56] On these towns and villages and their relationships with Cremona, see Chittolini, 'Centri minori del territorio'; and Gamberini, 'Rivendicazioni urbane, autonomie locali'.

[57] ASMi, *Carteggio* 1525, s.d.

[58] MURATORI, 'Capitula Pacis', cols. 1013–14: 'la giurisdizione e dominio resti ad essa Illustrissima Signoria di Venezia per la giurisdizione di Crema'.

60 BORDERS AND THE POLITICS OF SPACE IN LATE MEDIEVAL ITALY

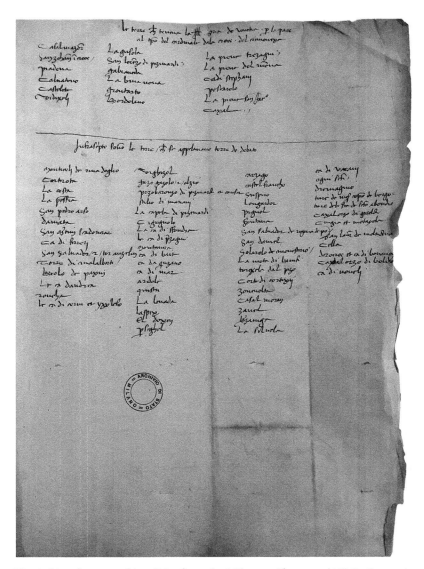

Fig. 4 List of contested localities from the Milanese Chancery (ASMi, *Carteggio* 1525, s.d.). Reproduced with permission from the Italian Ministry of Cultural Heritage

the two states. In doing so, the Milanese and Venetian delegations were able to move the negotiations from the level of the *districtus* to that of more compact bodies, such as the intermediate aggregation of the Geradadda. If these were not available, negotiators were left with no choice but to drill down to the level of individual localities, as in the case of the villages of the Cremonese mentioned above. In sum, much like the treaty of Ferrara, the peace of Lodi employed different spatial scales to describe the political geography of the 1450s, while again adopting the principle of jurisdictional affiliation to place small and large territories in relation to each other.

Trading Territories, Shifting Borders

The role of smaller territories in defining the new political geography of northern Italy can be explored further by looking at how the terms of the treaty were later implemented. Specifically, the moment in which the arrangement of state borders effectively shifted is traceable to a unique series of proceedings. Depending on the party recording the event, these are known in the sources as either *consignationes* or *acceptationes*. While they were ostensibly public ceremonies, they bore a remarkable resemblance to a practice normally conducted between private individuals. This practice is what medieval notaries called *confessio*: the deed through which a person acknowledged receipt of an agreed sum in fulfilment of a preceding transaction—a payment receipt, essentially.[59] At this stage, public treaties such as the peace of Lodi were still framed as an agreement between private parties. The negotiation of the treaty was led by deputies who acted in the name of the duke or doge, rather than as representatives of abstract political communities.[60] And with public treaties being modelled on private contracts, it should not come as a surprise that mechanisms such as the notarial *confessio* informed the proceedings through which authority over territorial units was effectively transferred.[61]

---

[59] A description of this practice and some detailed evidence of its longevity in the region can be found in Salvi, *Tra privato e pubblico*, 181–2.

[60] Scholars of international law have talked about sovereigns as 'treaty partners' to frame the role of rulers in transactions of this kind; see, in particular, Grewe, *The Epochs of International Law*, 196. Still, differences remained across Europe, starting with the practice of having treaties ratified by parliaments and assemblies in some kingdoms, as discussed by Meron, 'The Authority to Make Treaties', 2.

[61] On the intermingling of these different traditions, see Ziegler, 'The Influence of Medieval Roman Law on Peace Treaties'; and Lesaffer, 'The Medieval Canon Law of Contract'.

62 BORDERS AND THE POLITICS OF SPACE IN LATE MEDIEVAL ITALY

In practice, trading territories required two deputies (*procuratores*) to convene in the space that was the object of the transaction. Here, they would gather local representatives to witness the event. These were typically prominent landowners, members of the clergy, and often also people with sound knowledge of the landscape. In compliance with the terms of the treaty, one agent would then deliver (*consignare*; hence *consignatio*) the territory in question to his counterpart, who in turn would publicly acknowledge its receipt (*acceptare*; hence *acceptationes*—or indeed *confiteri*; hence *confessio*). One need only look at the language used to gain a sense of how much these ceremonies were shaped by contractual practices. Several clues can be found in the reports sent to Milan by deputies who were travelling 'from place to place to execute and bring to an end the restitution of all those localities of the Bresciano' and of the Bergamasco.[62] In these reports, the deputies presented their activities as involving the transfer of certain lands ('certe terre') which the duke owed ('debito') and the Venetians were meant to receive ('credito').[63] To put it simply, contemporaries saw the trading of territories as the act of balancing debit and credit in lands.

Although drawing on private practices, these proceedings served the same purpose as other public deeds, starting with the so-called acts of surrender (*deditiones*). These were the material result of the process through which a city framed its subjection to a higher power, typically a prince (the duke of Milan) or a dominant centre (the *commune* and later *signoria* of Venice). As seen in Chapter 1, acts of surrender allowed cities to bargain for their rights and duties within the larger polity, while the polity itself gained the opportunity to assert its authority over them publicly. In this sense, *deditiones* and *consignationes* had fundamentally the same function: they sanctioned a change in the ownership of jurisdiction over a subject body, while also recognizing its existence as a distinct unit. But where a *deditio* allowed cities to negotiate their place within the larger polity, a *consignatio* transferred territories from one power holder to another without much consultation. Thus, the proceedings discussed above kept together the double nature of *iurisdictio*—territorial and personal at the same time—by channelling territorial authority over a given body from the original power holder (the duke) to his deputy on site, then to the corresponding deputy for the other party, and finally to the new power holder (the doge).

---

[62] ASMi, *Carteggio* 341, 14 April 1454: 'de loco et loco per exequire et dare fine alla restitutione de quillli [sic] lochi de Bressana'.

[63] ASMi, *Carteggio* 341, 14 April 1454.

The proceedings were conducted by high-calibre representatives, documented by local notaries, and subsequently recorded by central chanceries. Given what was at stake, the Venetians deployed a large group of deputies to receive the remaining localities of the Bresciano and the Bergamasco. These were headed by one of the architects of the Lodi settlement, Paolo Barbo. In March 1454, while receiving his mandate to negotiate the treaty, the patrician had already been instructed to receive 'in manibus' any sort of territorial gain resulting from its application.[64] He was also responsible for updating the duke on the progress of the proceedings, as is evident from some of the numerous letters he sent him.[65] As he fulfilled his mission, Barbo issued the Milanese Chancery with written acknowledgements of the completion of the two most important proceedings: one for the Bresciano and another for the Bergamasco. The Chancery labelled them 'acts of acceptance' ('instrumenta acceptationis') and soon transcribed them in registers containing other official texts, such as the treaties themselves and the verdicts of preceding arbitrations.[66]

At first glance, the drafting of two distinct acts and, with that, the holding of two separate ceremonies may seem to reflect the sustained primacy of the two urban frameworks: the Bresciano and the Bergamasco. However, the headings assigned to these documents by Milanese chancellors already reveal which bodies they were really about. The first is entitled 'act of acceptance regarding the said localities of the Bergamasco';[67] the second is said to concern all the 'lands held by the most illustrious duke in the Bresciano'.[68] This shows that the *contadi* of Bergamo and Brescia were still used as the most inclusive references, even though the transaction only concerned smaller territories within the two *districti*. These were the *loca* and *terrae* still held by the duke in the area, despite Venice controlling the rest of the two *contadi* (not to mention the cities themselves). For this reason, referring to the *districtus* as a whole was not a viable option, so lower levels of description were adopted once again.

---

[64] ASMi, *Carteggio* 1524, 28 March 1454.

[65] Notably ASMi, *Carteggio* 1568, 17 April 1454; and ASMi, *Frammenti* 1, f. 12/4, 18 April 1454.

[66] ASMi, *Registri* 18, cc. 387r–388r. For more details on these registers, see Chapter 6.

[67] ASMi, *Registri* 18, c. 387r, 17 April 1454: 'instrumentum acceptationis infrascriptum locorum omnium Pergamensi'.

[68] ASMi, *Registri* 18, c. 388r, 29 April 1454: 'terrarum tenebantur per illustrissimo domino ducem in agro Brixiensis'.

64 BORDERS AND THE POLITICS OF SPACE IN LATE MEDIEVAL ITALY

The handover of the ducal possessions in the Bergamasco occurred on 17 April, only a week after the conclusion of the peace of Lodi (9 April 1454).[69] Although the document is said to concern all the localities still held by the duke in the area, the proceedings took place in the village of Calolzio, in the Val San Martino, and specifically in the garden of the Benagli family. Throughout the first half of the century, the valley had been fiercely contested because of its strategic position, just south of Lecco and on the eastern bank of the river Adda.[70] Having fought in the area himself, Francesco Sforza knew well the advantages of controlling a bridgehead on the opposite side of the river; in the end, however, the support lent to Venice by families such as the Benagli tilted the balance in favour of the Republic. Owing to the retreat of the ducal forces, the eastern boundary of the Val San Martino (not far from the river itself) was to become the new state frontier. This explains why the ceremony was held in Calolzio: both sides needed to engage with the territory in question, while also securing the support of local powers.[71] In light of this, it is not surprising that the families who had sided with Venice during the last war (notably the Benagli, Lazzona, and Rota) provided four of the five witnesses taking part in the proceedings. The notary in charge of the deed (Alberto Rota) was also a member of one of these families, whereas a second notary (the *magister* Giovanni Corti) was involved most likely on account of his professional acquaintance with the area.[72]

In the Bergamasque proceedings, the Val San Martino provided a spatial reference which was much more manageable than that of the entire *districtus* but also not as minute as that of individual villages. By contrast, the area of the Bresciano still controlled by the duke featured no intermediate bodies; as a result, deputies were left with no choice but to list all the individual villages ('loca'), fortifications ('castra'), and towns ('terrae') set to be transferred

---

[69] ASMi, *Registri* 18, c. 387r, 17 April 1454.

[70] Local historians have worked extensively on these vicissitudes. See especially Longoni, *Fonti per la storia dell'alta Valle San Martino*; and Bonaiti, 'Val San Martino: Una terra di mezzo'.

[71] The same could be said about Martinengo. Only a week later, the town was the object of a separate *consignatio* in the presence of local witnesses: ASVe, *Miscellanea* 39, 24 April 1454. Unlike the Val San Martino, Martinengo was not controlled by the duke at this stage but by the condottiere Bartolomeo Colleoni, who had recently abandoned Sforza to fight for Venice. A separate ceremony was thus necessary, since jurisdiction over the town had to be transferred first from the *condottiere* to the duke and then from the duke—or better still, his deputy—to the corresponding deputy sent by Venice.

[72] To judge by a surviving notebook, few others could match his familiarity with the lands and villages that made up the valley: ASBg, *Archivio notarile* 166.

2. WAR AND PEACE   65

from one party to the other.[73] This time, the ceremony took place in Brescia. Although the city itself had no part in the proceedings, the leaders of families with a significant stake in those territories, such as the Gambara and the Martinenghi, had taken up residency there. Much like the Benagli in the Bergamasque proceedings, they all feature prominently in the *consignatio* of territories where their influence was most felt. The localities still controlled by the duke in the area made up a consistent ring of settlements on the left bank of the river Oglio. In the early 1450s, this created a fluid frontier in the midst of what was traditionally regarded as the *contado* of Brescia. Francesco Sforza was personally involved in snatching these towns and localities from Venetian control, as shown by his correspondence with on-site officials. Some were brought under ducal control by deploying armies; others were acquired *cum littere*, that is, by enticing them with written promises of grants and privileges. By June 1452, the duke could boast of controlling over 25 localities beyond the river Oglio.[74] It follows that in enforcing the terms of the treaty, the proceedings of the *consignatio* were not only returning these territories to Brescia but also shifting the frontier between the two dominions back to the banks of the river.

Both documents show that the territorial modifications framed by Lodi were implemented not through top-down impositions but by performing the handover of individual units before the people who would be most affected by the change. Like the better-known *deditiones*, these proceedings asserted the primacy of regional powers over these lands, but they also ensured their jurisdictional identity, being as recognizable units within a *contado* or as legitimately separate bodies. Like the acts of surrender of some cities, they also acknowledged the role and position of local leaderships. As Sergio Zamperetti has shown for Vicenza and Gian Maria Varanini for Belluno, it was not uncommon for prominent families or local factions to play a key role in framing the surrender of urban centres.[75] It seems that the same can be said of the acts through which the territories of smaller bodies were annexed to a new dominion. Finally, in shaping the relationship between a polity and its new territories, these proceedings endorsed their spatial configuration. In the same way as the *deditiones* confirmed the integrity of the old city-states within the new regional dominions, the *consignationes* retained the individual status of smaller territorial bodies.

---

[73] ASMi, *Registri* 18, c. 388r, 29 April 1454.
[74] ASMi, *Missive* 13, cc. 146r–146v, 10 June 1452.
[75] Zamperetti, 'Vicenza e il Vicentino'; Varanini, 'I ghibellini di Belluno'.

66 BORDERS AND THE POLITICS OF SPACE IN LATE MEDIEVAL ITALY

Interestingly, the *instrumenta acceptationis* omitted any detailed descriptions of these territories, as if their contours were already evident to all. This goes to show that when the ownership of jurisdiction changed hands, even though the borders between the Duchy and the Republic shifted, the familiar boundaries of the traded territories remained untouched. Together, the necessary involvement of local representatives and the preservation of pre-existing territorial arrangements are a testament to the extent to which the specificities of the 'second Terraferma' informed the politics of space.

* * *

Taken as a whole, this chapter shows how the system of records preceding and even following treaties such as those of Ferrara and Lodi framed the establishment of a new political geography in northern Italy. They sanctioned the Venetian conquest of eastern Lombardy, but they also laid down, albeit in general terms, how it would affect the limits of the two dominions. This was not done by drawing a line of distinction between the Duchy and the Republic (from point A to point B, as we might do nowadays) but by listing the individual units under their rule (territories A, B, C, and D). From a legal perspective, these treaties were nothing but a public agreement through which the deputies of two private parties (the duke and the doge) reached an understanding over the content of such lists, often through the mediation of a third party (the papal legate). Since many of the geopolitical changes occurring in the first half of the Quattrocento were brought about by Venetian expansion, the process came down to listing the localities still held by the duke within areas now subject to the Republic (the Bergamasco, the Bresciano and, to a lesser extent, the Cremasco). In short, the objects of territorial negotiations were never the territories of the states themselves but rather the territories of the plurality of bodies which they controlled.

Both the final drafts of the treaties and the minutes of the negotiations relating to them employed a plurality of spatial references to describe territorial modifications. Where possible, they would adopt the city-state as the basic unit of description. They did this in two ways: by requiring the duke of Milan to pledge publicly to respect Venetian rule over Bergamo, Brescia, and later Crema, and by obliging him to return all the towns and localities which he held within their respective districts. This restored the original shape of the territories which had once been subject to the city, making them an ideal reference for the extended dimension of the Venetian dominion in the area. Another point worth noting is that this procedure reflected the seemingly spontaneous capitulation of the individual city-states. Proud as they were of their independent past, the *civitates* would not accept being treated as mere objects of a transaction, something that Venice, for its part, was more than happy to indulge, particularly if it led to an act of spontaneous surrender (*deditio*). This explains why both treaties appear to sanction a handover that had already taken place: they only confirm Venice's hold over Brescia, Bergamo, and Crema, since in the eyes of these *civitates*—let alone Venetian propaganda—they had already offered themselves spontaneously to the Republic.

Yet the territories of the former city-states were not the only units in play. Faced with the challenge of describing more subtle changes in territorial arrangements, the negotiators behind the treaties of Ferrara and Lodi made use of a broad array of spatial references. As the negotiation of each treaty unfolded, the description moved from the level of the *civitas* (Bergamo, Brescia, Crema) to that of the intermediate body (the Val San Martino, the town of Martinengo, the federation of the Geradadda) and finally to the level of the local community (as in the case of the contested villages of the Cremonese). This shows a clear understanding of the territorial hierarchies of the time. Most of these bodies could not claim to be giving themselves freely to the Republic, in the same manner as the cities had done earlier through an act of surrender, so the treaties themselves played a proactive role in prescribing which of the two powers should now rule over these lands. This process added spatial complexity to the texts of both treaties, as negotiators took care to list the individual bodies that, though formerly attached to a city-state, were now to be directly subject to a new regional polity.

Still, the treaties only went as far as to prescribe territorial modifications; they framed geopolitical changes but did not put them into operation. The effective transfer of territorial authority over these lands took place only after the conclusion of each treaty, following the proceedings known as *consignatio*. This required the deputies of the duke and the doge to meet publicly in front of local representatives to perform a ritual delivery of the territories in question. Thus, the boundaries between pre-existing bodies acquired a new, public significance (that of distinguishing regional dominions) only when the convention between superior powers was enforced in the localities. When the possession of certain units changed hands, the frontier between the two polities was redesigned; however, the boundaries of the single units remained unaltered. In the end, the cities, towns, and villages of eastern Lombardy joined the bulk of the Venetian dominion almost like tiles added to a mosaic. As such, they would retain their spatial configuration for years to come.

3

Confinium Compositio

Territorial Disputes and the Making of Borders

While Chapter 1 exposed the territorial culture underpinning the making of borders and the organization of political spaces in the Late Middle Ages, Chapter 2 uncovered the extent to which this shared conceptual framework informed the establishment of a new political geography in northern Italy. However, as the scholar of borders—whether medieval or modern—knows only too well, the negotiation of border disputes is often just as revealing as the peace-making process that first defined those very borders. Having seen how the theory was put into practice on the occasion of major treaties, let us then move on to investigate instances where this process broke down, mistakes occurred, and new conflicts arose. These instances gave contemporaries a chance to discern exactly which territories would be brought under their rule, namely where the frontier between states would fall; and they give us the opportunity to uncover the criteria they adopted to do so. In focusing on the principles they employed to correct errors and address failures in border negotiations, the chapter will bring the inquiry started earlier in the book to full fruition.

We begin by considering the immediate aftermath of the peace of Lodi and the circumstances that brought its terms into question, particularly following the implementation of the treaty through the proceedings of the *consignatio*. Indeed, the fulfilment of these procedures was not free from misunderstandings or outright errors; besides, it soon became clear that the peace of Lodi did not provide enough guidance on the fate of some contested areas. In the first half of the century, complications of this kind would have inevitably led to a renewal of the conflict between the Duchy and the Republic, further feeding a fire that for almost three decades had been continuously fuelled by family feuds and unwanted interventions in their respective spheres of influence. In the mid-1450s, however, at the time when the two polities were in the process of forming the Italian League, the resolution of territorial disputes was left to negotiation rather than war.

Borders and the Politics of Space in Late Medieval Italy: Milan, Venice, and their Territories. Luca Zenobi, Oxford University Press. © Luca Zenobi 2023. DOI: 10.1093/oso/9780198876861.003.0004

3. *CONFINIUM COMPOSITIO* 69

For the first time, special deputies were given the time and resources to carry out a thorough redefinition of the borders between regional states. In practice, the challenge was twofold: not only were they to rectify the mistakes made while implementing the Lodi settlement, but they were also tasked with solving controversies which the treaty had failed to address altogether. The entire process extended over two years, from the spring of 1454 to the summer of 1456, and required an amount of information and level of detail which was, in many ways, unprecedented. The final result was an official document named 'confinium compositio'.[1] In this context, the Latin word *compositio* stands for 'pact' or 'agreement' (concerning borders). However, *compositio* had a further meaning in late medieval Italy, which is that of an 'arrangement' or 'combination' (of borders). This chapter takes its cue from the twofold title of this document: it will explore the negotiations that led to its compilation whilst discussing how borders were, quite literally, composed in late medieval Italy.

Who Broke the Treaty?

Let us start by considering the mistake that first raised doubts over the terms of Lodi and later led to a reopening of the whole settlement. Although legally solid, the mechanism of the *consignatio* was far from straightforward. A first challenge was that the proceedings had to occur in the territory that happened to be the object of the transaction. Much of the negotiation that resulted in treaties such as those of Ferrara and Lodi was conducted by correspondence, with the duke and the doge making use of their respective chanceries to convey their wishes. When the parties did meet, this was typically done through appointed deputies, who would assemble in a designated place until the treaty was drafted (such as the court of Ferrara or the house of the papal legate in 1428). By contrast, the *consignationes* forced state deputies to be continually on the move, as they travelled from one territory to the next to perform the ceremony in front of local representatives. The second challenge was that state deputies operated on the basis of changing and sometimes conflicting information. In order to act legally on behalf of their masters, they first had to receive an official mandate (*littera credulitatis*), which had to be signed personally by the duke

---

[1] DUMONT, *Corps universel diplomatique* (vol. III), 241–3.

70   BORDERS AND THE POLITICS OF SPACE IN LATE MEDIEVAL ITALY

or by the doge. This was followed by a series of individual instructions sent by the two chanceries. Unlike the mandate, however, which existed only to legitimize the deputy's actions, the instructions could change several times. It was not uncommon to transmit new and sometimes divergent instructions to deputies who were already on the road, particularly as the terms of the treaty were finalized. Another opportunity for misunderstanding arose when deputies compared their instructions with those sent to their counterparts and finally when they presented their assignment to local representatives, who in turn were often prompt to exploit uncertainty in order to serve the interest of their communities. Small oversights were thus frequent and somewhat understandable, but even major errors were not impossible.

The most sensational mistake was made on 17 April 1454, only a week or so after the treaty of Lodi was finalized. On that day, Giovanni Giappani, the deputy of the duke of Milan, delivered all the lands that his master still held in the Bergamasco to the Venetian deputy.[2] The *consignatio* concerned a handful of localities situated alongside the ancient boundary between the *districtus* of Bergamo and that of the city of Milan. The trouble was that, over the second half of the fourteenth century, the boundary between Milanese and Bergamasque territories had somewhat faded in the minds of contemporaries. As seen in Chapter 1, by the time the Venetian armies converged on Bergamo, the *districtus* had lost ground to competing spatial frameworks. From above, the Visconti had established a direct rule over both the Bergamasco and the Milanese *contado* and were striving to enforce the same policies throughout their regional dominion. From below, a growing number of intermediate bodies (large federations, small towns, individual fiefdoms) had obtained some of the rights and duties lost by the city-state, thus gaining a spatial significance which was virtually comparable to that of the old *districtus*. However, when the time came to yield the Bergamasco to Venice—first at Ferrara (1428) and now, by way of confirmation, at Lodi (1454)—the old boundary between the *contado* of Bergamo and that of Milan acquired a new public significance, that of marking the frontier between the Republic and the Duchy. In practice, this involved disentangling the territories that used to be subject to Bergamo before the Visconti took over these areas from those that were traditionally attached to the city of Milan. Giovanni Giappani was thus left with the task of restoring

---

[2] Giappani's role is largely neglected in the local historiography, which tends to frame the matter as a mere difference of opinion between the two governments: Franceschini, 'Il confine fra Bergamasca e Valsassina'; Cappellini, 'Confini fra Venezia e Milano'.

3. *CONFINIUM COMPOSITIO* 71

the original shape of the two *districti* by returning all the 'loci Pergamensi' that the Milanese armies had come to control over the course of the war.[3]

It took the Milanese Chancery almost two months to realize Giappani's mistake: in his zeal to apply yet another set of instructions, the deputy had returned localities that were not meant to be returned. It is now hard to tell whether this was due to Giappani's misinterpretation of his orders or, more simply, to a clerical error. It is also possible that Giappani acted upon pressures exerted by local power holders and particularly by the representatives of territories that it was hoped would be handed over to the Venetians, a hypothesis supported by the lavish privileges then promised to them by the Republic.[4] By the time the controversy blew up, Giappani had at least fifteen years of experience as a diplomatic agent, having served both Filippo Maria Visconti and Francesco Sforza. He was also a qualified notary who would go on to serve as a secretary in the ducal chancery.[5] It is therefore likely that Giappani was reasonably familiar with the procedure he was about to perform, which makes it even more plausible that he was led into error by the commotion caused by locals. Whatever the reasons behind Giappani's mistake, the fact remains that the distinction between Milanese and Bergamasque territories was not entirely obvious at this stage.

At its origin, the controversy was not handled by specially appointed deputies. Having only just signed the treaty of Lodi, the duke and the doge did not expect to be drawn into a new series of territorial negotiations, so the issue was first tackled through the ordinary means of diplomacy. It was uncommon for the duke and the doge to approach each other directly. Although they appeared to act as equals in public treaties (they were both called 'princes' in official documents), constitutionally their role could not be more different. Where the duke professed to be the sole owner of a supreme jurisdiction over all the lands that made up his dominion, the doge could only claim to be the highest official of the Republic.[6] As such, the doge sent his instructions to the Venetian governors in Bergamo, while the duke had two ambassadors in the lagoon to negotiate on his behalf. In practice, this meant that two parallel negotiations were often taking place at the same time: one in Milan (between the duke and the Venetian governors)

---

[3] ASMi, *Frammenti* 1, f. 12/4, cc. 209r–209v, 17 April 1454.

[4] ASVe, *Senato Terra* (*Registri*) 2, cc. 111r and 132r, 9 June and 26 October 1449; BMBg, *Municipali* 2, c. 35r, 23 December 1455.

[5] Leverotti, *Diplomazia e governo dello stato*, 178–80.

[6] For this contrast, compare Black, *Absolutism in Renaissance Milan*, 84–92; and Tenenti, 'Il potere dogale come rappresentazione'.

72 BORDERS AND THE POLITICS OF SPACE IN LATE MEDIEVAL ITALY

and one in Venice (between the doge—and sometimes the Senate—and the Milanese ambassadors). A constant stream of letters, now scattered across multiple archival series, enabled the two groups to deal simultaneously with the same issues. When collated, these sources allow us to follow closely the unfolding of the dispute, while opening a window to the techniques used to claim rights over space in late medieval Italy.

To start with, the missive in which the duke first entrusted his ambassadors with the matter provides us with an accurate summary of the territories in dispute.[7] Giappani had mistakenly surrendered to the doge a handful of localities situated not far from Lecco. A flourishing market centre in the fourteenth century, the town was transformed into a frontier stronghold over the course of the Quattrocento. Although traditionally Milanese, Lecco sits on the eastern shores of Lake Como, which makes it closer to Bergamo. At the time, this placed it not only at the crossroads of the routes that linked Milan to the Alps but at the very intersection of the two *contadi*. The same placement that once ensured its prosperity had turned the area into a borderland.[8] To the Milanese castellan in charge of its citadel in 1452, Lecco's strategic value could not be more obvious: should the enemy capture the town by the lake, he once wrote to the duke, they would turn it into a little Venice ('Venetia piccinina') and then use it as a base to advance on Milan.[9] Lecco's strategic importance made Giappani's mistake hard to overlook, especially considering that amongst many villages of the Bergamasco the deputy had conceded some of the town's own defences. Except for the citadel, the fortifications that guarded Lecco were all located along the ancient boundary between the district of Milan and that of Bergamo. Relinquishing them would not only expose the town itself but provide the enemy with fortified positions on the new frontier between the two states. These ranged from the great fortress of Baiedo in the nearby Val Sassina, whose importance was such that Leonardo da Vinci was later asked to draw up a project for its renovation, to little suburbs of Lecco, such as Bione and Acquate, which protected the town from an attack by land, to family castles, such as Pizzino and Pianchello in the nearby Val Taleggio, and even to border fortifications, such as the *Chiusa* ('closure') of Vercurago, a wall that extended

---

[7] ASMi, *Registri* 18, cc. 397v–398r, 21 June 1454.
[8] On Lecco and its strategic importance in this period, see Pensa, 'Lecco e la Valsassina'; and Buratti Mazzotta, 'Le fortificazioni'.
[9] ASMi, *Carteggio* 660, 3 April 1452.

3. *CONFINIUM COMPOSITIO* 73

from the nearest mountain slopes to the banks of the river Adda, where it met the main road connecting Lecco to Bergamo.[10]

We can only imagine how the Venetians reacted to Giappani's offer to surrender some of these strategic locations so freely, but we know for certain that Sforza was well aware of their importance. Only a few months earlier, the duke had made sure that the treaty of Lodi stated explicitly that these territories were to remain under his rule. As a result, his ambassadors could now present a strong case to the Venetians: that these localities were Milanese, they were instructed to argue, is something that 'you can see and touch with your own hands through the ruling and words of the [treaty's] clause'.[11] Public agreements such as that of Lodi were the most immediate tool employed by contemporaries to assert territorial claims. The idea behind this was fairly simple: the matter had already been settled before all the parties involved, so the easiest way to go about solving the dispute was to restore what had been originally decided. Conversely, challenging the terms of the treaty meant challenging the powers that had agreed to ratify it—powers that Venice, for one, had no intention of antagonizing, at least not now that the Turks were threatening their possessions in the Adriatic. Still, having a recent treaty to use as benchmark turned out to be a mixed blessing on this occasion. As the duke sent a copy of the treaty to his ambassadors in Venice to support his claims, the doge provided the Venetian governors in Bergamo with their own copy.[12] This gave the Venetians the chance to compare the localities which the treaty described as Milanese with those that Giappani had mistakenly brought under their rule. It soon became apparent that while key fortifications such as the Chiusa of Vercurago were treated as Milanese in the text, some of the localities delivered by Giappani were not mentioned at all. As shown in Figure 6, these included the valleys of Torta and Averara, which were located between the Val Sassina (traditionally Milanese) and the Val Brembana (traditionally attached to Bergamo), and the castle of Pizzino, which guarded the mountain pass that, through the Val Taleggio, led down to Bergamo.

The Milanese party was thus faced with the challenge of proving that localities which they had offered freely to Venice were, in fact, theirs to hold. From the outset, their case was founded on a jurisdictional discourse.

---

[10] BAMi, *Codex Atlanticus*, c. 41v. Specifically on these fortifications, see the short studies by Borghi, 'Signorie di Valsassina'; Borghi, 'La chiusa di Lecco'.
[11] ASMi, *Confini* 270, 21 July 1454: 'secondo che largamente potreti videre et tocare con le mane per sententia et parole desso capitolo'.
[12] ASMi, *Carteggio* 341, 18 July 1454; BMBg, *Confini*, ms. 96 R 12, cc. 23r–24r, 23 July 1454.

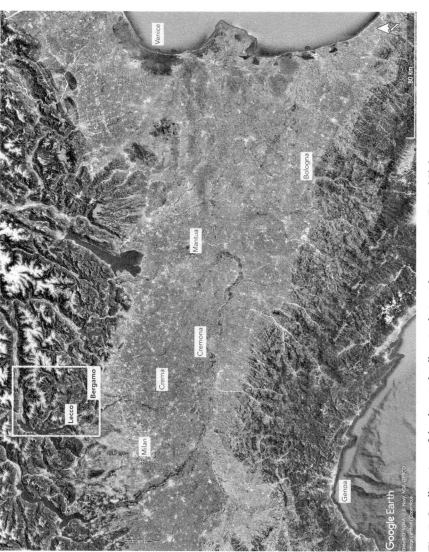

Fig. 5 Satellite view of the disputed valleys in their wider context. © DigitalGlobe

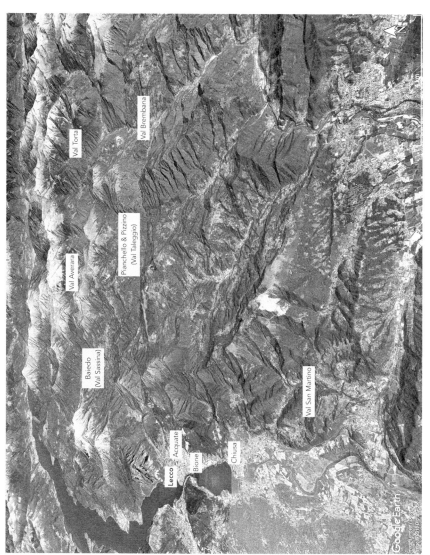

Fig. 6 Satellite view of the disputed valleys between Bergamo and Lecco. © DigitalGlobe

76   BORDERS AND THE POLITICS OF SPACE IN LATE MEDIEVAL ITALY

While in ancient times, they argued, the people of these valleys descended to Lecco to attend a Milanese court of justice, in recent years they had been subject to the jurisdiction of the Val Sassina, where a Milanese magistrate was known to pass judgment.[13] The treaty of Lodi declared that the Val Sassina was to remain part of the ducal dominion; therefore, Sforza hoped to solve the matter by finding proof that those localities were part of the Val Sassina and not of the Bergamasco.[14] To do so, the Milanese Chancery presented the Venetians with two complementary types of evidence. First, they retrieved a report from the magistrate who had been dispensing justice in the area before the war. In it, the magistrate confirmed that he had been in charge of the Val Sassina and of all the lands that pertained to it ('pertinentiarum'), including the valleys of Torta and Averara as well as that of Taleggio, which comprised Pizzino. These lands, he stated, 'were all obedient to Milan during his time in office'.[15] Secondly, they dispatched an envoy to Bergamo to transcribe a passage from the municipal statutes. As was tradition in Bergamo and many other cities, the passage twinned every community of the Bergamasco with one of the city gates; however, the Milanese envoy noted that the localities in question were not to be found among them.[16] Together, the two records proved not only that these

---

[13] BMBg, *Confini*, ms. 96 R 12, c. 23r, 17 August 1454; ASMi, *Carteggio* 341, 31 August 1454. In their attempt to secure the loyalty of these secluded territories, the Visconti had granted the valleys of Taleggio and Averara jurisdictional independence from any urban centre (namely Bergamo and Lecco), which meant that a Milanese magistrate would now be stationed on site to apply the law of the land: ANDERLONI, 'Statuti di Averara e Val Taleggio'. However, by the end of the fourteenth century, the Visconti had brought these valleys together with the Val Sassina to form a large jurisdictional body inhabited by around 7,000 people: Medolago, Oriani, and Sampietro, 'La Valsassina all'epoca della formulazione degli statuti', 24. More generally, for the overlapping of Milanese and Bergamasque jurisdictions on the border between the two *contadi* and for the establishment of a new geography of justice under the Visconti, see Gamberini, 'Il contado di Milano nel Trecento', 91 and 119.

[14] ASMi, *Carteggio* 341, 1 September 1454.

[15] ASMi, *Registri* 18, c. 408r, 16 July 1433: 'sibi obedientes durante eius officio'. Interestingly, local statutes are not mentioned here, despite the fact that they did validate the magistrate's testimony. Chapter 5, in particular, stated plainly that the *vicarius* of Val Sassina had the power to enforce the law in Taleggio and Averara by appointing local deputies in these territories: DE LAZARIS, *Statuta civilia et criminalia*. Another element that supported the Milanese case and yet was not brought to the table at this stage was the fact that the very structure of local statutes betrayed the original affiliation of these territories. While the statutes of the Val Sassina—and later those of Taleggio and Averara—bore a striking resemblance to those of Lecco, the statutes of the Val Brembana were clearly modelled on those of Bergamo: Varanini, 'La tradizione statutaria'.

[16] ASMi, *Registri* 18, c. 408v, 1 September 1454. 'The comune de Talliegio' is actually included in the municipal statutes of 1331 and so is the unquestionably Milanese 'comune de Valsasina': Storti Storchi, *Lo statuto di Bergamo*, 59. The discrepancy was probably brought forward from 1263, around the time when Bergamo had briefly gained control over Lecco and

3. CONFINIUM COMPOSITIO 77

territories were not part of the Bergamasco (and thus not part of the Venetian dominion) but that they were, in fact, subject to the Val Sassina, which in turn made them part of the Duchy.[17]

In keeping with the principle of jurisdictional affiliation, the Milanese party was adopting the same criteria that underpinned the negotiation of previous treaties. The peace of Lodi stated explicitly that the Chiusa of Vercurago would remain within the duke's domain because it had long belonged to the jurisdiction of Lecco; therefore, the same argument could now be applied to localities which were attached to the Val Sassina. In normal circumstances, the same principle that had informed the making of the treaty would have informed the resolution of the dispute. This time, however, the fundamental assumption that jurisdictional bodies should remain intact had been undermined by one of the two parties. This was not the Venetians, who actually tried, without much success, to find evidence that the jurisdiction of Bergamo extended over these localities (evidence which would have disproved the Milanese case).[18] Rather, it was someone who not only belonged to the Milanese ranks but who acted on behalf of the duke himself: Giovanni Giappani. By surrendering lands that had long been part of Milanese territories, the duke's deputy had *de facto* triggered the separation of long-standing jurisdictional bodies, a separation that became apparent as soon as the Venetians gained control of these localities and began to appoint their own magistrates to dispense justice in the area. In short, an agent of the party that would have most benefited from strict observance of the treaty had been the first to fail to comply with its terms. This nullified the possibility of turning to the treaty to clear up the matter, while questioning the very principle of jurisdictional affiliation.

In the end, the parties were left with no other option but to reopen the negotiations. The provisions of Lodi failed to mention a series of disputed

---

its subject territories. Nevertheless, the question remains whether the Milanese envoy was lying or whether the copy he examined in 1454 had been amended.

[17] In passing, it is worth noting that the fact that all these valleys had once been a fiefdom of the Milanese bishopric, which in turn had long been controlled by the Visconti themselves, was not offered as evidence. See Bognetti, 'Le miniere di Valtorta e i diritti degli arcivescovi'; and Meroni, 'Le parrocchie bergamasche'. This suggests that ecclesiastical districts had a limited territorial significance compared with those of secular jurisdictions. However, given what we learned in Chapter 1 about the strict equivalence between a community (*universitas*), its spatial extent (*territorium*), and the type of power that was exercised over it (*iurisdictio*), the fact that ecclesiastical districts were not deemed to provide legally valid borders should not come as a surprise. They did not correspond to a political community, so they were not seen as jurisdictional bodies.

[18] Their attempts are touched upon in ASMi, *Carteggio* 341, 31 August 1454.

78   BORDERS AND THE POLITICS OF SPACE IN LATE MEDIEVAL ITALY

localities, so it was not possible to rely on the treaty alone to establish which of the two regional polities should now rule over them. To make matters worse, Giappani had accidentally conceded some of the localities which the text treated as Milanese, thus denying the very principle adopted by the treaty to determine their status. As long as the matter remained unsettled, the precarious balance found at Lodi was at risk, as was Sforza's delicate position as duke of Milan. In the letter in which he charged his ambassadors with conducting the negotiations on his behalf, the new duke made no secret of how much this worried him: 'we came together and agreed over great things when the fate of Italy was a stake, yet in some measure it will be a failure on all parts if we cannot find an arrangement over these few differences.'[19] To the Venetians, whose reason for seeking peace in the first place was to be able to focus on the threat posed by the Turks, the matter appeared far less urgent; for nearly two years, they sought to settle things remotely. Finally, in the summer of 1456, the doge resolved to give his governors in Bergamo and Brescia a dedicated mandate to write and sign a new pact with the duke of Milan. This was meant to 'draw the boundaries between the parties' and finally bring peace and tranquillity to the area.[20]

To produce the final draft of what would then become the *confinium compositio* of 1456, the deputies of the two parties had first to deal with a number of outstanding matters. Some were issues arising from Giappani's ill-fated mistake, such as the case of the valleys between Lecco and Bergamo (Taleggio, Torta, Averara). Others were territorial disputes on which the terms of Lodi had already ruled but which were now back on the negotiating table due to the doubts which had been thrown on the reliability of the treaty itself. Significantly, the deputies of the two parties moved quickly to find an agreement on the most pressing matters. These included the fate of two key items of infrastructure which happened to be located by the new frontier between states: one was the *Fosso Bergamasco*, a shallow ditch marking the southern boundary of the Bergamasco; the other was the *Strada Cremasca et Cremonese*, a busy system of roads connecting the enclave of Crema to Bergamo and the communities of the Geradadda to Cremona. To deepen our exploration of the ideas and practices that went into negotiating borders in late medieval Italy, here we shall focus on the

---

[19] ASMi, *Carteggio* 341, f. 'Venezia 1454', s.d. but datable to the second half of the year: 'concordati et uniti in le cose alte e dove pende el stato de tucta Italia, pare quodammodo mancamento delle parte che non se accordano a cuore via queste poche differentie'.

[20] ASMi, *Confini* 255, 15 May 1456: 'designandum confinia ipsarum partium'.

dispute that the deputies of the two states found to be the hardest to resolve: that concerning the mountainous areas between Bergamo and Lecco. In keeping with the approach adopted so far, our focus will be the agency of both central deputies and peripheral actors, and the principles that informed the making of borders in late medieval Italy.

The Limits of Factional Allegiance

Not surprisingly, the dispute concerned some of the territories that Giappani had erroneously conceded to the Venetians. The hardest knot to unravel was undoubtedly the Val Taleggio. We have seen that the most common way to establish which polity should rule over a given territory was to determine its jurisdictional affiliation: should the parties agree that the valley formed part of the Bergamasco, for example, the whole territory would have been ceded to Venice. In this case, however, the vicissitudes of 1454 ruled out the possibility that the Val Taleggio could remain a unified territory under the same rule. Although the text of Lodi did not mention the valley itself, it stated explicitly that the castle of Pianchello was to remain with the duke of Milan. Tucked between the village of Vedeseta and the mountain pass that led from the Val Taleggio down to the Val Sassina, this remote fortification clearly had enough strategic importance to be included in a major peace treaty. The castle of Pizzino, on the other hand, had been spontaneously surrendered by Giappani, which gave the Venetians effective control over the opposite side of the valley and particularly over the village of Sottochiesa. In short, each of the two parties had a perfectly legitimate reason to claim control over at least part of the Val Taleggio. This led to a diplomatic impasse: should the valley be assigned to Venice, Pianchello would remain with Milan; should the valley be assigned to Milan, Pizzino would still be under the rule of Venice. Because of the valley's key location between Lecco and Bergamo, neither of the two parties was willing to waive its right to a foothold in the Val Taleggio. At the same time, neither was ready to force the matter by taking control of the whole valley, in case this prompted its counterpart to retaliate and, possibly, to break the peace.

To members of modern society, where nation-states claim to project an undisputed power over a seemingly neutral space, the solution to the entire issue may appear obvious; until not long ago, a dispute of this kind would have been settled simply by partitioning the territory in question into equal parts. In late medieval Italy, however, negotiating borders entailed much

80 BORDERS AND THE POLITICS OF SPACE IN LATE MEDIEVAL ITALY

more than simply drawing lines in the sand. As seen in previous chapters, the territorial culture of the time envisaged state frontiers as overlapping closely with the boundaries of long-standing jurisdictional bodies, not as cutting through them. Breaking up territories was an emergency solution, one dictated by the unique conditions under which state deputies found themselves to operate. It was the exception, rather than the norm; but it was also the exception that proved the rule. Indeed, when it came to dividing the Val Taleggio, this was not done by drawing borders from above but by locating the individual communities that could form the building blocks of two new jurisdictions: one to be assigned to Venice and one to be assigned to Milan. In reducing the spatial scale to the level of the villages that made up the valley, the deputies in charge of settling the dispute were following the same procedure that we encountered earlier when looking at the negotiation of major treaties. Just as the peace of Ferrara had moved from the level of the *districtus* (Bergamasco, Bresciano) to the level of intermediate bodies (Martinengo, Val San Martino), so now the deputies of Milan and Venice moved from the level of the intermediate body (the Val Taleggio) to that of the single villages that composed it. Once again, negotiating borders came down to identifying a list of communities that formed part of one of the various territories that made up each regional dominion.

How, then, to decide which communities should belong to the Venetian Val Taleggio and which, instead, should belong to the Milanese Val Taleggio? On the basis of the treaty of Lodi, Pianchello was clearly meant to be ruled by the duke of Milan; Pizzino, on the other hand, was already in Venetian hands due to Giappani's mistake. But what about the other communities of the Val Taleggio? What criteria did the deputies employ to determine their belonging to one or the other part of the valley? Given the new political climate in the peninsula, particularly following the creation of the Italian League, both parties were keen to find a solution that would bring stability to the area once and for all. Hence, the deputies of Venice and Milan thought twice before enforcing an arbitrary partition on the valley, even though, for once, they had been given a virtually free hand to do just that. Instead, they based their resolution on a careful consideration of the forces at play in the Val Taleggio, and particularly on the way in which the local population felt about the issue. Lucien Febvre explained choices of this kind very elegantly when he wrote that 'what engraves a frontier powerfully in the earth is not policemen or customs officers, nor it is cannons drawn up

3. *CONFINIUM COMPOSITIO* 81

behind ramparts; it is feelings, and exalted passions'.[21] In the Val Taleggio, these were the feelings that local families harboured towards each other and towards those who governed them. They were feelings of hatred and enmity as much as feelings of love and friendship. They were the 'exalted passions' of factional allegiance.[22] In the Val Taleggio, as in many other parts of Lombardy, the names of Guelphs and Ghibellines determined the relationship between ruled and rulers, as much as personal ties between individuals. More importantly, they fostered a deep sense of territorial belonging. In the valley, factions had a spatial quality to them; they shaped the way in which space was organized and so went on to inform the resolution of the entire dispute.

The Val Taleggio was far from unique in this respect. In the nearby Val Tellina, one's political affiliation often determined one's place of residence, and vice versa: people who identified as Guelph inhabited one side of the valley whereas people who identified as Ghibelline inhabited the other.[23] In the Alpine foothills north of Milan, the course of the river Adda divided a federation of Guelph villages (the Val San Martino) from a federation of Ghibelline villages (the Monte di Brianza).[24] In Brescia, Ghibelline families lived mostly in the fortified citadel built by the Visconti, whilst Guelphs dominated the rest of the city.[25] Yet perhaps nowhere else in Lombardy did factions have a more profound effect on the way in which space was organized than in the Bergamasco. This is because, over the course of the Middle Ages, Bergamo never managed to overcome competing forms of political and territorial organization. Two factors prevented the city from doing so. The first was the abundance of natural resources in the surrounding valleys (wool, metal, lumber), where most of the Bergamasco's population lived and worked. The city was highly dependent on these resources for its manufacturing but could not access them without the mediation of the locals.[26] During the thirteenth and fourteenth centuries, this position of strength allowed the valleys to protect some of their interests and ways of life against the agency of urban magistrates. The second factor was the Visconti's support of local autonomies, particularly when this served to balance the power

---

[21] Demangeon and Febvre, *Le Rhin*, 129.

[22] As if to prove this very point, Italian sources often use the word *passionati* to refer to Guelphs and Ghibellines, while Bartolus himself described the adherence to one of the two factions as *affectio*: Ferente, *Gli ultimi guelfi*, 242–5; Gentile, 'Bartolo in pratica', 245–7.

[23] Della Misericordia, 'Dividersi per governarsi', 738–45.

[24] Zenobi, 'Nascita di un territorio', 826–7.   [25] Pagnoni, 'Notariato, fazione', 184.

[26] On economic structures and demographic patterns in the Bergamasco, see Mainoni, *Le radici della discordia*, 132–44; and Albini, 'La popolazione di Bergamo e territorio', 213–55.

82 BORDERS AND THE POLITICS OF SPACE IN LATE MEDIEVAL ITALY

relations between the subject city (Bergamo) and its countryside (the valleys), as touched upon in Chapter 2. Some Visconti policies were explicitly aimed at promoting factions as an interface between urban and rural society, if not as a formal means of political participation. Famously, in 1394, in a period of violent clashes between Guelphs and Ghibellines, Gian Galeazzo ordered that each and every person residing in Bergamo or the Bergamasco must declare their formal adherence to one of the two parties. He then persuaded the families at the head of each faction to agree to a truce, which in turn had the effect of binding people across all strata of society to respect the peace and, ultimately, to refrain from changing sides.[27]

Perhaps in light of well-known Tuscan examples, Guelphs and Ghibellines are typically thought to reflect economic and social divisions.[28] A century or so earlier, Milan itself had seen the *pars nobilium* turn into the *pars ghibellinorum*, while the *pars populi*, which included lesser noblemen as well as merchants and artisans, transformed into the *pars guelforum*.[29] Yet the reasoning behind Gian Galeazzo's intervention highlights a different model: one in which Guelphs and Ghibellines cut across social groups and served as an organizing principle for both rural and urban society. It is precisely on account of this ubiquity that factions had such a profound effect on the way in which space was organized in the Bergamasco. As Guelphs and Ghibellines brought people from all backgrounds together, it became possible for an entire community to find itself united behind a common cause. People who identified with the same faction forged bonds of solidarity, established business connections, and gained access to the same web of social relations. In doing so, individuals came closer together, physically as much as figuratively, while people who identified with rival factions were driven further apart. In some cases, the conflict was such that entire communities were forced to disband. Not far from the Val Taleggio, the community of Zogno had to split itself into two separate villages: as precise boundaries between a Guelph Zogno and a Ghibelline Zogno were drawn, people were banned from moving to the territory of the opposing party.[30] Most frequently, however, the communities of the Bergamasco saw one

---

[27] The episode has recently been reappraised by Del Tredici, 'La popolarità dei partiti', 319–20. On the circumstances that led to Gian Galeazzo's order, see Grillo, 'Il territorio conteso'.

[28] Starting with Salvemini, *Magnati e populari*, 1–75; and now Diacciati, *Popolati e magnati*, 209–302.

[29] Grillo, *Milano guelfa*, 214–16.

[30] Mazzi, 'Zogno diviso'; Belotti, 'Controversie sui confini di Zogno'.

3. *CONFINIUM COMPOSITIO* 83

party or the other establishing a monopoly over the entire locality. This gives us an opportunity to evaluate the role of factions in shaping the territorial organization of these localities, while also reflecting on their supposed divisiveness for the politics of space.

Although the results of Gian Galeazzo's factional census have been lost, it is still possible to pin down the individual allegiance of most mountain communities by undertaking a close reading of contemporary chronicles.[31] As shown in Figure 7, communities that were controlled by the same party formed large and contiguous areas sitting opposite each other.[32] A Guelph or Ghibelline bloc would often extend over all the villages that made up a valley. By way of example, the villages of the Val San Martino (Erve, Carenno, Vercurago) were all Guelph, whereas those of the Val Brembilla were all Ghibelline.[33] Occasionally, however, the communities of a valley could display opposing loyalties. This was clearly the case in the Val Taleggio, where Ghibelline families gathered in the village of Vedeseta, while Guelph families clustered around Sottochiesa. Were the Val Taleggio placed in the heart of the Bergamasco, the persistence of sharp political divides with a distinct territorial connotation would not have posed much of a problem. If anything, the valley would have split peacefully into smaller federations, thus replicating the case of Zogno on a larger scale. This is precisely what happened to the nearby Val Brembana, where Guelph families retained control of the lower valley (San Giovanni, San Pellegrino, Dossena) whilst Ghibelline families nestled in the north (Lenna, Branzi, Piazzatorre).[34] Yet on account of its location, the Val Taleggio was bound to remain fiercely contested by members of the two factions. The same pattern can be found in all the valleys that sat on the boundary between the *districtus* of Bergamo and that of Milan, and now on the frontier between states. In the Val Averara, Guelphs hinged on the village of Olmo in order to challenge the dominance exerted by Ghibelline families over the rest of the valley (Cusio, Ornica, Santa Brigida); in the Val Imagna, Brumano formed a Ghibelline isle in a sea of Guelph villages; in the Val Torta, the Ghibelline hold over the entire valley was intermittent at best.

---

[31] CASTELLI, 'Liber mirabilium', cols. 841–1008; FINAZZI, *Cronaca Anonima*, 241–61.

[32] In addition to the chronicles mentioned above, information used to complete the map in question has been drawn from notarial records, following the work by Sato, 'Fazioni e micro-fazioni', 149–70. Community boundaries are based on the modern map of the Bergamasco developed by Oscar and Belotti, *Atlante storico del territorio bergamasco*, 347.

[33] Tagliabue, 'Come si è costituita la *communitas* di Val S. Martino'; Belotti, 'La cacciata dei Brembillesi', 211–32.

[34] Medolago, 'La comunità di Val Brembana Oltre la Goggia'.

Fig. 7 Guelph and Ghibelline communities in the Bergamasco, respectively in light and dark grey. © Provincia di Bergamo

3. *CONFINIUM COMPOSITIO* 85

However, what divided these valleys was more than just the presence of factions that grouped two or more communities together; it was the fact that their location linked them horizontally to networks which cut across state borders, in turn connecting them vertically with external powers (whether the duke or the Venetians).[35] On the border, Guelph and Ghibelline allegiances put the peripheries into communication with an alternative ruler. The Visconti had long fashioned themselves as the champions of Ghibellinism in northern Italy, notably by stressing their role as imperial vicars in the region.[36] Despite his attempt to pacify the Bergamasco, Gian Galeazzo himself had prescribed that his firstborn heir and his successors would inherit the Milanese dominion only 'on the condition that they would lead and defend the Ghibelline faction'.[37] Venice, on the other hand, was one of the few Italian cities which 'held no factions…or ever wished to hold them', as Bernardino of Siena famously noted.[38] Of course, this did not stop the Republic from drawing heavily on Guelph ideology or from joining forces with Florence to form a Guelph league against Milan.[39] Famously, when it came to rewarding the citizens of Bergamo who facilitated the taking of the city, Venice did not just call them their subjects but 'our Guelph partisans'.[40] In the valleys, Guelph became almost a synonym for *marchesco*, that is, a supporter of St Mark, whereas the Ghibellines were labelled *ducheschi*, after the duke of Milan. Depending on the power that controlled each valley at a given time, members of the two factions could also be *partisani* or *rebelli*. As one group was rewarded with tax exemptions and further forms of autonomy from the city, the other was obliged to take an oath of allegiance or rather go into exile across the border, waiting for their chance to return in force. Claiming their allegiance to one of the two factions was for local families a way to gain external support for their struggle against a rival group and then a way to legitimize their newfound position at the helm of the community. For major powers, on the other hand, flying the Guelph or Ghibelline flag was a means of upsetting the balance of power in

---

[35] A more extensive discussion of these two levels can be found in Gentile, '*Postquam malignitates*', 250–7. More broadly, see also Gentile, 'Factions and parties'.

[36] Not to mention the fact that their family's history included being excommunicated by more than one pope. On the Visconti's changing attitudes towards factions, see Gentile, 'Discorsi sulle fazioni'.

[37] CORIO, *Storia di Milano* (vol. II), 968: 'sotto condicione che lui e successori suoi fussino principi e difensori di gibellina factione'.

[38] DA SIENA, *Prediche volgari* (vol. II), 477: 'città, le quali non tengono niuna parte, delle quali è una Vinegia, né mai ne volse tenere'.

[39] On the 'ideological constellation' of Guelphism, see Ferente, 'Guelphs!'.

[40] As explored by Cavalieri, Qui sunt guelfi et partiales nostri, 19–92.

86   BORDERS AND THE POLITICS OF SPACE IN LATE MEDIEVAL ITALY

the peripheries and later of securing the loyalty of local residents in case of a takeover.[41]

It is only by following these developments in the Val Taleggio that it is possible to capture the territorial divisions that would then inform the resolution of the dispute. Around the mid-1420s, when Venetian troops first reached the Bergamasco, Guelph families took up arms and forced rival Ghibellines to flee to the Val Sassina (which would largely remain under Milanese control over the course of the conflict). In 1429, Venice honoured its Guelph supporters with a charter (*privilegio*).[42] This allows us to uncover their names and map where they lived: they were the Bianchi and Danioni families and all the inhabitants of Peghera, Olda, and Pizzino, where the noted castle of another Guelph family, the Bellaviti, was located. From then on, Pizzino would host the valley's magistrate, to be appointed by local residents in complete autonomy from the city, which of course had the desired effect of entrusting the valley to the members of yet another Guelph family, the Salvioni.[43] In 1431, the Guelph party of the Val Torta and the Val Averara accomplished a similar feat. Defeated, the local Ghibellines sought refuge in the Val Sassina, where they joined the *pars expulsa* of the Val Taleggio. Together, the Ghibelline families from all three valleys tried to retake the Val Taleggio, but they were beaten by a coalition of Guelph and Venetian forces, which took the extreme measure of levelling the castle of Pianchello with artillery ('positis bombardis').[44] In 1438, the Ghibellines came together once again to assist the short-lived recovery of the valleys by the ducal army. It was the duke's turn to reward his supporters with a charter granting the locals a complete tax exemption.[45] This time, the document is addressed specifically to the clan leading the Ghibelline front, the Arrigoni of Vedeseta, and generally to all the families who had been exiled from the Val Taleggio. As the ducal army retreated, the Venetians forced the rebels to take an oath of loyalty, which reveals that Ghibellines centred around the villages of Vedeseta, Lavinia, Avolasio, Pratogiugno, and Almanterga (now Regetto).[46]

---

[41] For the impact that this phenomenon had on social structures and power relations in the mountains, see respectively Zenobi, 'Itinerari di mobilità geografica e sociale'; and Della Misericordia, 'Relazioni interlocali lungo una frontiera alpina'.

[42] PREDELLI, *I Libri Commemoriali* (vol. IV), 150, 10 February 1429.

[43] ARRIGONI, *Documenti inediti*, 177.   [44] ASMi, *Registri* 18, c. 408r, 16 July 1433.

[45] ASMi, *Esenzioni* 381, f. 'Arrigoni', 13 January 1438.

[46] CALVI, *Effemeride sacra profana* (vol. III), 46–7 (12 September 1446).

3. *CONFINIUM COMPOSITIO* 87

As the conflict unfolded, the people of the Val Taleggio polarized into opposite camps. As we have seen, in order to locate the Guelph and Ghibelline portions of the valley, central chanceries referred either to individual villages or to the families that inhabited them. They did so interchangeably, which suggests that political, territorial, and familial identity overlapped very closely in the Val Taleggio. The same conclusion can be drawn from the analysis of the surviving notarial records, which confirm that families identifying with the same faction owned properties in the same villages.[47] As shown in Figure 8, Guelph families controlled the villages of the lower valley, which led to the Val Brembana and from there to Bergamo; Ghibelline families, on the other hand, controlled the villages of the upper valley, which put them in communication with the Val Sassina and Lecco. Guelph areas were thus directly accessible to Venetian territory, while Ghibelline areas were connected to Milan. The political and territorial division that marked the Val Taleggio must have been just as evident to contemporaries. In the valley, factions had shaped a strong correlation between political allegiances, people, and places. In so doing, they lent weight to the community as the most basic and irreducible unit of territorial organization. More importantly, factions provided a universal principle, distinguishing between rebels and loyalists, between *ducheschi* and *marcheschi*, and between communities that would refuse an external power and communities that would welcome it, the same principle that would then be used to determine the new frontier between states.

Mapping the Negotiations

It took several meetings, some extending well into the night, to reach an agreement on the final draft of what would then become the *confinium*

---

[47] A systematic analysis of Guelph lands has been conducted on the basis of little-known records now kept in BMBg, *Fondo Salvioni e Bellaviti* 1, notary Costanzo Salvioni from Sottochiesa (1455–63); and BMBg, *Fondo Salvioni e Bellaviti* 39, notary Cristoforo Bellaviti from Taleggio (1444–64). Around this time, other notaries must have worked for Ghibelline communities, but their records have not survived; this is possibly because they were then kept in the Val Sassina instead of Bergamo. However, we can still draw connections between Ghibelline families and individual villages thanks to a later map of the Val Taleggio which does exactly that. In it, the names of most villages of the valley are noted next to the name of the family that lived there: Vedeseta is linked to the Arrigoni, Lavinia to the Amiconi, Avolasio to the Rognoni, and Almenterga to the Quartironi. The map was probably made for the Milanese chancery around the year 1550 and can now be found in ASMi, *Miscellanea mappe e disegni* 20 A.

Fig. 8 Guelph and Ghibelline villages in the Val Taleggio, respectively in light and dark grey. © DigitalGlobe

compositio of 1456. The entire process took roughly a month, from the beginning of July to the beginning of August.[48] As the talks unfolded, the two parties compiled a number of provisional agreements, which reveal their changing attitudes towards the dispute and the sorts of solutions brought to the table. Initially, both Venice and Milan sought to enforce the criterion of jurisdictional affiliation to support their claims, as in the case of the Val Torta and the Val Averara. While the Venetians deemed the valleys to be part of the Bergamasco, the duke saw them as limbs (*membra*) of the Val Sassina, which in turn made them part of the *contado* of Milan and, by extension, of the ducal dominion. A similar argument was then put forward for the villages of Brumano and Morterone: although they were located in the Val Imagna, their inhabitants had long travelled to Lecco—and not Bergamo—to make use of a court of law.[49] However, communities that formed part of the same jurisdiction could still end up under the control of opposing powers. Except for the Val Taleggio, where Giappani had implicitly sanctioned the rule of Venice over Pizzino and the lower valley, situations of this kind were typically caused by war. As a result, both parties took to experimenting with alternative criteria to secure their military achievements. For example, while the Venetians agreed to concede the plain (*piano*) of Lecco, including the disputed lands of Acquate and Bione, they were reluctant to give up the so-called hill of Lecco, namely 'the things which belong to Lecco but are in the mountains', including Brumano and Morterone.[50] Thus, a geographical criterion was juxtaposed with the jurisdictional criterion evoked by the duke. This does not mean that the two parties had divergent visions of how borders should be established or that the Milanese were averse to similar reasoning, especially when it suited their claims. Notably, in an attempt to protect their jurisdiction over at least part of the Val Taleggio, the Milanese party suggested splitting the valley according to the course of a local river, the creek of Salzana, a proposal soon rejected by the Venetians on the grounds that they already controlled lands on both sides of it.[51]

The testing of alternative forms of territorial division in what was, in essence, a jurisdictional universe could not be any more evident than in the map shown in Figure 9. As we shall see in Chapter 7, this unique piece of

---

[48] ASMi, *Carteggio* 343, 7 July 1456; ASVe, *Miscellanea* 40, 4 August 1456.
[49] ASMi, *Carteggio* 343, 17 July 1456.
[50] ASMi, *Carteggio* 343, 18 July 1456: 'le cose de Lecho che sono in la montagna'.
[51] ASMi, *Carteggio* 343, 21 July 1456.

90 BORDERS AND THE POLITICS OF SPACE IN LATE MEDIEVAL ITALY

cartography contains valuable clues as to the way in which borders were imagined and committed to paper in this period. For now, however, let us focus on what it can tell us about the way in which contemporaries approached the dispute and finally settled it. At first glance, we are met with a familiar sight: from the heights of their respective positions, the castles of Pizzino (to the right) and Pianchello (to the left) dominate the Val Taleggio. The valley itself is depicted by a circle, which is split down the middle by the creek of Salzana. Beside the thumbnail sketches of Pizzino and its hill, the semicircle on the right includes only a smaller circle marking the community of Sottochiesa ('terra Subeclexia'). By contrast, the semicircle on the left contains the castle of Pianchello, the community of Vedeseta ('terra Vedexite'), and five smaller villages (Pratogiugno, Avolasio, Canto, Lavinia, and Olda). Together with the exaggerated size of the river, the comparative abundance of place names in the semicircle on the left (which is the portion of the valley that was controlled by the ducal army at this stage) shows that the map was chiefly an attempt to visualize the Milanese proposal to split the Val Taleggio following the course of the Salzana. In turn, this suggests that the map was made for or perhaps even by the Milanese Chancery in 1456. Surprisingly, the reason why the Milanese proposal proved to be unviable is also noted on the map: the village of Olda, which is located in the lower portion of the Milanese semicircle, is said to be currently held by the Venetians ('Olda que nunc tenetur per Venetos'). Indeed, the fact that another hand added notes and names to the map, including that of Olda, suggests that as the talks unfolded, the negotiators tested different views and alternative criteria on the map itself, leaving us with a layered representation of the dispute.

Although the solution embodied by the inflated course of the river Salzana is made to stand out, the underlying layer of this map nonetheless betrays a jurisdictional discourse. For this to be immediately evident, we first have to reappraise the map not just as a sketchy portrait of the Val Taleggio, but as a graphic representation of a complex system of interconnected valleys extending for more than 20 miles between Bergamo (in the bottom right-hand corner) and Lecco (to the far left). In its entirety, the system is depicted by a star diagram, one in which each point stands for a single valley and the Val Taleggio sits at the intersection of them all. Indeed, while the map singles out the distinctions that marked the two sides of the Val Taleggio, it also charts connections and highlights the valley's strategic location. It reveals, for example, that to reach Lecco from the Val Taleggio, people took the road through the disputed lands of Brumano and Morterone

Fig. 9 Fifteenth-century sketch of the Val Taleggio and the surrounding valleys (ASMi, *Confini* 290). Reproduced with permission from the Italian Ministry of Cultural Heritage.

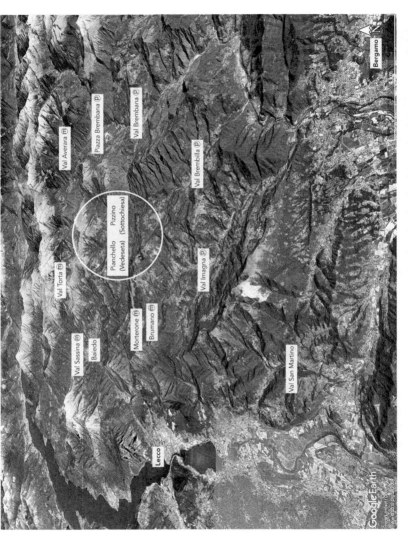

Fig. 10 Satellite view of the area and place names included in the sketch of the Val Taleggio. © DigitalGlobe

3. *CONFINIUM COMPOSITIO*   93

rather than through the Val Sassina. Similarly, the map shows that a mountain pass (the 'Forzela Pegarie', now Forcella di Bura) linked Sottochiesa to the Val Brembilla, which in turn is linked to the Val Imagna by the diamond-shaped body of the Val San Martino. With the exception of the last, every valley is branded with either the letter M or the letter P. This is to signal their jurisdictional affiliation with one of two city-states: *Mediolanum* and *Pergamum*. Accordingly, some the valleys are marked as part of the Bergamasco, thus accepting Venetian claim over them. These are the Val Imagna, the Val Brembilla, and the Val Brembana, which is accurately split into a lower valley ('Valis Brambana') and an upper valley ('Laplaza', now Piazza Brembana). On the other hand, the Val Sassina (with the fortress of Baiedo) and the valleys of Torta and Averara are marked as Milanese, thus visualizing the argument put forward by the duke. The same can be said for Brumano and Morterone, which are also labelled as part the territory of Lecco ('territorii Leuci'). It follows that the map reflects closely the unfolding of the negotiations: as the two parties sought to find an effective way to divide the Val Taleggio, the other valleys could be assigned to one of the two powers simply by adopting the criterion of jurisdictional affiliation.

In short, like the provisional agreements above, the map charts how the two parties approached the dispute and what kinds of criteria they sought to apply. But what can it tell us about the way in which the dispute was finally settled? This is where the final but also most consequential layer comes in. While other layers have identified the villages of the Val Taleggio and surveyed the jurisdictional affiliation of the surrounding valleys, this layer adds local families to the picture. It does so in two ways: by tracing their spatial distribution across the valley and by locating their presence at one moment in time. Not surprisingly, the families that we know to be the leaders of the Guelph front are shown to be living in the portion of the valley controlled by the Venetians, between Pizzino and Vedeseta ('hic morantur Salvioni et Belaviti'). On the other hand, the Ghibelline families are shown as having lived in the other portion of the valley, between Pianchello and Vedeseta ('hic morabant Arigoni, Quartironi, Amiconi, et Rognoni'). As we know, this is because of the events of the 1430s and 1440s, when the Ghibelline families were repeatedly forced out of the valley by a coalition of Guelph and Venetian forces. The same vicissitudes are echoed in the annotations to Pianchello and Vedeseta, which are briefly described as lying in ruins at this stage ('Plancelum nunc derupatum', 'terra Vedexite derupata'). Years had passed since the exiled families had been fully in control of the upper valley, but the distinction between Guelph and Ghibelline

94 BORDERS AND THE POLITICS OF SPACE IN LATE MEDIEVAL ITALY

villages was evidently still in place. By incorporating a temporal dimension, the map reveals how the factional past of the valley informed not only the present power balance but also the very future of the dispute.

In the end, the *confinium compositio* encompassed all these layers into its text.[52] Much of the mountain border was established by assigning the entirety of a jurisdictional body to one of the two powers. Brumano and Morterone were deemed to be subject to Lecco, so they were given to the duke as part of the town's territory. Conversely, the valleys of Torta and Averara were brought under the jurisdiction of Bergamo, thus becoming part of the Venetian dominion.[53] While jurisdictional powers changed hands, the boundaries of the valleys and other mountain territories remained largely the same. As such, they could be combined to form the new state frontier. The Val Taleggio, on the other hand, posed a different set of problems: circumstantial factors and serious mistakes had driven a profound wedge between two sides of the valley (upper and lower, Ghibelline and Guelph). In the interest of bringing stability to the area, the negotiators were left with no choice but to elevate this political and territorial division to a formalized distinction between the two states. Rather than the external boundaries of the whole valley, the internal boundaries between its two sides were adopted as the new state borders. To define these borders, the agreement established a direct equivalence between local families and their communities, which it then used to delimit the extent of each dominion in the area. While the Venetians retained Pizzino, Sottochiesa, Olda, and much of the lower valley (with the Salvioni and Bellaviti families), the duke gained control over the Arrigoni, Rognoni, Amiconi, and Quartironi families and all the villages they inhabited (Pianchello, Vedeseta, Lavina, Almanterga, Avolasio, Canto, Pratogiugno, and S. Bartolomeo). Just as the rest of the border was the result of the aggregation of pre-existing boundaries between

---

[52] The final version of the treaty was drafted in Milan (ASMi, *Registri* 39, cc. 37r–38v, 4 August 1456) and ratified in Venice a week later (ASVe, *Miscellanea* 40, 12 August 1456).

[53] Understandably, Francesco Sforza was far from content with this outcome. A few months after the treaty was signed, he was still writing to his ambassadors in Venice complaining that there was no doubt that those territories 'belong to us, for they clearly are places of the jurisdiction of the duchy of our city of Milan... This truth is worth more than a thousand records, especially when these are made by mistake' (referring to Giappani's ill-fated *consignatio*): ASMi, *Registri* 18, cc. 463r–463v, 29 October 1456: 'spectavano a nui perché sonno lochi della iurisditione del ducato de questa nostra città... debbe più valere la mera veritate che mille scripture, maxime quando sonno facte per errore'. However, 'to show goodwill and courtesy towards Venice', as he would then write when taking leave of his loyal subjects of the Val Torta, the duke had no choice but to act against his own interest: ASMi, *Registri* 18, c. 464r, 20 January 1457: 'non riguardando ad nostro interesse per usare de cortesia et liberalitate verso de lei'.

3. *CONFINIUM COMPOSITIO* 95

mountain territories, in the Val Taleggio it was the product of the existing divide between local communities.[54]

* * *

The case of the Val Taleggio was undoubtedly exceptional. Here, rather than treating the valley as a unified territory, negotiators built on the existing partition of local society to define the new state borders. Yet the handling of the dispute also bears a striking resemblance to the way in which major treaties were negotiated, since it reflects the same abiding principles and negotiation practices discussed in Chapters 1 and 2. The first is the role played by the local community as the basic unit of territorial organization. Although the division of the valley was rooted in family rivalries, it also exhibited a visible spatial dimension. As communities became more politicized, factions became increasingly territorialized. Whilst people identified with Guelphs and Ghibellines, factional identities were mapped out onto the most fundamental spatial layer, that is, onto the boundaries between villages. This charged the distinctions between individual communities with a whole new meaning, a political meaning—so political, in fact, that Milanese and Venetian deputies could then use it in the making of state borders. Once again, the true objects of negotiation were not the borders of the state as a whole but the boundaries of its constituent units—of territories shaped by communities of people.

The second element that reminds us of the negotiation of major peace treaties is the interplay of a plurality of spatial references, particularly when that plurality served to describe borders in more detail and at different scales. While the issue of the Val Taleggio was settled at the level of single families, these were then defined in relation to local communities (the villages), which in turn were made part of intermediate bodies (the two half-valleys) and urban territories (the *contadi*). All these levels are also depicted in the map: the families (with their names), the villages (as small circles), the valleys (as semicircles), and finally the urban centres (with M and P). What emerges from this is the significance ceded to the boundaries of

---

[54] As often happened, the Milanese and Venetian governments were drawn into further disputes over the valleys between Lecco and Bergamo for much of the early modern period (even though, of course, the duchy was now part of the Spanish empire). The disputes concerned the one and only stone which the two parties left unturned in 1456. This was the fate of the extensive pastures and woods that the people of the valley used to exploit together as common land before the establishment of new state borders. See Cozzi, 'Politica e diritto in alcune controversie confinarie'; and Martin, 'The Venetian Territorial State: Constructing Boundaries in the Shadow of Spain'.

96 BORDERS AND THE POLITICS OF SPACE IN LATE MEDIEVAL ITALY

former city-states, coupled with the fact that the most consequential units were actually smaller than that and might also be linked to other powers (as in the case of the Bergamasco, which then contained assets that were under the duke's authority).

The third and last element is the widespread adoption of the culture and language of *iurisdictio*. We have seen the extent to which this underpinned the allocation of entire territories. But even when it came to dividing a jurisdictional body, this was not done by drawing an arbitrary line but by splitting—or rather doubling—the Val Taleggio into two distinct corporations. The mapmaker mirrored this decision by marking both halves of the valley with the same name (*Taegium*). In jurisdictional terms, there were now two distinct Val Taleggios: one to be assigned to Venice, the other to be assigned to Milan.

Furthermore, the analysis of the Taleggio dispute allows us to make some broader points about inter-polity relations and about the way in which space was constructed and negotiated through the intervention of both state and non-state actors. Establishing a new frontier between states was initially a matter of describing the territorial modifications first caused by war (and particularly by the Venetian conquest of eastern Lombardy) and then ratified through peace-making (notably through the treaty of Lodi). Yet the fact that peace treaties provided only some generic guidance as to which territories should change hands and particularly as to how such change should actually take place—not to mention that their terms could still be applied incorrectly—meant that this first phase of border-making was far from exhaustive. At a later stage, the initial terms of the treaty had to be reconciled with the realm of practice. The current state of affairs might force some to work energetically towards a resolution (Milan), while others might decide to delay action (Venice), thus shaping the times and modalities of border politics.

In addition, the case of Giappani's mistake shows that the negotiation of borders could be driven to a great extent by localized exigencies. In spite of the seemingly authoritative character of the proceedings, the implementation of territorial modifications was far from a top-down process imposed by the leaderships of the two polities. Rather, it was the result of a sustained dialogue with local agents and of a careful consideration of their interests, motives, and ways of doing things with space. In the valleys between Lecco and Bergamo, it was the culture of factions which put the local and the regional in communication with each other—which made the existing organization of space available for higher purposes. While the antagonism between Venice and Milan allowed local parties to perform on the stage of inter-polity relations in the first half of the Quattrocento, their spatial dimension gave the two polities an organizing principle which could inform and sustain the establishment of new state borders in the second half of the century. The same factions that were once strengthened by war were now used to strengthen the peace. In this context, peripheral exigencies were addressed not for the sake of internal cohesion, but because they provided a stable territorial platform upon which the state's spatial dimension could be projected. As the shared language and discourse which connected local instances with regional designs, the culture of factions thoroughly informed the politics of space in late medieval Italy and is a perfect illustration of its interactive nature.

4

From Macro to Micro and Back Again

Constructing Borders in the Localities

Chapter 1 shed light on the genealogy and practical ramifications of a shared territorial culture in late medieval Italy—one that sanctioned the coexistence of a variety of corporate bodies (*universitates*) exerting varying degrees of power (*iurisdictiones*) over their spaces (*territoria*). That culture underpinned how people envisioned the territorial landscape of the peninsula: as an expanse of communities over which superior forms of political and social organization (first city-states, then regional states) came to extend their jurisdiction. But what made these communities so resilient? Chapter 2 established that the boundaries of local communities were often used as building blocks in the making of new state borders. But why would the leaderships of larger polities trust the demarcations made by local actors? Chapter 3 showed that even when such demarcations followed personalized logics, as in the case of factional allegiance, these were still mapped onto a grid of discrete communities. But how did people distinguish these communities from one another? This chapter answers these outstanding questions. It does so by exploring the intersection of micro practices of territorial demarcation, namely the definition of local boundaries, and macro practices of border-making, as seen in the book so far. In so doing, the chapter seeks to investigate the integration of multiple territorial scales across the Late Middle Ages and assess the role of local communities in the making of Italian society.

In conducting this analysis, we shall draw on both constructivist and relational theories of space (and thus of borders and territories). As discussed in the Introduction, this book is informed by the idea that space is not just a mere container for human agency. Rather, space is a construct which is continuously challenged and redefined by people's actions, including usage, representation, movement, and exchange. In short, space is seen as the ever-changing product of relational practices. Philosophers and social theorists such as Henry Lefebvre and Michel de Certeau have introduced a

Borders and the Politics of Space in Late Medieval Italy: Milan, Venice, and their Territories. Luca Zenobi,
Oxford University Press. © Luca Zenobi 2023. DOI: 10.1093/oso/9780198876861.003.0005

4. FROM MACRO TO MICRO AND BACK AGAIN   99

whole generation of historians to the notion that human interactions have shaped space, but they have also noted how space has helped people to attach meanings to things.[1] The idea here is that space—and thus territories and borders—is always invested with social significance and this has substantial ramifications for the world at large: spatial constructs evoke group narratives, ground complex memories, denote a sense of self, and even provide a pivot for collective identification. To put it briefly, space shapes human agency as much as it is shaped by it.

In this chapter, this constructivist and relational understanding of space will be applied to examining the most fundamental unit of territorial organization: the local community. In addition to those mentioned earlier, two notions have informed the development of the chapter. The first is the notion of 'appropriation', as developed by the Swiss geographer Claude Raffestin. Influenced by Foucault's writings on power and Deleuze's philosophy on territorialization, Raffestin framed territory as a space in which an actor has performed an appropriative action, whether this has been concrete (marking, delimiting) or abstract (representing, imagining).[2] The second notion is that of the 'production of locality', as formulated by anthropologist Arjun Appadurai. This concept's potential for historical analysis is best exemplified by Angelo Torre's work on early modern Piedmont. Drawing on Appadurai, Torre framed locality as a cultural and social framework generated over time through activities such as the enforcement of community rights, the exploitation of collective resources, and the performance of rituals.[3]

Building on the methodological platform provided by these works, the chapter's first section will consider the practice of defining local boundaries in the context of collective appropriations of space. In so doing, we shall respond to those outstanding questions regarding the production of late medieval localities, while also considering some of the issues underpinning the notions introduced above. These include matters such as agency (who performed territorial demarcations?), materiality (what objects and tools did they use?), knowledge (how did they inscribe their desired outcome?), law (what made demarcations legally binding?), and memory (to what extent did local boundaries affect long-term identities?). After considering

---

[1] Lefebvre, *La production de l'espace*; de Certeau, *L'invention du quotidien*.
[2] Raffestin, *Pour une géographie du pouvoir*; but see first Klauser, 'Thinking through Territoriality'.
[3] Torre, *Luoghi. La produzione di località*; Appadurai, *Modernity at Large*, 178–99.

100 BORDERS AND THE POLITICS OF SPACE IN LATE MEDIEVAL ITALY

how border- and community-making took place from below, the chapter's second section will explore how local boundaries were then adopted, from above, to function as state borders. In aligning the chapter with the rest of the work, we shall look especially at the interactions through which space and borders produced in the margins were then made available for higher purposes, while also examining how local practices were legitimized by central agencies. In conclusion, the chapter will discuss the reciprocity between bottom-up and top-down practices of border-making and place it in the context of our wider investigation into the spatial fabric of Italian society.

Collective Action and Space Appropriation

If locality is the space within which a community practices its activities, what, then, is a community and how did it appropriate such a space? Like locality and space itself, the term 'community' has been widely adopted by scholars of the peninsula only in the last few decades. In Italian, the adoption of the term (*comunità*) has been accompanied by the dwindling use of 'village' (*villaggio*) and 'rural commune' (*comune rurale*). While the former was dear to scholars interested in questions of demography and settlement growth, the latter had informed the vocabulary of a whole series of studies over the course of the twentieth century. At first, rural communes were seen chiefly as institutions built around a strictly regulated assembly and governed by a set of elected officers. According to scholars such as Romolo Caggese, rural communes became progressively more defined only through a class-like confrontation with local lords (*domini loci*).[4] This institutional formulation might have survived to this day but for the injection of a fresh interpretation by Chris Wickham. In a seminal book on twelfth-century Tuscany, the British historian highlighted the internal hierarchies and social relationships that bound together and at the same time divided the peasants, while also presenting cases where the commune developed independently from seigneurial powers.[5]

Whatever their origin, it is now accepted that rural communes had already acquired a well-defined spatial dimension by the year 1200 and that

---

[4] Caggese, *Classi e comuni rurali*. On this theme and on the reception of Caggese's thesis, particularly by eminent Italian historians such as Giovanni Tabacco and Andrea Castagnetti, see Taddei, 'Comuni rurali e centri minori', 321–4.

[5] Wickham, *Community and Clientele*. Given its relevance to the topic at hand, consider also Wickham, 'Frontiere di villaggio'.

4. FROM MACRO TO MICRO AND BACK AGAIN   101

this was the product of social as much as institutional practices.[6] In other words, peasants came to appropriate their space not only through becoming organized (whether on their own or in opposition to local lords) but through doing things together. What fostered a sense of belonging was not simply electing officers or voting in assemblies but taking part in a range of social activities. While some of these, such as the carrying out of religious ceremonies, only partly affected territorial identities, others did much to foster a sense of territorial belonging. Taxes, for example, were now collected not from the labourers working the scattered lands of a *dominus* but from the people who resided in a community's territory—a territory which might or might not have been part of a seigneurial jurisdiction. Similarly, the collective management of common resources, such as woodlands and pastures, increased the need for a precise definition of those areas, which soon went from sitting at the margins of communal territories to forming an integral part of them.[7]

As urban communes incorporated their rural counterparts into their dominions, the territories of local communities were further sanctioned by superior powers. Communities could be arranged around a main nucleus or even be fragmented in a myriad of neighbourhoods and minute hamlets. However, regardless of their settlement type, the spatial dimension of local communities was now seen as the only form of territorial organization which was truly alternative to—and, in fact, constitutive of—that of the *civitates*. As anticipated in Chapter 1, this was the outcome of two concurrent processes: the marginalization of competing forms of political and social organization (notably rural lordships) and the intellectual framing of rural communes as sister corporations of the *universitas civium* (the urban commune). Significantly, this happened as the cities themselves saw their *contadi* recognized by the emperor, which laid the foundation of a hierarchical territorial order in central and northern Italy.[8]

---

[6] The debate about how exactly these processes took place in different regions of Italy—let alone Europe—remains open. For our purposes, it should suffice to refer to the reappraisal undertaken by Sergi, 'La territorialità e l'assetto giurisdizionale'; and Lazzari, 'Campagne senza città e territori senza centro'.

[7] The literature on these topics is vast and spans multiple decades. A first phase coincided with the publication of studies such as Violante, 'La signoria *territoriale*'; and Castagnetti, *Le comunità rurali*, 7–76. More recently, a new generation of Italian historians has taken to placing rural communities in a new methodological context, enriching the institutional outlook of previous studies with cultural analysis. See, by way of example, the research conducted on Piedmont by Guglielmotti, *Comunità e territorio*; and Provero, *Le parole dei sudditi*.

[8] On these processes, compare Nobili, 'I contadi organizzati'; with Taddei, 'L'organizzazione del territorio'.

102   BORDERS AND THE POLITICS OF SPACE IN LATE MEDIEVAL ITALY

By the beginning of the Quattrocento, communities were almost universally identified with their territories and, by extension, with their boundaries. At least in northern Italy, there remained pockets where horizontal solidarities were weak and local populations chose to identify with some lordly power (*dominatus loci*).[9] Commonly, however, the association of residents was now seen as the holder of a bundle of undisputed rights over their territory, while also being expected to fulfil certain duties in relation to it. Communities were free to choose their representatives, to endow the incomes and properties of local churches, and to regulate the use of natural resources in any way they saw fit. At the same time, however, they were required to impose tariffs on the consumption of certain goods, to maintain roads and police the area, and even to patrol fords and mountain passes. As Massimo Della Misericordia has put it in a recent reappraisal, these activities 'created rights and duties that extended towards delineated horizons'.[10]

An evocative example of the equation of a community and its territory is their close association in the lexicon of notarial records. In fifteenth-century Lombardy, the community was still far from transforming into an administrative division of local government—an abstract entity separate from the individuals who formed it in the first place. In fact, the congregation of communal assemblies was recorded by notaries both as the meeting of a corporate body and as the gathering of a group of people (*convocata et congregata universitate communis et hominum*).[11] While the community was embodied in the sum of its members in notarial parlance, the people themselves were presented as those who inhabited the community: as the residents not just of a material settlement (*villa, locus, burgus*) but of a territory headed by the community itself (*territorium communis* or, simply, *commune*).[12] In short, communities were now seen as the fundamental units around which not only social life pivoted but space itself was organized.

How, then, did local communities ensure that the space they had appropriated remained in their possession? In this respect, it was not so much the intrusion of rural lordships or urban powers which posed a threat but the

---

[9] This was notably the case of the peripheries of far from cohesive *contadi* such as that of Reggio, as demonstrated by Gamberini, 'La territorialità nel Basso Medioevo', 47–72.

[10] Della Misericordia, 'The rural Communities', 278; though see also Mori, 'Territorial Identities', 330–2.

[11] On this particular formulation and its equivalents in fifteenth-century Lombardy, see Del Tredici, 'Loci, comuni, homines', 280–1; and Della Misericordia, 'Decidere e agire in comunità', 308–9.

[12] On these other formulations, see Della Misericordia, *Divenire comunità*, 350–1; and Lazzarini, *Il linguaggio del territorio*, 25–31.

4. FROM MACRO TO MICRO AND BACK AGAIN 103

encroachment of adjoining communities. Italian archives are replete with sources recording legal clashes and even violent confrontations between members of opposing communities. Following Wickham and Grendi respectively, scholars of medieval and early modern Italy have long unlocked the potential of court records to study how communities defended the limits of their territories, while also uncovering how they envisioned their collective rights—and duties—over space.[13] Yet the 'practice of borders', to use Grendi's noted expression, entailed more than just conflict. Communities defined their boundaries on a regular basis. The goal was to distinguish one's territory against that of one's neighbours, thus ascribing lands and assets unequivocally to those who were meant to control them. While the periodic definition of community boundaries is often mentioned in writings stemming from conflict resolution, the proceedings were first recorded in dedicated documents. Sometimes called *instrumenta confinationum* or simply *confinationes*, these were notarial records attesting the placing of new boundary markers or, more typically, certifying the statements of people who knew about their location.

Unlike the perambulation of parish bounds in England, the process recorded in the *instrumenta* was a fully fledged legal procedure.[14] Across Lombardy, communities of all sizes can be found resorting to the service of notaries to formally inscribe the arrangement of their boundaries. As a rule, these records would then remain in the custody of the notary who wrote them and, at his death, be passed on to a nearby colleague or simply to his heirs (should they choose to take up their father's occupation). The written memory of local boundaries was thus bound to stay in the locality along with other records documenting the activities of the community and of its members—from deeds validating the sale or rent of common lands to minutes noting the matters discussed in general assemblies. This renders these sources rather arduous to retrieve; it also prevents us from estimating how often local communities conducted these proceedings on their own initiative. At times, however, notaries in the service of superior powers could make authenticated copies of the *instrumenta* and collect them in specially created manuscripts. As we saw in Chapter 1, this was notably the case of the so-called books of borders (*libri finium*).

---

[13] Grendi, 'La pratica dei confini'; Wickham, *Courts and Conflict*, 81–5, 139–44, and 183–5. Two pieces of research following in their footsteps are Provero, 'Una cultura dei confini'; and Stopani, 'Pratiche di mantenimento del possesso'.

[14] Hindle, 'Beating the Bounds of the Parish'. Still, the custom is not unique to England, let alone Europe, as shown by Radcliffe, 'Marking the Boundaries'.

104 BORDERS AND THE POLITICS OF SPACE IN LATE MEDIEVAL ITALY

In Lombardy, the practice is especially well documented for Bergamo, where numerous *instrumenta* were gathered by the city's own chancery on a regular basis. For the period 1392–1492, over 300 records have survived. These were written by roughly 100 different notaries for almost 170 different communities.[15] The Bergamasco is a geographically diverse region, straddling a large area from a narrow plain, where communities were few and somewhat weak, to densely populated hills, where communities were set in direct opposition to Bergamo itself, to an intricate network of valleys, where communities were strong and often united in federations. This makes the Bergamasco representative of other regions and subregions of Italy where equivalent social structures and political institutions can be found, including many areas of Lombardy. The plain of Brescia, for example, bore a striking resemblance to that of the Bergamasco, as did the northern suburbs of Milan. Similarly, the valleys of the Bergamasco had a political and social organization analogous to that of valleys once subject directly to other cities, such as the Val Tellina (Como) and the Val Camonica (Brescia)—not to mention the nearby Val Sassina.

The rest of this section will build on the unique corpus of records gathered in Bergamo to investigate how the proceedings of the *confinationes* consolidated the extent of a community's territory in late medieval Italy. In looking at these proceedings, we shall consider how they intersected with the realms of agency, materiality, knowledge, law, and memory, thus maintaining the approach laid out in the chapter's introduction.

To turn first to the issue of agency, it is clear that defining boundaries in the localities involved the vast majority of the politically active population. In the Quattrocento, the community was first embodied in the assembly of all the heads of households. Summoned periodically by the sound of church bells, the assembly had as its main duty to approve deliberations by a majority. The most frequent deliberations concerned the election of officers and smaller councils, who in turn were responsible for the day-to-day running of the community. Typically, a small group of notaries, merchants, and large landowners dominated these posts, but their decisions were still framed as

---

[15] The records dating to the fourteenth century are all collected in the so-called *Codice Patetta* (BAVa, *Fondo Patetta*, ms. 1387), which has been transcribed and published in full by MARCHETTI, *Confini dei comuni*. The records dating to the fifteenth century are in a separate manuscript, which is now held in BMBg, *Salone Cassapanca* I, ms. 4 47/1–2. A working list of all the communities concerned by these records can be found in Oscar and Belotti, *Atlante storico del territorio bergamasco*, 344. As the *instrumenta* are highly formulaic, what follows does not cite individual examples but tries instead to extrapolate a general model.

4. FROM MACRO TO MICRO AND BACK AGAIN   105

being made in the name of the whole community (*nomine communis*).[16] It was from these people that the deputies in charge of settling disputes were appointed, the same method used for the selection of the protagonists of our *confinationes*. In the records, their position in the institutional apparatus would always be noted first by notaries. They could be executive officers (*consuli*), specially appointed agents (*sindaci*), or members of the community's largest council (*anziani*). Their involvement was generally limited to sharing their knowledge about the location of boundary markers, though sometimes they were made directly responsible for placement. This often determined the venue where the deputies of the community met the notary to draft the *instrumentum* itself, which could range from the local church square or the house of some official to the site of one of the recently placed markers.

This brings us to the issue of materiality. In essence, defining a community's territory meant tracing a polygon connecting boundary markers. In writing the *instrumenta*, notaries translated this practice into a description not of the boundaries themselves but of the virtual journey which the parties performed to visit all the markers. When possible, the deputies would adopt evident features of the landscape as markers. These included natural elements, such as a peculiar tree or a spring, as well as artificial ones, such as a crossroads or a noticeable building. Typically, however, boundary markers were a combination of the two, as in the noted case of carved stones bearing writings or other signs, such as crosses. Having sketched the appearance of the first marker (*primus terminus*), the notaries went on to pinpoint its position. As a rule, they did so by resorting to the same technique they used to identify pieces of land (in deeds of sale, for example, or in wills), namely by locating the marker in relation to its surroundings.[17] In practice, this came down to integrating the marker in question with the topography of everyday life (the marker flanks a road to the north, a river to the south) and even with the geography of property (the marker borders common pastures to the west, the estates of some community member to the east). Combined with this set of well-known references, boundary markers came to form a system of signs which was cognitive as much as visual, mental as much as

---

[16] For the functioning of representative as well as executive institutions in fifteenth-century communities, see also Della Misericordia, 'Decidere e agire in comunità', 291–378; and, with particular reference to borders, Della Misericordia, 'I confini dell'economia', 253.

[17] On the delimitation of rural areas on behalf of specialists of the written word, see Coste, 'Description et délimitation de l'espace rural'; and Portet, 'La mesure géométrique des champs'.

106 BORDERS AND THE POLITICS OF SPACE IN LATE MEDIEVAL ITALY

practical.[18] Through their materiality and location, these artefacts were incorporated into people's experience of the space of their community, which in turn helped to fix the spatial coordinates of local boundaries.

After placing or identifying the first boundary marker, the reader of the *instrumentum* is taken on an excursion to the next one. To do so, the notaries strung an imaginary wire between the two markers (*per lineam rectam*) and then grounded its location in a sequence of notable sites (a peculiar boulder, a fortified wall, a water well, a church square, and so on). As with the markers themselves, when evident features were available, they were normally adapted to reify the line connecting two markers. These could be the course of a river, the profile of a mountain ridge, or simply a trail route. As the record unfolds, the notary treads with the deputies along these lines (*veniendo, recidendo*), thus moving from one marker to the next, until they find themselves back at the marker they first encountered, thus closing the polygon. This method allowed the notary to follow closely the activities of the deputies who had placed or known the markers. Additionally, it enabled the reader to trace their steps, if needed, thanks to the use of a common set of points—and lines—of reference.[19]

At the same time, the peripatetic definition of community boundaries allowed notaries and deputies alike to encompass the whole of the locality within a visible and physical framework, thus contributing to its spatial cohesion. By the end of the *confinationes*, a network of site markers and linear features of the landscape had been transformed into the legal bounds of the locality. In turn, this moulded a compact space, setting aside the community's territorial possessions from those of its neighbours. In the *instrumenta*, the outcome of this process is sometimes brought into focus in the final section of the records. Here, to keep using the language of photography, the notaries zoomed out to reveal the overall shape and limits of a community's territory. As with the markers and indeed any compact piece of land, the notaries did so by locating the community in relation to its surroundings (our territory borders that of community X to the north, that of community Y to the south, and so on). In so doing, they effectively treated the newly defined locality as an exclusive unit of territorial organization.

---

[18] On the 'sensorial' and 'semantic' experience of encountering boundaries in the countryside, see respectively Della Misericordia, 'I confini dell'economia', 263; and Francesconi, 'Scrivere il contado', 527.

[19] On the materiality of boundary markers and their definition, consider Della Misericordia, 'Significare il confine'; together with the analogous practices found by Degrassi, 'Dai confini dei villaggi ai confini politici'; and Bordone, 'I confini della comunità'.

4. FROM MACRO TO MICRO AND BACK AGAIN 107

The proximity of neighbouring communities and the threat this posed to the control of lands and assets was possibly the first reason behind the periodic redefinition of local boundaries. Like other small-scale societies in history, such as those studied by Appadurai, late medieval communities 'seem to assume that locality is ephemeral unless hard and regular work is undertaken to produce and maintain its materiality'.[20] If communities never took their locality as given, how then did they ensure that future generations sustained this ceaseless work of spatial appropriation? This brings us to consider how the proceedings of the *confinationes* intersected with matters of knowledge and law and, from there, with the issue of memory and identity.

The knowledge of local boundaries lay first with the deputies who marked them or simply knew them over the course of their lives. Through the mediation of a notary, knowledge of territorial arrangements was then translated into a set of well-known references and finally codified into a legally binding document. Like the French notaries studied by Daniel Lord Smail in Marseilles, not only did Italian notaries develop their own spatial language, but they inscribed it in 'verbal maps' which were widely understood by contemporaries.[21] Through the undisputed validity that notaries were able to impart to their records, the written rendition of community boundaries was elevated as the official image of the locality, thus taking part in its shared construction.[22] By the end of this process, individual knowledge of space had been turned into the legal foundation of collective possession. In this sense, it is fair to say that 'knowledge of the territory is a production of the territory itself'.[23] Jacques Revel wrote these words to frame the capacity of pre-modern kingdoms to gather spatial information and then use it to sanction their territorial authority. Yet his methodological suggestion applies just as well to the proceedings through which local communities defined their territories. In late medieval Italy, granular knowledge of space was first acquired and legitimized at the level of the locality.

In shaping localities and local knowledge, these processes were also shaping 'local subjects', to retain Appadurai's terminology; these were people who knew 'how to produce and reproduce locality under conditions of anxiety and entropy, social wear and flux, ecological uncertainty and cosmic

---

[20] Appadurai, *Modernity at Large*, 180.

[21] Smail, *Imaginary Cartographies*; but consider also his reflections on public notaries as cartographers in Smail, 'The Linguistic Cartography of Property and Power'.

[22] On the ability of local notaries to classify and thus structure society through cultural processes, notably writing, consider the extensive study by Della Misericordia, *Figure di comunità*.

[23] Revel, 'Knowledge of the Territory', 134.

108 BORDERS AND THE POLITICS OF SPACE IN LATE MEDIEVAL ITALY

volatility, and the always present quirkiness of kinsmen, enemies, spirits, and quarks of all sorts'.[24] To put it another way, while relying on the participation of much of the local population and their direct knowledge of space, the definition of community boundaries also shaped people's sense of responsibility towards them. The maintenance and visitation of boundaries was entangled with practices which had long driven both the process of community formation and that of space appropriation, including the collection of taxes and the exploitation of local resources within an area. Boundaries provided a framework within which people conducted these practices and, in so doing, grounded the process through which individual members of the community came to identify with its territory. Like the practices they framed, boundaries were thus deposited into the collective memory; they became part of one's past and heritage. By extension, boundary markers became places of remembrance, sites were artefacts with a strong mnemonic character signalled the limits of the locality whilst also embodying the long history of the interactions between the people and their spaces.[25]

Together, the involvement of much of local society, the development of inclusive techniques on behalf of notaries, and the significance of boundaries for collective activities and identities gave local communities an unparalleled spatial cohesion among other territorial bodies. As we have seen, constructing borders in the localities was first and foremost a matter of community participation. In Chapter 2, we noted how local representatives often acted as witnesses in the legal ceremony through which jurisdiction over a territorial body was occasionally transferred from one power holder to another (*consignatio/confessio*). Their presence legitimized the transaction and ensured, to some extent, that the local population would promptly accept its judicial and fiscal ramifications. Yet local representatives did not exert any agency on these occasions; it was not their transaction but the state's. On the other hand, the *confinationes* were proceedings which not only happened periodically but which also saw notaries and local representatives take full responsibility for their outcomes.

Community participation became ever more meaningful because notaries moulded the proceedings of the *confinationes* around the world of the residents. As seen in Chapter 3, the negotiation of borders employed a

---

[24] Appadurai, *Modernity at Large*, 181.

[25] The literature on this topic has grown exponentially over the last few decades, particularly following the publication of the monumental survey directed by Nora, *Les lieux de mémoire*. One study in particular which incorporates the issue of social memory into a broader examination of the 'practice of borders' as first defined by Grendi is Stopani, 'La memoria dei confini'.

variety of spatial references to describe territorial modifications, ranging from the cities' *contadi* to intermediate bodies and individual villages. This enabled state deputies to capture the big picture while still referring to the shape of the units they mentioned to provide further details. It was the language of late medieval geopolitics, a discourse developed to relate change to space. While this language may have been seemingly foreign to most peasants, the inhabitants of rural communities were far from spatially illiterate. They spoke a different language, which in turn had been developed by notaries to suit their own motives. Like that of geopolitics, this language was grounded in its own set of spatial references, the same references which already underpinned the topography of everyday life. It is quite possible that many people were not able to read the *instrumenta* drafted by notaries; yet most were able to read the landscape. Unlike the recording of territorial modifications at a higher level, this made the definition of local boundaries conducted by notaries immediately accessible to residents.

Finally, the involvement of the vast majority of the population and the use of an inclusive language on the part of notaries aligned the definition of local boundaries with practices which had long fostered a sense of place. Defining boundaries mattered to territorial identities because it framed the activities through which the process of space appropriation was continually conducted—because it provided a framework within which locality could be produced and reproduced. The *instrumenta confinationum* were more than just written descriptions of local boundaries; they were acts of possession, legal deeds through which the community asserted ownership over its territory and collectively identified with it. In this sense, it is important to remember that while the *instrumenta* distinguished the territory of a community from that of its neighbours, they did so not by drawing a line between two or more localities, thus imparting an image of division and fragmentation, but by drawing a polygon around a single locality, thus conveying a sense of unity and cohesion. In the long run, it was this sense of unity and cohesion, coupled with collective practices and identities as much as individual actions and recordings, that gave local communities their spatial solidity.

Empowering Interactions and Border-Making

If local boundaries were fundamentally the framework of community life, what then made them suitable for being transformed into the new state

Fig. 11 An illustration from Bertrand Boysset's fifteenth-century copy of the *Traité d'Arpentage* by Arnaud de Villeneuve (1240–1315) showing people at work by boundary markers (BICa, ms. 327, c. 157v). © Irht.cnrs.fr

4. FROM MACRO TO MICRO AND BACK AGAIN   111

frontiers? In what ways, to put it differently, were micro practices of territorial demarcation combined with macro practices of border-making? And what can this process tell us about the nature of borders and territoriality in late medieval Italy? The short answer to these questions is 'interactions', particularly between communities and state institutions (such as chanceries, office holders, and courts). The long answer is the section that follows.

Like space, borders are always built on interactions; the more people acknowledge them, the more universal their meaning for the way a society is territorially organized. This aligns borders with other constructs which rely on widespread acceptance to operate, starting with the state itself. Long gone are the days when state formation was seen as a one-sided process imposed by ministers, dynasties, and their generals. Rather than in terms of coercion and resistance, state formation is now framed as a matter of negotiation between the state and a plurality of other bodies—in short, as an interactive process. Notably, in 2009, a volume edited by Wim Blockmans, André Holenstein, and Jon Mathieu proposed the notion of 'empowering interactions'.[26] The volume's premise was that the interests of central agencies and peripheral players were not necessarily at odds but could in fact meet and overlap, thus paving the way for mutually beneficial exchanges between state and non-state actors. Members of local societies called on the state to uphold their claims and settle their conflicts, thus gaining the backing of a superior authority; in turn, the state saw the nature and extent of its power recognized by a broadening social base. As the state legitimized the interests of local actors, its function was simultaneously legitimized by them.

While the paradigm of 'empowering interactions' was one of the first methodological attempts to frame these dynamics, scholars from all over Europe had been looking at reciprocal relationships in political life for quite some time.[27] In Italy, historians such as Giorgio Chittolini and Elena Fasano Guarini called for a reappraisal of the interplay between centres and peripheries, while also blurring the boundaries between public and private interests within the framework of a new history of pre-modern forms of political

---

[26] Blockmans, Holenstein, and Mathieu, *Empowering Interactions*. For the deep history of this historiographical shift, see Blockmans, 'Les origines des états modernes en Europe'.

[27] The examples could be many, but perhaps the most illustrative is the work done on the English kingdom, starting with Braddick, *State Formation*, who argued that 'a study of the process by which the state acquired agency is simultaneously a study of the uses of state power' (90). For a late medieval perspective on English politics, see the classic essay by Carpenter, 'The Duke of Clarence and the Midlands'; together with the case made for an integrated and, indeed, interactive political community made by Watts, 'The Pressure of the Public'.

112 BORDERS AND THE POLITICS OF SPACE IN LATE MEDIEVAL ITALY

organization.[28] Concurrently, scholars influenced by the practice of micro history endeavoured to invert this paradigm and look instead at political formations from the perspective of peripheral bodies and private ties (such as kinship, factions, and clientage).[29] Yet despite the breadth of historiographical interest, interactions are yet to be fully incorporated into our understanding of spatial constructs. On the one hand, as previous chapters have shown, treaties and diplomatic letters outlined the fundamental features of late medieval political geography, while also revealing the images of territorial authority projected by major powers. On the other, as we have seen with the present chapter, the records produced by notaries reflected a profound knowledge of local spaces, whilst also capturing a collective sense of territorial belonging. Even so, we know little about ways in which these two levels related to each other, thus leading to the integration of different territorial scales—an element which, as seen in the book so far, was one of the defining features of the spatial fabric of Italian society.

Exceptions remain, starting with Grendi's pioneering inquiry into the 'practice of borders' in early modern Italy.[30] In examining how communities of the Ligurian Apennines made use of state institutions to settle territorial disputes, Grendi noted that judges and magistrates alike were not merely acknowledging the rights of a community at the expense of its neighbours; they were also translating an ensemble of collective spatial practices into a set of recognized legal rights. To use the words of André Holenstein, one of the editors of the volume on empowering interactions, this was a situation in which 'local groups [made] use of the authoritative and legitimizing resources that the state offered through its office holders, courts and laws'.[31] While Holenstein did not have Grendi in mind when he wrote these words, they do a good job of capturing the kinds of processes which lay at the heart of the micro historian's interests. As Angelo Torre has put it while reviewing Grendi's method, his focus was on instances where communities made 'pragmatic use of institutions', which in turn triggered broader 'processes of cross-legitimation between power holders and their subjects'.[32]

---

[28] Two essays, in particular, are often cited as seminal for these developments: Chittolini, 'The *Private*, the *Public*, the State'; and Fasano Guarini, 'Center and Periphery'.

[29] Among many influential essays, consider Raggio, 'Visto dalla periferia'; and Levi, 'The Origins of the Modern State'.

[30] Grendi, 'La pratica dei confini'.

[31] Holenstein, 'Introduction: Empowering Interactions', 30.

[32] Torre, 'La produzione storica dei luoghi', 451.

4. FROM MACRO TO MICRO AND BACK AGAIN   113

The following section will adapt this approach to study how communities utilized state resources to sanction their ownership of space in late medieval Italy. Conversely, we shall also consider how the state itself made 'pragmatic use' of local communities to construct better-defined borders at its peripheries. Indeed, local communities had long been interlocutors with superior forms of political organization: the city-states, the regional polities, and even intermediate bodies such as townships and rural federations. Upon their incorporation into larger polities, their fiscal and judicial responsibilities were determined through negotiation. Thereafter, communities could enter into conversation with the state and its institutions on an everyday basis: by writing petitions, for example, or simply by turning to the closest state representative (*vicari, commissari, rettori, provveditori*).[33] In the context of this constant dialogue between communities and the state, particularly as embodied in its offices and office holders, it is possible to discern three sets of interactions which cross-legitimized both local and regional spaces.

The first set of interactions revolved around the sharing of records. As mentioned, rural communities defined their boundaries autonomously, but the written product of these proceedings (the *instrumenta confinationum*) could sometimes be extracted from the miscellaneous registers of local notaries to form uniform compilations (the *libri finium*). In Bergamo, we know that a first 'liber instrumentorum confinium' was compiled as early as the 1220s.[34] At the time, the city was looking to strengthen its hold over the *districtus*, while also refining its shape and limits. Bergamo's project rested on a key principle: all the communities of people populating the countryside (*vicini, rustici, homines*) had to identify with an exclusive territory, one within which they were responsible for paying taxes, maintaining infrastructures, and providing a share of their produce to be sold on the urban market. For this to work, communities were instructed to conduct a careful definition of their boundaries, so that there would be no territory left without a community. As the process unfolded, the city acquired a systematic description of the borders of its *contado*, while the communities had access to urban magistrates who could settle any existing controversy between them.[35]

---

[33] On such exchanges, see Della Misericordia, '*Per non privarci de nostre raxone*'; and generally Hattori, 'Community, Communication'.

[34] On this first initiative, see Mazzi, 'I confini dei comuni'; and Nobili, 'Appartenenze e delimitazioni'.

[35] It is worth nothing that these practices are not unique to Bergamo and the Bergamasco. While much remains to be done to highlight equivalent traditions in other regions, a first consideration of southern Tuscany has already been cast by Redon, *Lo spazio di una città*, 147–9.

114   BORDERS AND THE POLITICS OF SPACE IN LATE MEDIEVAL ITALY

In 1353, a little more than a century after this first series of *confinationes*, Bergamo's new municipal statutes reiterated that communities were expected to 'define clearly, publicly, and without any doubt the boundaries of their localities and territories'.[36] The resulting records were meant to be entrusted to the archives of the city of Bergamo, where the municipal governor (the *podestà*) would remain available to arbitrate any disagreement. It is now hard to assess the extent to which the ruling of the statutes was followed by the communities, for only a couple of *instrumenta* from the 1350s have survived;[37] but thanks to another episode, we know that this sort of prescription could sometimes be carried out at once by dozens of communities. In 1391, the ruler of Bergamo, Gian Galeazzo Visconti, passed a decree which adopted the ruling of the statutes almost word for word. These had been recently reissued, which suggests that cities might have collected the records of local boundaries just as routinely as the communities did and that superior powers (in this case, the prince) had an interest in making sure that operations of this kind were effectively conducted. With the support of the Visconti, the city was able to collect over 130 *instrumenta*, thus covering the vast majority of its territory.[38]

The initiatives undertaken in the 1220s and then again in 1353 and 1391 can all be ascribed to Bergamo's long-lived desire to shape the communities of the surrounding countryside into a compact *contado* serving the interests of the city, starting with the territorial allocation of taxes and other collective burdens. These initiatives were launched concurrently with the enactment of new municipal statutes, which proves that they were part of broader and indeed repeated attempts at affirming Bergamo's hold over its *districtus*.[39] At the same time, the operations launched in 1391 marked a change to the way in which these initiatives were promoted. This is because a third actor features alongside the urban centre and the rural communities: Gian Galeazzo Visconti, the soon-to-be first duke of Milan. In supporting the city in its effort to refine the shape and limits of its *contado*, Visconti's

---

[36] FORGIARINI (ed.), *Lo statuto di Bergamo*, 282: 'diffinire clare et aperte et sine aliqua obscuritate confines sui loci et territorii' (*collatio* XII-11). This was soon reiterated in a new edition of the statutes dating to 1374: BMBg, *Sala* I, ms. D 7 29 (*collatio* XII-7).

[37] Notably those of Gandino and Albano, which were then included in the *liber finium* from the early 1390s: BAVa, *Fondo Patetta*, ms. 1387.

[38] For a brief discussion of these proceedings, see the introduction to MARCHETTI, *Confini dei comuni*; together with Della Misericordia, 'I confini dell'economia', 264–5.

[39] On the statutes of Bergamo and their place in the city's attempts to control the surrounding countryside, see Storti Storchi, *Diritto e istituzioni a Bergamo*, 264–71; and generally Menant, *Campagnes lombardes*.

4. FROM MACRO TO MICRO AND BACK AGAIN   115

intervention reveals that, by the end of the fourteenth century, the spatial configuration of rural communities was already relevant beyond the level of the locality and even beyond that of the *contado* itself. In this sense, the decree issued by Visconti in 1391 was no different from the ordinance through which, only a few years later, he required all the people of the Bergamasco to declare their factional affiliation (as seen in Chapter 3). Both allowed him to utilize the social structures of the localities—the factional organization of political spaces and the close identification of every community with its territory—to strengthen the peripheries of his dominion.

The pragmatic use of local structures on behalf of superior powers became even more evident through two further initiatives. The first was carried out in the spring of 1456, in preparation for the *confinium compositio* signed a few months later. The initiative produced 93 records in total. While some *instrumenta* were drafted from scratch to fill the gaps left by previous initiatives, most updated the *confinationes* performed in the 1390s. This shows that although local boundaries underwent geographical changes over the span of a generation, their legal significance (for the communities themselves as much as for the state now collecting these records) did not change. In 1387, for example, the Bergamasque community of the Val Torta bought a little hill named Monte Stavello from the Milanese community of Perledo, located between lake Como and the Val Sassina.[40] At first, the transaction had no ramifications beyond the level of the two localities; in 1456, however, the Val Torta was recognized as part of the Bergamasco and thus as Venetian territory. It was thus essential that the new record of community boundaries documented the Val Torta's possession of Monte Stavello, for this ultimately shifted the boundaries between the Bergamasco and the Milanese and thus between the Republic and the Duchy.[41]

Ultimately, thanks to the initiative of 1456, much of the Bergamasco was newly mapped by the actors who were best acquainted with its territorial arrangements: the local communities and their notaries. Although the area was now subject to Venice, the archives of the Republic are yet to return evidence that a decree comparable to that sponsored by Visconti in 1391 was ever issued. The fact remains that the *confinationes* of 1456 unfolded at

---

[40] BMBg, *Confini* 96 R 30, cc. 1r–11v, 31 December 1387.

[41] For this and many other reasons, including the resistance mounted by the locals, the valley's handover was far from uneventful. These vicissitudes can be followed by collating letters exchanged between Milan, Venice, and Bergamo over the issue: most notably *Registri* 18, cc. 462v–463r, 27 October 1456; ASMi, *Carteggio* 343, 15 November and 3 December 1456; ASMi, *Registri* 18, c. 464r, 20 January 1457; ASMi, *Carteggio* 344, 29 January and 2 March 1457.

116 BORDERS AND THE POLITICS OF SPACE IN LATE MEDIEVAL ITALY

the same time as the negotiations that then led to the *confinium compositio*. As discussed in Chapter 3, these negotiations were mainly concerned with localities in the Bergamasco. The same can be said for the second initiative launched under Venetian rule (which was actually the fifth in the overall series but only the second of the fifteenth century). This took place in 1481, producing a total of 76 new records. Following the death of Galeazzo Maria Sforza, the relationships between the Duchy and the Republic had deteriorated and were about to be put under further stress by the impending war of Ferrara. It is then quite likely that, as in 1456, the execution of new *confinationes* in the peripheries was solicited from the centre to prevent further conflicts at a higher level.[42]

The five instances discussed so far (1220s, 1353, 1391, 1456, and 1481) were all set in motion by superior powers, first by the city-state and subsequently by the princely or republican authorities. By interacting with local actors, regional and sub-regional powers could better survey the extent of their dominions. In addition, they could outsource the precise definition of local borders to the people most familiar with them. However, the interactions between central powers and peripheral actors did not result merely in the exploitation of local resources on behalf of the state. Local communities, in turn, took advantage of the initiatives launched by the state to settle ongoing controversies between them and generally to inscribe a legally recognized image of their territory. Indeed, unlike the *confinationes* performed autonomously by those communities, which would mostly remain in the private registers of local notaries, the *instrumenta* drafted on these occasions had to be deposited in public repositories. Thus, state resources offered communities a further form of validation, one that their neighbours would think about twice before challenging. As the communities empowered the territorial authority of the state, the state empowered the control exercised by the communities over their respective territories.

Further evidence for the centrality of this dynamic is the fact that local communities and central offices would continue to interact regarding the provision of records concerning boundaries throughout the early modern period. This is particularly evident from the activities of Bergamo's *Camera dei confini*, the magistracy which Venice put in charge of gathering documentation that could settle border disputes from the late sixteenth century. For more than two-hundred years, the *Camera* continued to extract records

---

[42] The *instrumenta* made in 1456 and 1481 were all collected in a volume now held in BMBg, *Salone Cassapanca* I, ms. 4 47/1–2.

4. FROM MACRO TO MICRO AND BACK AGAIN   117

from the localities themselves as well as maintaining pre-existing collections. An act originally made on 14 June 1456, for example, was extracted from a 'register of records of the borders of the Bergamasco existing in the chancery of the city of Bergamo'.[43] Another from the same year was said to have been written first by a notary serving a local community, then copied by a notary working for the city's offices, and finally copied again and even translated from Latin into the vernacular by yet another notary working for the *Camera*.[44] The same could be said about the Milanese equivalent of the Venetian *Camera dei confini*, which was established around the mid-eighteenth century. In the *contado* of Milan, the tradition of compiling *instrumenta confinationum* on a regular basis was not as strong as in the Bergamasco. As a result, the Milanese magistrates took to gathering other notarial records that could prove a community's possession of the surrounding territory, such as deeds of sale or wills written by notaries at the behest of residents.[45]

While the first set of interactions centred on the sharing of records, the second revolved around the presence of state officials in the localities. Whenever they initiated a *confinatio* of some relevance, the deputies of Milan and Venice would often attend the proceedings or even direct them. An illustrative example comes from the summer of 1456, during the fourth initiative discussed above. This was launched to gather information that could help settle the dispute over the mountain borders between the *contadi* of Bergamo and Milan. While many of the contested localities lay in the valleys of the Bergamasco, some were located on the left bank of the river Adda, between the town of Lecco, which was traditionally Milanese, and the Val San Martino, which was traditionally Bergamasque and thus Venetian. The matter was further complicated by the fact that the boundary between the upper communities of the valley and the lower part of the territory of Lecco ran past two key fortifications. The first was the so-called Chiusa, a border wall which extended from the banks of the river to the nearest mountain slopes, which in turn gave it full control over the road connecting Bergamo and Lecco. The second was the castle of Vercurago, a fortified post sitting on a nearby hill, from which it towered over the Chiusa itself. In determining where the Lecchese ended and the Val San Martino

---

[43] BMBg, *Confini*, ms. 96 R 23, cc. 1r–7v: 'registro instrumentorum confinium agri bergomensii esistente in cancellaria magnifice civitatii Bergomi'.

[44] BMBg, *Confini*, ms. 97 R 9, cc. 2r–7r, 8 June 1456.

[45] See, by way of example, two registers compiled with records extracted from notarial registers from the Val Taleggio: ASMi, *Confini* 288.

118 BORDERS AND THE POLITICS OF SPACE IN LATE MEDIEVAL ITALY

began, the deputies of Venice and Milan were also establishing who should hold the two fortifications. Coupled with the fact that the *confinatio* concerned the boundaries between intermediate bodies rather than mere localities (a township and a valley federation), the presence of key assets explains why the deputies of the two polities were so keen to supervise the process.

Like the *consignatio* which, two years earlier, handed over the Val San Martino to the Venetians, the proceedings took place in the garden of the Benagli family, near the village of Calolzio. To record the outcomes of the operation, a local notary was appointed, by the name of Alberto Rota, a member of yet another influential affinity from the area. The same can be said about the dozens of witnesses featuring in the final *instrumentum*, who belonged to families such as the Cattaneo and the Zonca, all leaders of the valley's dominant Guelph party. Besides the choice of the venue, the selection of the notary and the participation of members of the local gentry as witnesses, another moment which allowed for the interaction between deputies and residents was the collection of depositions from people who were said to be knowledgeable about the surrounding area. In the *instrumentum*, the deputies acknowledged explicitly 'having listened to many different people' from both the valley and the Lecchese.[46] By doing so, they were able to gather information not just from local representatives but from the wider population. In addition, their interactions with the residents legitimized their decision in the eyes of a much larger portion of local society, particularly when it came to settling potential disputes. For their part, by interacting with state deputies, the members of the local gentry had their position at the helm of their community recognized by a superior power, while also taking advantage of their presence to settle ongoing controversies with their neighbours.

Aside from their intervention in exceptional *confinationes*, state officials interacted with locals on a regular basis to protect the borders of the dominion. Most of these interactions revolved around the coordination of frontier defences. A good example comes from the territory of Monte Brianza, a federation of communities located north of Milan, on the right bank of the river Adda. Here, the defence of local borders, like their periodic definition,

---

[46] As mentioned, the *instrumentum* was originally drafted by a local notary, but authenticated copies would later be made for the chanceries of Milan (ASMi, *Confini* 270, 17 April 1454), Bergamo (BMBg, *Municipali* 2, c. 28v), and Venice (ASVe, *Memorie antiche per servire al vacuo dei Commemoriali* 2, p. 385): 'auditis multis et diversis personis'.

4. FROM MACRO TO MICRO AND BACK AGAIN   119

was almost entirely outsourced to local families. Over the years, these families had built dozens of towers to guard the nearby borders. These functioned primarily as family residences, imposing fortifications from which their owners exerted their influence over the surrounding communities, thus serving private interests. But because of their location, these fortifications also guarded the limits of the ducal dominion, thus serving the public interests of the whole state. Like their neighbours from the Val San Martino, the families of Monte Brianza gained both political influence and social prestige by interacting with state officials, while these officials were able to rely on local resources to protect the borders of the dominion.[47]

In addition to overseeing *confinationes* and managing frontier defences, the presence of state officials could sometimes generate practices which, borrowing from Patricia Seed, could be described as 'ceremonies of possession'.[48] These were formal procedures conducted jointly by state officials and local residents to claim ownership over space. A wonderful example comes again from the banks of the river Adda and from the area near the fortress of Trezzo in particular. At the time, this fortress guarded a strategic stone bridge connecting Milan's own hinterland to the Bergamasco. Here, the residents shared an interesting tradition with the official in charge of the local fortification. Every year, on Easter Sunday, they joined a deputy sent by the ducal castellan to patrol the banks of the river Adda. Since the treaty of Lodi had established that the entirety of the river was to be controlled by the Duchy, the deputy and residents were looking specifically for violations of this rule. More often than not, these took the form of water mills or fishing facilities built by subjects of the Republic on the left bank of the river, towards the Bergamasco, which the group went on to survey and, at times, demolish outright. As part of their itinerary, they also visited several river islands, where the deputy would place ducal banners with the assistance of the residents. As the castellan explained to the duke, this was done 'to retain [the duke's] possession and right over the river'.[49] However, it is crucial to

---

[47] Much work remains to be done on the mechanics through which local communities were actively involved in the state's military endeavours. An initial view, including a more extensive treatment of the Brianza case, can be found in Zenobi, 'Guerra, stato e poteri locali'. See also Della Misericordia, 'Politiche della difesa e territorio'; and, for a more wide-ranging discussion, Ansani, 'Oltre i signori, dopo i mercenari'.

[48] Seed, *Ceremonies of Possession*, 16–40. More broadly, see also the scholarship reviewed by DeSilva, 'Taking Possession'.

[49] ASMi, *Confini* 255, 28 March 1477: 'per continuare et parseverare alla possessione et ragione de questo vostro fiume d'Adda'. Background information is provided by two earlier letters, dated 10 and 20 March 1468.

120 BORDERS AND THE POLITICS OF SPACE IN LATE MEDIEVAL ITALY

realize that staking possession over islands and riverbanks served the interests of the local population as much as those of the duke. As the castellans utilized their manpower and spatial knowhow, the residents gained control of the entirety of the river using state resources (the ducal banners and, more broadly, the presence of ducal officials). This allowed them to stake a more authoritative claim to the ownership of local assets, such as the plentiful fish available in the vicinity and the energy generated by running water—assets which, otherwise, might have remained in the hands of rival communities across the river.

Aside from the sharing of records and the presence of state officials, a third set of interactions took place in the context of conflict resolution. While much has been said already about border disputes, it is essential to frame them anew as an instance in which the interests of states and communities were largely aligned. The city-states of northern Italy had long positioned themselves as the chief mediators of contentions between local communities, especially when this enabled them to replace seigneurial powers as the main judicial point of reference in the countryside.[50] In arbitrating disputes, urban magistrates asserted the city's jurisdictional primacy over the *contado*, whereas local communities had their claims of possession recognized by a superior power. Despite the rise of regional polities in the Late Middle Ages, the resolution of territorial conflicts continued to hinge on the interactions between the old city-states and rural communities. This was true of the Bergamasco as well as of other areas of Lombardy. Crema, for instance, appointed deputies for the settlement of border conflicts on a regular basis in the second half of the fifteenth century.[51] In 1450, the Lombard town had been promoted to the rank of *civitas* by Venice; therefore, it was especially keen to refine the limits of its long-coveted *districtus*. In turn, local communities were able to protect their territories against the encroachment of their neighbours, particularly when these lay beside the new borders with the Duchy of Milan (in the Geradadda and in the Cremonese).

As a rule, the officials of regional polities stepped in only when the magistrates of the city had failed to find a suitable agreement. At times, they did take the lead on their own initiative, but normally the intervention of

---

[50] While the literature devoted to this theme is extensive, see, in particular, the study by Milani, 'Lo sviluppo della giurisdizione'; together with his overview of recent research in Milani, 'Diritto e potere'.

[51] E.g. BCCr, *Provisioni* 2, c. 54r, 28 June 1458 (Gera d'Adda); BCCr, *Provisioni* 5, cc. 170r–170v, 1 March 1469 (Cremonese).

4. FROM MACRO TO MICRO AND BACK AGAIN 121

state officials was urged by the communities themselves. Whenever they were unsatisfied with the ongoing settlement or simply exasperated by the lengthy procedures of urban offices, communities were prompt to turn to superior interlocutors. Initially, these interlocutors were simply the most immediate representatives of the state. In the 1470s, for example, a bitter controversy between the burghers of Caravaggio, in the Geradadda, and the people inhabiting nearby villages of the upper Cremasco was brought to the Milanese officer posted there (the *commissario* of Caravaggio) and to the closest Venetian governor (the *rettore* of Crema). From there, the two officials interacted with local communities in several ways: they evaluated the records the communities presented to prove their ancient possessions ('antiquissima possessione'); they visited the contested lands and took measurements with their representatives ('mensurazione'); they interrogated well-informed local noblemen ('gentiluomini pratici de la causa'); and they even held a general discussion ('parlamento').[52] However, when the parties involved rejected the solutions offered by state officials, these officials were left with no choice but to bring the matter to even higher authorities. In the case of the dispute discussed above, those were the Venetian Senate (and from there the doge) and the Milanese Secret Council (which, in turn, would involve the Milanese ambassador in Venice and the duke himself). In the months and years that followed, all these actors engaged in correspondence about the fate of the contested lands between Crema and Caravaggio.[53] Conflict had thus transcended the localities to form part of the interplay between regional actors. The empowering interactions between local communities and state representatives had set in motion processes of cross-legitimation between the two polities as much as between the polities and their subject territories.

*　*　*

The unfolding of this dispute brings us back to the diplomatic negotiations discussed in previous chapters, namely to macro practices of border-making. At the same time, the dispute reminds us that agreement—and indeed disagreement—over territorial arrangements was negotiated first on

---

[52] ASMi, *Confini* 296, 16 June 1474.

[53] The unfolding of the dispute can be followed by collating records from the ducal archives and the archives of Crema: BCCr, *Provisioni* 5, cc. 146r–146v, 6 November 1468; ASMi, *Confini* 296, 16 June 1474, including a comprehensive report and copies or mentions of many relevant letters; BCCr, *Ducali* 1, cc. 135v–136r, 12 November and 8 December 1474; ASMi, *Confini* 296, 13 October 1492.

122 BORDERS AND THE POLITICS OF SPACE IN LATE MEDIEVAL ITALY

a micro level. As the first section of this chapter has shown, boundaries were first and foremost a local construct. They were the framework of communal activities, the tools of spatial appropriation, the markers of territorial possession, and the signifiers of collective identities. Much like locality itself, however, local boundaries were simultaneously shaped by the very practices and dynamics which they framed and underscored. In other words, boundaries were both determinant of and determined by community life. Their peripatetic demarcation was nothing but a reflection of the community's desire to bring its territory together and protect its assets. The very method of this demarcation, drawing on the geography of property and on the topography of everyday life, was developed by notaries with the interests of the community in mind. The result was a careful, precise, and, most importantly, meaningful redefinition of local boundaries. This translated a shared patrimony of spatial knowledge into legally binding records, sanctioning the community's territory (and its solid character) before the wider world.

On a micro level, boundaries were constructed chiefly through the interactions between notaries and community members. On a macro level, state offices and office holders came into play. As the second section of this chapter has shown, the interactions between local communities and state representatives played out simultaneously in three different realms. First, the two interacted over the provision of certain records, the *instrumenta confinationum*. These were not just documents concerning the position and materiality of local boundaries but fully fledged legal deeds ratifying the shape and limits of a community's territory. When collated in specially designed manuscripts, they provided urban chanceries with an accurate and lawful picture of the compound boundaries of the *districtus*. While the creation of these records would escalate in times of political or territorial change, the second set of interactions took place on a regular basis. This revolved around the presence of state officials in the localities, where they would supervise *confinationes* of particular importance and join the local population in conducting ceremonies of possession. Both instances served as a stage for interactions between the residents, who sought recognition of the territorial extent of their communities, and state officials, who were seeking better-defined boundaries in the peripheries of the dominion. Finally, empowering interactions between local and central actors occurred on the occasion of conflict resolution: the settlement of territorial disputes validated a community's possessions while also confirming its subordination to the space of a superior power.

In all, this discussion complements previous chapters in showing that late medieval borders were constructed from below as much as from above and

4. FROM MACRO TO MICRO AND BACK AGAIN   123

through the appropriation of space on a micro level as much as through its negotiation on a macro level. More specifically, this chapter highlights the importance of empowering interactions between local communities and central agencies for the functioning of the politics of space. Late medieval territoriality was not a mere byproduct of the state-building process, nor was it solely an outcome of community formation. Rather, it was constructed through a process of cross-legitimation, one taking place at different levels and involving a variety of different actors. In addition, the chapter delivers a first blow to the notion that pre-modern borders were invariably fuzzy and ill-defined. From the peripatetic definition of local boundaries to their recording in the *instrumenta confinationum*, the activities described in the first half of the chapter show that borders could be precisely located and widely understood. Crucially, however, this precise understanding and definition of borders was not limited to the localities. Through the interactions examined in the second half of the chapter, knowledge of territorial arrangement was further legitimized in the eyes of not one but multiple polities (first city-states, as in the case of Bergamo, then regional powers, like the Duchy and the Republic). In the end, their shape and nature could not have been clearer in the minds of contemporaries.

5
Borders as Sites of Mobility
Crossing External Frontiers and Internal Boundaries

The Romans had a god, Terminus, to watch over borders and border markers. The protector of private properties as much as public boundaries, his corporeal manifestation was the very artefact that bore his name: *terminus*, the boundary stone. He was a god of rules, norms, and constraints—almost the divine embodiment of fixity and limitation. However, like many other societies throughout history, the Romans themselves acknowledged that demarcation does not exhaust the nature of borders. Every border is a beginning as much as an end, a space of contact as much as one of separation. The Romans placed this contradictory and yet simultaneous function of borders under the protection of a different deity, called Janus. He was the god of motion and the guardian of all spaces of transition, including doors, gates, passageways, and of course border crossings.[1] The Romans had clearly developed an exhaustive mythology to address both the making of borders and the experience of crossing them. Yet anthropologists have suggested that the twofold function of borders may be fundamental to all cultures.[2] Following specialists such as Henk van Houtum, geographers now talk expressively of the 'Janus-face character of borders'.[3] Not just constructions denoting a strong demarcation between two spheres (inside and outside, legitimate and illegitimate, us and them), borders are understood to be spaces where dichotomies may be blurred—sites of contact, exchange, and mobility.

So far, this book has looked at borders as *termini*, namely as the limits of both old and new territorial bodies: from villages and federations to towns

---

[1] On borders, the Romans, and their gods, see Piccaluga, *Terminus*; and Holland, *Janus and the Bridge*.

[2] For an anthropological perspective on borders, see the classic essay by Cohen, 'Culture, Identity, and the Concept of Boundary'; and now Wilson, 'Territoriality Matters in the Anthropology of Borders'.

[3] E.g. Sohn, 'Navigating Borders' Multiplicity', 184. On Janus and related theories of the border, see van Houtum, 'The Mask of the Border', 58–9.

Borders and the Politics of Space in Late Medieval Italy: Milan, Venice, and their Territories. Luca Zenobi, Oxford University Press. © Luca Zenobi 2023. DOI: 10.1093/oso/9780198876861.003.0006

and cities, to entire states. To fully appreciate their double nature, this chapter will now go on to explore phenomena that cut across those same boundaries: the movement of groups and individuals (in the first section of this chapter) and the circulation of objects and goods (in the second section). Once more, we shall look specifically at eastern Lombardy, with the Bergamasco, Bresciano and Cremasco. As discussed in previous chapters, this area had long belonged to the Lombard Duchy before the wars and negotiations of the first half of the fifteenth century made them part of the Venetian Republic. Even today, these territories are sometimes dubbed *Lombardia veneta*—a label that evokes the image of two overlapping sets more than that of two distinct worlds. By looking at borders as sites of mobility, it will be possible to assess the endurance of trans-regional connections, especially following the treaty of Lodi and the *confinium compositio* of 1456. Since crossing borders was the most common way in which contemporaries encountered boundaries and frontiers, by looking at how they functioned as spaces of control and power (for the rulers) and as sites of movement and empowerment (for the ruled), it will also be possible to survey how people interacted with them and with the authorities which such borders objectified.

The first section of the chapter examines how the leaderships of Milan and Venice channelled and monitored access to their respective dominions, while also exploring how people across the social spectrum negotiated their will to move. Drawing—or better still 'composing' borders, as discussed in Chapter 3—was always an arbitrary process. When jurisdiction over a given territory was transferred from one power holder to another, the frontier between the two states was moved, but pre-existing patterns of contact and exchange were also affected. Some people found themselves at the cross-roads of new networks, traffic, and allegiances; others were disconnected from the political, social, and economic contexts to which they were most accustomed. This was especially evident in times of war, as in the early 1450s, when the frontier between the two states shifted several times, rendering safe conducts a necessary requisite for moving freely across the region. The second section of the chapter shifts its focus from inter-state mobility to movement across internal boundaries. It does so by considering the mechanics by which Italian polities regulated traffic flows in times of peace, as in the late 1450s. By tracing the itineraries of people who had obtained a licence to trade across some of the many territories which made up a state, the section will study how rulers levied duties on products and controlled their circulation. In so doing, the composite structure of late

126 BORDERS AND THE POLITICS OF SPACE IN LATE MEDIEVAL ITALY

medieval borders and the coexistence of multiple units within the same polity (as discussed in Chapter 1) are brought back to the fore.

Negotiating Movement in Times of War

Nowadays, crossing borders is almost synonymous with passports and visas. Indeed, border crossings may now be invisible or even be permanently displaced, as in the case of airport terminals, but they still require the exhibition of valid papers.[4] Just like borders, however, travel documents have always existed. In the Late Middle Ages, they took the form of letters of passage (*litterae passis*), a patent through which ruling powers granted supplicants licence to enter their territories. With access may come the guarantee of safe travel, which is why such patents are sometimes known as safe conducts (*salvi conducti*). Although the level of safety they ensured varied considerably between regions, similar customs can be found across much of Europe. In England, kings were known to grant letters of immunity and judicial protection to their subjects.[5] In Spain, both single individuals and entire institutions could be given a formal promise of guidance and security (*guidaticum*).[6] In Germany, travellers could buy themselves an escort (*Galeit*) or simply be honoured with one, a practice which made the right to accompany people within one's territory both a prized source of income and a potent medium of seigniorial authority.[7] In the Mamluk sultanate, Christian visitors could obtain a document (*amān*) guaranteeing their freedom of movement.[8] More broadly, safe conducts were sometimes granted to categories of travellers in late medieval Europe, typically in conjunction with patents of recommendation, courtesy charters, or simple letters of credence. Notable examples include aristocratic hostages, foreign emissaries, and people en route to courts of law, as well as merchants, pilgrims, and minority groups.[9]

---

[4] On the mechanics of modern surveillance and its bureaucratic development, see the classic essay by Torpey, 'Coming and Going'; together with the recent overview by Higgs, 'Change and Continuity'.

[5] Lacey, 'Protection and Immunity'.   [6] Burns, 'The *Guidaticum* Safe-Conduct'.

[7] Historians of the Holy Roman Empire have written much on the subject, starting with De Craecker-Dussart, 'L'évolution du sauf-conduit'; Schaab, 'Gleit und Territorium'; and Müller, *Das Geleit*.

[8] Rizzo, 'Travelling and Trading through Mamluk Territory'.

[9] For Italy, an array of examples from the earlier and especially Central Middle Ages can be found in Bognetti, *Note per la storia del passaporto*. But the practice has an even older history, as shown in Purpura, '*Passaporti* Romani'.

5. BORDERS AS SITES OF MOBILITY   127

By the end of the Middle Ages, safe conducts and letters of passage in general had become ubiquitous. More importantly, they had evolved from a rare tool used to ensure people's safety and public peace into an instrument deployed on a regular basis to control movement. Significant variations remained. In Germany, as studied most recently by Luca Scholz, safe conducts would retain their focus on lordly protection well into early modernity, turning border crossings into contested sites at which travellers were handed over from one authority to another.[10] In France, as first discussed by Daniel Nordman, safe conducts evolved in conjunction with the notion of national citizenship, thus paving the way for the development of fully fledged identity documents (*passeports*).[11] Italy differed from both these models. First of all, protection from threats and travel hazards was rarely the purpose of Italian safe conducts. Escorts were sometimes deployed to accompany foreign dignitaries but certainly not the holders of regular safe conducts. If anything, the patents themselves placed much emphasis on protecting their holders from the interference of local officers, and notably from those in charge of custom duties. In short, Italian safe conducts did not warrant their bearers protection by public authorities but rather from them. They also did not serve the purpose of establishing the identity of individuals. As Valentin Groebner has convincingly argued, late medieval authorities undoubtedly had the means of identifying travellers, either through a description of their clothing or physical features (such as scars, moles, or tattoos); however, these details were almost never included in letters of passage and were certainly absent from Italian safe conducts.[12]

What, then, was the purpose of safe conducts in late medieval Italy? They existed neither for protection nor for identification but simply to enable and regulate movement. This was especially true in times of war, when obtaining a safe conduct was ostensibly the only way one could hope to cross borders. In this respect, these ancient patents served the same two basic functions as our modern passports and visas: they ensured people's 'rights of passage'[13]

---

[10] Scholz, *Borders and Freedom of Movement*. See also Wiederkehr, *Das freie Geleit*; and now Kintzinger, 'Cum salvo conductu'.

[11] Nordman, 'Sauf-conduits et passeports'. More recent studies include Noiriel, 'Surveiller les déplacements'; and Judde de Larivière, 'Du sceau au passeport'.

[12] Groebner, 'Describing the Person'. Specifically on the issue of identification in Italy, see, for the Middle Ages, Hubert, 'Identificare per controllare'; and, for early modernity, Geselle, 'Domenica Saba Takes to the Road'. On the so-called bureaucracy of movement in Italy, see also the recent study by Saletti, 'How Foreigners Entered Italian Cities'.

[13] The reference is to Salter, *Rights of Passage*. Another noted volume emphasizing these continuities is Torpey, *The Invention of the Passport*.

128   BORDERS AND THE POLITICS OF SPACE IN LATE MEDIEVAL ITALY

and they provided authorities with a certain degree of control over those looking to move. In fact, following a tradition in sociological studies, medieval and modern papers alike could be framed as boundary objects: 'they are both plastic enough to adapt to local needs and constraints of the several parties employing them, yet robust enough to maintain a common identity across sites'.[14] Much like borders themselves, travel documents may mean different things to different groups and institutions, but they remain recognizable to all. For some, the granting of safe conducts and thus the prospect of crossing borders was the first step towards a business opportunity or a family reunion; for others, it was a way to control movement at the frontiers of the state. It follows that by looking at borders and mobility through the lens of safe conducts, it is possible to highlight both the individual experiences and motivations behind border-crossing and the collective restraints that were imposed upon them.

From a material perspective, the double value of safe conducts was reflected in the practice of drafting them twice: the actual patent (equivalent to our modern papers) travelled with the individual who had requested it, while a written record of its issue (equivalent to an entry in a modern database) was filed by the authorities. While most individual safe conducts have been lost, the Italian archives hold numerous series of what, in essence, was medieval databases: chancery registers. Between 1452 and 1465, the Milanese Chancery kept track of most of the safe conducts they released in a single volume.[15] This register alone contains over two thousand documents, which equates to a safe conduct being granted every three or four days.[16] Scrolling through its endless series of grants, one can retrace the upheavals of the first part of the decade and then observe how the treaty of Lodi and the subsequent definition of state borders in 1456 allowed for a renewal of trade and connections across the region. Between 1452 and 1454, when the frontier between Milan and Venice was shaken by conflicts, the main reason people sought safe conducts was war itself. Looking through the patents granted at

---

[14] The term was introduced by Star and Griesemer, 'Institutional Ecology', 393. For its use in current border studies, see Häkli, 'The Border in the Pocket'.

[15] Earlier registers existed but were mostly destroyed with the Visconti archives. A surviving volume for the years 1441–4 was uncovered by Bognetti, 'Per la storia dello Stato visconteo', 294–347. Further examples can be found in VITTANI, *Inventari e regesti*, 255 (s.v. *passaporti*) and 267 (s.v. *salvacondotti*).

[16] ASMi, *Registri* 151. While the register in question is entirely devoted to mapping all the individuals who had gained permission to enter the territories of the duchy, safe conducts are recorded in at least ten other miscellaneous registers for this period, which indicates that numbers could have been even higher: ASMi, *Registri* 98, 100, 126, 129, 154, 155, 161, 162, 164, and 166.

5. BORDERS AS SITES OF MOBILITY 129

this stage, one encounters soldiers travelling home from enemy lands, Venetian exiles in search of protection, diplomats sent from elsewhere in the peninsula, and other situations of this kind. By contrast, the number of people looking to cross state borders for economic reasons grew considerably after 1454. One finds craftsmen looking for new customers, contractors chasing up their debtors, as well as merchants and labourers of all sorts: from manual workers seeking employment on the other side of the border to Jewish traders looking to set up new businesses.

If we join the stream of people crossing borders at this stage and consider the safe conducts granted on the Venetian side, similar trends and dynamics can be found. Each month, hundreds of people from all backgrounds left the territories of the Duchy for those of the Republic. To do so, they first had to gain permission from the Venetian authorities. Unlike in Milan, these tended to be local rather than central offices. As a rule, the Republic deployed two governors in each of its major cities (including Bergamo and Brescia) and at least one in smaller towns (as in the case of Crema). While Venice's central offices retained the power to direct the politics of mobility for the entire polity, the governors based in mainland cities were given the authority to accord safe conducts at their discretion. Much as in the Milanese Chancery, their concessions were tracked by clerks in dedicated registers. While they seldom received the same care and attention as the main archives of the Republic, surviving fragments can still be extremely revealing. A little-known example is the register of safe conducts granted by one of the patricians in charge of Bergamo between 1430 and 1432 (possibly no less than the noted humanist Francesco Barbaro).[17] In it, the governor's clerks recorded all the patents granted to Venetian officials travelling through Milanese territories, as in the case of castellans and men-at-arms moving to their lodgings or magistrates with properties and investments close to state boundaries (such as mines in frontier valleys and mills on border rivers).

But how could these people voice their desire and sometimes their need to cross state borders? And how could the authorities monitor the resulting movement? To answer these questions, it is crucial to realize that recording a safe conduct in chancery registers was but the final act in a long series of negotiations. First, it was a negotiation between a petitioner and an authority. To move across borders in fifteenth-century Lombardy, one had first to

---

[17] BMBg, *Cancelleria pretoria* 1.

130 BORDERS AND THE POLITICS OF SPACE IN LATE MEDIEVAL ITALY

move a significant amount of paper. Nobody, not even local lords or state officials, was born with an absolute right to move, especially in times of war. Permission had to be solicited in writing, justified in front of the relevant office, and sometimes even lobbied for at court. This placed the mechanics through which a safe conduct was granted at the intersection of two of the most distinctive traits of late medieval politics. The first is what some scholars refer to as 'the paradigm of exception'.[18] This is the idea that pre-modern government rested not only on the legal foundations of the polity (as inscribed in statutes and decrees) but also on the direct and indeed exceptional intervention of a prince or republican magistrate (in the form of licences, privileges, or immunities). In a world where the polity was embodied in a prince or republican governor, derogating from the law in a systematic way fostered a special relationship between the rulers and the ruled—between petitioners and authorities. Making exceptions, to put it briefly, was in itself a form of government. By granting safe conducts, princely and republican regimes were effectively governing movement, while also asserting their power over a unified dominion under their rule.

A second trait of late medieval politics shown in the mechanics through which a safe conduct was granted is what a growing body of literature calls 'governing through grace'.[19] If someone wanted a prince or a republican magistrate to accord them a safe conduct, they first had to ask for their gracious intervention and this was done primarily on paper. The general principle was that nobody could automatically cross state borders, especially when war raged; yet anyone with enough influence, money, and sometimes literacy could gain permission to do so just by writing to the relevant office. In this sense, petitions and supplications are but the natural complement to the paradigm of exception introduced above: they gave rise to a textual space in which the 'quest for a direct relationship with the authorities'[20] could take place—a space in which movement could be negotiated. For the ruled, writing petitions was a way to make their voice heard; for the rulers, their enactment or refusal was a way to state and wield their power. Where supplicants gained access to their benevolence, princely and republican regimes gained a flexible tool of government, together with the opportunity

---

[18] On this first trait, particularly in relation to Italy, see Vallerani, 'Paradigmi dell'eccezione'; and now Della Misericordia, 'Nondimeno. Una nota sul linguaggio della circostanza'.

[19] On this second trait, see particularly Millet, *Suppliques et requêtes*; and, for an Italian take, Covini, 'Pétitions et suppliques'.

[20] I borrow this fitting expression from Nubola, 'Supplications between Politics and Justice', 36. See also Holenstein, '*Rinviare ad Supplicandum*'.

5. BORDERS AS SITES OF MOBILITY   131

to present their authority as superior to that of preceding institutions. People at all levels of society utilized this system to voice their desire and sometimes need to move, while princely and republican governments used it both to monitor movement across borders and to assert their control over it.

Once permission to move had been discussed between a petitioner and an authority, a further series of negotiations took place. This time, it was a negotiation between different and sometimes competing authorities. In wartime especially, the release of safe conducts was affected by a continuous routine of push and pull: one ruler was willing to grant permission to enter their territory to a number of people subject to an enemy only if the enemy agreed to do the same for some of their own. The practice is called simply 'exchange' in the sources (*contracambio*), while the patents it prompted are sometimes labelled 'reciprocal safe conducts' (*reciproci salvocondotti*). Both terms figure prominently in the correspondence of the early 1450s.[21] This is true for the letters exchanged between the Sforza duke and his frontier officials as well as for their Venetian counterparts: the governors of Brescia, Bergamo, Crema, and, exceptionally, the condottiere Jacopo Piccinino. In times of war, the patricians stationed in each urban centre would sometimes share their responsibilities with military commanders based in the countryside. Much like a governor's clerks, their travelling secretaries would also keep registers of safe conducts.[22] Much of their work has not survived, but we can still learn a great deal by looking at their correspondence with offices more inclined to preserve letters of this kind, starting with the Milanese Chancery.[23]

Let us zoom in on the years 1452 and 1453, at the time of the last conflict between the Duchy and the Republic.[24] Fundamentally, this was a fight between condottieri and their men-at-arms: Francesco Sforza, who had recently proclaimed himself duke of Milan, and Jacopo Piccinino, who was at the head of the array of forces siding with Venice. However, it was also a subtler political and economic confrontation, one taking place in the main centres of power as well as in the localities most affected by the clash.

---

[21] Letters which are especially rich in terminology include ASMi, *Missive* 12, c. 498r, 28 July 1453; and ASMi, *Missive* 13, c. 148v, 27 June 1452.

[22] A little-known but excellent example is the register of 'littere salviconductus, littere licentie, and littere recomendatorie' granted by Niccolò Piccinino between 1437 and 1438: ASMi, *Frammenti* 11, f. 160.

[23] On condottieri and their travelling chanceries, see Covini, 'Guerre e relazioni diplomatiche'. On the flow of letters reaching the Milanese chancery, see Covini, 'Scrivere al principe'.

[24] On the vicissitudes of this period, see Peyronel, 'Un fronte di guerra nel Rinascimento'; and Chittolini, 'Guerre, guerricciole e riassetti territoriali'.

132 BORDERS AND THE POLITICS OF SPACE IN LATE MEDIEVAL ITALY

Here, Sforza and Piccinino fought not only to gain new territories but also to retain the support of those they already controlled. On a political level, the allegiance of local communities was won by propaganda exposing the enemy's supposed lies and false threats.[25] On an economic level, loyalty was secured by promising privileges which most communities held very close to their hearts: fiscal immunity and the right to move across borders. With the war reaching its peak, Sforza and Piccinino could not afford to lose the support of local residents, so they took to exchanging safe conducts on a regular basis. The number of patents they granted was such that the Milanese Chancery began compiling lists of all the people, groups, and communities who possessed a safe conduct at a given moment. Each list featured two separate groups. The first comprised people and localities that were subject to the enemy but had obtained a safe conduct from the duke; the second was made up of the corresponding patents granted by Venice to inhabitants of Milanese territories. These were updated as soon as new concessions were granted and soon shared with officials stationed in frontier areas. Some were even sent to Venetian governors, which suggests that it was not uncommon for the two polities to monitor cross-border mobility jointly.[26]

If exchanging safe conducts in a systematic, informed, and yet careful manner was fundamentally the way in which the two polities opened their borders, withdrawing safe conducts had the opposite effect, namely border closures. Rather than being the product of bilateral negotiations, this was often the result of one-sided resolutions. There were, first of all, real states of emergency. In June 1452, Francesco Sforza allowed the people of Cremona to request safe conducts from the Venetian authorities so they could travel to villages that used to be subject to the Duchy but had recently been acquired by the Republic. Despite the ongoing war, the Venetians were more than happy to allow the Cremonesi to visit their territories, for they did so to sell grain and fodder—goods which the area chronically lacked. However, as soon as news broke that a plague might be spreading, the Cremonesi were forbidden to cross state borders entirely.[27] Another circumstance that

[25] Consider, for instance, some of the letters sent to Cremonese communities at this stage: ASMi, *Missive* 7, cc. 159v–160v (5 July 1452), cc. 164r–164v (7 July 1452), c. 185v (28 July 1452), cc. 192v–193r (31 July 1452), c. 211r (19 August 1452), cc. 357r–357v (1 November 1452), and c. 475v (18 December 1452).

[26] By way of example, consider the many letters sent between 21 and 22 August in ASMi, *Missive* 12, cc. 193r–194v.

[27] ASMi, *Missive* 7, cc. 41v–42r (18 June 1452) and c. 162r (6 July 1452). An overview of countermeasures of this kind can be found in Albini, 'Il controllo della sanità'; and in Palmer, *The Control of Plague*.

5. BORDERS AS SITES OF MOBILITY   133

led authorities to close their borders was when groups or individuals abused safe conducts. In the summer of 1453, many subjects of the duke were accused of having exploited their permission to enter Venetian territories from the Cremonese in order to plunder the land. In his complaint to the duke, Jacopo Piccinino noted that the number of such subjects was so great that the damage they caused cost the Venetians more than the amount they earned by allowing free transit. In the end, all the safe conducts granted to fetch supplies from enemy territory were revoked, except for those concerning activities less likely to be abused, such as hunting and fishing. Without valid documentation, Piccinino made clear at the end of his letter, 'everyone will be sent back'.[28]

Beyond emergencies and abuses, the most common motives for border closures were political contingencies. Just as the politics of mobility were directed towards gaining the support of certain parties and people, both inside and outside a ruler's territories, steps were taken to prevent the movement of constituent groups and bodies from the rival polity. In September 1453, for instance, following the poor results of the partial withdrawal he had enacted a few weeks earlier, Jacopo Piccinino decided to revoke every safe conduct granted to the people of the Cremonese.[29] While policies of (im)mobility were thus often aimed at restricting the movement of local groups and communities, they could also be directed against entire states. In August of the same year, Venetian troops took control of Castelleone with a cunning stratagem: they granted a huge number of safe conducts to its inhabitants, thus emptying the town and rendering it easier to capture. In a letter to his wife, the duke explained that the only suitable response to such subterfuge was to revoke all the safe conducts granted to the communities of the Bergamasco, Bresciano and Cremasco, which essentially meant closing the borders to all the people who lived in the frontier provinces of the Terraferma. It took Piccinino only two days to retaliate by withdrawing all concessions granted to 'men-at-arms and single individuals of any social condition' subject to the duke, effectively closing the borders between the two polities until a new exchange of safe conducts could be negotiated.[30]

---

[28] ASMi, *Carteggio* 340, 3 and 10 August 1453: 'se remanda indietro tuti quanti'. Subjects of the republic equally perpetuated abuses in Milanese territories, as reported in ASMi, *Missive* 12, c. 330r, 14 February 1453.

[29] ASMi, *Carteggio* 340, 4 and 5 September 1453.

[30] ASMi, *Missive* 16, cc. 23v–24r, 13 August 1453; ASMi, *Carteggio* 340, 15 August 1453: 'gentedarme et singular persone de che condictione se voglia'.

134 BORDERS AND THE POLITICS OF SPACE IN LATE MEDIEVAL ITALY

But why exactly did people move so much? Having explored the causes behind the opening and closing of borders on behalf of the authorities, let us now focus on the reasons that prompted people to seek permission to cross them. To do so, it is vital to look more closely at the documents that set that very process in motion: petitions. By collating petitions with the registers and day-to-day correspondence employed so far, one can survey the full array of motives that led to people asking for a safe conduct. First, there were people looking to vote with their feet, namely individuals and often entire families who were willing to relocate to a different polity to protect their interests. This was often the case after periods of intense conflict, as in the early 1450s, when several groups and communities found themselves under a power which they had openly opposed during the war. Together with pardons for rebels and exiles, safe conducts were always among the first demands met by new authorities. The rulers of the time knew well how precious these patents were to the locals and often used them extensively to secure their support. A withdrawal or mere denial could sometimes lead villagers to outright disobedience. In the summer of 1452, the repeal of a series of safe conducts by the Milanese authorities led some localities of the Bresciano to declare themselves loyal to the enemy by swearing allegiance to a Venetian deputy and even chanting the name of St Mark from their bell towers ('marcho marcho').[31] Others went as far as rejecting the authority of both powers. Frustrated by the insecurity brought about by the war of Ferrara, in the early 1480s, people working across the boundary between the Cremasco and the Cremonese began claiming to need no regular safe conduct from secular authorities; instead, they placed themselves under the protection of St Anthony and, much to the dismay of local officers, began threatening to invoke the revenge of the saint every time they were stopped at the border.[32]

A second group looking to cross borders was made up of state agents. Regardless of their public role, people employed directly by the authorities had to ask for permission if they wished to enter the territories of another polity. Even the Venetian diplomat and noted humanist Paolo Morosini had to obtain a safe conduct to go to Milan.[33] For the patrician governors sent to Venetian Lombardy, writing to the duke to ensure that that they could safely reach their place of employment was often their first official act. Crema, in particular, was then a Venetian enclave among Milanese territories, to the

[31] ASMi, *Carteggio* 1566, 8 August 1452.   [32] Galantino, *Storia di Soncino*, 307–9.
[33] ASMi, *Carteggio* 344, 20 September 1457 and 5 October 1457.

5. BORDERS AS SITES OF MOBILITY 135

point that travelling there without a safe conduct was virtually impossible in times of war. The same went for trips that began in Crema but extended beyond the limits of its district. A good example is the periodical coming and going of the *oratores* who were despatched by the Cremaschi to represent their interests. If we are to believe the numerous complaints they made upon being stopped at the border, their activities were almost entirely dependent on the duke's goodwill.[34] While Crema's case was exceptional, officials travelling to or from Venetian Lombardy could still undergo a similar treatment. To get to Bergamo, Venetians would rarely journey across the Terraferma; instead, they would board a ship in Venice and sail up the river Po to Cremona. This meant traversing Milanese territories and, as several petitions testify, securing a safe conduct beforehand.[35] Water routes were similarly key to relocating armies and military officials. Since much of the rivers Po and Adda fell under the control of the duke, the Milanese archives are full of requests from Venetians seeking permission to use them.[36]

Still, the most common motive behind petitions for safe conducts was the need to work and trade across borders. In general terms, a concession from the authorities would shield petitioners from the risk of being held at the border by local magistrates, and especially by those in charge of custom duties. Together with fiscal exemptions, granting safe conducts was one of the principal ways in which the regimes of the time encouraged the presence of foreign traders (in Lombardy, mostly Catalans and Germans).[37] It was also a tool used to protect the transfer of precious goods. While distinguished merchants appear frequently in fifteenth-century petitions, the shipment of valuable objects under a safe conduct was often arranged by the authorities themselves. From Crema, the Venetian governor Andrea Dandolo hoped to secure a safe conduct for 'that nice codex and many other writings' he promised to send to his son in Venice.[38] From Ravenna, the Milanese secretary Antonio Guidobono planned to ship some peregrine falcons to the duke, but only as long as the Venetians agreed to a safe conduct.[39] From Venice itself, Milanese traders worked tirelessly to supply the

---

[34] An illustrative episode, among others, is discussed in ASMi, *Carteggio* 343, 10 March 1453.

[35] Again, to give but one typical example: ASMi, *Carteggio* 341, 2 August 1454.

[36] These are especially frequent after the peace of Lodi, when Venice began transferring some of its forces to its eastern frontiers: e.g. ASMi, *Carteggio* 342, 11 February 1455.

[37] Barbieri, *Economia e politica*, 70–9; Mainoni, *Mercanti lombardi*, 13 and 38.

[38] ASMi, *Carteggio* 341, 23 January 1454: 'quello bello codego et altri molti scripsti'.

[39] ASMi, *Carteggio* 341, 27 September 1454.

136 BORDERS AND THE POLITICS OF SPACE IN LATE MEDIEVAL ITALY

princely court. Aside from drapes and dresses for the duchess,[40] safe conducts were often employed to protect the most fragile merchandise of all: glassware. The correspondence exchanged with the Milanese Chancery is replete with people pleading for a patent which would allow them to safely transfer their delicate goods. Examples include 'beautiful vases adorned with crystal and silver', enamelled cups for the prince's table, and even a model of Sforza's own castle in Milan.[41] Sometimes a safe conduct was simply denied, but that did not stop some agents from entrusting their purchases to other people. In the summer of 1454, an agent of Cicco Simonetta took advantage of the imminent departure of the Milanese ambassadors to send his master a whole set of tableware from Murano.[42]

Yet moving across borders was not restricted to wealthy merchants and princely agents. Individuals from poor backgrounds and marginal communities petitioned the authorities at all times seeking permission to move. This was especially true for minorities such as the Jews and generally for rootless people. When they could afford to send any, we can track their desired itineraries via their petitions; however, the correspondence that different authorities exchanged about such petitioners is often even more informative. In 1457, the Venetian governor of Crema advised the duke of Milan about the movements of an unnamed poor man ('povero huomo').[43] He had spent the summer harvesting crops in the fields around Lodi and was now looking to travel back to Bergamo to share with his mother the little wheat he had gleaned. This tells us that a few months earlier the man had left the territories of the Republic for those of the Duchy and was now asking for a safe conduct which would allow him to walk the route back without being troubled by local officials. But as the letter explains, this was almost inevitable, for the poor man had to cross multiple boundaries to travel from Lodi to Bergamo. The Venetian governor had readily allowed him to enter the Cremasco from the Lodigiano, but to reach Bergamo from Crema he had to travel once again over Milanese territories. As he had not sought permission to do so, the ducal officials seized his goods, which in turn prompted the Venetian governor to intervene in his favour.

---

[40] E.g. ASMi, Carteggio 341, 14 September 1454: a 'damaschino [sent] per uno correro de merchandanti milanesi'.

[41] ASMi, Carteggio 342, 14 February 1455: 'bellissimi vaxi lavorati de cristallo et de argento'; ASMi, Carteggio 341, 4 November 1454.

[42] ASMi, Carteggio 1568, 24 July 1454; ASMi, Carteggio 341, 2 August 1454.

[43] ASMi, Carteggio 344, 24 July 1457.

5. BORDERS AS SITES OF MOBILITY   137

Petitions and letters of this kind open a window not just on the array of activities performed by people on the move but also on the degree of interest taken by both central chanceries and local officials in monitoring their movement across state borders. As much literature has shown already, petitions were a crucial source of information for late medieval regimes: they gave rulers valuable data about the needs, goal, and intentions of the people over whom they ruled.[44] Together with chancery registers, safe conducts allowed authorities to trace the itineraries of both single individuals and entire groups. Some patents even went as far as to prescribe a detailed route. A safe conduct granted by Jacopo Piccinino to 65 residents of Rivolta, in the Geradadda, listed for each of them the specific locality they were permitted to visit.[45] Similarly, in granting a safe conduct to a group of friars who were looking to travel from Brescia to Milan for a meeting of their order, the Milanese Chancery noted that the concession would apply only when crossing the border at the bridge over the river Adda in Lodi.[46] And although only some safe conducts had spatial restrictions, all of them had time constraints. As the numerous requests for extension suggest, these limits were rigorously enforced. In December 1453, Piccinino was about to transfer his troops from Crema to Bergamo, but he was worried that the upcoming Christmas festivities would slow his men down; eventually, he resolved to ask Sforza to extend the safe conducts he had granted him by just a few days, so that his men could complete their journey in time.[47]

The amount of detailed information which was available to the authorities shows that the control exercised over cross-border mobility through the negotiation of safe conducts could be very careful and systematic. This was true for central magistracies (the duke and the Milanese Chancery, the Venetian governors and their condottieri) as well as for the officials stationed in frontier posts. The lists which chanceries shared with such officials are a testament to their role in monitoring movement in the peripheries. And while the who, where, and when of cross-border mobility were clearly well known to the authorities, the same could be said about the people applying for a safe conduct in the first place. Their understanding of the procedures and costs involved could sometimes rival that of secretaries and chancery clerks. Once again, a good example can be found in the

---

[44] For an overview, see Ormrod and Dodd, *Medieval Petitions*; together with Almbjär, 'The Problem with Early-Modern Petitions'.

[45] ASMi, *Carteggio* 340, 30 July 1453.   [46] ASMi, *Missive* 12, c. 435v, 5 June 1453.

[47] ASMi, *Carteggio* 340, 21 December 1453.

138 BORDERS AND THE POLITICS OF SPACE IN LATE MEDIEVAL ITALY

correspondence of the early 1450s, specifically from the letters exchanged between two rural noblemen: the *miles* Antonino Martinenghi in Brescia and the *dominus* Marco Secchi in the Geradadda.[48] The two families had long shared an interest in investing in the grey zone around Crema's enclave, but their access to local properties was now threatened by the establishment of new state borders in the area. To counter this, Martinenghi and Secchi began their own form of *contracambio*, where each nobleman successfully petitioned his government to obtain a safe conduct for his counterpart.

Much like the authorities of the time, we have no way of tracking how many eluded the system altogether, perhaps by bribing officials or simply by crossing the border at less obvious sites. But the abundant documentation discussed above, together with the fact that individuals from all walks of life were represented in it, suggests that in times of war at least, a large portion of the population had to request a safe conduct if they wished to move. At the same time, it confirms that, rather than being an exceptional instrument of protection, Italian safe conducts were a tool used routinely to negotiate movement. Since the patents themselves did not describe those who were expected to carry them, we also have no way of assessing how many exploited a safe conduct granted to others. Commenting on records from Spain and England, Adam Kosto has talked about these absences as a sign of 'ignorance about the traveler'.[49] However, it might be more accurate to say that the authorities of the time were safe in the knowledge that patents of this kind were hard to fabricate: for every safe conduct they granted, they knew that a corresponding number of people would now be given access to their territories. Indeed, border officers were only required to authenticate the document, not their holder. After all, Italian safe conducts were devices designed to control movement, not forms of identification; they were the medieval equivalents of modern visas, not the antecedents of our passports. They were not about who you are but about where you come from.

More broadly, safe conducts were a tool in the hands of the people, who used them to express their desire to travel, as much as an instrument in the hands of the authorities, who employed them to monitor movement across state frontiers. In Italy, the functioning of borders as sites of mobility relied extensively on this interaction—sometimes on paper, sometimes in person—between the polity and its subjects. When a concession was granted, the tension between the artificial fixity enforced by the authorities and the

---

[48] ASMi, *Carteggio* 341, 20 March 1454. [49] Kosto, 'Ignorance about the Traveler'.

natural mobility pursued by the people was relieved. However, safe conducts should not be seen simply as a safety valve but rather as a conduit, one through which movement across borders was unlocked and channelled. In times of war, they enabled economic and social practices which rendered the new frontier between Venice and Milan exceptionally permeable to movement, but they also provided peripheral as much as central authorities with a great deal of control over cross-border mobility. Just like borders themselves, safe conducts signified the power that made them, while offering people across all strata of society a framework within which to move. In keeping with their Janus-face character, they show that borders functioned both as the end of the state and as the beginning of a journey.

Trading across Borders in Times of Peace

The new frontier between the Duchy and the Republic was far from being the only existing border at this time. As we saw in the first half of the book, late medieval Italy featured multiple scales of territoriality and a dense network of pre-existing boundaries. These were notably the boundaries of long-standing territorial bodies, such as cities and towns or even fiefs and rural federations. In the Quattrocento, these bodies made up the internal provinces of the two dominions. In addition, they often happened to be peripheral bodies; therefore, sections of their local boundaries came to serve also as the new borders between regional states. Yet this does not mean that the rest of their boundaries (those facing inwards, to put it simply) were doomed to fall into disuse. For a start, justice was still organized around the boundaries of older territories. Urban and rural communities had long exercised jurisdictional rights over their respective spaces. With the rise of regional powers, these rights were transferred from local bodies to the princely or republican state, which would now deploy or simply appoint new deputies in the localities to administer justice in their name. However, the limits of each deputy's jurisdiction were still defined locally by the limits of the same jurisdictional units, that is to say, by the borders of pre-existing territorial bodies.[50] Similarly, the collection of taxes on moving

---

[50] On the territorial ramifications of the administration of justice in Lombardy, see Zenobi, 'Nascita di un territorio', 834–6; and Della Misericordia, 'Essere di una giurisdizione', 105–8. For comparison, consider the Florentine perspectives in Zorzi, *La trasformazione di un quadro politico*, 181–280.

140   BORDERS AND THE POLITICS OF SPACE IN LATE MEDIEVAL ITALY

goods was still largely based upon the boundaries of former urban territories. The Italian *civitates* had long levied duties on people entering or leaving their *contadi* with valuable possessions. In doing so, as Massimo Della Misericordia has put it, they 'loaded their political spaces with economic overtones'.[51]

Jurisdictional and fiscal boundaries overlapped so closely that the new regional powers made little to no effort to disentangle them. The Venetians never sought to replace the system of duties traditionally levied by single municipalities with a uniform system of regional taxation. Instead, they limited their fiscal policies to facilitating the flow of resources that were essential to Venice's own market, such as grain for the citizens, armour for the militia, and timber for the Arsenale. This promoted the role of the lagoon as an entrepôt for the entire mainland, but it also preserved a fiscal organization based upon the contours of urban territories.[52] In comparison, first the Visconti and later the Sforza pursued policies of more direct intervention in the Milanese dominion; however, the perimeters within which goods were moved and duties collected remained virtually the same. The lords and then dukes of Milan granted privileges of immunity to vast areas in order to reduce transaction costs and mobilize local produce. They centralized the gabelle tax on salt, which was now handled by private contractors dealing directly with central officers. They weakened the economic control exercised by the cities over their respective *contadi*, thus promoting a more balanced circulation of resources between individual cities and between single economic hinterlands (wood and iron from the valleys of Como and Lecco, grain and hay from the plains around Piacenza and Cremona, etc.). While these could be seen as the first steps towards a more integrated regional economy, the dukes actually did very little to dismantle fiscal boundaries between the internal provinces of their dominion.[53] People leaving Piacenza for Cremona, for example, were still expected to pay duties on the goods they carried when looking to cross the boundaries between the two *contadi*, just as the travellers from the Bresciano or the

---

[51] Della Misericordia, 'Spazi politici e spazi economici', 25. On the urban dimension of indirect taxation, which endured well into the latest stages of the Middle Ages, see also Mainoni, 'Una fonte per la storia dello stato visconteo-sforzesco', 70.

[52] On Venetian economic policies, see Knapton, 'Il fisco nello stato veneziano', 28–32; and generally Pezzolo, *Una finanza d'ancien régime*.

[53] As discussed by Mainoni, 'Fiscalità signorile e finanza pubblica', 115–23. See also Epstein, 'Town and Country', 462–5.

5. BORDERS AS SITES OF MOBILITY 141

Bergamasco were expected to contribute their share to the Venetians when leaving their provinces.[54]

Internal boundaries, to put it simply, went on serving as administrative borders and customs barriers. As such, they offer a promising angle for analysing mobility inside regional dominions, namely across the boundaries of their many provinces. To map and examine movement across internal borders, this section will look at the internal circulation of people and goods. In contrast to the first section of the chapter, we shall focus especially on the period of renewed peace and stability brought about by the treaty of Lodi, so as to investigate the everyday practice of cross-border mobility outside the exceptional measures adopted in wartime. We shall start by considering how late medieval polities regulated the movement of supplies from one territory to another and how they levied duties at local boundaries. We shall then look at the ways in which the itineraries of people who were involved in these traffics can be mapped, before moving on to discuss the wider implications of this analysis for a treatment of borders as sites of mobility in late medieval Italy.

Channelling and taxing the movement of people and goods, both from and to their territories, had long been a major concern of the Italian city-states. As Laura Bertoni has recently noted, a sustained effort in regulating the circulation of resources went hand in hand with the very process through which the *contadi* were made.[55] A booming population, flourishing trade, and infrastructure development had transformed every Italian city into a pole of attraction for rural products. Yet these products could still be lured away by the demand of nearby centres or simply sold on the spot in exchange for other products. To prevent this, urban authorities enforced two complementary policies: they prohibited new fairs and markets outside the city walls and they imposed higher taxes on the export of goods from their *contadi*. Together, these two policies fostered the subordination of rural production to the needs of the city while at the same time establishing clear fiscal boundaries within which goods were encouraged to move.[56]

---

[54] The model of Lombardy and the Veneto is often contrasted with that of Tuscany, where Florence achieved a greater economic integration by asserting its position as the monopolistic centre of trade and manufacturing in the region: Malanima, 'La formazione di una regione economica'. For a comparative overview, see now Scott, 'The Economic Policies of the Regional City-States'.

[55] Bertoni, 'I regimi di popolo e la vigilanza annonaria', 127. See also the case study by Pucci Donati, *Il mercato del pane*; and the overview by Magni, 'Politica degli approvvigionamenti'.

[56] On policies directing goods to urban centres in medieval Italy, see Della Misericordia, *I confini dei mercati*, 53–7; and generally Mainoni, 'La fisionomia economica delle città'.

142   BORDERS AND THE POLITICS OF SPACE IN LATE MEDIEVAL ITALY

Additional rules applied to the internal circulation of foodstuffs, such as legumes, hay (which was then associated with basic food provisions) and especially grain. As Fabien Faugeron has shown for Venice, feeding a late medieval city was a highly complex task, one that mobilized public actors as much as private individuals from all backgrounds and concerned a supply area that often extended far beyond the city's sphere of influence.[57] Between the thirteenth and early fourteenth centuries, when the proportion of the population residing in urban centres reached its peak in Italy, securing a constant flow of supplies also became a matter of public order. To prevent local produce from being sold in other markets, export duties were raised even further and customs barriers became more strictly enforced. In addition, most centres began forcing their subject communities in the countryside to supply a set amount of produce to the city each year. In many cases, the system remained fully in place throughout the Late Middle Ages and often well into the early modern period. The city of Cremona, which could boast a population of over 40,000 people around 1500, revised the quota of grain assigned to each community on a periodic basis over the course of the Quattrocento. On such occasions, city deputies went from house to house in all the communities of the countryside to compile a list of all the hay, flour, and legumes available in their territory.[58]

Still, descriptions of this kind accounted only for the share of supplies going straight into the urban market; the city gates, where officials took note of all the goods entering the city on a given day, were supposedly the only border that these provisions would ever cross. People who sought to export goods outside the boundaries of a *districtus* or other constituent territory of the dominion were subject to a different set of regulations. In the context of fifteenth-century Lombardy, it is possible to build up a picture of internal border-crossing by combining two series of sources: one is the general ordinances on the circulation of foodstuffs issued by the Visconti and Sforza dukes; the other is the specific instructions supplied to local officials in the

---

[57] Faugeron, *Nourrir la ville*. For a Tuscan perspective, see Dameron, 'Feeding the Medieval Italian City-State'. The surviving sources do not really allow similar studies for Milan, although consider Parziale, *Nutrire la città*.

[58] ASCr, *Annona* 8, f. 7: 'Liber bladorum consignandorum pro imposta in platea comunis Cremone' (1487). Additional censuses were then conducted when nearby territories suffered from war damage and were thus particularly keen to extract an extra portion of supplies from the Cremonese: e.g. in 1427, on the occasion of the first major conflict between Milan and Venice (ASCr, *Annona* 11, f. 1) and similarly in 1477, following the assassination of duke Galeazzo Maria (ASCr, *Annona* 11, f. 2). Analogous practices were carried out in many cities of the Venetian dominion, starting with Crema: BCCr, *Provisioni* 1, c. 23r, 7 June 1450.

5. BORDERS AS SITES OF MOBILITY   143

form of fiscal handbooks.[59] Marco Lunari has convincingly argued that this set of laws and guidelines was generated to respond to the needs of the moment rather than to an organic administrative design[60]. However, with the power of the duke growing stronger, the rules governing the movement of goods inside his dominion became progressively more refined, as did the functioning of internal boundaries as customs barriers. By 1463, the duties collected on moving goods, both inside and outside the Duchy, contributed the largest single share to state revenues.[61] Together, these sets of laws and guidelines provide us with plenty of details about the process through which products were taxed, as well as about the locations where duties were supposed to be levied.

If we exclude the quota of supplies that rural communities were expected to bring straight to the closest urban centre and the share of produce heading directly to the city, which was normally exempt from any form of duties, moving goods eventually had to cross either one or two types of borders: the external frontiers of the Duchy as a whole and/or the internal boundaries between its many provinces. Ducal ordinances maintained a formal distinction between these two movements: some decrees concerned goods coming from any land or territory under ducal rule but headed outside the ducal dominion ('extra dominium nostrum'); others were directed at goods moving from one province to another ('de uno districto nostro ad alium nostrum districtum').[62] It is striking, however, that the two were broadly subject to the same set of rules. All people carrying marketable products were expected to perform their journey via the most direct and well-known route: whatever their origin or destination, travellers were not allowed to cut across the main itineraries ('de loco ad locum, de burgo ad burgum,

---

[59] The first of these has been the subject of a detailed analysis by Lunari, 'I decreti visconteo-sforzeschi'; while the second has recently been the focus of a study by Bertoni, 'Strade e mercati'.

[60] Lunari, 'I decreti visconteo-sforzeschi', 116.

[61] Chittolini, '*Fiscalité d'état* et prérogatives urbaines', 159. On the Venetian mainland, by way of comparison, indirect taxation made up between 60 and 80% of all the revenues collected by the state: Varanini, 'Il bilancio d'entrata', 80.

[62] Plenty of examples for this distinction come from a collection of ducal ordinances in BTMi, ms. 1230, which is also the main source employed by Lunari, 'I decreti visconteo-sforzeschi'. The same can be extended to Venetian decrees by using a similar collection kept in BMVe, ms. It. VII 489 (8147). For the purposes of this analysis, these manuscripts have also been collated with the equivalent collections compiled by the chanceries of single municipalities, in particular Crema (BCCr, *Ducali* 1, cc. 61r–69r) and Cremona (BSCr, ms. AA 4 30 and ms. Albertoni 222).

144 BORDERS AND THE POLITICS OF SPACE IN LATE MEDIEVAL ITALY

de terra ad terram').[63] Partly, this was to prevent the produce from being sold before reaching its final destination or, worse, from being diverted into enemy markets by local smugglers. But generally, regulations of this kind were aimed at channelling moving products towards designated customs points, that is, sites at which the movement of goods and people could be closely monitored and the collection of duties could reliably take place. The most established customs points were situated around the gates of urban centres. Here, ducal agents had long joined city officials in overseeing the collection of duties on incoming goods, which was typically outsourced to private contractors.[64] More generally, custom points were located alongside internal as well as external borders. If urban checkpoints were placed around city gates, their rural counterparts were located where the territorial border intersected with either trading hubs, such as market towns, or transit areas, such as roads and river crossings (fords, ports, bridges).[65] People were expected to visit the closest customs point immediately after crossing a state's frontiers or when they were about to leave one of its territories. Travellers hoping to trade their goods inside the territory they were entering would only be expected to pay import taxes, but travellers hoping to then export their goods outside the territory—or even outside the Duchy— were required to pay taxes both upon their entrance ('pro introitu') and upon their leaving ('pro exitu').[66] People travelling with marketable products were thus charged for crossing internal boundaries as much as external frontiers: when it came to collecting duties, both functioned as watertight compartments.

Another dynamic which equated internal and external borders was the fact that both could be crossed with valuable products by first obtaining a licence from the duke himself. As we have seen, transporting grain and other provisions had long been regulated by individual city-states, particularly through the channelling of a sufficient share of the produce directly to the urban market. However, when the lords of Milan began extending their power over adjacent city-states, new outlets for a potential surplus were

---

[63] As discussed by Bertoni, 'Strade e mercati', 136, drawing on a collection of fourteenth-century ordinances now in BBMi, ms. A E XII 39.

[64] On custom barriers outside city gates, see also Pult Quaglia, 'Early Modern Tuscany', 136–7; and Jütte, 'Entering a City', 213–14. On the practice of selling the rights to collect duties to local nobles and businessmen, particularly when in need of generating cash, see Chittolini, 'Alienazioni d'entrate e concessioni feudali', 153–4.

[65] These are listed in NOTO, *Liber datii mercantie*, 98.

[66] As noted by Bertoni, 'Strade e mercati', 138. More broadly on the practices taking place by rural checkpoints, see Paganini, 'Notule sulle vicende dei transporti'.

5. BORDERS AS SITES OF MOBILITY   145

created. By the time their expansion in northern Italy had come to a halt, the Visconti had formed an intermediate market between the most fertile lands of their dominion, which were concentrated in the Po Valley, and areas that were chronically unable to sustain themselves, starting with the populous valleys of the Lombard Alps.[67] Just as single cities had long struggled to retain local produce against the attraction of nearby centres, the Visconti and then Sforza dukes were forced to put special measures in place to prevent resources from being dispersed on the way to their destination. Next to increasing or lowering duties on specific products, issuing dedicated licences became the main way in which they channelled the circulation of products across their dominion.

Like safe conducts, trade licences were issued in the form of letters, that is, formal patents which travellers were required to present for inspection when looking to leave the Duchy with their goods or, more commonly, when trying to cross the boundaries between its many provinces. And again, much like safe conducts, trade licences allowed people and authorities to interact with each other and negotiate their respective needs. For the ruled, obtaining a licence to move things either inside or outside the Duchy meant being exempt from duties and also safe from the intrusion of border officers. For the rulers, issuing licences was but another way of allowing for the prince's exceptional intervention in matters governed by a pre-existing set of customs and norms. Trade licences gave people the option of eluding the existing duties by exploiting their influence and connections at court, while the prince gained the opportunity to direct another aspect of the politics of mobility.

Before 1466, when Galeazzo Maria Sforza agreed to create a dedicated office, the issuing of trade licences was delegated to the Milanese Chancery.[68] The Venetians had a comparable system in place, although, as in the case of safe conducts, trade licences were not granted by the Republic's central offices but by the governors of each province.[69] The earliest source documenting the operations of the Milanese Chancery in this area dates back to

---

[67] On the development of a regional economy in Lombardy, see Mainoni, 'The Economy of Renaissance Milan'; and Chiappa Mauri, 'Le merci di Lombardia'.

[68] Lunari, 'Forme di governo nella Milano sforzesca'.

[69] By way of example, consider the decrees with which the Venetian governors of Crema ruled that local provisions could not be exported outside its territory without first obtaining a licence from them: BCCr, *Ducali* 1, c. 105v (29 May 1455) and cc. 176r–176v (29 May 1483)— something that surely enraged the Cremaschi, given that both in 1443 and in 1447, in his quest to secure the loyalty of the locals, the duke had promised to abolish all custom barriers between the territory of Crema and that of Milan: BCCr, *Finanza* 19, fs. 164 and 165.

146   BORDERS AND THE POLITICS OF SPACE IN LATE MEDIEVAL ITALY

the period immediately following the peace of Lodi. At this time, the Chancery recorded every licence they granted in a *Liber Albus* (that is, quite literally, a 'white book').[70] This is probably the first of a new series of registers documenting this practice, the rest of which are largely lost.[71] The *Liber Albus* itself only survives as a fragment of what must have been a much larger manuscript. Yet the period it covers, between July 1454 and March 1455, is extremely relevant to this analysis, for it contains data on the movement of goods and people following the enactment of the treaty in the spring of 1454. Just as safe conducts have helped us to uncover the mechanics of cross-border mobility in times of war, trade licences offer a consistent source base for investigating mobility in times of peace. The added bonus is that trade licences concerned movement through the polity as much as to and out of the polity: they chart mobility across internal boundaries as much as across external frontiers.

In addition, this source base offers several other advantages. First of all, the *Liber Albus* was probably the sole register employed by the Chancery to record trade licences at this stage. This means that the 335 concessions it contains represent a sizeable portion of the people involved in moving products across borders in the period in question—except, of course, for those who were not able to obtain a licence and thus were forced to pay duties at the border or simply smuggle their goods, which must have been a considerable phenomenon in its own right but also one that is now hard to estimate.[72] Secondly, extracting data from this manuscript is relatively easy. Its entries record only essential pieces of information: the date on which the licence was granted, its duration, the name of the person who requested it, the quantity of goods, their origin and destination, and sometimes also the itineraries and custom points they should visit. Finally, the key advantage of the *Liber Albus* is that its data is multidimensional. It tells us something about the people crossing borders in this period, about the goods they carried, and about their reasons for travelling; but it also tells us something about

---

[70] ASMi, *Frammenti* 1, f. 15.

[71] The only exception being the *Liber licentiarum bladorum* covering the years 1455–8, although this is probably only a slightly more formal successor to the *Liber Albus*. Perhaps improperly, the manuscript can now be found in the archival series of registers of letters: ASMi, *Missive* 33.

[72] The mechanics of smuggling between the Duchy of Milan and the Republic of Venice have been studied by Costantini, 'Commercio e contrabbando di cereali'. A more general treatment for the early modern period can be found in Cavallera, 'Questioni di dazi e di contrabbandi'. So far, scant attention has been paid to the Late Middle Ages, save for local studies such as Aldeghi and Riva, 'Adda fiume di confine'. For an initial discussion of the phenomenon for the Quattrocento, see Zenobi, 'Il rovescio della medaglia'.

5. BORDERS AS SITES OF MOBILITY   147

the timeframe within which they moved, about the routes they followed, and about the places they visited. In short, the *Liber Albus* is both about things and people and about time and space.

For the purposes of what follows, 35 of the 335 licences in question have been set aside, typically due to incomplete data or to place names which were impossible to identify. The remaining 300, covering a little less than one year, have been mapped out using *Palladio*, which is an online toolset combining data analysis with digital visualization. This allows for a systematic treatment of the multiple dimensions introduced above. First, by putting names and objects in a table, we can identify patterns in the phenomenon of border-crossing: how many people requested a licence every month? Were they private individuals or public officials, men or women, lay or secular? What sort of goods were they looking to move across borders? How many people sought to cross state boundaries and how many were just moving from one province to another? Second, by putting places of origin and destination on a map, we can make out the overall shape of the network of food trade, and visualize the flow of resources inside and outside the region. Finally, we can uncover the connections between its many nodes and assess the degree of border-crossing it involved.

Let us start by looking at the temporal dimension of these licences. If we include the group of documents that have been excluded from consideration due to their unreliability, the Milanese Chancery granted on average 42 licences per month, that is more than one a day, and between three or four times the number of safe conducts granted only a couple of years earlier. As trade licences were mostly concerned with foodstuffs, one would expect their temporal distribution to reflect seasonal trends of production and demand. But with the exception of a relative spike in March 1455, perhaps due to shortages of supplies at the end of the winter, this was simply not the case: as Figure 13 shows, a constant stream of traders and provisions was moving across borders at all times. The vast majority of the licences expired within one or two months. This gave their holders only enough time to perform their journey once or, at most, twice before the licence expired. However, a small minority of licences extended to as much as five or even twelve months. This was often the case when the applicant was employed directly by the state: Stefano and Tormello, who are said to be both originally from Florence, obtained a five-month licence to export wheat from Cremona to the Bresciano to make bread for soldiers, while Giacomo Policastri, who was the ducal officer in charge of the castle of Vigevano at the time, obtained a year-long licence to transport

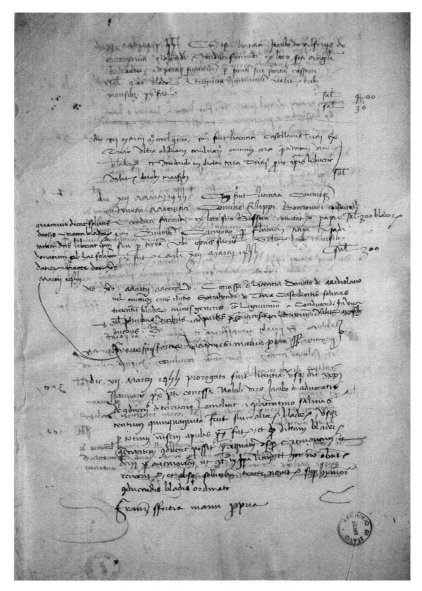

Fig. 12 The last page from the fragment of the *Liber Albus* (ASMi, *Frammenti* 1, f. 15, c. 24v), including a transcription of the duke's own signature at the end. Reproduced with permission from the Italian Ministry of Cultural Heritage

5. BORDERS AS SITES OF MOBILITY   149

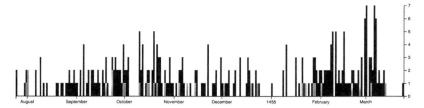

Fig. 13 Temporal distribution of the licences of the *Liber Albus* (July 1454– March 1455). The light-coloured bars represent the portion of licences granted to legal representatives rather than to the person nominally applying for them. © Luca Zenobi

hay and wine from any place in the Duchy, provided that this was solely to equip his fortress.[73]

Sources of this kind can tell us a great deal about the objects being moved, and thus about aspects such as food consumption and price patterns; but they also provide us with valuable insight into the people they empowered, their individual itineraries, and, sometimes, their personal motivations. As we have just seen, the first group of people who figure prominently in the *Liber Albus* were state officials. These were typically low-ranking castellans,[74] like our Giacomo Policastri, or condottieri looking to secure enough provisions for their soldiers and hay for their horses.[75] Alongside them, we find the governors of entire provinces, such as the Venetian governors of Bergamo and Crema, two areas that despite their new allegiance to the Republic were still heavily dependent on importing grain and other food supplies from the most fertile areas of the Duchy.[76] Catering for the needs of their subjects, so as to prevent the discontent of the ruled, was a primary concern of neighbouring rulers such as the doge of

[73] ASMi, *Frammenti* 1, f. 15, cc. 1r (25 July 1454) and 3r (1 September 1454).

[74] E.g. the castellans of Caravaggio, San Lorenzo (Cremona), Santa Croce (Parma), and Trezzo: ASMi, *Frammenti* 1, f. 15, cc. 4v (19 September 1454), 6r (30 September 1454), 14v (10 Janurary 1455), and 24v (12 March 1455). On the licences granted specifically to castellans and other military officials to cater for their garrisons, see also Covini, 'I castellani ducali', 559 and 578.

[75] E.g. the condottieri Giovan Antonio Gattamelata, Donato del Conte, Micheletto Attendoli, Sagramoro da Parma, Giovanni da Tolentino, and Tiberto Brandolini; see ASMi, *Frammenti* 1, f. 15, cc. 1r (30 July 1454), 1v (1 August 1454), 6v (3 October 1454), 13r (10 December 1454), 17v (7 February 1455), and 20v (18 February 1455).

[76] ASMi, *Frammenti* 1, f. 15, cc. 3v (7 September 1454), 4r (14 September 1454), 10v (29 October 1454), 20r (19 February 1455), 20v (23 February1455), and 22r (28 February 1455).

150 BORDERS AND THE POLITICS OF SPACE IN LATE MEDIEVAL ITALY

Genoa.[77] In a similar way, the marquis of Mantua applied for as many as five licences in the period in question, which makes him the most frequently recurring figure in the *Liber Albus*. Most of the goods he looked to transfer came from the Duchy itself, such as the 300 wagons of wheat and hay that his men extracted from the provinces of the Po Valley that year. Others, such as the 200 carts full of Monferrato wine mentioned by the *Liber Albus*, came from beyond the Duchy, which means that they had to cross its borders twice: first when entering the ducal dominion and then when leaving it on the way to Mantua.[78]

Nevertheless, the vast majority of people seeking permission to transfer goods across the Duchy were private individuals. Many of them were simply trying to meet day-to-day needs: to provide for their families and then retail any surplus within their communities. Some, however, were only granted a licence so that they could transfer goods for other people. Members of aristocratic families, such as Torelli, Scotti, and Borromeo, were unlikely to perform the journey themselves, but their agents (*nunzi*) can be found all over the *Liber Albus*, either transferring goods to their masters' lands or taking excess produce from their lands to nearby markets.[79] The same could be said about the five members of the clergy who secured a licence in the period under consideration. Among them, we find three prioresses, who also happen to be the only women featured in the *Liber Albus*.[80] Women could nominally ask for a licence with complete independence, although often they did so only after seeking the intercession of local authorities. The prioress of Santa Giulia in Brescia, for instance, had a reliable ally in the Venetian governors. One of the governors of Brescia even wrote to the duke of Milan suggesting that 'indulging said women' in transferring the fruit of their extensive lands in the Cremonese 'will certainly be a very merciful act'.[81] Next to noblemen and nuns, special deputies were most often employed to buy and transfer supplies for entire communities, such as the steep-sided valleys of the Bergamasco and the thriving towns of the

---

[77] ASMi, *Frammenti* 1, f. 15, c. 5r, 22 December 1454.

[78] ASMi, *Frammenti* 1, f. 15, cc. 2v (20 August 1454), 5r (23 September 1454), 12v (27 November 1454), 14v (8 January 1455), and 18v (10 February 1455).

[79] E.g. counts Cristoforo Torelli, Alberto Scotti, and Filippo Borromeo: ASMi, *Frammenti*, f. 15, cc. 2v (29 August 1454), 16r (1 February 1455), and 24v (13 March 1455).

[80] ASMi, *Frammenti* 1, f. 15, cc. 5v (27 September 1454), 7v (16 October 1454), and 13v (17 December 1454).

[81] ASMi, *Carteggio* 343, 26 January 1456: 'se degni compiacere ditte donne... che certo serà opera molto pietosa'. On the same issue, see also ASMi, *Carteggio* 341, 25 September 1454 and ASMi, *Carteggio* 342, 20 September 1455.

Geradadda (mainly Treviglio, Caravaggio, and Rivolta). These populous communities appointed two or more deputies at regular intervals to secure a constant flow of provisions from more fertile areas. For the Bergamaschi, these were mainly the lowlands around Pavia, a territory with which the mountain dwellers had long forged very close links, notably by virtue of the age-old tradition of wintering their herds in the area.[82] For their part, the townspeople of the Geradadda would normally send their deputies to the markets of the Cremonese, the fertile *contado* to which most of these communities used to be subject before the Visconti granted them jurisdictional and fiscal autonomy.[83]

This brings us to the last but also most relevant dimension of the *Liber Albus*, which is that of space. The itineraries followed by the deputies of both mountain communities in the Bergamasco and small towns in the Geradadda are typical examples of the wider network of food trade in this period: they extended over a regional space, they connected fertile lands to areas that were densely populated, and they involved the crossing of multiple borders. To reach Pavia from the mountains, for instance, the Bergamaschi had first to cross the boundary of the Duchy by stepping into the territory of the Geradadda, then return to the Venetian dominion by traversing the enclave of Crema, and finally cross state frontiers once more when leaving the Cremasco for the Lodigiano; once inside the Duchy for the second time, the Bergamaschi still had to cross the boundaries between its internal territories when leaving the *contado* of Lodi for that of Pavia. Although typical, this was far from the only itinerary described by the *Liber Albus*. Let us then exploit the full potential of *Palladio* and start visualizing the spatial dimension of the itineraries recorded by our source.

Figure 15 pinpoints the origins and destinations of the 300 itineraries extracted from the *Liber Albus*. The size of each dot reflects how many licences mention the locality in question, that is to say the magnitude of movement to or from that locality. From this, we can note that the points of origin (light grey) are concentrated in the south-west: from the Monferrato and the Lomellina to the lowlands surrounding the centres of Pavia, Lodi, Piacenza, and Cremona. By contrast, the points of destination (dark grey) are largely located in the north-east, alongside the left banks of the river Adda, with Crema and the Geradadda (located around Treviglio), and throughout the *contadi* of Bergamo and Brescia. When superimposing the

---

[82] Roveda, 'Allevamento e transumanza'.
[83] Di Tullio, *The Wealth of Communities*, 36–42.

Fig. 14 Area covered by the *Liber Albus*, shown in Figure 15 in greater detail. © Luca Zenobi

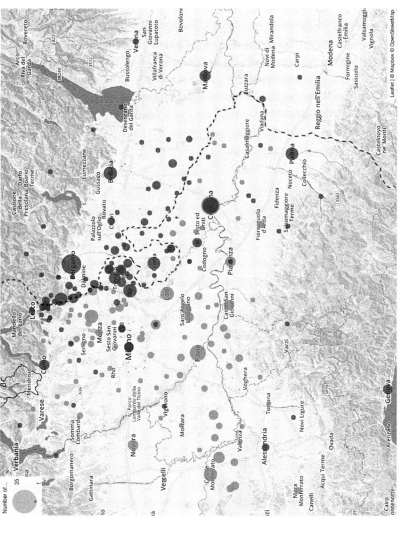

Fig. 15 Origins and destinations of the itineraries of the *Liber Albus*. The dotted line distinguishes the two polities' spheres of influence. © Luca Zenobi

154   BORDERS AND THE POLITICS OF SPACE IN LATE MEDIEVAL ITALY

political geography discussed in Chapter 2 onto this map, it becomes clear that resources flowed not only from the most fertile lands of the Po Valley to the populous centres lying at the foot of the Alps but from territories that formed part of the Duchy of Milan to territories which were now subject to the Republic of Venice.

Combined with the *Liber Albus*, the letters through which Venetian officials petitioned the Milanese Chancery for a licence confirm how desperately these territories depended on importing much of their food supplies from the Duchy.[84] From Crema, they lamented that due to scant sowing in the previous season, most people could not afford to buy any type of flour.[85] From Brescia, one Venetian governor admitted that importing grain from the Cremonese was key not just to keeping prices down but to having enough produce to feed all the citizens.[86] From Bergamo, another patrician wrote begging for a licence that would allow him to transfer enough hay and wheat to face a period of famine.[87] The same could be said about Milanese officials, though in opposite terms. In reporting to the duke about various attempts to smuggle goods across the river Adda, the castellan of Brivio explained that this should not really come as a surprise, for the *contado* of Bergamo was poor and barren while 'the duke's backyard [i.e. the Milanese *contado*] is the most beautiful garden in the world'.[88]

Figure 16 pushes our enquiry one final step further, by combining the dimension of space with that of mobility. In this map, points of origin and destination retain their shape and size but now function as the nodes of a network: the network of food trade in fifteenth-century Lombardy. The arc of each line represents the flow of the relationship between single nodes, which in this case is the direction of travel between points of origin and points of destination. By mapping the overall shape of the network and by depicting the consistency of its web of connections, this chart provides us with a more comprehensive picture of cross-border mobility. An array of short-range itineraries, often linking localities in nearby territories, is now just as visible as the heavy flow of resources that moved from the Duchy to

---

[84]   This remained true in the following centuries. In 1565, the Venetian governor of Bergamo reported that his territory was dependent for nine months every year on grain imported from its neighbours: TAGLIAFERRI, *Relazioni dei rettori veneti*, 79. For an early modern overview, see now Costantini, 'One City, Two Economic Areas'.

[85]   ASMi, *Carteggio* 341, 21 July 1454.   [86]   ASMi, *Carteggio* 342, 8 August 1455.

[87]   ASMi, *Carteggio* 343, 27 September 1456.

[88]   ASMi, *Comuni* 14, f. 'Brivio', 27 April 1474. Indeed, based on Figure 15, it is clear that Milan did not import much produce, especially considering the size of the Lombard capital. This shows that the Milanese *contado* and particularly its southern section (the so-called Bassa) was so rich and fertile that there was little need to introduce supplies from outside the boundaries of Milan's own province.

5. BORDERS AS SITES OF MOBILITY 155

the Republic (that is to say, across the frontier between the two states). These short-range itineraries connected localities that were all subject to the duke of Milan but happened to be placed in different provinces of his dominion, such as Piacenza and Parma, Lodi and the Geradadda, Pavia and Como. To move between any of these nodes, people and their goods had first to cross the internal boundaries of the Duchy (that is to say, the boundaries between its territories) and thus apply for a trade licence.

Besides uncovering the multiple dimensions (internal and external) of cross-border mobility, this analysis shows how central the experience of border-crossing was to two concurrent phenomena. The first is the great volume of people, goods, and objects travelling across the Po Valley at this time, despite the establishment of new state borders between the Duchy of Milan and the Republic of Venice. The Pavia–Cremona corridor, among others, was clearly a crucial mobility channel not just for the Duchy but for all the neighbouring polities. Even fertile areas such as the Mantovano depended heavily on importing goods from the core areas of the Milanese dominion. This attached a strong political connotation to the granting or refusal of a licence to foreign deputies, that is to say, to the opening or closure of borders—a dynamic which scholars are yet to fully incorporate into our understanding of diplomatic relations in this period.

The second phenomenon is the sustained level of exchange between the Bresciano and the Cremonese, and between the Bergamasco and the Milanese. These were all territories that used to form part of the same dominion (the Duchy of Milan) but now happened to be subject to two different polities (the Duchy and the Republic). It is now agreed, as Tom Scott has recently put it, that 'Venice's penetration into Lombardy brought about no palpable reorientation...The principal cities west of the Mincio, in essence Brescia and Bergamo, retained their economic and commercial attraction towards Milan.'[89] Their dependence on supplies coming from the Milanese dominion reflected historic ties cutting across the new state frontier as much as structural deficiencies of local produce. Thanks to the system of trade licences, border crossings became the channels through which contacts and exchanges could be maintained, albeit under the watchful eye of state authorities.

*   *   *

---

[89] Scott, 'The Economic Policies of the Regional City-States', 229. On the Bresciano, see Varanini, 'Per la storia agraria della pianura bresciana', 88. On the Bergamasco, see Costantini, In tutto differente dalle altre città, 53.

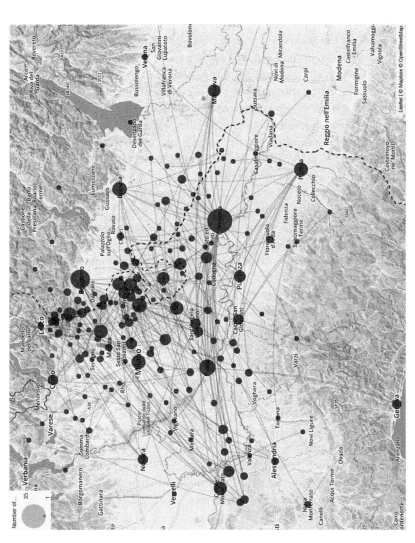

Fig. 16 Network of food trade in fifteenth-century Lombardy, based on data extracted from the *Liber Albus*. © Luca Zenobi

5. BORDERS AS SITES OF MOBILITY 157

Overall, this chapter's inquiry into the Janus-face character of pre-modern borders suggests that just as we should refrain from seeing a border as a mere line, we should also be wary of reducing cross-border mobility to a single arrow. In fifteenth-century Lombardy, a multifaceted regime of movement featured internal boundaries (e.g. when leaving Lodi for the Geradadda) as much as external frontiers (i.e. when travelling from the Duchy to the Republic, and vice versa). This conclusion lends support to the argument developed earlier in the book, by confirming once more the solidity of pre-existing units vis-à-vis the spatial dimension of new regional polities, although from the angle of mobility now. The patterns on display in the *Liber Albus* exemplify this point very clearly. Coupled with the granting of safe conducts, issuing trade licences allowed the dukes of Milan to effectively centralize the politics of mobility. It is striking, however, that the implementation of such politics was not accompanied by the development of new infrastructures and control systems but by the widespread adoption of those already in existence, starting with the boundaries and custom points of the old city-states.

In addition, the chapter aligns with the rest of the book in challenging the idea that pre-modern borders were irreducibly muddled lines surrounding the territories of inattentive polities. Safe conducts and trade licences alike show that contemporaries encountered borders on a daily basis and that the spatial coordinates of border-crossing were very evident to them. At the same time, they show that people's ability to move went hand in hand with a certain degree of control on behalf of the authorities. Late medieval rulers exercised this in two ways: by subjecting the movement of people and goods to the issuing of a special permit (a safe conduct in time of war or, more commonly, a trade licence) and by presiding over a system of border posts located at both internal boundaries and external frontiers. Here, multiple dimensions of mobility interacted, as locals and foreigners came into contact with one another and with state officials. In the end, this significant amount of movement was enabled not by the supposed porosity of late medieval borders but by the deliberate adoption of open-border policies on behalf of the authorities. Fifteenth-century borders were indeed permeable but only because rulers were content with channelling people and goods through specific checkpoints rather than preventing them from entering their territories altogether. Using movement as a category of analysis, it is thus possible to question traditional views of medieval borders as fluid and porous lines and show that they were in fact precisely located, widely understood, and carefully governed.

6
Committing Borders to Paper
Written Memory and Record-Keeping

Like space more broadly, borders were made by ideas, practices, and movement; but they were also made by records. So far, we have explored how the world of boundaries and frontiers intersected with a unique territorial culture built around the jurisdictional notion of power over space, with pre-existing social practices and especially the collective action of local communities, and with the circulation of goods and people. We have also witnessed how borders were constructed and sometimes reshaped by specific records, such as the texts of major treaties, the *instrumenta confinationum*, and the registers of safe conducts and trade licences. All these records had a performative effect on the world of borders. For a start, putting borders on paper afforded them a further level of significance, that of memory and belief. Contemporary records did not feature borders just as they were, being in their geographical or legal dimension, but as people imagined them and often wished them to be. More importantly, for the scope of this chapter, committing borders to paper did more than simply reflect changes in border arrangements; rather, it was itself a moment of change for the ways in which borders were understood, arranged, and organized. A prime example is the process of cross-legitimation explored in Chapter 4, where we first encountered the *instrumenta confinationum*. In recording the boundaries of individual communities, these notarial deeds were legally sanctioning the collective use of a defined territory. However, as cities and regional states began to acquire copies of these records for their own archives and then used them to settle territorial disputes, the *instrumenta confinationum* came to sanction change also in the borders between *contadi* and larger dominions. As municipal and later regional authorities employed these records to legitimize territorial claims, individual communities saw the extent of their collective spaces legitimized by a superior power. This goes to show how, while reflecting the arrangements of local boundaries, these records could also have a direct impact on the shape of state frontiers.

Borders and the Politics of Space in Late Medieval Italy: Milan, Venice, and their Territories. Luca Zenobi,
Oxford University Press. © Luca Zenobi 2023. DOI: 10.1093/oso/9780198876861.003.0007

6. COMMITTING BORDERS TO PAPER 159

While records made borders, they were, in turn, also made by them. Making, challenging, and even crossing borders generated maps and a variety of written documents in fifteenth-century Italy. As seen in Chapter 3, the *confinium compositio* of 1456 was nothing but the end point of a well-recorded series of negotiations. As these unfolded, the negotiators produced a large corpus of correspondence, extracted documents from both local and central archives, and even commissioned visual representations. In addition, the text of the *compositio* itself and the documentation that led to its final form would then serve as the starting point for future disputes. As such, they were referenced or simply copied entirely in several chanceries across the region.[1] Given the potential for further conflicts, actions concerning borders were constantly written about and filed away. It follows that, while intersecting with the realms of ideas, mobility, and social practice, borders also shaped and were shaped by the mechanisms of record-keeping. Let us then consider how borders were committed to paper in late medieval Italy and how the resulting documentation was then stored and made available for future negotiations.

In considering borders *sub specie scripturarum*,[2] the chapter will adopt the methodological suggestion that the way in which records came to be and were then archived is a profitable field of inquiry in its own right. In truth, archivists and historians alike have long seen archives as sites where knowledge and information are not only ordered and stored but also challenged and newly produced.[3] But it is only in the last two decades, inspired by the cultural turn in the humanities, that scholars have begun to explore more fully contingent practices of record-keeping not just as a useful guide for navigating the archives but as products and at the same time producers of the defining characteristics of an era.[4] Just recently, specialists have drawn attention to the material dimension of archives and to their role as sites of power, conflict, and interaction for a wide range of social groups.[5] In Italy, the same sensitivity towards the way in which records were produced,

---

[1] ASVe, *Miscellanea* 40, 4 August 1456; ASMi, *Registri* 39, cc. 37r–38v; BAMi, ms. L 90 suss, cc. 150r–165v; BMBg, *Confini*, ms. 98 R 27, cc. 22r–24v; BCCr, *Ducali* 1, 109r–110v.

[2] To paraphrase Lazzarini, 'Transformations documentaires'.

[3] Ketelaar, 'Archival Turns and Returns'; Bastian, 'Moving the Margins to the Middle'.

[4] Perhaps the most coherent contribution to the development of the field was made by the publication of three successive special issues of the journal *Archival Science*: Cook and Schwartz, *Archives, Records, and Powers*; Blair and Milligan, *Toward a Cultural History of Archives*; and Head, *Archival Knowledge Cultures*.

[5] Consider in particular two other special issues: de Vivo, Guidi, and Silvestri, *Archival Transformations*; and Corens, Peters, and Walsham, *The Social History of the Archive*.

160 BORDERS AND THE POLITICS OF SPACE IN LATE MEDIEVAL ITALY

stored, and rearranged has been combined with a vast inquiry into the growth and development of the distinctive polities of the peninsula. The emergence of city-communes has thus been placed side by side with the appearance of a new documentary system run by notaries.[6] Equally, historians of the fourteenth and fifteenth centuries have established a strong correlation between the development of regional states and the affirmation of their chanceries as laboratories in which innovative documentary practices were developed: the introduction of new written forms, the adoption of a shared language, the establishment of a continuous flow of letters between individual states and between central chanceries and peripheral officials, and finally the adoption of tools that allowed them to navigate this booming 'world of paper' in the longer term.[7] Following Isabella Lazzarini, Italian historians have framed this line of inquiry as the 'documentary history of institutions', a careful definition that places emphasis on the multiple forms of political organization (*istituzioni*) that took part in this process.[8]

When it comes to borders, however, their intersection with the history of record-keeping has been addressed to the greatest extent only by early modernists.[9] This is due to the availability of extensive series left behind by magistracies which were set up exclusively to deal with border matters. By the time the Italian Wars came to an end in the late 1550s, France had renounced its claims over the peninsula, while Spain had strengthened its hold over both Milan and the South. Yet once the dust had settled, it became clear that although new actors were now running the show, the internal perimeters of the Italian stage had hardly changed. While the borders between regional polities were already well established, the presence of new foreign powers prompted Italians to set up magistracies that could prevent future disputes—and, thus, conflicts in which they knew they had little hope of prevailing. This was especially true of the Republic of Venice, which had gone from facing a state of comparable size, wealth, and population (the Duchy of Milan) to bordering directly the mighty Spanish empire.

---

[6] Maire Vigueur, 'Révolution documentaire'; Bartoli Langeli, 'Notariato, documentazione'.

[7] Senatore, Uno mundo de carta. On these developments, see generally Lazzarini, 'Le Pouvoir de l'écriture'; and Lazzarini, 'De la *révolution scripturaire*'.

[8] The term was first introduced in Lazzarini, 'La nomination des officiers'. A programmatic manifesto can be found in Lazzarini, 'Introduzione: scritture e potere'.

[9] It must be noted that bringing the written dimension of medieval borders to the fore was perhaps the most innovative approach adopted in the recent volume edited by Guglielmotti, *Distinguere, separare, condividere*. For the medieval period, however, that remains an approach that is still far from being fully explored, as noted by Tigrino, 'Azioni, trascrizioni, archiviazioni'.

6. COMMITTING BORDERS TO PAPER 161

In 1554, Venice became the first Italian polity to establish an office devoted to the preservation of state borders.[10] The office was held by two patricians appointed by the Senate, who took the title of *provveditori ai confini*. They conducted much of their affairs in the doge's palace, where they were given a room with direct access to the Republic's secret archive, the *Camera dei confini*.[11] It was a technical rather than an executive office, whose primary duty was the acquisition, arrangement, and provision of maps and documents concerning borders. The power to implement border policy remained with the Senate, but the senators could now call on the *provveditori* to provide practical information. In the cities of the mainland dominion, the task of preserving the memory of state borders and visiting the peripheries to obtain new records was assigned to sister offices. By way of example, between 1585 and 1795, Bergamo's own *Camera dei confini* gathered enough documentation to fill more than a hundred bulky tomes.[12] The size and systematic organization of these archives explain why scholars have been able to study early modern borders in close connection with contemporary practices of record-keeping.[13]

Rightly, historians have related the establishment of these offices to the growth of central bureaucracies and generally to the development of early modern statehood. Inevitably, however, this has also led them to characterize the documentary history of borders and border-making as a belated phenomenon, positing that little attention had been paid previously to managing their written memory. Compared with the systematic means by which sixteenth-century *camere* organized their archives, the ways in which

---

[10] Venice was followed closely by Florence, where an equivalent magistracy was set up in 1560: Benigni and Vivoli, 'Progetti politici e organizzazione d'archivi'. Perhaps inhibited by Spanish and then Austrian government, the Milanese took almost two centuries to follow their example: Adami, 'La magistratura dei confini'. In 1753, when a *commissario ai confini* was finally appointed, there was so much to catch up with that local officers were forced to copy seminal documents and even entire inventories from the archives of Brescia and Bergamo: e.g. in ASMi, *Confini* 238 and 271.

[11] Adami, *I magistrati ai confini*; Pitteri, 'I confini della Repubblica di Venezia'.

[12] Cavalieri, 'L'Archivio della Camera'. Consider also the detailed inventory compiled by one of the *Camera*'s chancellors, Giovanni Maironi da Ponte: BMBg, *Salone Furietti* Ar 22; and the decrees which directed officeholders to take proper care of the local archive and then prepare a register of all maps and charts concerning borders: BMBg, *Confini*, ms. 96 R 2, 17 February 1628 and 16 May 1648.

[13] In addition to those mentioned in the footnotes above, examples include the *Assunteria di Confini* in Bologna, whose archive has recently been studied by Carbonara, *Between Cartography and Representation*; Lucca's *Offizio sopra le differenze dei confini*, on which see the notes in Sabbatini, 'L'occhio dell'ambasciatore', 111–20; the *Giunta dei Confini* in Genoa, on which see Gardini, 'The Use and Reuse of Documents'; and the equivalent institutions of the Savoyard state, on which see Mongiano, 'Delimitare e governare'.

162 BORDERS AND THE POLITICS OF SPACE IN LATE MEDIEVAL ITALY

fifteenth-century Milan, Venice, and other polities recorded information about their borders may indeed appear inattentive, almost an indicator of the alleged fluidity and muddled nature of medieval borders themselves. Yet the absence of dedicated offices, with the resulting lack of a unified archive, does not mean that concerted efforts to collect, store, and share information about borders were not prevalent already in the Late Middle Ages. Rather than judging the efficiency of late medieval systems against early modern standards, this chapter will explore the distributed handling of records concerning borders in the context of contemporary practices of record-keeping. In so doing, the chapter will test once again the main premise behind this book, which is that medieval borders should be understood in the light of the distinctive features of the society to which they belonged. We opened the chapter by suggesting that, due to its performative nature, the making of records was in itself a form of border-making: committing borders to paper was a way to inscribe and advance one's claims over space. By investigating the role played by different actors in managing the records of borders, the chapter will also add a new dimension to our inquiry into the participative framework in which late medieval territoriality was constructed.

At the Centre

For much of the medieval period in Italy, the world of writing and archiving revolved around notaries. Originally just trusted professionals offering their services to the newborn city-communes, notaries soon became the centre of civic bureaucracies. However, over the fourteenth and fifteenth centuries, the formation of large regional polities saw notaries replaced by secretaries and chancellors as the new masters of public records.[14] More importantly, princely and republican chanceries extended their sphere of influence way beyond that which had previously fallen under the remit of urban chanceries. They handled a constant flow of correspondence with both local magistrates and diplomatic agents, ensured that paperwork was shared efficiently between offices, and took care of preserving the surge of records they wrote and received in a way that would then allow for efficient consultation. Compared with their predecessors, fifteenth-century chanceries lay also at

---

[14] For this transformation, consider the classic essay by Bartoli Langeli, 'La documentazione degli stati italiani'; together with the recent overview by Lazzarini, 'Records, Politics and Diplomacy'.

6. COMMITTING BORDERS TO PAPER 163

the centre of the decision-making process. Not only did they handle the day-to-day documentary practice of government, but they were themselves a direct extension of it. More than just a technical expression of princely or republican power, the Renaissance chancery was widely regarded as the very heart of the state (*cor status nostri*).[15] It is thus at the chancery that we should first look in our search for a centralized effort to produce, store, and circulate records concerning borders.

While the analysis that follows seeks to draw a broad picture of how Italian chanceries wrote about borders and preserved their memory in the Quattrocento, it is important to note that constitutional differences and circumstantial factors led to the survival of fundamentally different archives in Venice and Milan. Compared with its Milanese equivalent, the Venetian Chancery was less of a direct extension of the authority of the prince and more of a separate office at the disposal of the Republic's major councils: the Council of Ten, the Senate, and the Great Council. The Chancery made no official transcripts of the internal discussions held by these councils, but it was responsible for passing on their resolutions (*deliberazioni*) to the specific magistracies entrusted with their execution. The Chancery would then transcribe each paper into parchment volumes (*registri*) so as to secure their immediate conservation and facilitate their future use.[16] As Elisa Della Mea has shown for the sixteenth century, it is especially in the volumes of the Senate that one may find resolutions concerning borders; these included the appointment of special deputies, the commission of frontier inspections, and the instructions sent to mainland governors on the matter.[17] In the fifteenth century, by contrast, records of this kind remained scattered across the *senato* series, which suggests that the appointment of the *provveditori* (in the 1550s) was the Senate's first centralized attempt to take care of documentation concerning boundaries and frontiers.

This does not mean that the Venetian Chancery paid little or no attention to the written memory of state borders. A separate branch of the Chancery, the *Cancelleria secreta*, was devoted to managing sensitive records, including those resulting from diplomatic activity.[18] Established at the beginning of the fifteenth century, the Secret Chancery was gradually transformed into

---

[15] De Vivo, 'Cœur de l'état'.

[16] On the operations of the Venetian chancery and archive, consider Viggiano, 'Le carte della repubblica'; and de Vivo, 'Ordering the Archive'.

[17] Della Mea, *La sicurezza incerta*, 16–21.

[18] On the Secret Chancery, see de Vivo, 'Cœur de l'état', 717–19; and generally Pozza, 'La Cancelleria'.

164   BORDERS AND THE POLITICS OF SPACE IN LATE MEDIEVAL ITALY

the documentary centre of foreign policy—a development that can be seen in particular from the 1460s, when the Council of Ten, which had risen to manage the Republic's relations with its neighbours, brought the *Secreta* under its control.[19] In the 1570s, two consecutive fires caused serious damage to its archive; however, inventories compiled during the 1530s and 1540s reveal that the Secret Chancery housed several records concerning borders, including treaties with foreign powers and dispatches sent to ambassadors abroad, governors in the peripheries, and finally special deputies, such as those charged with settling borders disputes.[20] The near complete loss of both internal and external correspondence for the Quattrocento makes it virtually impossible to gauge the documentary practices adopted by the Chancery for dealing with the recording of border negotiations. Yet the fact that the *provveditori ai confini* were later given a chamber with direct access to the *Secreta* confirms that the Secret Chancery was undoubtedly the place where records concerning borders were stored and collected in fifteenth-century Venice.

Given the patchiness of the Venetian *Secreta*, the analysis that follows will draw primarily on material held in Milan. This is not to deny that the Milanese archive also suffered from dramatic losses in the fifteenth century. Following the death of duke Filippo Maria, in 1447, most of the Visconti holdings were destroyed or dispersed by riots.[21] In the 1450s, however, the operations of the Milanese Chancery were relaunched on a much larger scale by the arrival of two new actors on the scene: the first is Francesco Sforza, the new master of the city; the second is Cicco Simonetta, his first secretary.[22] Following his many years as condottiere, the first Sforza duke was determined to set up and maintain an efficient system for the collection and management of diplomatic information, an obsession that soon earned him the title of 'master of news' (*signore de novelle*).[23] The rise of Sforza coincided not only with the development of new forms of diplomacy but also with a political and institutional process that turned the Milanese

---

[19] On the Council of Ten and Venetian foreign policy, consider the classic essay by Knapton, 'Il Consiglio dei Dieci'; together with Conzato, 'Sulle *faccende* da *praticare occultamente*'.

[20] ASVe, *Secreta* (*Indici*) 573 and 804. On these inventories and the broader project of *renovatio archivii* which caused their compilation, see Lazzarini, 'Materiali per una didattica delle scritture', 82–5; and Salmini, 'Buildings, furnishing, access and use', 102–4.

[21] The vicissitudes of the Visconti archives have been followed closely by Leverotti, 'L'archivio dei Visconti'. On the wider motives and significance of such episodes, see De Vincentiis, 'Memorie bruciate'.

[22] Broadly on these developments, see Leverotti, 'La cancelleria dei Visconti e degli Sforza'.

[23] On Francesco Sforza and his avid interest in information-gathering, see Lazzarini, *Communication and Conflict*, 69–85; and Senatore, Uno mundo de carta, 251–63.

6. COMMITTING BORDERS TO PAPER   165

Chancery into the epicentre of both his power over the Duchy and his influence over the rest of the peninsula.[24] Cicco, for his part, had a real talent, if not an obsession of his own, for ordering records all kinds and for compiling accurate lists of events, names, and expenditures. As first secretary, he was able to recover part of the Visconti archive and established what, at the time, was arguably the most advanced system for the management of diplomatic records.[25] By the death of Francesco Sforza in 1466, the joint will and predisposition of the duke and his first secretary had turned the Milanese Chancery into a well-oiled machine where records concerning borders were given special attention and have partly survived for our consideration.

By far the most ubiquitous way in which borders were discussed and committed to paper in Quattrocento Italy was the letter. Developed in conjunction with the growth of central chanceries and information networks, the *littera clausa* soon became the most common form of political communication.[26] Diplomatic letters sat at the intersection of public and private documents: they were not as private as the correspondence of wealthy merchants nor were they as public as humanistic correspondence designed to be copied and circulated. While they were flexible records conceived primarily for everyday use, they had to follow strict formal patterns in order to guarantee their authenticity. These included the inclusion of appropriate seals and the use of a recognizable structure.[27] Among other recommendations, the Milanese Chancery would often exhort the duke's ambassadors to write letters that dealt concisely with a single issue (*lettere separate*), as opposed to letters that engaged with several subjects at once (*lettere miste*).[28] As a result, it is not uncommon to find dispatches that addressed the matter of borders specifically.

Letters concerning borders were typically the product of ongoing negotiations. As talks unfolded, the deputies in charge of settling a given dispute (*procuratori*) or the diplomats liaising with the other party (*oratori*) reported to the Chancery about their progress. Every letter opened with a brief

---

[24] A development first discussed by Fubini, 'Appunti sui rapporti diplomatici'; and later reassessed by Leverotti, '*Diligentia, obedientia*'.

[25] On Simonetta and his role in the Milanese chancery, see Simonetta, *Rinascimento segreto*, 127–51; and now Covini, *Potere, ricchezza e distinzione*, 211–30.

[26] On the political use of correspondence more generally, consider Boutier, Sandi, and Rouchon, *Politique par correspondance*; and Giorgi and Occhi, *Carteggi tra basso medioevo ed età moderna*.

[27] On diplomatic letters, see Lazzarini, 'L'informazione politico-diplomatica'; and now Covini, Figliuolo, Lazzarini, and Senatore, 'Pratiche e norme'.

[28] Senatore, Uno mundo de carta, 231–4.

166   BORDERS AND THE POLITICS OF SPACE IN LATE MEDIEVAL ITALY

reference to the proposal they had been instructed to bring forward, followed by an account of how the other party had received it. When more than one issue was under discussion, the letter would be divided into multiple paragraphs (*capitoli*) so as to address each matter individually. For instance, in the weeks leading up to the *confinium compositio* of 1456, the dispatches reporting on the negotiations taking place in Venice addressed a whole bundle of disputes, including those about the valleys between Lecco and Bergamo, those about the roads through the Cremasco, and others concerning lands along the river Adda and the Fosso Bergamasco.[29] While deputies and diplomats reported regularly to central chanceries, they were in turn the recipients of written instructions concerning borders. These included the official mandates through which legal deputies were given the authority to negotiate in the name of their masters (*mandati*)[30] and the instructions sent to individual diplomats following their designation (*istruzioni*).[31] In addition, both deputies and diplomats were sent further missives on a regular basis over the course of their mission. At the height of the negotiations for the *confinium compositio*, for example, the duke might send his representatives in Venice up to three letters in a single day.[32]

Still, the fact that borders and border negotiations, in particular, were regularly discussed in letters is not in itself evidence of a centralized effort to produce, collect, and store documentation concerning borders. In this respect, the correspondence of the Milanese Chancery is no different from the deliberations of the Venetian Senate: both addressed borders in writing and kept plenty of copies of such records, but they did so only as part of the everyday practice of documenting government. In essence, records

---

[29] ASMi, *Carteggio* 343, 7, 18 and 28 July 1456.

[30] When registered in paper volumes, the texts of *mandati* can still be found in the midst of other records. The original parchment document, on the other hand, was meant to be carried by the bearer, so only a handful of these have survived. Among these, there is the *mandatus* issued by the doge to the governors of Bergamo and Brescia in 1456 so that they could find a settlement in his name regarding the borders with the duchy. As the two deputies reached the Milanese court, their mandate must have been presented to the Milanese chancery—if not to the duke himself. This explains its survival in the ducal archive, where it was found by the *provveditori ai confini* in the late eighteenth century (ASMi, *Confini* 255, 14 May 1456).

[31] Like other forms of *litterae*, the *instructio* evolved to meet new diplomatic needs in the Quattrocento, as discussed by Lazzarini, 'Lettere, minute, registri', 454. A prime example comes from the late 1460s, when Galeazzo Maria Sforza, Francesco's son and heir to the duchy, entrusted Giovanni Arcimboldi, then bishop of Novara and Milanese envoy for the renewal of the Italian League in Venice, with patching up an ongoing quarrel between the community of Quinzano (Bresciano, on the northern bank of the river Oglio) and that of Bordolano (Cremonese, on the southern bank of the river): ASMi, *Confini* 239, 9 April 1469.

[32] ASMi, *Carteggio* 343, 21 July 1456.

6. COMMITTING BORDERS TO PAPER 167

regarding borders were treated in the same way as every other record issued by these offices; as such, they were left scattered throughout the series of diplomatic correspondence (in Milan) or the volumes of the Senate (in Venice), where one may still find them today. Like the Venetian *Secreta*, however, the duke's own Secret Chancery had specific strategies in place for the extraction and preservation of documentation concerning borders.

On a temporary basis, the Milanese secretaries compiled short dossiers on the subject. Sometimes called *sommari*,[33] these dossiers served to keep track of the grievances raised by frontier communities and neighbouring powers, as well as to monitor ongoing disputes. To compile them, secretaries drew on two main sources of information: the first was the two-way correspondence between the Chancery and its agents; the second was the petitions sent by individual subjects and foreign dignitaries. Once redacted, most dossiers would remain in the Chancery for both immediate use and future reference. In 1472, for example, the ducal secretaries drafted a detailed report of every incident in which Venetian subjects had trespassed upon Milanese dominions over the past few years.[34] While this particular *sommario* focuses specifically on the boundary between the Bresciano and the Cremonese, it presents nonetheless the full range of border controversies which the Chancery was intent on recording. Perhaps half of the quarrels included stemmed from the improper use of the river Oglio, such as building irrigation ditches, calling at unlicensed ports, and setting up unauthorized fishing facilities. The other half featured more common border disputes, including those about the circulation of people, the collection of tax and duties, and the exploitation of properties located on both sides of the boundary. Dossiers of this kind could then to be used to share information on borders with other branches of government. A few months later, for example, the document was sent to some of the Milanese diplomats stationed abroad, while in 1475, the duke's councillors used it to devise a new plan of action for settling controversies about the river Oglio.[35] The compilation of *sommari* of border disputes was thus not only a way of preserving their immediate memory but also a means of informing policies that would then lead to their resolution.

On a more permanent basis, the Milanese Chancery compiled bound registers. Compared with the *sommari*, which were typically written on

---

[33] More broadly, on the chancery's use of *sommari* in the preparation of diplomatic dispatches, see Senatore, 'Ai confini del *mundo de carta*', 48–50.

[34] ASMi, *Confini* 314, s.d. but datable to 1472 on the basis of circumstantial information.

[35] ASMi, *Confini* 239, 9 August 1475.

168   BORDERS AND THE POLITICS OF SPACE IN LATE MEDIEVAL ITALY

everyday paper, these were originally made of parchment. They also comprised hundreds of pages, as opposed to the four or five that made up the average *sommario*. More importantly, chancery registers did not contain original material, that is, writings that drew together information from other records; instead, they included copies of the full text of records. While *sommari* were routinely made by the Chancery, registers concerning borders were generally prepared when the need became most pressing. In Milan, this had never been truer than in the 1450s and 1460s. As Cicco Simonetta launched his programme of reforms, the Chancery was already at the centre of Francesco Sforza's diplomatic attempts to see his newfound position as duke of Milan recognized by other major powers. In addition, the reformed Chancery was immediately placed in charge of handling the documentary dimension of the negotiations that then led to the peace of Lodi in 1454—not to mention the *confinium compositio* of 1456. Due to the dissolution of the Visconti archive, the Chancery was forced to take on this crucial role without being able to rely on much of the material that had framed pre-existing relations between the Duchy and other neighbouring powers (pacts, treaties, *arbitramenta*) and between the Duchy and the terri-tories that were now the object of contention (donations, privileges, *deditiones*). Mindful of this rocky start, Simonetta soon pushed forward with his programme of reforms: he hired new scribes, divided the Chancery into further branches, and sent to Pavia to recover what remained of the Visconti's private archive.[36]

Building on these records, the Chancery produced several registers which were specially designed to house the written foundations of ducal power. Given the circumstances, strong emphasis was placed on retrieving documents that supported the Sforza claim to the Duchy or helped to hold it against external competitors, starting with Venice. As new pacts were signed and disputes settled, the registers were updated with further mater-ial, thus holding both past and current documents concerning the relation-ships between the Duchy and its neighbours. The material remnants of these practices are sometimes evident from brief annotations left on the original documentation. The two *instrumenta acceptationis* discussed in Chapter 2, for example, namely the records that first sanctioned the delivery of ceded territorial bodies after the peace of Lodi, survive both as standalone documents and as registered copies. On the back of each original, one can

---

[36] On these developments, see Leverotti, '*Diligentia, obedentia*'; and Behne, 'Archivordnung und Staatsordnung'.

6. COMMITTING BORDERS TO PAPER 169

still read the note left by one of Simonetta's scribes: 'registratum in registro'.[37] The practice of updating registers became less regular after the death of Francesco Sforza; however, further registers were made under his son, Galeazzo Maria, mainly thanks to Cicco's determination.[38]

Of these,[39] the most relevant to this inquiry is register 18. This features the most notable records at the beginning. They were the pacts, treaties, rulings, and charters that evidenced the duke's legal position in relation to other powers.[40] Pacts and treaties were followed by letters reporting on their negotiation, that is, by the records that most mentioned borders. When present, the Milanese secretaries would also transcribe the documents that the duke and his deputies exchanged as part of their correspondence. These could take the form of informal texts as well as authentic excerpts from previous treaties. In the summer of 1454, for instance, the duke wrote a letter to his ambassadors in Venice attaching not only a *sommario* discussing passages drawn from the Visconti archive but also some of his own memories ('ricordi vecchi') of the time he acted as an arbiter for the peace of Cremona.[41] Finally, the register included much of the paper trail left behind by the rearrangement of state borders. In addition to diplomatic correspondence, this included the *instrumenta acceptationis* as well as the many drafts and counter-ratifications of the *confinium compositio*.[42] It is clear, then, that records concerning borders did not feature as mere attachments to a uniform series of prominent pacts and treaties; rather, they were organically integrated into what was essentially a functional collection of multiform records documenting the territorial modifications that, from the start of the Lombard Wars in the mid-1420s to the aftermath of the

---

[37] ASMi, *Carteggio* 1526, 17 April 1454 (Bergamasco) and 29 April 1454 (Bresciano).

[38] These registers were first discussed in some detail by MANARESI, *Inventari e regesti del R. archivio di stato di Milano* (vol. I), xxv–xxvii. See now Covini, *Potere, ricchezza e distinzione*, 227; and especially Lazzarini, *L'ordine delle scritture*, 310–7.

[39] ASMi, *Registri* 35, 37, 39, and 42.

[40] ASMi, *Registri* 18, cc. 100r–153r (Ferrara), 198r–208v (Cremona), 248r–251v (Rivoltella), and 379r–386v (Lodi). In this sense, the register in question could almost be likened to one of the books of rights (*libri iurium*) compiled by single city-states to preserve their foundational records: Rovere, 'I *libri iurium*'. Perhaps more appropriately, it could be likened to one of the Venetian memorial books (*libri commemoriali*), a series of volumes containing transcripts of the most consequential acts of the republic—a comparison already made by Somaini, *Geografie politiche italiane*, 110.

[41] ASMi, *Registri* 18, cc. 406v–409v. By way of example, the original letter is still kept in the main series of correspondence between Milan and Venice: ASMi, *Carteggio* 341, 1 September 1454.

[42] ASMi, *Registri* 18, cc. 387r–388r (17 and 29 April 1454) and cc. 458r–462r (12 and 27 August 1456).

170 BORDERS AND THE POLITICS OF SPACE IN LATE MEDIEVAL ITALY

peace of Lodi in the mid-1450s, had changed the shape and extent of the Milanese dominion.

The consideration which the Chancery gave to collecting records in these registers suggests that they functioned not only as repositories of information but also as tools of government. Transcribing records onto their pages was certainly a way of ensuring their conservation and allowing for their recovery. While loose papers were susceptible to water and could easily be mislaid or burnt by fire, records copied in chancery registers were made to withstand serious damage. Besides, they were typically rearranged chronologically and then listed in *rubriche* (indexes of subject matter) so as to facilitate their swift retrieval. However, registers could also inform the operations of the Chancery and, as a result, inspire the very practice of government. As Filippo de Vivo has noted with regard to the Venetian archives, records such as written reports of negotiations were kept not only to document diplomatic activity but also 'to serve as guides to foreign policy itself'.[43] As we saw in Chapter 5, fifteenth-century registers were efficient databases to which any member of the Chancery and the wider government could turn when the need arose.[44]

Chancery registers also functioned as separate archives in their own right. When registers collected the same kind of documentation (letters of appointment, patents and licences, outgoing missives, decrees and ordinances) they reflected the specific tasks of a distinct branch of the Chancery, thus forming an institutional archive of their distinct documentary practices.[45] On the other hand, when registers collected records concerning borders and the state's relations with neighbouring powers, they formed a virtual archive, that is, a purposely designed collection drawing together documents of all sorts:[46] from letters sent and received to the text of pacts and treaties, to specific legal records like the *instrumenta acceptationis*. Indeed, as a repository of all things borders, registers of this kind prefigured the much larger collections of the Venetian *camere dei confini*. As such,

---

[43] De Vivo, 'Archives of Speech', 537.

[44] On fifteenth-century registers and especially diplomatic archives as functional 'databanks', see Dover, 'Deciphering the Diplomatic Archives', 299.

[45] See also Lazzarini, 'Registres princiers'.

[46] The distinction between collections and archives proper is drawn from archival science. Italian archivists, in particular, have long theorized that what defines an archive as such is the existence of an original bond linking together all the documents produced and naturally deposited by an institution while conducting its ordinary business. The theory was introduced by Cencetti, 'Il fondamento teorico'; critiqued by Pavone, 'Ma poi è tanto pacifico'; problematized further by Romiti, 'Riflessioni sul significato del vincolo'; and later adapted to digital records by Duranti, 'The Archival Bond'.

their function was not only technical but symbolic.[47] They were the place where documents concerning borders were gathered, stored, and sometimes retrieved to settle controversies; they were the functional repository from which the duke could draw to evidence his territorial claims. At the same time, they were the immediate manifestation of chanceries' deliberate and conscious effort to preserve and put to further use the memory of borders and border negotiations in fifteenth-century Italy.

In the end, fifteenth-century Italian polities did not develop institutions such as the *provveditori ai confini*. Yet it would be wrong to take the absence of a specialized magistracy as a sign that these polities were not interested in the written memory of borders. Records concerning borders were seen as part of the wider corpus of texts documenting a power's relationships with its neighbours, including pacts and treaties as well as diplomatic correspondence. As such, they were not handled by a separate magistracy but rather organically integrated in the documentation of the centralized office which was then responsible for managing the written outputs of foreign policy, the Secret Chancery. Similarly, the fact that the Chancery never built a separate archive or even a room to house records concerning borders (a *camera dei confini*, as it was called later) does not mean that they failed to build repositories of readily available information on the subject. This becomes immediately evident when we consider the habit of drafting dossiers on border disputes (*sommari*) or collecting relevant documentation in chancery registers. These represented a major step forward from the *libri finium*, since they encompassed not just descriptions of community boundaries but records that acknowledged the more complex territorial hierarchy of the Late Middle Ages: from the borders of the state as a whole to the boundaries of its constituent territories (such as cities, townships, fiefs, and federations).

In the Peripheries

While central chanceries were undoubtedly the driving force behind an effort to collect, preserve, and circulate documentation concerning borders, a variety of bodies carried out parallel and sometimes converging practices

---

[47] On pre-modern archives functioning on both a functional and a conceptual level, see Head, 'Knowing like a State'; as well as the classic essay by O'Toole, 'The Symbolic Significance of Archives'.

172 BORDERS AND THE POLITICS OF SPACE IN LATE MEDIEVAL ITALY

in the peripheries. Some had developed documentary tools to handle the written memory of borders long before Renaissance chanceries asserted themselves as the heart of the state. As touched upon in Chapter 1, the offices of individual city-states compiled *libri finium*. These 'books of borders' collected descriptions of the boundaries of all the villages that made up the *contado*.[48] The practice built on the custom of recording community boundaries in the form of legal records, the so-called *instrumenta confinationum*. As explained in Chapter 4, by piecing together detailed descriptions of the boundaries of individual villages, cities were effectively documenting a legal picture of the borders of their *contadi*. As individual cities were then annexed to large regional formations, such as the Duchy of Milan and the Republic of Venice, urban centres lost their independence but retained much of their written material. Conquest, to put it another way, was not accompanied by the transfer of muniments to the centre of the new dominion. Although few have survived, it is likely that most *libri finium* remained stored in close proximity to the city hall—if not inside it, where the records of board meetings, fiscal surveys, and judicial archives would also continue to be kept.[49] This suggests that even after Renaissance chanceries began taking care of the written memory of state borders, individual city-communes kept handling documents concerning their own boundaries.

Smaller centres, such as towns and walled boroughs, present a slightly different picture. Although they were sometimes in charge of a limited district, this was never recognized as a true *contado*. As a result, their influence over the surrounding area did not translate into compiling collections such as the books of borders developed by cities. However, this does not mean that smaller centres had no interest in managing equivalent documentation, particularly when they were placed in frontier areas. Around 1490, for instance, the town of Lecco compiled a *catasto* of all the properties situated by the *Chiusa* of Vercurago. This took the form of a bound register of all the lands located by the barrier that marked the border between the Lecchese and the Bergamasco, that is to say, between Milanese and Venetian territories.[50]

---

[48] Given the present state of knowledge, the only surviving example of a *liber finium* for the area under consideration is Bergamo's *Codice Patetta* (BAVa, *Codice Patetta*, ms. 1387). On the survival and use of one such *liber* in the fifteenth century, see Francesconi, 'Il confine archiviato'.

[49] As discussed by Varanini, 'Written Public Records', 385–405; and now Lazzarini, 'La memoria della città'.

[50] As a local initiative, there is no doubt that the records of this *catasto* were kept in Lecco. Although they have not survived, we can still learn about them through the operations of Milan's *provveditori ai confini*, who extracted data from the archive in the late eighteenth century: ASMi, *Confini* 270, f. 'Muro della Chiusa', s.d.

6. COMMITTING BORDERS TO PAPER 173

The town of Crema was possibly the most attentive to the matter, especially after the peace of Lodi transformed the Cremasco into a Venetian enclave surrounded by Milanese territories. In 1473, following a fire that destroyed much of the municipal archive, the council appointed four deputies (one for each of the town's four gates) to search for surviving records regarding the matter of borders and then copy them in bound registers. As the councillors put it in their deliberations, this was done not only to preserve the memory of those records but to avert future conflicts and disorders.[51] For towns such as Lecco and Crema, namely for centres placed in the interstices between large regional formations, gathering and preserving the written memory of borders were key to protecting their territory against the encroachment of neighbouring powers.

Outside cities and towns, documents concerning borders were sometimes kept by single individuals. Family archives followed the course of dynastic events and so have survived only in exceptional cases.[52] However, it is still possible to glean some details on people's documentary practices by considering the correspondence between public authorities and private individuals. In 1468, for example, Bartolomeo Martinenghi came under fire from the Milanese toll keepers in Soncino, so he wrote a letter to the local officer (*commissario*) to defend his position. Although he was a member of a noble family from Brescia, Martinenghi owned lands on both sides of the river Oglio: on the Soncino side, in the Cremonese, and on the Orzinuovi side, in the Bresciano. The toll keepers accused him of regularly using a boat to transfer goods across the border, a manoeuvre that allowed him to evade the duties which were normally levied on the nearby bridge. Martinenghi responded by stating that he had personally inspected the text of the treaty (the peace of Lodi), which allowed him to claim that no measure against the use of such boats could be found in its terms.[53] While Martinenghi was part of an elite who appreciated the value of written records in advancing their claims, this episode shows that local noblemen had access to documents concerning borders and perhaps even owned copies of them.

In the countryside, however, documents concerning borders were most typically kept by entire communities. Just like small city-republics and large regional formations, rural communes looked after their territories and

---

[51] BCCr, *Provisioni* 7, c. 18v, 23 January 1473.

[52] On family archives and their distinct documentary practices, see Gamberini, 'La memoria dei gentiluomini'; and broadly Varanini, 'Archivi di famiglie aristocratiche'.

[53] ASMi, *Carteggio* 1517bis, 5 March 1468. On the *milites* Martinenghi and their long-term economic prominence in the lower Bresciano, see Nardini, 'I signori della pianura'.

174   BORDERS AND THE POLITICS OF SPACE IN LATE MEDIEVAL ITALY

guarded them against their neighbours. It follows that they had a vested interest in retaining records that documented their spatial dimension. As Massimo Della Misericordia has shown with regard to the communities of the Lombard Alps, these records ranged from the minutes of general assemblies, which elected surveyors and border patrols, to lists and notebooks recording the use of local roads and common lands.[54] In addition, the communities of the countryside employed specific records to inscribe the memory of their own boundaries, namely the *instrumenta confinationum*. As seen in Chapter 4, these records were more than a mere description of the village's perimeters; they were a requisite part of the procedure through which the community commemorated the use and possession of its territory. For the purpose of these proceedings, making the record was just as important as physically marking the boundary. Drafting the notarial deed served to legitimize the deed itself (that is, what actually happened) in front of a wider audience: from neighbouring villages to local magistrates and central powers. People died and lands changed hands, but the record protected the memory of the community's continuous use of space. In this sense, just as record-making was an essential component of border-making, record-keeping played a fundamental role in the protection of borders.[55]

While in cities and towns documentation concerning borders was produced and stored by the local chancery, in the communities of the countryside it was entrusted to the care of notaries. In the case of large community federations, such as the Val Camonica, notaries were hired directly by the *universitas* to handle the documentation produced by routine administration and to attend to the records defining the community's position in relation to superior powers (such as tax estimates, jurisdictional privileges, and local statutes).[56] For most rural communities, however, the occasional services of professionals fulfilled all their documentary needs. These came down to two essential tasks. The first was to guarantee the legitimacy of their written business. As long as they met some formal criteria, all notarial records enjoyed universal credibility, so the documents produced for the community were lent the same degree of trustworthiness. The second was

---

[54] Della Misericordia, 'Mappe di carte'.

[55] The intersection between records, identities, and the legitimation of local uses of space has been explored mostly by early modernists. This is particularly true of scholars influenced by the practice of micro history, such as Stopani, 'La memoria dei confini'; and Tigrino, 'Castelli di carte'. For an initial medieval perspective, consider the emphasis placed on written testimonies by Provero, 'Una cultura dei confini'; together with the attention drawn to the manipulation of community memory by Varanini, 'L'invenzione dei confini'.

[56] Signaroli, 'Per una storia archivistica'.

6. COMMITTING BORDERS TO PAPER 175

to ensure the conservation of those records. Thankfully, notaries were already responsible for retaining copies of each and every document they produced. Originally, notarial records were redacted as standalone deeds, so that they could be handed over to the notary's clients, but by the end of the Middle Ages notarial records were seldom written in full; more commonly, they were kept as extended summaries in what was essentially notarial registers, also known as cartularies. Just like chancery registers, cartularies offered an organized repository from which documentation concerning borders could be drawn. Besides, the habit of transmitting registers from father to son or, occasionally, from colleague to colleague ensured the long-term preservation of documents such as the *instrumenta confinationum*.[57] Since notaries lived locally and had deep family roots, the records that documented the community's rights over the surrounding territory were always within reach.[58]

Notaries and noblemen, cities and towns—in the peripheries, a variety of actors were engaged in retrieving, preserving, and sometimes making new records regarding borders. Many of these practices had been in place for decades, if not centuries, and would continue to exist alongside the novel documentary systems developed by Renaissance chanceries: even when they had been annexed to a superior power, territorial bodies kept on managing records documenting rights over their pre-existing claims over space. It was never the intention of central chanceries to replace local practices of record-keeping or to interfere with established modes of knowledge production and preservation in the localities. However, the chanceries' reluctance to pre-emptively draw to the centre documentation concerning borders should not be seen as a mark of neglect but rather as an indication of the trust placed in the existing practices of record-keeping carried out by individual bodies. The same argument should be extended to the documentary practices of individual communities. In the Late Middle Ages, most villages did not possess a genuine archive; yet this does not mean that records documenting community boundaries were not made or kept. Rural communities entrusted the written knowledge of space to the care of notaries—private professionals whose documentary practices were so

---

[57] On the conservation of notarial records in northern Italy and its relation to community memory, see Meyer, 'Hereditary Laws'; as well as Giorgi and Moscadelli, *'Cum acta sua sint'*.

[58] From a number of cases arising in the late sixteenth century, we know that some villages of the Bergamasco were able to retrieve records dating back one or two centuries earlier in order to document their rights over the surrounding countryside: e.g. BMBg, *Confini*, ms. 97 R 5, cc. 1r–11v, 10 October 1292; and BMBg, *Confini*, ms. 96 R 30, cc. 11r–12r, 31 December 1387.

176 BORDERS AND THE POLITICS OF SPACE IN LATE MEDIEVAL ITALY

reliable and universally trusted as to make a community archive, even one that preserved the records of local boundaries, wholly superfluous.

On the Move

It is clear, then, that in late medieval Italy, different records concerning borders were produced and managed in different ways, in different places, and by different actors and bodies. At the centre, state chanceries used periodic dossiers to keep track of ongoing disputes, while also compiling bound registers to collect the written foundations of their territorial authority, such as pacts with foreign powers and border treaties. In the peripheries, documents concerning borders were sometimes collected by the offices of small towns or even by single individuals, while rural communities relied on the expertise of local notaries to manage the memory of their territorial rights, including the *instrumenta confinationum*. Yet it would be wrong to conclude that the two levels (the centres and the peripheries) did not intersect. As the first half of this book has shown, the making of new state borders in the fifteenth century was the result of a composition of the boundaries of pre-existing territories. The arrangement of local boundaries was thus immediately relevant to the establishment of regional frontiers. Whenever discord arose, Milanese and Venetian negotiators settled the dispute by grounding their claims in the existing organization of political spaces. This was done by tracing the jurisdictional affiliation of individual bodies through the political and territorial hierarchy of the time: from the territories of city-states to those of intermediate bodies (such as towns and federations), to those of individual villages. By extension, documenting the disposition of local boundaries became a way to ground one's claims in actual territorial practices. Before drawing some conclusions from this discussion of central and peripheral record-keeping, let us then look more closely at how documentation concerning borders was retrieved and circulated to achieve these aims.

Rural communities were arguably the most basic territorial units of the Italian Middle Ages. In such localities, wealth could be unevenly distributed and social structures could disproportionally favour certain families, yet the community's territory remained uniform and compact. This was accurately reflected in the ceremonial drawing of community boundaries, as recorded by notaries in the *instrumenta confinationum*. Although documents of this kind were produced regularly to protect one's territory from claims by

6. COMMITTING BORDERS TO PAPER   177

neighbouring villages, they often acquired a whole new significance when the territory in question happened to be located at the borders between two regional polities. In Chapter 4, we learned that the boundaries of frontier villages were sometimes recorded in new and updated *instrumenta* in order to provide negotiators with an accurate picture of local territorial arrangements. While the *instrumenta* were produced locally, copies were then acquired by the archives of both Venice and Milan, as well as by the magistracies of the cities whose *contadi* would be directly affected by the displacement of local boundaries. Crema, among others, was especially concerned with the retrieval of records concerning borders from the localities. Not only was this Venetian town an enclave in Milanese territory but its recent promotion to the rank of *civitas* made protecting the integrity of its newfound *districtus* the most pressing task. In the late 1450s, for example, the communities of Capralba and Vailate were drawn into a dispute over the exact location of the boundaries between them. Since these marked the end of the Cremasco (Capralba) and the beginning of the Geradadda (Vailate), which formed part of the Milanese dominion, the town's councillors ordered the local magistrate to gather as much information as he could find, put everything in writing, and send it to Crema.[59] Perhaps enlightened by disputes of this kind, the council later commissioned authentic copies (that is, replicas validated by a notary) of all the *instrumenta* concerning places where the Cremasco bordered Milanese territories (namely the Geradadda, the Lodigiano, and the Cremonese) for storage in the municipal archive.[60]

While local communities were clearly the main provider of written material concerning borders, central powers retrieved information from a number of other sources. An illustrative example of these practices comes from the summer of 1454, when the Milanese Chancery was desperately trying to obtain records that could support the duke's claims to the community of Brivio. The village was strategically located on the Adda's western bank, just south of Lecco, where the Visconti had built a defensive castle and ducal officers manned a bridge over the river. Between the twelfth and thirteenth centuries, thanks to its position on the lower end of the waterway that connected the Alps to the Milanese countryside, Brivio flourished to the point that a new hamlet was established on the eastern bank of the river. This was named Brivio de là (literally, 'Brivio over there'). Although the hamlet was technically located in the *contado* of Bergamo, the two Brivios

---

[59] BCCr, *Provisioni* 2, cc. 194r–194v (28 June 1457) and c. 54r (28 June 1458).
[60] BCCr, *Provisioni* 3, c. 154v, 30 June 1461.

178   BORDERS AND THE POLITICS OF SPACE IN LATE MEDIEVAL ITALY

coexisted peacefully as part of the unified Visconti dominion for much of the fourteenth century. However, as Venice launched its expansion in Lombardy and Milanese territories were divided from those that were once subject to Bergamo, the two Brivios met with opposite fates: the original village and castle remained with the ducal army, whereas the hamlet across the river was brought under Venetian control. As seen in the first half of this book, the territorial culture of the time called for the integrity of spatial units rather than for their disintegration. Accordingly, both parties were able to use the one Brivio they already held to stake a claim over the one they did not. This would allow the victor to place the new state border around the whole of Brivio, gaining control over both banks of the river Adda. The duke's case was based on documentation that a chancery envoy had gathered in Milan and Bergamo. We are not told how he gained access to the archives of a city now subject to a foreign power, but the relations between Venice and Milan were not as tense at this stage, so it is possible that the visit was granted out of diplomatic courtesy or simply thanks to informal backchannels. To demonstrate that it was Milan and not Bergamo which had jurisdiction over the whole of Brivio, the envoy transcribed passages from the municipal statutes of the city. Among other things, he discovered that Brivio was not listed with the communities that were required to introduce fish to the city market. This proved that the jurisdiction of Bergamo did not apply to Brivio or to either bank of the river. Having refuted the Venetian argument, the envoy turned to documentation held in Milan to prove that Brivio was in fact subject to Milanese jurisdiction. He found the answer he needed by searching the papers of the ducal office in charge of collecting state revenues. This showed that Brivio had been paying its share of taxes directly to Milan, thus providing the duke with the evidence required to settle the dispute in his favour.[61]

Documents gathered this way were not only brought to the centre (that is, to the princely or republican chancery) but were also copied and deployed throughout the dominion. In 1454, for instance, the negotiations led by the Venetian governors of Bergamo with the deputies of the duke of Milan were informed by records extracted both from the municipal archives of Bergamo and from the main deposits of the Republic.[62] Local magistrates and specially appointed officers were similarly equipped with supplementary

---

[61] ASMi, *Registri* 18, cc. 408v–409r. On the vicissitudes of the two Brivios, see further Medolago, 'Abitati scomparsi', 72–6.

[62] BMBg, *Confini*, ms. 96 R 12, c. 23r, 17 August 1454.

6. COMMITTING BORDERS TO PAPER   179

information once they reached their posts. Studies by Nadia Covini have shown that architects and engineers possessed extensive knowledge of territorial arrangements, derived from records provided by central chanceries as much as from consultation with local experts.[63] Details of the configuration of local borders were sometimes included when discussing the upkeep of fortifications or the regulation of traffic flows via rivers and roads. More commonly, records concerning borders were sent to the peripheries when controversies arose. In 1485, for example, one of the ducal officers stationed in Cremona was sent copies of the treaty of Lodi so that he could show them, together with letters from the duke himself, to another member of the Martinenghi family, who was also grappling with the fact that the Bresciano and the Cremonese were now divided by a state border.[64]

On occasion, records concerning borders could be sourced in the peripheries only to be passed on to other local actors. In 1452, for example, Francesco Sforza was called upon to exert his newfound authority as duke of Milan in settling a dispute over the boundaries between one of the fiefs which made up his dominion, the county of Fontanellato, and one of the small principalities which bordered the southern edges of the Duchy, the marquisate of Soragna. While the frontier with the territories headed by the Emilian nobility was not as clearly defined as that with the territories held by Venice, the issue was not different in nature from any of the disputes discussed above: since the county of Fontanellato was located in the peripheries of the Duchy, by upholding its boundaries the duke was also upholding those of his dominion. In the end, it became apparent that the issue could be settled by a certain *instrumentum* kept in the archive of a local abbey (San Giovanni di San Donnino). As soon as he heard about it, the duke wrote to the bishop of Parma asking him to make sure that the abbess sent the document in question to the Chancery so that it could then be shown to all the parties involved in the quarrel.[65] Recording borders was thus also a means of information-sharing. In this respect, the Renaissance chancery lived up to its reputation as a site of negotiation and as the true heart of the state in that it put different and sometimes conflicting subjects in communication with each other.

*   *   *

---

[63] Covini, '*Studiando el mappamondo*'; Covini, 'L'Amedeo e il collettivo degli ingegneri'.
[64] ASMi, *Comuni* 12, f. 'Bordolano', 21 February 1485.
[65] ASMi, *Missive* 11, cc. 51v–52r, 17 April 1452.

180 BORDERS AND THE POLITICS OF SPACE IN LATE MEDIEVAL ITALY

In summary, this chapter demonstrates that the record of borders was constantly being committed to paper, reassembled, and preserved for future use by multiple actors and at multiple levels in late medieval Italy: centrally, by chancellors and secretaries recording everything they deemed relevant for future use; in the peripheries, by frontier towns and rural communities preserving the written memory of local boundaries; and on the move, by specially appointed deputies and negotiators. More importantly, the chapter shows that the distributed handling of records concerning borders can be understood as characteristic of contemporary documentary practices—practices that envisaged the involvement of a multiplicity of actors in the creation and keeping of records. Taken as a whole, these documentary practices lend support to two more arguments advanced in this book. The first is that, when explored from an Italian perspective at least, late medieval borders appear to have been more widely acknowledged and clearly situated than is commonly supposed. Indeed, this chapter has shed light on a diffused familiarity with the written memory of medieval borders: from notaries and surveyors to state officials and chancery scribes, records concerning both community boundaries and state frontiers were handled simultaneously and with great care by many different hands.

The second argument advanced by this chapter in unison with the rest of the book is that, more than as an authoritative projection on behalf of the state, the making of late medieval borders should be seen as the product of interactions between a plurality of different actors. As this treatment has shown, painting a more precise picture of borders was the result of a collective effort. Like borders themselves, records concerning borders were not simply constructed from below as well as from above; they were the product of a dialogic process. In the Renaissance chancery, borders were discussed and committed to paper in many different forms: from diplomatic letters to pacts with foreign powers. Yet the image of state borders drawn in these records did not just overlap or obliterate the memory of local arrangements. As we noted in the first half of the book, the boundaries of pre-existing bodies formed the building blocks of the new frontier between regional polities; it was therefore only natural that the memory of state borders was continually supported, if not fully integrated, with records concerning the disposition of local boundaries. As long as multiple sets of borders existed side by side, records as different as major diplomatic treaties between regional powers and series of *confinationes* between local communities could all be used concurrently, and indeed complementarily, to commit borders to paper in late medieval Italy.

7

Drawing the Line?

The Visual Representation of Territorial B/orders

In the history of Italian cartography, the fifteenth century was a time of extraordinary changes. In the Middle Ages, as Paul Harvey famously noted, Italy was already 'the most map-conscious part of Europe'.[1] Coastal centres such as Venice were home to flourishing map-making traditions, including portolans, *mappae mundi*, and charts of the Holy Land. In the Quattrocento, however, Italy came to play a leading role in the transformation not just of Italian map-making but of European cartography more broadly. Change was driven by technical as much as by cultural developments: as fifteenth-century science came to place added value on quantification and precise measurements, the rediscovery of Ptolemy's geography grounded the emergence of a new cartographic culture in the classical world. By the end of the century, the growing print industry and the expansion of humanist networks had already spread that new culture across much of Europe. Coupled with the invention of linear perspective, these novelties paved the way for a new way of making maps, which has thrived to this day.[2]

While these developments were profoundly transformative, the fifteenth century was also a period of remarkable continuity for the history of cartography. Older traditions of Italian map-making were thoroughly informed by Ptolemaic ideas, but they retained nonetheless a medieval substrate. Perhaps the most famous example of this dynamic is Fra Mauro's *Mappa Mundi*, which drew on classical authors and Renaissance humanism as much as on scholasticism and medieval travel literature.[3] A similar blend of cultural influences was almost certainly featured in another pre-existing tradition of

---

[1] Harvey, *The History of Topographical Maps*, 58. More broadly, on the place of Italy in medieval map-making, see Milanesi, 'La cartografia italiana'; and Morse, 'The Role of Maps'.

[2] On the intersections between the circulation of Ptolemy's geography and the diffusion of the printing press within the framework of Renaissance court culture and humanism, see Gentile, 'Umanesimo e cartografia'; and Bouloux, 'La géographie à la cour'.

[3] For the complex intellectual history of Fra Mauro's map, see especially the detailed study by Cattaneo, *Fra Mauro's Mappa Mundi*.

Borders and the Politics of Space in Late Medieval Italy: Milan, Venice, and their Territories. Luca Zenobi, Oxford University Press. © Luca Zenobi 2023. DOI: 10.1093/oso/9780198876861.003.0008

182 BORDERS AND THE POLITICS OF SPACE IN LATE MEDIEVAL ITALY

Italian cartography: the painted wall maps of the peninsula, which are now largely lost. Although surviving evidence suggests that these maps drew on Ptolemy's precise method, their function was not only practical but also rhetorical. In keeping with medieval influences, wall maps were populated with views and symbols that conveyed propagandistic visions of society and allegorical images of power—pictorial elements that were alien to Ptolemy's geography but would have been right at home in medieval cartography.[4]

Scholarship used to frame the measured maps of the Renaissance as the decisive step towards the development of modern cartography—particularly in contrast to medieval influences, which were long dismissed as remnants of an outdated world. Nowadays, however, specialists hold a more balanced view: the entanglement of styles both old and new is now seen as the defining feature of Quattrocento cartography.[5] This paradigm has an obvious heuristic value, providing specialists and non-specialists alike with an overall interpretation of the period in question; yet it runs the risk of overshadowing maps which do not quite fit the narrative which emphasizes the complex mix of continuity and change featured by the fifteenth century. These maps are what anglophone historiography calls regional and district maps, since they focus on a small area and are often centred on a single city.[6] Besides their scale, what sets these maps apart from other fifteenth-century products is the fact that they developed and declined independently of the rediscovery of Ptolemy's geography. While regional and district maps did not partake in the key cartographic transformation of their time, they were not truly representative of a sustained medieval tradition either, for evidence suggests that they flourished only in the Quattrocento. In short, regional and district maps belong to a different tradition of Italian cartography. This is a tradition which is now difficult to grasp, for it was ephemeral and largely confined to painted parchments, but also a tradition which is typical of its time and place of origin, which makes it the ideal object of inquiry for the present chapter.

While doubts have been raised over the reliability and even effectiveness of regional and district cartography, it is clear that these maps were widely put to use in Quattrocento Italy. Scholars often note that, by the

---

[4] On the 'lost world' of painted map cycles before the sixteenth century, see Milanesi, 'Cartografia per un principe senza corte'; and Rosen, *The Mapping of Power*.

[5] Two compelling arguments against progressive interpretations of the history of fifteenth-century cartography can be found in Gautier Dalché, 'Pour une histoire du regard géographique'; and Woodward, 'Cartography and the Renaissance'.

[6] For an overview, see, for now, Harvey, 'Local and Regional Cartography'.

7. DRAWING THE LINE? 183

beginning of the sixteenth century, Renaissance princes were actively counselled to commission maps of the areas they visited and generally to think topographically.[7] Machiavelli's advice to the political and military leader included having 'the country through which he marches described and mapped in such a way that he will know the places, the population, the distances, the roads, the mountains, the rivers, the swamps, and all their characteristics'.[8] Although we do not know whether analogous counsel was given to fifteenth-century rulers, we do know that many of them were already following it. In Ferrara, the Este family can be found drawing 'practical topographies' of regions and districts throughout the Quattrocento. For the first half of the century, we have references to maps of the Ferrarese, maps of Modena and its territory, and maps of Padua, Venice, and other nearby cities. In the second half of the century, we know that the Este commissioned maps of the Polesine of Rovigo (on the border with the Venetian dominion) and even maps of the whole of the Romagna.[9]

While the cartographic paradigm of continuity and change has generally masked the presence of this autonomous tradition of Italian map-making, specialists have offered two initial lines of interpretation for regional and district maps. The first goes back to Paul Harvey, who framed them as an instance of topographical maps.[10] Ptolemy would have seen this in opposition to geography proper and called it simply 'chorography': the rendering of the landscape in pictorial form, typically using symbols and other graphic signs. Following Harvey, emphasis has been placed on the ways in which regional and district maps charted roadways and watercourses, noted the presence of natural resources, and located castles and villages—particularly as opposed to nearby cities, which were often drawn larger than their proportion. Inevitably, this has also led scholars to emphasize the absence of scale and the fact that measured surveys played virtually no part in the preparation of these maps, thus raising questions of accuracy and practical use.[11]

By contrast, the second line of interpretation sees the presence of regional and district maps in Italy as a sign of the early rise of the 'cartographic state',

---

[7] Notably Hale, 'Warfare and Cartography', 720; and Kagan and Schmidt, 'Maps and the Early Modern State', 664.

[8] MACHIAVELLI, *Chief Works*, 674.

[9] On the use of district and regional maps in fifteenth-century Ferrara, see Donattini, 'Confini contesi', 205–6; and Folin, 'De l'usage pratico-politique', 265–6, from which the term 'topographies pratiques' is borrowed.

[10] Harvey, *The History of Topographical Maps*, 58–62.

[11] See, by way of example, the views expressed by an expert such as Milanesi, 'La rappresentazione cartografica', 26–7; Milanesi, 'Introduzione', 7–8.

184   BORDERS AND THE POLITICS OF SPACE IN LATE MEDIEVAL ITALY

thus making a case for their administrative and military value.[12] Attention has been drawn to the abundance of strategic details, such as fortifications or river crossings, and also to the fact that the vast majority of the maps in question were made in the Venetian mainland in the second half of the fifteenth century. Between the 1450s and 1470s, the period when most of the surviving maps were made, the Republic took three related initiatives: it defined its borders with the Duchy of Milan, it embarked on an extensive fortification programme, and, in 1460, it issued a decree requiring all officials stationed in the mainland to commission maps of the provinces under their rule.[13] Although it is far from clear which, if any, of the surviving examples were the result of Venice's decree, scholars such as Emanuela Casti have been quick to relate the making of regional and district maps in the Terraferma to the expression of a 'new intellectual mastery of the world' and to 'the ability of a state to govern the territory over which it exercised sovereignty'.[14]

Still, the novelty of the Venetian decree should not be overstated. Scholars often cite it as evidence of Venice's precocious realization of the potential of maps as tools of government.[15] The degree's opening text does lament a lack of knowledge about the size and the limits of the dominion; however, we know that Venice had commissioned regional and district maps long before the mainland provinces were acquired. A famous example comes from 1407, when a painter was hired to draw a map of the borderlands between Verona and Mantua, along the river Mincio, where Venice envisioned a possible line of defence.[16] Equally, scholars have often placed emphasis on Venice's ambition to map the whole of the dominion.[17] The decree was addressed to all the officials of the Terraferma: from the patrician governors stationed in cities to the castellans of walled towns and frontier fortifications. Although this covered the entirety of the Venetian state, the very text of the decree suggests that Venetians themselves did not think of cartography in such terms. Their wish was not to construct a map of the dominion

---

[12] The reference is to the book by Branch, *The Cartographic State*. The most notable example of this second line of interpretation is possibly Marino, 'Administrative Mapping'.

[13] On the Venetian decree and its historical context, see Mazzi, 'La conoscenza per l'organizzazione delle difese', 117–23; and Concina, '*In vera pictura*', 151–5.

[14] Casti, 'State, Cartography, and Territory', 874.

[15] Notably Harvey, *The History of Topographical Maps*, 60–1; following Almagià, *Monumenta Italiae cartographica*, 11–12.

[16] Mazzi, 'Agli esordi della difesa', 16–20.

[17] By way of example, see the views of two specialists such as Milanesi, 'Cartografia per un principe senza corte', 198–9; and Mazzi, 'Governo del territorio e cartografia', 19–21.

7. DRAWING THE LINE? 185

but to assemble a cartographic corpus covering all the individual territories under their rule ('omnium civitatum, terrarum, castellorum, provinciarum et locorum nostrorum').[18]

On its own, the distinction above may appear trivial, but it is important to remember that a variety of written sources employed the same vocabulary to describe the constituent components of regional states. As seen in previous chapters, these could be city-states, townships, fiefs, or local communities but never just a single regional space defined by Venice's ownership. It is also worth noting that a map of the whole dominion is simply not mentioned in the decree. In 1476, the Venetians had a map of the whole of Italy painted in the doge's palace, where it might have formed a backdrop to diplomatic negotiations.[19] This indicates that the painters employed by the Republic would have been perfectly capable of capturing the extent of the dominion in a compact but comprehensive map. Yet the Venetians never asked them to, not in 1460 or at any other point in the Quattrocento. By contrast, a century or so later the illustrious architect and cartographer Cristoforo Sorte was appointed by the Senate to draw not only a set of maps of the mainland provinces but an enlarged map of the whole Venetian state.[20] In short, while the decree was undoubtedly an early example of state-sponsored cartography, reading its text in light of the territorial culture of the time might offer a more nuanced interpretation.

This hypothesis is also the chapter's starting point. Mindful of the complex picture of late medieval territoriality drawn in the rest of the book, the chapter posits that the development of an independent tradition of regional and district maps in fifteenth-century Italy should not be mechanically linked to the rise of the state. While it is agreed that Quattrocento cartography was inescapably bound up with the dominant polities of the era, the chapter builds on the assumption that regional and district maps expressed more than just state territoriality. In this respect, the chapter's methodological premise is not different from that underpinning the whole book: regional and district maps should be studied in their own right, as objects belonging to the world from which they originated, born from the demands

---

[18] ASVe, *Dieci Misti (Registri)* 15, c. 197r, 27 February 1460.

[19] The map was painted on the walls of chambers in which decisions were taken and foreign envoys received, as discussed by Milanesi, 'Nelle stanze di palazzo', 109. It was then copied by painters in the service of the marquis of Mantua, which suggests that it was valuable and accurate enough for its purposes: Bourne, 'Francesco II Gonzaga and Maps', 65–7.

[20] On Sorte's maps and appointment, see the classic studies by Schulz, 'Cristoforo Sorte and the Ducal Palace'; Schulz, 'New Maps and Landscape Drawings by Cristoforo Sorte'.

186 BORDERS AND THE POLITICS OF SPACE IN LATE MEDIEVAL ITALY

of specific actors and responding to specific uses. To put it briefly, all maps are imbued with their own territorial zeitgeist. Regional and district maps represent more than just a given space; they represent the way in which such space was perceived by society. As such, they transcend reality to illuminate attitudes and can tell us much about the way in which contemporaries envisioned territories and borders.[21]

While testing that hypothesis, the chapter will also draw on some of the acquisitions of critical cartography to explore the performative value of regional and district maps. Here, the assumption is that these maps did not merely reflect late medieval attitudes and realities; they also helped to communicate them and, by extension, define them.[22] Like texts and indeed every form of written and visual language falling within the remit of cultural analysis, maps do more than just describe the order of things; they reorder things. All maps reify space and borders as they are understood by their makers, thus normalizing their propositions. In this sense, maps embody power relations between political players as much as spatial relationships between physical places.[23] It follows that by exploring the performative value of regional and district maps it is possible to uncover not only how maps presented the extent and the limits of Italian polities but also how the political and territorial order of the time was shaped by visual representation. In so doing, we shall add one final dimension to our inquiry into the nature of late medieval borders, while uncovering how territoriality itself and, more broadly, the spatial fabric of Italian society were visually constructed.

From District Maps to Imagined Territories

Let us then look more closely at what the surviving corpus of regional and district maps can tell us about the way in which contemporaries pictured

[21] On the nexus between knowledge and representation, as well as the many contingent meanings of maps, see, for northern Italy, Grendi, 'La pratica dei confini', 134–45; and especially Raggio, 'Immagini e verità'.

[22] On the role of maps in the dialectic construction of the world, see especially the theorization by Casti, *Reality as Representation*; Casti, 'Cartographic Semiosis'. On postmodernism, performativity, and the cultural turn in cartographic history, see Nash, 'Performativity in Practice'; and Cosgrove, 'Cultural Cartography'.

[23] A Foucauldian genealogy of power in mapping practices was famously advocated by Harley, 'Maps, Knowledge, and Power'; however, consider also his other essays in Harley, *The New Nature of Maps*. For a more recent take on maps as sites of power/knowledge, see Crampton, 'Maps as Social Constructions'; and the extensive reassessment of Harley's intellectual influences offered by Edney, *The Origins and Development*.

7. DRAWING THE LINE? 187

political spaces and later, in the chapter's final section, visualized borders. In 1929, when Roberto Almagià published his seminal survey, *Monumenta Italiae cartographica*,[24] around a dozen of these maps were already known. Since that time, a few others have been discovered, which suggests that the Italian archives could hold even more which are still unknown.[25] The earliest example is a small map of the territory between Asti and Alba in eastern Piedmont, dated to the late thirteenth century.[26] For the fourteenth century, the only known piece is a map of Lake Garda, on the border between the Bresciano and the Veronese, showing the lakeside settlements and several fortifications.[27] For the fifteenth century, we have regional and district maps for much of northern Italy.[28] These include maps of the territories of Verona, Padua, Crema, and Parma,[29] three others showing the whole of Lombardy or the Veneto,[30] and finally three maps of Brescia and its *contado*. Since these last three maps cover much of the period under consideration and the Bresciano is immediately relevant to our inquiry into the borders between Venice and Milan, this section will be based on their analysis. In so doing, we shall follow the development of this autonomous tradition of Italian cartography throughout the Quattrocento, while searching for recurring features which may reveal how contemporaries visualized territoriality in this period.

The first example of the cartographic corpus depicting the Bresciano is a map dating to the rule of Pandolfo Malatesta, which ran from 1406 to 1416 (Figure 17). Following the death of Gian Galeazzo Visconti and the temporary disintegration of the Milanese dominion, Malatesta managed to piece together a buffer state for himself by drawing on his experience as a condottiere and

[24] Almagià, *Monumenta Italiae cartographica*, 7–13.

[25] See the list put together in the late 1980s by Harvey, 'Local and Regional Cartography', 498. However, even this second list, following Almagià's, is now due for an update. A notable absence is the unique map of the area between Reggio and Correggio showing the dense network of roads connecting the two Emilian centres in remarkable detail (Figure 22). Although its origins have been lost, the map currently hangs on a wall in the Archivio di Stato di Reggio Emilia. It could perhaps be linked to a smaller map now held in the *Notai Pittori* series depicting the pathways taken by shepherds leaving Tuscia for Emilia, on which see Rombaldi, 'Carpineti nel Medioevo', 81.

[26] Almagià, 'Un'antica carta del territorio di Asti'.

[27] Filippi, 'Carta trecentesca del lago di Garda'.

[28] For an overview, compare Mazzi, 'Governo del territorio e cartografia veneta'; with Scotti, 'La cartografia lombarda'.

[29] Bertoldi, 'Topografia del Veronese'; Puppi, 'Appunti in margine all'immagine di Padova'; Roncai and Edallo, 'Un territorio in forma di città'; 108–9; Zanichelli, 'La committenza dei Rossi', 205–6.

[30] Baratta, 'La carta della Lombardia di Giovanni Pisato'; Pirovano, 'Carta militare della Lombardia'; Gallo, 'A Fifteenth Century Military Map of the Venetian Territory'.

188 BORDERS AND THE POLITICS OF SPACE IN LATE MEDIEVAL ITALY

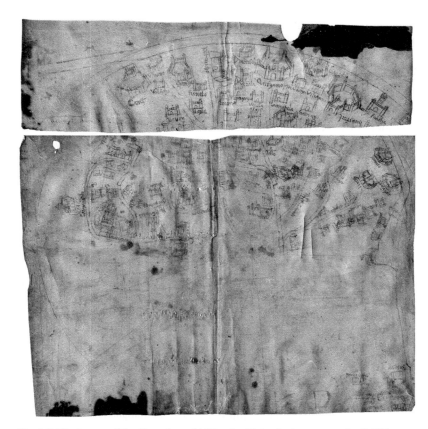

Fig. 17 First map of the Bresciano (ASBr, *Archivio storico comunale* 434/2). Reproduced with permission from the Italian Ministry of Cultural Heritage

his lands in central Italy to become master of Brescia and Bergamo as well as Lecco and the Lecchese.[31] As opposition against him weakened, Malatesta commissioned a revision of fiscal quotas (known as *estimi* in Italian) owed by every community of the Bresciano.[32] While the records do not mention the compilation of a map, the fact that the piece in question bears Pandolfo's name on the back and that it was later sewn to a copy of the revised fiscal contributions points to the map having being drawn on this occasion.

---

[31] On Malatesta and his short-lived dominion in Lombardy, see the essays collected by Chittolini, Conti, and Covini, *Nell'età di Pandolfo Malatesta*.

[32] ASBr, *Archivio storico comunale* 434/2. On the so-called *estimi malatestiani*, see especially Bonfiglio Dosio, 'Condizioni socio-economiche di Brescia'.

As Nathalie Bouloux noted in the only extensive study on the subject, the map might have had a practical application for the Malatesta entourage, men who came predominantly from central Italy and thus had little or no knowledge of the Bresciano.[33] In addition, the map could have fulfilled a celebratory purpose. Malatesta had to conquer the communities of the Bresciano almost one by one, so it is reasonable to believe that the map could have served to display the ruler's new dominion. If that was indeed the case, then Bouloux is right to relate the making of the map to other visual projects launched by Malatesta, starting with the transformation of Brescia's city hall into a lordly residence adorned by propagandistic frescoes.[34]

However, it is essential to note what forms of political and territorial organization the map actually expresses. Given what we have learned so far about late medieval territoriality, a radically different interpretation could be offered. Although the map is unfinished and now largely discoloured, its underlying design is still recognizable: an array of variously portrayed villages connected by roads and waterways is encased in a carefully drawn circle. In painting villages, however, the mapmaker is doing more than just listing visually all the localities that once formed the *districtus*; he is establishing a hierarchical order for them. While most of the villages are drawn indiscriminately as small castles, some show architectural features that set them apart: a series of bastions (Asola, Pontevico), a watchtower (Quinzano, Orzinuovi), and even an inner citadel (Pontoglio, Palazzolo). The circle, on the other hand, represents a superior form of territorial organization. It embodies not just the imagined boundaries of the *contado* but the harmonious unity between the *districtus* and the *civitas*. By signifying the territorial extent of urban jurisdiction, the circle brings together a constellation of sister *universitates* (both the small and the large communities of the countryside) to form a single corporation (the city-state). Thus, the subject of the map is not just the Bresciano area, nor it is simply a symbolic depiction of a lord's passing dominion in the region; instead, it represents the ancient *comitatus* of Brescia, as articulated through all the localities over which the city, before Malatesta even entered the stage, had extended its power.

Comparative analysis suggests that presenting the *contado* as an enclosed array of villages had long been common in Italian cities and would continue to be so even after the rise of regional polities. The earliest known example

---

[33] Bouloux, 'Trois cartes territoriales de Brescia', 106.
[34] On Malatesta's pictorial commissions, see Seccamani, 'Dati e rilievi sui resti della cappella di San Giorgio'.

190   BORDERS AND THE POLITICS OF SPACE IN LATE MEDIEVAL ITALY

of a district map, the 1291 map of Asti and the surrounding area, is also the earliest example of that same imagery, with the city at its centre and a total of 164 localities depicted all around it.[35] Significantly, the map was originally attached to a manuscript recording charters granted to Asti by the emperor and records sanctioning Asti's privileges and status of *civitas*. As in the case of Brescia's *estimi*, the collection was designed to celebrate the city's jurisdiction over the surrounding countryside, so it would only make sense for the accompanying map also to work as a signifier of civic power and identity. An even more intriguing example is the map of Padua and the Padovano drawn by Annibale Maggi da Bassano.[36] This was commissioned by the city council in 1449, only a decade before the Venetian decree of 1460. As in the case of the sketch of Asti and the Astigiano, the map presents an enlarged city surrounded by smaller centres. In this case, however, all settlements are also encased in a double circle, much as they are in the first map of Brescia. This goes to show how common it was, even decades, if not centuries apart, to use the same territorial imagery—an imagery that does not point to the spatial dimension of lordly or even state power but rather encapsulates the world of corporate and modular territoriality shaped by the communes.

The political and territorial culture underpinning cartographic representations of this kind is possibly even more evident in the second map of the Bresciano (Figure 18). Following Almagià, this second example was long considered one of the few surviving products of Venice's 1460 decree and dated to around 1470.[37] In recent years, however, a new generation of map historians has challenged this conclusion, noting that the criteria set out by the Council of Ten are simply not met by the map in question.[38] Missing are the distances between places ('distantiam de loco ad locum et loca vicina nobis et distantiam eorum') and so is any indication of the map's orientation ('signa ventorum et orientis et ponentis').[39] Yet no alternative reading has been offered as to the source, purpose, and imagery of the map in question.

---

[35] The original map of the Astigiano is now a badly damaged fragment from the *Codice Alfieri* of the Biblioteca Nazionale Universitaria di Torino. A reproduction from a copy dating to the mid-fourteenth century can be found in SELLA, *Codex Astensis*, tab. VII.

[36] The map is now lost, but a sixteenth-century copy has survived in BAMi, ms. 940 inf. Unlike that of Asti and the Astigiano, this map has been the object of some studies, starting with Puppi, 'Appunti in margine all'immagine di Padova', 163–5.

[37] Almagià, *Monumenta Italiae cartographica*, 12.

[38] Mazzi, 'Governo del territorio e cartografia veneta', 28–9; but see also Bouloux, 'Trois cartes territoriales de Brescia', 112–13.

[39] ASVe, *Dieci Misti (Registri)* 15, c. 197r, 27 February 1460.

7. DRAWING THE LINE? 191

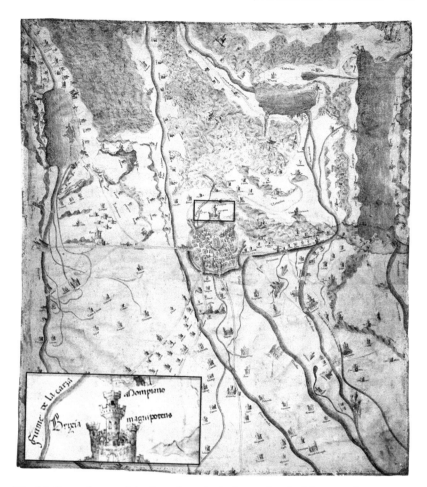

Fig. 18 Second map of the Bresciano, including a detail of the city of Brescia and the motto 'Brixia magnipotens' (BEMo, *Carte geografiche* A 8). © edl.beniculturali.it

Let us start with its imagery, so as to be able to assess this second map of the Bresciano in relation to our first example. To do so, it may first be helpful to disentangle what is arguably the fundamental layers of any map. One is a geographical layer, concerning the map's orography (the shape and pattern of mountains, which here are largely undifferentiated), its hydrography (the river Oglio and Lake Iseo to the left, the river Mincio and Lake Garda to the right), and finally its topography (including artificial features, such as

192   BORDERS AND THE POLITICS OF SPACE IN LATE MEDIEVAL ITALY

the dense network of roads leaving Brescia for the Cremonese or the irrigation channels flowing next to the city).[40] Once these details have been pushed into the background, what we are left with is the map's remaining layer. This is what we might call the territorial layer, concerning the contingent modes of territorial organization exhibited by the map; it is the cartographic rendition of the political and territorial order as envisioned by the mapmaker and, through him, by his patrons. As in the first map of the Bresciano, here territoriality is expressed through two synoptic elements: the villages and the city. Where the first map used a circular iconography to establish a relational hierarchy between the two, this second map employs the instrument of scale. As a *universitas* itself, Brescia is no different from all the other localities: like the rest of them, it is depicted as a fortified settlement linked to a system of roads and waterways. Comparatively, however, Brescia is drawn much larger and is also placed at the very centre of the map, signalling its dominant position over the surrounding countryside.

While the map's territorial imagery is analogous to that of the first map of the Bresciano, what are we to make of the source and purpose of this second example? First, it is possible that the map was prepared a few decades earlier than specialists, both old and new, have commonly supposed. Two elements recommend an earlier dating: the Gothic script, which would be unusual in a product of the later decades of the Quattrocento, and the limited use of perspective, which is evident from the flat depiction of mountains and from the skewed towers of Brescia. Should the map predate the 1460s or even the 1450s, a new take could be offered, one that pushes aside the Venetian decree to consider what the map itself can tell us about its origin and destination. The clue is in the way in which the city of Brescia is labelled on the map: 'Brixia magnipotens' (Figure 18). In the first half of the fifteenth century, this motto formed part of the rhetoric adopted by Brescia to rebrand itself as 'Venice's most loyal city'.[41] In 1440, the motto appeared on the celebratory banner presented by Brescia to the Venetians, following the city's strenuous resistance to the siege laid by the armies of the duke of Milan.[42] Yet like the banner itself, featuring St Mark alongside Brescia's own patron saints, the motto encapsulated the city's determination to continue to act

---

[40] All features are already abundantly described by the scholar who first drew attention to the map in question: Baratta, 'Sopra un'antica carta'.

[41] The reference is to the book by Bowd, *Venice's Most Loyal City*; however, see also the invariably valuable narrative drawn by Pasero, 'Il dominio veneto'.

[42] On the 1440 episode and many others in which the motto 'Brixia magnipotens' is used, see Bowd, *Venice's Most Loyal City*, 40–4; and now Cotti, 'I santi all'assedio', 127–8.

independently; it voiced a rhetoric of civic pride other than one of loyalty. In this respect, Brescia's motto was similar to the rhetorical devices adopted by several other cities in the fifteenth century: faced with an ostensibly irreversible future as subject centres, cities were nonetheless determined to defend their status as *civitates*.[43] Despite its annexation by the Venetian Republic, Brescia's leadership still saw their polity as a city-state and conceived its authority over the surrounding territory as integral to their autonomy. Rather than as the result of a Venetian commission, this second map of the Bresciano should therefore be interpreted in the same way as the banner of 1440—as a visual representation of the city's persisting political vision and pre-existing territorial identity.

Having established that the territorial layer of district maps is a visualization of the territorial order as envisioned by the old city-states, further conclusions can be drawn as to the way in which competing forms of territorial organization are depicted in them. To do so, let us turn our attention to the third and final map of the Bresciano to be considered in this section (Figure 19). This presents a similar imagery to that of our second example. If anything, the common nature of urban and rural *universitates* is perhaps even more evident here, since the city is portrayed as nothing but a scaled-up version of the largest corporations of the countryside: a seemingly empty settlement surrounded by mighty walls. The other notable difference is that the localities of this map are labelled with a series of capital letters (M, G, etc.). The presence of these letters can be explained in view of the manuscript to which the map was originally attached: a miscellaneous collection of records and especially fiscal privileges granted to some of the feudal families of the Bresciano.[44] Stephen Bowd has framed this manuscript as a 'site of memory' and argued that its function was to normalize Brescian–Venetian relations after the revision of civic statutes in 1470.[45]

Yet the manuscript, and with it the map once attached to it, could also be framed as an attempt to reshape the memory of the last few decades and thus assert a new balance in the Bresciano. Following the wars of the first

---

[43] On *civitates potentes* and generally 'the rights of a virtual *small state* within a larger state', see Chittolini, 'Dominant Cities', 26.

[44] BQBr, ms. H V 5. With regard to the manuscript, see two studies by Ferraglio, 'Il libro dei privilegi'; Ferraglio, 'Aristocrazia, territorio e regime fiscale'. A more recent reading, placing the manuscript in opposition to cartularies compiled by the families, can be found in Parola, Per diffender le rexone de sua magnificentia, 60–1 and 69–70.

[45] Bowd, *Venice's Most Loyal City*, 30; however, consider also the more balanced interpretation offered by Bouloux, 'Trois cartes territoriales de Brescia', 109–10. As for 'sites of memory', Bowd's reference is to the classic work by Nora, 'Between Memory and History'.

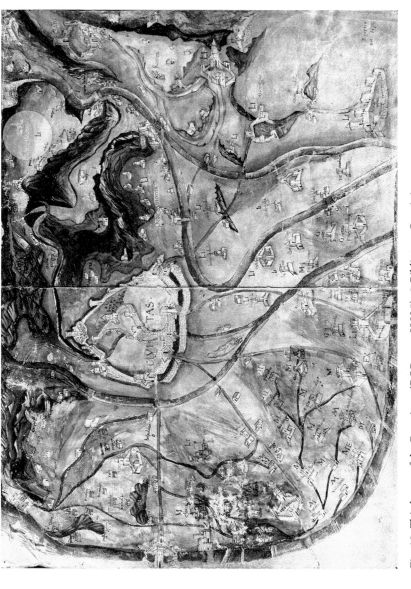

Fig. 19 Third map of the Bresciano (BQBr, ms. H V 5). © Biblioteca Queriniana

7. DRAWING THE LINE? 195

Fig. 20 One of the illuminations of the manuscript to which the third map of the Bresciano is attached (BQBr, ms. H V 5, c. 64v), showing the lords of the Bresciano plucking the winged lion of Venice. © Biblioteca Queriniana

196   BORDERS AND THE POLITICS OF SPACE IN LATE MEDIEVAL ITALY

half of the fifteenth century, the noble families whose privileges are included in the manuscript had profited from political instability to secure tax exemptions in exchange for their support to the Republic. In the 1470s, Venice was still content with relinquishing a portion of its revenues to appease the lords of the Bresciano. The citizens of Brescia, on the other hand, held a different view: they saw the fiscal immunities granted to seigneurial families as detrimental not only to Venice's income but also to the city's common good.[46] It is possible, then, that the map could have then been used together with the manuscript to advocate the cause of the citizens against the lords. It certainly conveys the citizens' position in at least two ways. First, it exposes the extensive lands held by seigneurial families in the countryside by labelling the villages where they exercised some prerogatives with their initials: M for Martinenghi, G for Gambara, and so on. Second, the map denies these lordships a spatial dimension. Once again, it is to the city's political and territorial project that we should look to understand these visual messages. In the world envisioned by the city, personal privileges can only exist if superimposed onto the only unit which the *civitas* saw as alternative or indeed complementary to itself: the subjugated rural community.

But what of other forms of territorial organization? How does this map cover their presence? For a start, there is clearly no reference to the presence or spatial extent of Venice's authority. The Bresciano had been part of the Republic for almost half a century by the time the map was made, not to mention that the map itself may have been made to be shown to Venetian authorities. Yet the map does not present the Bresciano as a province of the Venetian state but as the territory of the city of Brescia. We know, however, that between the fourteenth and the fifteenth century, the old *contado* had lost ground to a number of intermediate bodies. As seen in Chapter 1, these sat between the village and the *districtus* in the territorial hierarchy of late medieval Italy. With the rise of polities such as the Duchy of Milan and the Republic of Venice, their autonomous spatial dimension was explicitly recognized by regional powers, often by way of denying the city's original claim over them. In Chapter 2, for example, we noted how the Val Camonica, notwithstanding its original affiliation with the Bresciano, was treated as a separate territory during the negotiation of the treaty of Ferrara.

How, then, does a map commissioned by the city deal with the presence of competing territorial bodies in its *contado*? Like our second example, the

---

[46] On the seigneurial families of the Bresciano, their alignment with the Venetians, and their conflictual relationship with the citizens, see Ferraro, 'Proprietà terriera e potere'; Montanari, *Sommersi e sopravvissuti*; and Valseriati and Viggiano, 'Venezia in Lombardia'.

7. DRAWING THE LINE? 197

third map of the Bresciano reflected the city's claim of full jurisdiction over the surrounding countryside. In keeping with this claim, the mountain villages are mapped as part of the *contado*. Simultaneously, however, the map silences the spatial dimension of valley federations such as the Val Camonica. These are broken up into the individual villages of which they were composed and ultimately blurred as mere geographical references in the wider *contado*. It is hard to think of more compelling evidence of the extent to which these maps represent the interests and worldview of the city: in denying the spatial dimension of valley federations as much as rural lordships, the makers of the third map of the Bresciano were advancing their vision of a uniform *comitatus* subdued to the power of the *civitas*. Once more, comparative analysis allows us to appreciate the meaning of these cartographic choices even more. Figure 21 shows a detail from a map of Lombardy drawn around the same time as our third map of the Bresciano. While the origins of this regional map are unknown, its depiction of forms of territorial organization alternative to the city and its subject communities are extremely revealing. In particular, the map depicts two valleys of the Bresciano (the 'Val Tropia' and 'Val Sabia') as compact communities. They are still relatively smaller than Brescia, but they are also comparatively larger than the single villages of the Bresciano. This shows that the mapmaker acknowledged them as recognizable territorial bodies, something that certainly cannot be said for the third map of the Bresciano.

In conclusion, one might note that all these maps were made at moments of change: the rise of a new master (Pandolfo Malatesta), the political reorientation of the Bresciano under a new ruler (the Venetian Republic), and the assertion of a new balance between social groups (the citizens and the lords). At the same time, however, they all point to remarkable continuities. First, they all show continuity in terms of spatial imagination. Cartographic techniques were visibly improving over the course of the century, as is immediately clear when we compare the first map of the Bresciano with the last one above. But what is also clear is that all these maps drew from the same territorial imagery, with the city occupying an area far in excess of its actual size and the *contado* rendered as a patchwork of fortified settlements.[47] In essence, the maps of the Bresciano are all examples of the same cartographic genre, one that visualized the spatial fabric of society as

---

[47] Significantly, the same imagery can still be found in the first printed map of the area, which may have been partly derived from the second or third map of the Bresciano. The map is attached to the *Chronica de rebus Brixianorum* by Elia Capriolo, printed in Brescia by Rondo de Rondi (Arundum de Arundis) around 1505: BAMi, ms. S N N III 2, cc. 1v–2r.

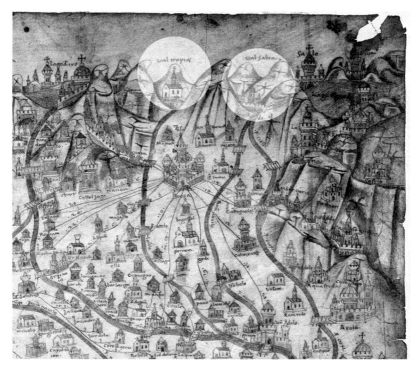

Fig. 21 The Trompia and Sabbia valleys in a fifteenth-century map of Lombardy (BNFr, *Cartes et plans* Ge C 4090). © Images.bnf.fr

it was imagined by the city. For the singularity of this cartographic tradition to be immediately evident, we need only to consider maps depicting not a city-commune with its *contado* but an urban centre with the surrounding countryside. A little-known example is the fifteenth-century map from Reggio (Figure 22). In comparison with the district maps of the Bresciano, here the city is positioned in the upper right-hand corner rather than the centre, while the surrounding communities are represented as sparse settlements rather than as fortified villages. Although the map is still awaiting a thorough study, its focus was plainly the local road system and its purpose purely practical.

This brings us to the second mark of continuity featured by these maps, which is their consistent performative value. When considering their source and origin, it becomes immediately evident that they were pragmatic artefacts, built on extensive and reliable records to be fully operational; yet their

7. DRAWING THE LINE? 199

Fig. 22 Fifteenth-century map of the road system near Reggio (ASRe). Reproduced with permission from the Italian Ministry of Cultural Heritage

use and destination suggest that they also played a performative function. Their modes of description and systems of classification were directed towards exalting the centrality of the city, flaunting the size and connectedness of its subject communities, and marginalizing competing organizations (whether these were personal, such as feudal families, or properly territorial, such as valley federations). In short, more than mere administrative tools devised to govern reality, district maps were partisan depictions of that reality. In articulating visually the territorial order as envisioned by the old *civitates*, mapmakers asserted the aspirations of a specific group of people: the citizens. What these maps offer to the viewer is more than a mere cartographic representation of the city's territory; it is an idealized vision of it—an imagined territory. As such, district maps provide a window into

200 BORDERS AND THE POLITICS OF SPACE IN LATE MEDIEVAL ITALY

how long-standing bodies and their leaderships, notwithstanding their submission to new regional powers, continued to view their spatial dimension and lay claims of territoriality.

The Lion, the Viper, and the Border

Where does this leave borders? At first glance, our examination of the three maps of the Bresciano may seem to suggest that they are simply not part of the picture. If anything, the borders depicted there are fictitious, as in the case of the perfect circle encompassing the area once subject exclusively to Brescia in the first map. In the second and third map, the drawing is only as large as the *contado* was: the limits of the *contado* are equated with the most peripheral village subject to the city and placed on the fringes of the map itself, where the end of the Bresciano is marked by a blurred landscape, one devoid of any life. Indeed, while district and regional maps were relatively widespread, it is impossible to deny that borders were more often written than drawn. As we noted in previous chapters, the most common way to visualize borders on the page was not a set of symbols or lines but a series of written devices. As David Wood put it, 'it would be a form of *cartocentricity* to imagine that spatial relationships have to be embodied in map form.'[48] However, given what we learned in Chapter 3 about the verbal mapping carried out periodically by local notaries when recording the boundaries of rural communities, the predominance of written forms of representation should not come as a surprise. Throughout this investigation, we have also encountered another device used to map borders in writing: the list. Typically compiled in the form of written successions of place names, lists conveyed a real sense of space to contemporaries, one which was virtually analogous to that which modern maps convey to us. By anchoring the position of borders to the familiar topography of a catalogue of localities, lists embodied spatial relationships just as any map would now do.[49] Together, the marginality of identifiable borders and the relative abundance of their written descriptions, especially vis-à-vis their elusive cartographic representation, have led many scholars to argue that depicting borders was

---

[48] Wood, 'P.D.A Harvey and Medieval Mapmaking', 53.

[49] On the interchangeable use of written and visual devices in the description of borders and space in the Late Middle Ages, see Gautier Dalché, 'De la liste à la carte'; and, more broadly, Boucheron, 'Représenter l'espace féodal'.

something that medieval maps simply did not do. Explanations vary, though generally they invoke at least one of the following: the shortcomings and predominantly aesthetic purpose of medieval cartography and the supposed lack of interest on behalf of medieval states to accurately map their territories (often coupled with their technical inability to do so).[50]

Yet when looking at late medieval Italy, a different picture emerges. On the one hand, it is clear that contemporaries did not think about maps as such: the very word map (*mappa*) was extraneous to their vocabulary. On the other, we have several references to drawings (*disegni*) depicting not just a region, a district, or a portion of the local landscape but the borders of territories. There was no such thing as a state cartographer in late medieval Italy; maps of frontier areas were typically commissioned from military architects and engineers or, more commonly, from private contractors. In 1373, a drawing by a local painter, Jacopo Dondi, was employed to settle a territorial dispute over one of the areas where the Venetian dominion and that of the Carrara of Padua met (between Chioggia and Caverzere, north of the Po Delta).[51] Similarly, in 1487, the celebrated architect Francesco di Giorgio Martini was hired by Siena to prepare a drawing of the area between Montepulciano and Chianciano, on the southern frontier of the Florentine dominion.[52] Unlike the written records of borders, which were committed to paper on an everyday basis, cartographic representations were commissioned only in exceptional circumstances. In 1492, the map ordered by the Aragonese of Naples to chart a section of their borders with the Papal States followed the signing of a new agreement with Rome and was presumably carried out under the aegis of one of the treaty's chief negotiators: Giovanni Pontano, the famous Neapolitan humanist.[53] Together with the technical prowess that went into the making of such maps, the timing of these instances proves that maps depicting borders were far from merely decorative in late medieval Italy; in fact, they had immediate utility and needed to be exact.

The writings of Italian rulers further support this hypothesis. Their letters, in particular, show that power holders saw these maps as a way of picturing the contours of their dominion, or at least of part of it. However, it is

---

[50] Two illustrative examples of these dismissive views are the one paper devoted to cartography from the latest collection of essays on medieval frontiers: Iwanczak, 'Borders and Borderlines'; and the scholarly dialogue imagined by Hiatt, *Dislocations*.

[51] Lazzarini, 'Di una carta di Jacopo Dondi'.

[52] Rombai, 'Cartografia e uso del territorio', 109.

[53] Valerio, 'Cartography in the Kingdom of Naples', 951–3.

202   BORDERS AND THE POLITICS OF SPACE IN LATE MEDIEVAL ITALY

crucial to appreciate that smaller references remained pivotal. In 1471, the duke of Milan asked his engineers for 'a drawing... of the borders of our state', but he also stated that the map would have to show 'the borders we have with the Venetians, thus in the Lodigiano and the Cremonese, as well as in the Geradadda and in any other locality where we have borders with them'.[54] What better way to remind ourselves that borders were not articulated around the territories of states at this stage but around those of urban and rural communities? There is no reference to maps commissioned by Venice to chart its borders with Milan, but we know that the Republic used drawings occasionally during diplomatic activities. In 1487, following the negotiation of its new frontier with the Ottomans in the Balkans, Venice commissioned a map of the territory of Dulcigno, on the borders of Venetian Albania (now Ulcinj, in Montenegro). The map was exchanged as part of the correspondence between the capital and the Venetian diplomat in charge of establishing the local boundaries, together with various 'records containing details about those lands'.[55] This allows us to make a further preliminary point, which is that maps of this kind circulated as part of the wider documentary corpus describing territories and borders in late medieval Italy, as discussed in Chapters 2 and 6. As a rule, maps were sent independently of text only when someone could be sent along with them to contextualize what they represented. In 1493, for example, the governor of Bergamo had a drawing of the borderlands between the Bergamasco and the Geradadda made, but he would only ship it to Venice accompanied by a knowledgeable individual ('cum persona experta').[56] In essence, despite including the same plurality of spatial references, late medieval maps would never become alternatives to oral knowledge or even to written material such as the list.

And circulate they did, particularly when multiple polities were drawn into the same dispute. A prime example can be found in 1477, when a bitter controversy divided the people of Pietrasanta, a community located in

---

[54] Beltrami, *Il castello di Milano*, 272. Beltrami extracted these notes from two letters sent by Galeazzo Maria Sforza to Bartolomeo da Cremona on 14 June and 11 July 1471. While these are said to be found in ASMi, *Registri* 100, c. 105v and c. 195r, the registers were then renumbered and the original source of the two records could not be found. Still, Beltrami's transcription seems reliable: 'el designo havemo ordinato se faci delli confini del stato nostro'; 'uno designo de li confini che havemo con venetiani, cosi in lodesana che cremonese come in Giuaradadda et qualuncha altro loco dove confiniamo con loro'.

[55] BMVe, ms. It. VII 2581 (12473), cc. 377r–380v, 7 March 1487: 'el desegno del territorio de Dolcigno ve mandai, cum le scripture dele informationi delle terre, unido sotto della cerada'.

[56] ASMi, *Comuni* 6, f. 'Bergamo', 1493 May 13.

northern Tuscany but traditionally subject to Genoa, and a series of villages located in the peripheries of the republic of Lucca (Montignoso, Camaiore, and Monteggiori).[57] While the dispute arose out of historical enmities inherent to local society, it still threatened the balance between Italian powers because of the number of major parties which had a stake in it. On the one side, there was the duke of Milan, who at the time held Genoa on behalf of the French and was thus expected to protect the interests of Pietrasanta. On the other, there was Florence, which had been applying increasing pressure on the southern borders of Lucca and saw this area as a buffer for its own state, if not as its natural direction of expansion. As we know, defining the boundaries between local communities meant also defining the frontier between regional dominions, so a third party was brought in to settle the dispute. This was the marquis of Mantua, Ludovico Gonzaga, who happened to be treating his aching legs in the nearby thermal baths.[58] Perhaps drawing on information gathered on the spot by some of his agents, the marquis commissioned a map of the area in dispute. His verdict was to depend on the agreement of the duke of Milan, but Galeazzo Maria Sforza had recently been killed by a group of rebellious noblemen, so the decision fell to his wife, Bona of Savoy, who was then acting as regent. Finally, the map or perhaps a copy of it was sent to the Mantuan ambassador in Milan, who presented it to the duchess and to members of the Secret Council, promptly summoned by the ever-powerful Cicco Simonetta. Following the 'exhibition of the drawing', the duchess finally agreed to comply with Gonzaga's ruling.[59]

Maps depicting borders were thus made by professionals, commissioned on the occasion of major diplomatic agreements—or incidents, and circulated alongside written descriptions of territorial arrangements. But what did they look like? Save for the map of the borders between Naples and Rome, which survives in a dubious late copy,[60] all the examples mentioned above have been lost. However, we can still learn much about the place of borders in fifteenth-century Italian cartography by considering the surviving corpus of regional and district maps. On the basis of the examples

---

[57] On the structural tension existing in this area, following Pietrasanta's rebellion against Lucca and its consequent acquisition by Genoa in 1436, see Bratchel, *Lucca, 1430–1494*, 235–55.

[58] The dispute of 1477 is recounted by TOMMASI, *Sommario della storia di Lucca*, 336–7; while Gonzaga's visits to the Tuscan hot springs are noted by Lazzarini, 'Ludovico III Gonzaga', 417–26.

[59] NATALE, *Acta in Consilio Secreto* (vol. I), 101: 'cum la dimostratione del dessegno'.

[60] Almagià, *Monumenta Italiae cartographica*, 12; Almagià, 'Studi storici di cartografia napoletana', 233.

204 BORDERS AND THE POLITICS OF SPACE IN LATE MEDIEVAL ITALY

discussed in the first section of this chapter, one could be forgiven for thinking that borders, as noted at the beginning of this section, are simply not part of the picture. Precisely drawn lines dividing the territories of compact polities do not appear, nor do evenly applied colours marking their geometrically measured spaces. Now universally adopted to depict the extent of any political aggregation, these patterns of representation were actually developed in the early modern period, when cartography began to reshape territory by depicting it as a homogenous space delimited by clear-cut borders.[61] In Italy, these new models were already quite common by the mid-sixteenth century but remained alien to the Late Middle Ages. Still, the absence of colour-filled areas and bounded political entities is not in itself proof that borders were not depicted in fifteenth-century maps. As we have learned, political spaces were not defined by a uniform authority and linear perimeters at this stage but by a plurality of overlapping bodies exercising different degrees of jurisdictional power over them. When searching for borders in fifteenth-century maps, it is thus essential to set aside our spatial understanding of the world (as divided into mutually exclusive nation-states) and consider instead the distinct nature of late medieval territoriality.

What, then, should we expect to find? For a start, it is worth noting that even when borders are plainly the reason why a certain map was made, they were normally superimposed onto an existing grid formed not by latitudes and longitudes but by the array of corporations (urban as much as rural) which composed the area in question. Significantly, the map which the marquis of Mantua sent to the duchess of Milan in 1477 was not described as map of borders but as a drawing of the territory in which the dispute lay ('picturam territorii in quo est differentia confinium').[62] And on the face of it, territories—not borders—are precisely what Figure 23 shows. Drawn by the mysterious Giovanni Pisato, this map exhibits the same spatial imagery as the three examples of the Bresciano: an array of fortified villages linked by roads and waterways is catalogued by twisting their scale and painting details of their military architecture. Yet this time, the area included on the map is not limited to a single district but covers an entire region. Being west-facing, the map ranges from the river Po (along the left margin) to the Alps (on the right-hand side) and from Pavia and Como (respectively in the top left and top right corners) to Mantua and Verona (near the bottom

---

[61] For the role of early modern cartography in the construction of a new notion of territorial state, see Biggs, 'Putting the State on the Map', 374–405; and Branch, 'Mapping the Sovereign State', 1–36.

[62] NATALE, *Acta in Consilio Secreto* (vol. I), 101.

Fig. 23 The so-called map of Lombardy by Giovanni Pisato, including a detail of various territorial markers (BCTv, ms. 1497). © Biblioteca comunale di Treviso

206 BORDERS AND THE POLITICS OF SPACE IN LATE MEDIEVAL ITALY

margin). Having been made in 1440, the map was undoubtedly used to inform political and military decisions. Not only does it depict the theatre of the so-called Lombard Wars between Venice and Milan; it also offers an overall survey of strategic details, including the presence of defensive structures, an indication of fortified bridges, and the distance between individual settlements (shown in miles).[63]

On closer inspection, however, the map reveals a supplementary set of symbols and notes, one signifying the contours of polities and, by extension, marking borders. The symbols are the banners waving from the towers of settlements or the coats of arms painted on their walls. Save for Mantua, which flies the Gonzaga banner, a great number of settlements display the Visconti viper (for Milan) or the winged lion of St Mark (for Venice). Thus, a symbolic overlayer is superimposed onto the grid made up by territorial units to signal their belonging to one polity or the other. The notes serve the same function, though they were not part of Pisato's original design and were added later by different hands, as evidenced by the varying script (that of Pisato being predominantly Gothic and booklike, while the subsequent additions are more cursive and typical of Renaissance chanceries). The notes range from a simple *S M* (sometimes spelled out as *Sancto Marcho*) to full-length sentences noting the changing status of a given piece on the political chessboard. The Venetian conquest of Cremona, for example, is noted as happening in 1499; the Visconti viper is simultaneously erased from the city's banner to make space for *Sancto Marcho*.

On its own, Pisato's attempt to distinguish the territories of the Republic from those of the Duchy by applying symbols could been seen as unusual, perhaps even as unique.[64] However, the addition of further notes from 1440, when Pisato finished his work, to 1500, when the latest change in territorial arrangements is marked on the map, opens up a different interpretation. We know from Sanudo's diaries that following the disastrous defeat of

---

[63] The strategic nature of the Pisato map had already been emphasized by Baratta, 'La carta della Lombardia', 577–93; and recently by Casti, 'State, Cartography, and Territory', 893–5.

[64] Save for the example of the Cremasco map discussed below (Figure 24), the only other district or regional map using banners on a comparable scale to Pisato's is the late thirteenth-century map of the Astigiano mentioned earlier. This is significant because the Astigiano map is the oldest known example of this independent tradition of late medieval Italian cartography, which suggests that many more maps might have adopted banners or other signs to mark the contours of territorial aggregations before the Quattrocento: SELLA, *Codex Astensis*, tab. VII; Almagià, 'Un'antica carta del territorio di Asti'. While a full study has yet to be devoted to this practice, it is interesting to note that it did not stop with the end of the Middle Ages but continued well into the early modern period. See, by way of example, the Castilian standards placed in maps of the New World: Padrón, 'Charting Shores', 33–7.

7. DRAWING THE LINE? 207

Agnadello, in 1509, the Venetian senators could trace the withdrawal of their armies on a large map of Italy painted on the walls of the doge's palace.[65] The map by Pisato could have been used in exactly the same way, though over an even longer period and perhaps even on the move, given its small format. Besides, the predominance of settlements marked as Venetian and the map's current location in the civic library of Treviso suggest that its origin may have been Venice itself. In 1440, when Pisato laid down his pen, Venetian galleys had defeated the Milanese fleet on the shores of Lake Garda; this enabled the enduring expansion of the Venetian dominion to the west of the lake itself, in eastern Lombardy. The map may have been commissioned by the Venetians to survey local infrastructures and gain a detailed picture of the area. If that was indeed the case, the inclusion of symbols and the addition of notes might have had a cognitive as well as a mnemonic function. Over a period of sixty years, including the time of the debated ordinance of 1460, the Venetians may have used this map to mark their shifting frontier with the Duchy of Milan: from the Lombard wars of the 1440s to the establishment of new state borders in 1450s, and finally to the French descent and temporary loss of the Terraferma at the turn of the century.[66]

The use of banners as badges of territorial belonging is also featured in a smaller map depicting Crema and the surrounding area, but with a twist (Figure 24). Given the architecture of the city's fortifications, it is possible to date this example to the period between 1454 and 1469.[67] As with the drawing by Pisato, it is reasonable to believe that this map was made and used in Venice: it represents Venetian territories and is still held at Venice's Museo Correr. Besides, the map depicts Crema and its territory as an

---

[65] SANUTO, *I diari* (vol. VIII), col. 247. This was, in all likelihood, the same map painted by Antonio Leonardi in 1476, on which see Gallo, 'Le mappe geografiche del palazzo ducale', 51–2; and Bianchi, 'Notizie del cartografo veneziano', 189–90.

[66] While maps delimiting political entities using equivalent devices appear only sporadically in the rest of Europe, a suggestive parallel is the wall of arms (*Wappenwand*) created by Frederick III in the same years as Pisato's map. This charts all the Habsburg territories by identifying them with their coats of arms and by surrounding them by even more coats of arms from the rest of the world and even fictional places in the Far East: Schauerte, 'Heraldische Fiktion als genealogisches Argument', 345–64.

[67] The map was first dated to the beginning of the second half of the fifteenth century by Verga, *Crema città murata*, 14–15. A case for the end of the 1490s was later made by Caniato, 'Mappa del territorio cremasco'. More recently, Giuliana Mazzi has pointed to 1454 as its *terminus post quem*, given the presence of ravelins built after this date, and to 1469 as its *terminus ante quem*, given the detached representation of the gatehouse of Porta Serio, which was incorporated into the city's walls after this date: Mazzi, 'Governo del territorio e cartografia veneta', 39–40.

Fig. 24 Map of Crema and the Cremasco showing the thin red line as well as localities with the Visconti viper painted on their walls (MCVe, *Cartografia* 35). © Fondazione Musei Civici di Venezia

independent *civitas*, a condition which Milan had long denied to the Lombard centre (mainly to indulge Cremona's more ancient claim over the territory) but which Venice had promptly granted to secure its hold over this crucial enclave. As a district map, the map exhibits a familiar picture: a network of roads and rivers runs through an area populated by a large urban centre and countless settlements of varying size and architecture. But as a map charting borders, this example seeks also to disentangle the communities belonging to the Cremasco from those that fell outside this Venetian enclave, which conversely made them Milanese. Like the map of Lombardy, borders are superimposed on the territorial layer of the depicted area by placing symbols (banners) on some of its constituent components (villages, castles, and towns). A series of settlements is thus marked with the Visconti's viper to set them aside from those which were part of the Cremasco. Yet the maker of this map went a step further than Pisato: he enclosed all the communities he knew to be subject to Crema within an area marked by a thin red line.[68] While this technique for mapping borders is undoubtedly more familiar to our modern eye, it is important to note that the curve of the line is still rather vague and fundamentally predetermined by the position of the individual localities on the map. Rather than as a direct representation of the border between the Duchy and the Republic, this line should be seen as an expedient to lump together all the communities belonging to the same territory (the Cremasco). Like Pisato, the mapmaker was merely superimposing the political order onto the same familiar imagery of the spatial fabric of late medieval Italy.

Finally, a demonstration of what maps depicting borders might have looked like in late medieval Italy comes from the sketch of the valleys between Lecco and Bergamo we first encountered in Chapter 3 (Figure 25).[69] Although this is the only example deviating from the spatial imaginary and visual patterns discussed above, two elements suggest that the drawing may well be the only survivor of an otherwise common sub-tradition of what we might call local maps.[70] First, while all the surviving regional and district maps were drawn on parchment by specially hired artists, the sketch of the Lombard valleys was drawn on paper by an ordinary chancery hand. This means that similar maps were cheap and quick to make but also prone to fire and water damage, which together may have destroyed most of such objects over the years.[71] Second, while the map is unquestionably a product of the 1456 negotiations, the minutes and correspondence recording the

---

[68] Exceptionally, it is the map-maker himself who tells us what to make of his representation of borders in a note left in the lower margin of his creation:

> se voy intenender questo desegnio de Crema et del Cremascho, drizalo su li venti et guarda verso Tremontana e volze le spalle a Ostro, et conoserai de dentro dal segnio rosso per finir a Ada esser Cremascho, teritori de Crema, et tuti li lochi circondanti ch'ano le bisse eno del ducha de Milano, de Lodesana, Geradada, Cremonise e parte de Milanise. (MCVe, Cartografia 35)

[69] The map is still held among the papers of count Roghendorf, who was appointed 'deputy for the resolution of borders' by the Milanese government (on behalf of Austrian empress Maria Theresa) in 1777. In the following years, Roghendorf managed to get to the crux of the Taleggio matter by building his inquiry around numerous documents from the ducal archives, some of which remain within his dossier, alongside the map itself: ASMi, *Confini* 290. So far, the only study of the map and its documentary *traditio* is that by a local historian: Pesenti, 'Conflitti locali, poteri centrali e cartografia'.

[70] Significantly, a similar tradition has been identified in Burgundy and the south of France. See Paviot, 'Les cartes et leur utilisation'; Dauphant, 'Entre la liste et le terrain'; and Fermon, *Le peintre et la carte*. Recent studies have painted an even richer picture, especially Gomis and Flauraud, *La cartographie ecclésiastique*; and Dumasy-Rabineau, Serchuk, and Vagnon, *Pour une histoire des cartes locales*.

[71] However, it is entirely possible that some have survived and are now buried in the huge corpus of diplomatic correspondence. Two notable examples are the sketches of towns

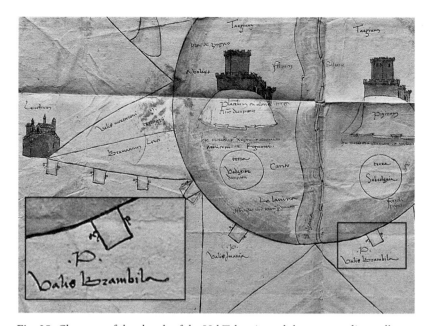

Fig. 25 Close-up of the sketch of the Val Taleggio and the surrounding valleys showing border stones painted on the lines marking the contours of local bodies (ASMi, *Confini* 290). Reproduced with permission from the Italian Ministry of Cultural Heritage

talks make no mention of it.[72] This may be a sign that similar maps, being easily drawn, were routinely made for the temporary needs of the Chancery, only to be disposed of or simply mislaid when they had outlived their purpose, the way other ephemeral records were. Writing in 1355, Bartolus himself recommended making sketches and diagrammatic maps to resolve territorial disputes, particularly when these concerned the mutable meanders of rivers and the resulting legal challenges.[73]

Despite its unique nature, the sketch of the Lombardy valleys enables us to shed some light on the way in which contemporaries visualized borders in greater detail. While all the maps examined in this section have been

and besieging armies contained in STORTI, *Dispacci sforzeschi da Napoli* (vol. IV), XXIII (26 October 1461); and NATALE, *I diari di Cicco Simonetta*, 132–3 (7 August 1474).

[72] As discussed in Chapter 3, minutes and correspondence are now scattered throughout multiple series of the Milanese archives: ASMi, *Registri* 18; ASMi, *Confini* 270; ASMi, *Carteggio* 341 and 343.

[73] On Bartolo and the origin of a 'cartographie juridique' which is now largely lost, see de Dainville, 'Cartes et contestations', 118–21.

prospective views, the sketch of the Lombardy valleys is a topographical chart; where the former depicted a defined area from an aerial viewpoint, the latter captures spatial relationships using a flat diagram. However, the sketch does more than simply outline their position in relation to the disputed Val Taleggio (represented here as a circle). This is because it depicts the valleys not as geographical features but as units of territorial organization, namely as discrete corporate bodies. Like the castles and villages on the map of Crema or even the towns and cities on that of Lombardy, these units can be used to signal the location of state borders. This time, the spatial description is moved from the level of regional polities (lions and vipers) to that of individual city-states. On the map, the jurisdictional power of the *civitates* over the local units is signalled by adding the letter M (for Milan, meaning part of the old Milanese *districtus* and now of the Duchy) or the letter P (for *Pergamum*, that is Bergamo and thus part of the Venetian Republic). As in the map of Crema, where the linear representation of local boundaries is determined by the position of individual communities, here the border is determined by the spatial configuration of individual territories.

This book has spent a great many words explaining how and to what extent state borders came to overlap with the boundaries of pre-existing territories. By placing border stones marked with Ms and Ps on the lines representing the limits of local bodies, the mapmaker provides us with a concise but enlightening representation of this phenomenon as well as new way of thinking about the relationships between space and power in late medieval Italy. The map is also a brilliant depiction of another dimension central to this book: the vertical interactions shaping the politics of space. After all, what is this map if not an effort by state chancellors to make sense, through symbols and geometry and much humanistic flair, of the intricate geography established by local parties and communities in the Lombard Alps?

* * *

It is clear, then, that besides being technical and artistic products, regional and district maps from late medieval Italy were artefacts rooted in the political and territorial culture of their time. The maps examined in this chapter epitomize the territorial order as it was understood by contemporaries, thus challenging our preconceptions of the ways in which territoriality could be visually depicted. To begin with, none of the examples above presents a uniform political space, one bounded by linear borders and under the authority of an exclusive power. Regional states do appear in this corpus of

212   BORDERS AND THE POLITICS OF SPACE IN LATE MEDIEVAL ITALY

fifteenth-century maps: they are embodied in the vipers, lions, words, and letters marking territorial possession. However, their spatial extent is never pictured in its entirety; regional states, in other words, are never rendered as territories themselves. While Pisato's work is traditionally labelled as a regional map, its spatial framework is not a single regional dominion but rather the area (Lombardy) where two or more polities (the Duchy and the Republic) became entangled.

If the examples examined above chart less than the full dimension of regional states, they also chart more than mere landscapes or series of places. As we have seen when discussing the three maps of the Bresciano, a geographical layer made up of mountains, rivers, and infrastructures was always coupled with a territorial layer displaying multiple units of territorial organization (such as villages, towns, *contadi*, and, when not silenced, intermediate federations) which were then arranged hierarchically according to their jurisdictional power. To the makers of these maps and their contemporaries, these units were more than just places on a map; they were *universitates*, corporate bodies exercising a bundle of rights and duties over a jurisdictional space. The focus of regional and district maps, to put it briefly, was neither states nor places. It was territories or, more accurately, *territoria*. Territories, not states, were the spatial frames of reference of the Venetian decree of 1460; and territories, not places, were the communities through which the citizens of Brescia visually constructed their imagined *contado*.

Although they were hired by major power holders and state officials, the makers of regional and district maps could not help but give emphasis to the smaller units in which territoriality lay. Even when emphasizing the prominence of Brescia or Crema within their wider *contadi*, they still placed cities in relation to a constellation of smaller corporations. Similarly, when it came to drawing borders, that is, to applying a political overlayer onto the geographical and territorial layers described above, mapmakers first had to consider the location of these units and their political affiliation. They did so in a number of ways: by tracing imaginary circles encompassing the communities making up the *districtus*, by leaving empty spaces in the margin of a drawing, by using heraldic badges and other signs of territorial belonging, by adding words and letters, and even by painting border stones. Whatever the written or pictorial element used to signify the limits of the state, it was the position of the unit to which that element was attached that allowed them to draw the line. It was neither the mapmaker nor his clients (the polity, the lord, the city) who determined the location of state borders but the spatial configuration of a plurality of pre-existing territories.

Conclusion

Over the course of this book, the world of borders has been explored from a variety of angles. We discussed the intellectual notions and discourses which both framed them and shaped them (Chapter 1). We uncovered the principles and diplomatic practices through which they were negotiated (Chapter 2) and disputed (Chapter 3). We tracked the most important actors and interactions behind their definition (Chapter 4) and examined the flows of people and objects by which they were crossed (Chapter 5). Finally, we studied the techniques through which they were recorded (Chapter 6) and mapped (Chapter 7) and highlighted the range of people involved in doing so. These last few pages will discuss the importance of these findings for three broader fields: the history of medieval borders, and especially their supposed porosity and muddled nature; the study of pre-modern forms of territoriality, as seen through the framework of the politics of space; and the paradigm of the territorial state in Italy, now reappraised from the perspective of borders.

Borders

Unlike some of their European equivalents, the borders of late medieval Italy were not vague zones of contact, conflict, and exchange; nor were they merely porous or muddled lines. When we assume that all borders were fluid and uncertain before modernity, we are effectively oversimplifying historical conditions and refusing to allow for the complexity of a system other than our own. Instead, this book has shown that borders were widely understood, carefully located, and often also strictly controlled in late medieval Italy—just not in the way we understand, locate, and control borders today.

Firstly, borders were not seen as dividing lines or as connecting points; rather, they were conceived of as the perimeters of territories or, more accurately, as the limits of *territoria*. While they might also have happened to set states apart, borders were more commonly what brought people

Borders and the Politics of Space in Late Medieval Italy: Milan, Venice, and their Territories. Luca Zenobi, Oxford University Press. © Luca Zenobi 2023. DOI: 10.1093/oso/9780198876861.003.0009

214   BORDERS AND THE POLITICS OF SPACE IN LATE MEDIEVAL ITALY

together—what encompassed the territory over which a community (*universitas*) exercised its rights. As with *iurisdictio* itself, this meant that different types of territories could exist side by side or even overlap. The same went for their borders. The land and boundaries of a village could be part of a fief or federation, which in turn could be part of a town or city district; similarly, an urban district could form part of a larger polity, as in the case of the Duchy of Milan and the Republic of Venice. It follows that before being seen as an issue for states and authorities to regulate, borders were understood as a matter of communities and jurisdictional rights.

As such, Italian borders were often precisely situated. But again, precision was not dictated by some absolute requirement for linear distinctions between states. Rather, precision was made necessary by the need to define the spatial prerogatives of different communities: where a village could lead its herds to pasture, where a town could fell trees or exploit streams, where a city could levy duties over passing goods. This made for an acute awareness of the limits of local spaces, one based not on carefully drawn maps but on mnemonic artefacts (border stones), written devices (notably lists and notarial records), and social activities (including the itinerant definition of community boundaries, the official visitations of state deputies, and the regular encounters with frontier posts). While precision in the location and knowledge of borders was not a byproduct of the rise of new states, such polities promptly capitalized on this entrenched spatial consciousness to define their own borders. As has been noted many times in this book, in the expanse of overlapping corporations that formed the territorial landscape of the time, power holders needed only to enumerate the territories that were effectively under their jurisdiction to define the contours of their dominions.

Once local boundaries had been adopted as state frontiers, Italian rulers joined local groups in their governance. Although trading territories on the occasion of major peace treaties was first conducted at a higher level, every other aspect of border policy hinged upon a sustained level of exchanges between state and non-state actors. Firstly, localized exigencies often drove border disputes, but they also settled them. The case of the communities of the Lombard valleys, where the territorial organization of factions dramatically shaped local spaces, shows well the extent to which pre-existing divisions imparted strength and stability to state frontiers. Secondly, spatial knowledge was originally inscribed in the peripheries, from which it was constantly retrieved by central chanceries. Using different scales and different techniques, notaries and chancellors compiled accurate information concerning border arrangements. Lastly, while the actual marking of

CONCLUSION 215

borders was outsourced to local communities, Italian rulers established their presence at both external frontiers and internal boundaries. Through these border posts, they oversaw a dense system of crossings designed to channel the flow of resources and monitor the circulation of people.

The Politics of Space

Having established that borders were widely understood, carefully located, and sometimes also strictly controlled in late medieval Italy, we can draw further conclusions as to the historical conditions that brought them into being. This book has investigated the contingent nature of borders—and of the territories they bounded—in the context of the politics and culture that shaped them. That politics was not just the process through which the state organized its territories; it was the ensemble of political exchanges and social activities which surrounded and sometimes hindered that process. While constructing state borders was not always a concerted endeavour, it was inevitably an interactive one, involving community representatives and local notaries alongside state deputies and central chanceries. In late medieval Italy, these actors interacted in different ways and on different stages: the transfer of jurisdiction over multiple territories, specifically on the occasion of proceedings such as that of the *consignatio*; the formulation of arrangements drawing on existing divisions of local society, as in the case of Guelphs and Ghibellines; the definition of local boundaries, notably using the knowhow and manpower of rural communities; the mechanics of border-crossing and, in particular, the negotiation of travel documents; and finally the making of records and maps concerning borders, which in turn was driven by the same need for dialogue between centres and peripheries over territorial divisions.

What guided these interactions, thus shaping the politics of space, was a shared territorial culture, that is, a common understanding of the ways in which spatial relationships should be conceived, constructed, and challenged. In late medieval Italy, this culture encompassed multiple elements. One was the theory of territorial pluralism developed by jurists—a theory both framing and reflecting the realities of their time. Building on the flexible notion of *iurisdictio*, jurists were able to conceptualize the coexistence and overlapping of multiple territorial bodies within the same polity, all equipped with their own boundaries. Another element was the set of criteria applied to negotiate and dispute borders. These criteria included the use of a

216   BORDERS AND THE POLITICS OF SPACE IN LATE MEDIEVAL ITALY

range of spatial scales to describe territorial changes and the adoption of the principle of jurisdictional affiliation to place territories in relation to each other. Finally, several other elements of this territorial culture were drawn from other types of cultures, such as a writing culture and a negotiating culture. At its foundation, however, much derived from a culture of possession (as exemplified by the close identification of a community and its space, and by a patrimonial understanding of personal dominions) and from a culture of practice (seen in the belief that borders were never established once and for all but rather needed to be continuously experienced and reified).

By placing borders and territories within the broader framework of the politics and culture that shaped them, a new understanding of pre-modern forms of territoriality is gained. This reveals that territoriality, like political power, was constructed through performances as much as through authoritative projections—through representation (mapping, listing) as much as through practice (crossing, marking, negotiating). It also reveals that, like power itself, territoriality lay simultaneously with different bodies. The state was not the only promoter of territorial changes, nor was it the only border maker: countless communities of different shapes and sizes asserted their own claims over space and drew their own borders. This made for a form of territoriality that was fundamentally modular, composite, and non-exclusive but nonetheless effective. Indeed, much as late medieval power holders were undoubtedly powerful in relative terms, late medieval territoriality was, to all intents and purposes, territorial; but it was so in a contingent way, one that does not resemble modern modalities of territorial control. Finally, while it is essential to recognize that the workings of territoriality mimicked those of political power, it is also important to appreciate that the two did not always go together. Some bodies were more potent than others, as was undoubtedly the case with the Italian states, but were they also the most territorial?

Milan, Venice, and their Territories

The answer is no. In the Late Middle Ages, the political landscape of the Italian peninsula underwent profound changes. Most of the old city-states were incorporated into more extensive dominions, while small principalities and feudal pockets were either dissolved or forced to accept the same fate as the ancient *civitates*: submission. In the book's Introduction, this picture was framed as the 'narrative of simplification'; it was suggested that it may have shaped our understanding of the spatial fabric of Italian society far more than we realize. Indeed, from a political perspective, the familiar account of the rise of a small number of 'territorial states' is hard to question. Smaller independent powers did survive, but now they were inescapably yoked to a system of feudal and political bonds which, while defending their seeming independence, ultimately reinforced their subordination to a few larger powers. However, from a territorial perspective, the narrative of simplification shows more than one crack.

The evidence presented throughout this book demonstrates that by the end of the Middle Ages, the network of borders running through the peninsula had got denser rather than thinner, while the spatial fabric of Italian society had become even more intricate. Counter-intuitively, for the modern observer at least, the undeniable decrease in the number of dominant polities was not accompanied by a corresponding decrease in the number of territories. This was due to two factors. The first was the establishment of novel territorial aggregations, notably the dominions of new regional powers (such as the Duchy of Milan and the Republic of Venice) and the territories of new intermediate entities (such as townships, fiefs, and community federations). The second and most crucial factor was that these new bodies did not erase pre-existing forms of territorial organization, nor did they cancel their borders: territorial states did not efface the old city-states and intermediate entities never fully replaced the localities which they encompassed.

This raises the question of what, then, was the territorial footprint of the new bodies. In the case of intermediate entities, the answer is simple: they aligned with and sometimes replaced the old *contadi*. As the spatial frameworks within which taxes were collected and justice administered, these new bodies came to serve both as superior units of social organization for the localities and as arenas in which states could exert their prerogatives. With regard to regional dominions, however, our answer needs to be more nuanced. This is not only because of their size, but because the question of their territorial power is inescapably bound up with questions about their political power. One problem is that state territoriality was more often imagined than asserted, a dynamic which we have explored throughout this book: by studying maps, for example, but also through various examples of linguistic imagery. Another is that even when a degree of territorial control was actually asserted, as when monitoring movement flows or dispatching officials to frontier posts, the extent to which this promoted a new form of territoriality remains debatable.

In Italy, the process of state formation involved an interesting mixture of continuity and discontinuity. Among the novelties, one could count the establishment of centralized magistracies, extensive chanceries,

218   BORDERS AND THE POLITICS OF SPACE IN LATE MEDIEVAL ITALY

and diplomatic networks—all conversing using a shared idiom and common written devices. Territoriality, however, does not seem to have been among those novelties, for it generally remained with smaller bodies: from city-states or intermediate entities to local communities. To appreciate this fact more fully, one need only compare the territorial strategy of the old city-states with that of the new polities. Although both were fundamentally non-exclusive, the city-states would only recognize local communities as alternative forms of territorial organization. At first, when they enjoyed full independence, the cities strove to assimilate rural lords into the territorial order they envisioned; later, having become part of larger dominions, they never truly accepted the competition of intermediate entities. By contrast, the rulers of fifteenth-century Italy did none of these things: they allowed and even promoted enfeoffments, and they fully legitimized the territories of townships and federations. As long as these bodies brought strength and stability to their dominions, starting with their borders, Italian rulers preferred to rely on pre-existing forms of territorial organization rather than devising some of their own.

In the end, the Italian states were only territorial in so far as their constituent bodies had already undergone a process of territorialization. Better still, the state was effectively territorial without being a solid territory in itself. It follows that thinking about the Duchy of Milan as a territorial principality may not be the best way to appreciate its spatial dimension: territorially, the Duchy was more like a micro empire than a miniaturized kingdom. Similarly, a new vision of the Venetian Terraferma is gained: again, territorially speaking, the mainland state was a constellation of areas which were more like Venice's overseas possessions than the territorial expanse of the state itself. These polities may therefore be best understood not as territories themselves but as networks: regional systems connecting spaces made by local communities. In turn, this suggestion invites a new conceptualization of Italian society, one that moves away from established paradigms to develop a new picture of the spatial fabric of the peninsula. In the Introduction, we outlined two of these paradigms and discussed the maps which epitomize them: those depicting an Italy of cities and an Italy of states. Having reached the end of this investigation, we can safely say that neither truly captures the territorial order of the time. Politically, late medieval Italy was undeniably made up of a system of regional states, most of which had been built on the power of an individual city. But spatially, the map of Italy was actually very different and, arguably, far more complex: it was not an Italy of cities, nor was it one of states; it was an Italy of territories or, one last time, *territoria*.

Bibliography

1. Unpublished Primary Sources

Archivio di Stato, Bergamo (ASBg)

Archivio notarile 166: notebook of the notary Giovanni Corti, active in the Val San Martino in the first half of the Quattrocento.

Archivio di Stato, Brescia (ASBr)

Archivio storico comunale 434/2: manuscript copy of the fiscal estimates to which the earliest map of Brescia and the Bresciano was originally attached (1406–16).

Archivio di Stato, Cremona (ASCr)

Annona 8, f. 7: census of local food supplies for the year 1487.

Annona 11, f. 1 and f. 2: censuses of local food supplies for the years 1427 and 1477.

Archivio di Stato, Milano (ASMi)

Atti di governo (*Esenzioni*) 381, f. 'Arrigoni': collection of fiscal privileges granted to the family from the fifteenth century onwards.

Carteggio 217: diplomatic correspondence between Milan and Naples for the year 1468.

Carteggio 340, 341, 342, 343, and 344: diplomatic correspondence between Milan and Venice for the years 1450–6, mostly letters to and from the duke's ambassadors based in the lagoon.

Carteggio 660 and 662: internal correspondence between the duke, his officers, and subject bodies for the years 1452 and 1453.

Carteggio 1517bis, 1566, and 1568: further correspondence relevant to Milanese–Venetian relations for the 1450s, 1460s, and 1470s.

Carteggio 1524, 1525, and 1526: minutes, copies, and originals of other public records drafted in the 1450s (*pactae, consignationes, investiturae*).

Comuni 6 (f. 'Bergamo'), 12 (f. 'Bordolano'), 14 (f. 'Brivio'), and 17 (f. 'Caravaggio'): petitions sent to the Milanese Chancery in the second half of the Quattrocento.

Confini 238, 239, 255, 270, 271, 288, 296, and 314: records concerning borders originally made or received by the Milanese Chancery and then extracted by the *provveditori ai confini* in the late eighteenth century.

Confini 290: map of the valleys between Lecco and Bergamo (1456).

Frammenti 1, f. 15: fragment of the *Liber Albus*, collecting trade licences granted by the Milanese Chancery between 1454 and 1455.

Frammenti 11, f. 160: register of 'littere salviconductus', 'littere licentie', and 'littere recomendatorie' granted by Niccolò Piccinino between 1437 and 1438.

Miscellanea mappe e disegni 20 A: map of the Val Taleggio (*c*.1550).

220 BIBLIOGRAPHY

Missive 2, 4, 7, 11, 12, 13, and 16: registers of outgoing correspondence, typically letters sent by the Milanese Chancery in the duke's name to both home and foreign officials, rural communities, and individuals.

Missive 33: 'Liber licentiarum bladorum', comprising trade licences granted by the Milanese Chancery between 1455 and 1458.

Panigarola 1: register of ducal ordinances issued under the Visconti, including decrees from the late fourteenth century.

Registri 18, 35, 37, 39, and 42: chancery registers comprising the written foundations of ducal power (investitures, donations, *deditiones*) mixed with records framing the relationships between the Duchy and neighbouring powers (pacts, treaties, *arbitramenta*).

Registri 98, 100, 126, 129, 151, 154, 155, 161, 162, 164, and 166: chancery registers comprising copies of safe conducts granted by the Milanese Chancery between 1452 and 1465.

Archivio di Stato, Reggio Emilia (ASRe)

Untitled fifteenth-century map of the area and road system between Reggio and Correggio.

Archivio di Stato, Venezia (ASVe)

Copie dei Pacta 6: manuscript copy of a chancery collection of pacts and treaties between Venice and neighbouring powers.

Dieci Misti (Registri) 15: register of deliberations taken by the Council of Ten between 1454 and 1460.

Memorie antiche per servire al vacuo dei Commemoriali 2: miscellaneous compilation of records made by the Venetian Chancery to fill the gaps left by the *Commemoriali* series, including pacts, treaties, trial records, and other public documents.

Miscellanea 35, 39, and 40: miscellaneous boxes of charters granted to local bodies and treaties signed with neighbouring powers.

Secreta (Indici) 573 and 804: inventories of Venice's Secret Chancery compiled during the 1530s and 1540s.

Senato Secreti (Registri) 10 and 12: registers of secret deliberations taken by the Venetian Senate between 1426 and 1433.

Senato Terra (Registri) 2: register of deliberations concerning the mainland dominion taken by the Venetian Senate between 1446 and 1451.

Biblioteca Ambrosiana, Milano (BAMi)

Codex Atlanticus: bound set of drawings and writings by Leonardo da Vinci, including a project for the renovation of the fortress of Baiedo.

ms. 940 inf: sixteenth-century copy of the map of Padua and the Padovano drawn by Annibale Maggi da Bassano in 1449.

ms. L 90 suss: miscellaneous collection of records extracted from the Milanese archives, notably public treaties and ducal decrees from the fourteenth and fifteenth century.

ms. S N N III 2: printed copy of the *Chronica de rebus Brixianorum* by Elia Capriolo (Brescia 1505), including the oldest printed map of the Bresciano.

BIBLIOGRAPHY   221

ms. Z 227 sup, f. 'Guerra co' Veneziani e col marchese di Monferrato 1452–4': miscellaneous collection of records extracted from the Milanese archives.

Biblioteca Apostolica Vaticana, Roma (BAVa)

Fondo Patetta, ms. 1387: Bergamo's earliest surviving *liber finium*, comprising records describing the boundaries of over 120 Bergamasque communities (1392–5).

Biblioteca Civica Angelo Mai, Bergamo (BMBg)

Cancelleria pretoria 1: excerpt of a register of safe conducts granted by one of the two Venetian governors of Bergamo between 1430 and 1432.

Confini, ms. 96 R 2, ms. 96 R 12, ms. 96 R 23, ms. 96 R 30, ms. 97 R 5, ms. 97 R 9, and ms. 98 R 27: miscellaneous volumes comprising documentation concerning borders collected in the early modern period by the *provveditori* of Bergamo's *Camera dei confini*.

Fondo Salvioni e Bellaviti 1 and 39: records by the notary Costanzo Salvioni from Sottochiesa (1455–63) and the notary Cristoforo Bellaviti from Taleggio (1444–64).

Municipali 1 and 2: register of normative resolutions sent to Bergamo's governors and other local magistracies by Venice's central offices.

Sala I, ms. D 7 29: 1373 statutes of Bergamo, including a section on the duty of rural communities to delimit their respective boundaries (*collatio* XII–7).

Salone Cassapanca I, ms. 4 47/1–2, manuscript collection of around 180 *instrumenta confinationum* concerning Bergamasque communities (mostly dating to the years 1456 and 1481).

Salone Furietti Ar 22: inventory of the archive of Bergamo's *Camera dei confini*, compiled by the chancellor Giovanni Maironi da Ponte in 1795.

Biblioteca Civica Queriniana, Brescia (BQBr)

ms. H V 5: the so-called *Libro dei privilegi di Venezia per la nobiltà bresciana*, including the third oldest map of Brescia and the Bresciano (*c.*1472).

Biblioteca Civica Trivulziana, Milano (BTMi)

ms. 1230: Milanese collection of ordinances regulating the circulation of food supplies (1386–1485).

Biblioteca Comunale, Crema (BCCr)

Ducali 1: register of resolutions sent to local authorities by the central powers (notably the doge of Venice) mixed with formal documentation relevant to the city's jurisdictional and fiscal position (charters, privileges, conventions).

Finanza 19, f. 164 (1433) and f. 165 (1447): documentation recording Visconti's pledge to abolish all custom barriers between the district of Crema and that of Milan.

Provisioni 1, 2, 3, and 5: registers of resolutions adopted by Crema assemblies and councils, including decrees regarding the circulation of goods, the administration of records concerning borders, and the appointment of deputies for the resolution of territorial disputes.

222 BIBLIOGRAPHY

Biblioteca Comunale, Treviso (BCTv)
ms. 1497: map of Lombardy by Giovanni Pisato (1440).

Biblioteca Nazionale Braidense, Milano (BBMi)
ms. A E XII 39: a collection of ordinances concerning the collection of duties and the circulation of foodstuffs issued by the Visconti between 1331 and 1446.

Biblioteca Nazionale Marciana, Venezia (BMVe)
ms. It. II 119 (4843): 'Iura iurisdictionum octo vallium bergomensium', compilation of fiscal and jurisdictional privileges granted by Venice to the valleys of the Bergamasco.

ms. It. VII 498 (8147): Venetian collection of ordinances regulating the circulation of food supplies (fifteenth and sixteenth centuries).

ms. It. VII 762 (7668): miscellaneous collection of records, including a long letter sent by Paolo Morisini to Cicco Simonetta (n. IV).

ms. It. VII 1827 (7620): annals for the period 1237–1509, focusing especially on Venice's involvement in the Lombard Wars of the first half of the Quattrocento.

ms. It. VII 2540 (12432): sixteenth-century chronicle including data extracted from the Venetian archives, notably fifteenth-century demographic censuses and lists of revenues and expenses.

ms. It. VII 2581 (12473), Venetian chronicle covering the years up to 1457, including miscellaneous records extracted from the Venetian archives.

Biblioteca Statale, Cremona (BSCr)
ms. AA 4 30 and ms. Albertoni 222: fifteenth-century series of local ordinances regulating the circulation of food supplies.

Biblioteca Universitaria Estense, Modena (BEMo)
Carte geografiche A 8: second oldest map of Brescia and the Bresciano (c.1440).

Bibliothèque Municipale de l'Inguimbertine, Carpentras (BICa)
ms. 327: fifteenth-century Provençal copy of the surveyor's manual by Arnaud de Villeneuve (1240–1315).

Bibliothèque Nationale de France, Paris (BNFr)
Cartes et plans Ge C 4090: the so-called Carta militare della Lombardia, dating to around the mid-fifteenth century.

ms. Latin 6467: philosophical treatise from Pavia's ducal library, including a manuscript illumination depicting the Visconti dominion as a catalogue of cities.

Museo Correr, Venezia (MCVe)
Cartografia 35: map of Crema and the Cremasco from around the mid-fifteenth century.

BIBLIOGRAPHY 223

2. Printed Primary Sources

ANDERLONI, E. (ed.), 'Statuti di Averara e Val Taleggio degli anni MCCCXIII e MCCCLXVIII', in *Corpus Statutorum Italicorum* (vol. III), ed. by P. Sella, Rome, 1913.

ARRIGONI, G. (ed.), *Documenti inediti riguardanti la storia della Valsassina e delle terre limitrofe*, Milan, 1857.

CALVI, D., *Effemeride sacra profana di quanto di memorabile sia successo in Bergamo* (vol. III), Bergamo, 1676.

CASTELLI, C., 'Liber mirabilium, sive Chronicon successuum guelforum et gibellinorum ab anno MCCCLXXVIII usque ad annum MCCCCVII', in *Rerum Italicarum Scriptores* (vol. XVI), ed. by L. A. Muratori, Milan, 1730, cols. 841–1008.

CORIO, B., *Storia di Milano* (vol. II), ed. by A. Morisi Guerra, Milan, 1978.

DA SIENA, B., *Prediche volgari sul Campo di Siena: 1427* (vol. II), ed. by C. Delcorno, Milan, 1989.

DE LAZARIS, J. D. (ed.), *Statuta civilia et criminalia communitatis Vallissaxinae*, Milan, 1674.

DEL MONTE, G., *Tractatus de finibus regendis civitatum, castrorum*, Venice, 1574.

DEL POZZO, G., *Allegationes celeberrimorum doctissimorum iurisconsultorum Iacobi de Puteo pro Communitate terrae Valentiae et Luchini de Curte pro Communitate Sancti Salvatoris in materia confinaria*, Venice, 1574.

DE SAXOFERRATO, B., *Super secunda parte Digesti Novi*, Lyons, 1504.

DE SAXOFERRATO, B., 'Tractatus super Constitutionem ad reprimendum', in *Consilia et Tractatus*, Venice, 1635.

DE UBALDIS, B., *In usus feudorum*, Lyons, 1550.

DUMONT, J. (ed.), *Corps universel diplomatique du droit des gens* (vols. II and III), Amsterdam, 1726.

FINAZZI, G. (ed.), *Cronaca anonima di Bergamo degli anni 1402–1484*, Bergamo, 1870.

FORGIARINI, G. (ed.), *Lo statuto di Bergamo del 1353*, Spoleto, 1996.

LÜNING, J. C. (ed.), *Codex Italiae Diplomaticus* (vol. I), Leipzig, 1725.

MACHIAVELLI, N., 'Discorsi sopra la prima deca di Tito Livio', in *Opere* (vol. I), ed. by S. Bertelli and F. Gaeta, Milan, 1960.

MACHIAVELLI, N., *Chief Works and Others* (vol. II), trans. by A. Gilbert, Durham, NC, 1965.

MACHIAVELLI, N., *The Prince*, ed. by Q. Skinner and R. Price, Cambridge, 1988.

MANARESI, C. (ed.), *Inventari e regesti del R. archivio di stato di Milano* (vol. I), Milan, 1915.

MARCHETTI, V. (ed.), *Confini dei comuni del territorio di Bergamo (1392–1395)*, Bergamo, 1996.

MURATORI, L. A. (ed.), 'Raphayni de Caresini cancellarii Venetiarum Cronica a. 1343–1388', in *Rerum Italicarum Scriptores* (vol. XII), Milan, 1728, cols. 1–524.

MURATORI, L. A., 'Capitula Pacis Factae in Civitate Laudeae die IX Aprilis Anno MCCCCLIV', in *Rerum Italicarum Scriptores* (vol. XVI), Milan, 1730, cols. 1009–20.

224 BIBLIOGRAPHY

NATALE, A. R. (ed.), *I diari di Cicco Simonetta*, Milan, 1962.
NATALE, A. R. (ed.), *Acta in Consilio Secreto in castello Portae Jovis Mediolani* (vol. I), Milan, 1963.
NOTO, A. (ed.), *Liber datii mercantie communis Mediolani*, Milan, 1958.
OSIO, L. (ed.), *Documenti diplomatici tratti dagli archivi milanesi* (vol. II), Milan, 1872.
PREDELLI, R. (ed.), *I libri commemoriali della Repubblica di Venezia: regesti* (vol. IV), Venice, 1896.
SANUTO, M., *I diari* (vol. VIII), Venice, 1882.
SELLA, Q. (ed), *Codex Astensis qui de Malabayla nuncupatur*, Rome, 1887.
STORTI, F. (ed.), *Dispacci sforzeschi da Napoli* (vol. IV), Salerno 1998.
TAGLIAFERRI, A. (ed.), *Relazioni dei rettori veneti in Terraferma: podestaria e capitanato di Bergamo* (vol. XII), Milan, 1978.
TOMMASI, G., *Sommario della storia di Lucca dall'anno MIV all'anno MDCC*, Florence, 1847.
VITTANI, G. (ed.), *Inventari e regesti del R. Archivio di Stato di Milano* (vol. II), Milan, 1929.

3. Printed Secondary Literature

Abulafia, D., *Mediterranean Encounters: Economic, Religious, Political, 1000–1550*, London, 2000.
Abulafia, D. and N. Berend (eds.), *Medieval Frontiers: Concepts and Practices*, Aldershot, 2002.
Adami, V., 'La magistratura dei confini nello Stato di Milano', *Archivio storico lombardo*, 37/2 (1913), 126–57.
Adami, V., *I magistrati ai confini nella Repubblica di Venezia*, Grottaferrata, 1915.
Agnew, J., 'The Territorial Trap: The Geographical Assumptions of International Relations Theory', *Review of International Political Economy*, 1/1 (1994), 53–80.
Agnew, J., 'Sovereignty Regimes: Territoriality and State Authority in Contemporary World Politics', *Annals of the Association of American Geographers*, 95/2 (2005), 437–61.
Agnew, J., 'Borders on the Mind: Re-Framing Border Thinking', *Ethics and Global Politics*, 1/4 (2008), 175–91.
Airò, A., C. Caldelli, V. De Fraja, and G. Francesconi, 'Italia, italiae, italicae gentes. Particolarismi, varietà e tensioni all'*unitas* nella cronistica tardomedievale', in *Unità d'Italia e Istituto storico italiano. Quando la politica era anche tensione culturale*, ed. by A. Airò, E. Caldelli, and V. De Fraja, Rome, 2013, 33–55.
Albini, G., 'Da castrum a città. Crema fra XII e XV secolo', *Società e storia*, 42/4 (1988), 819–54.
Albini, G., 'La popolazione di Bergamo e territorio nei secoli XIV e XV', in *Storia economica e sociale di Bergamo* (vol. II), ed. by G. Chittolini, Bergamo, 1999, 213–55.
Albini, G., 'Crema tra XII e XIV secolo. Il quadro politico-istituzionale', in *Crema nel Trecento: Conoscenza e controllo del territorio*, Crema, 2005, 13–44.

BIBLIOGRAPHY 225

Albini, G., 'Il controllo della sanità. Gli officiali del ducato di Milano nel XV secolo', in *La polizia sanitaria: dall'emergenza alla gestione della quotidianità*, ed. by L. Antonielli, Soveria Mannelli, 2015, 7–18.

Aldeghi, G. and G. Riva, 'Adda fiume di confine. Contrabbando e spionaggio tra Olginate e la valle di S. Martino nella seconda metà del Quattrocento', *Archivi di Lecco*, 17/4 (1994), 63–128.

Almagià, R. (ed.), *Monumenta Italiae cartographica. Riproduzione di carte generali e regionali d'Italia dal secolo XIV al XVII*, Florence, 1929.

Almagià, R., 'Un'antica carta del territorio di Asti', *Rivista Geografica Italiana*, 58/2 (1951), 43–4.

Almagià, R., 'Studi storici di cartografia napoletana', in *Scritti geografici (1905-1957)*, Rome, 1961, 231–324.

Almbjär, M., 'The Problem with Early-Modern Petitions: Safety Valve or Powder Keg?', *European Review of History*, 26/6 (2019), 1013–39.

Anderson, J., 'The Shifting Stage of Politics: New Medieval and Postmodern Territoriality', *Environment and Planning D: Society and Space*, 14 (1996), 133–55.

Anderson, M., *Frontiers: Territory and State Formation in the Modern World*, Oxford, 1996.

Andreozzi, D., *Nascita di un disordine. Una famiglia signorile e una valle piacentina tra XV e XVI secolo*, Bologna, 1993.

Ansani, F., 'Oltre i signori, dopo i mercenari. Per una rilettura del rapporto tra istituzioni militari e stato rinascimentale', *Annali dell'Istituto Italiano per gli Studi Storici*, 33 (2021), 29–101.

Antonini, F., 'La pace di Lodi e i segreti maneggi che la preparano', *Archivio storico lombardo*, 57 (1930), 233–96.

Appadurai, A., *Modernity at Large: Cultural Dimensions of Globalisation*, Minneapolis, MN, 1996.

Appuhn, K., 'Inventing Nature: Forests, Forestry, and State Power in Renaissance Venice', *The Journal of Modern History*, 72/4 (2000), 861–89.

Arcangeli, L., *Gentiluomini di Lombardia. Ricerche sull'aristocrazia padana nel Rinascimento*, Milan, 2003.

Ascheri, M., 'Beyond the *Comune*: The Italian City-State and its Inheritance', in *The Medieval World*, ed. by P. Linehan and J. L. Nelson, London, 2001, 451–68.

Ascheri, M., 'La cité-état italienne du Moyen Âge. Culture et liberté', *Médiévales*, 48/1 (2005), 149–64.

Austin, J. L., *How to Do Things with Words*, ed. by J. O. Urmson, Oxford, 1962.

Avesani, R., *Verona nel Quattrocento. La civiltà delle lettere*, Verona, 1984.

Baratta, M., 'La carta della Lombardia di Giovanni Pisato (1440)', *Rivista geografica italiana*, 20 (1913), 159–63, 449–59, and 577–93.

Barbiche, B., 'Les *diplomates* pontificaux du Moyen Âge tardif à la première modernité. Office et charge pastorale', in *Offices et papauté (XIVe–XVIIe siècle). Charges, hommes, destins*, ed. by O. Poncet and A. Jamme, Rome, 2005, 357–70.

Barbieri, G., *Economia e politica nel ducato di Milano, 1386-1535*, Milan, 1938.

Bartlett, R. and A. MacKay (eds.), *Medieval Frontier Societies*, Oxford, 1989.

226 BIBLIOGRAPHY

Bartoli Langeli, A., 'La documentazione degli stati italiani nei secoli XIII–XV. Forme, organizzazione, personale', *Publications de l'École française de Rome*, 82/1 (1985), 35–55.

Bartoli Langeli, A., 'Notariato, documentazione e coscienza comunale', in *Federico II e le città italiane*, ed. by Id. and P. Toubert, Palermo, 1994, 264–77.

Bastian, J. A., 'Moving the Margins to the Middle: Reconciling *the Archive* with the Archives', in *Engaging with Records and Archives: Histories and Theories*, ed. by F. Foscarini, H. Macneil, B. Mak, and G. Oliver, London, 2016, 3–19.

Bauder, H., 'Toward a Critical Geography of the Border: Engaging the Dialectic of Practice and Meaning', *Annals of the Association of American Geographers*, 101/5 (2011), 1126–39.

Baumgärtner, I., *Martinus Garatus Laudensis: Ein italienischer Rechtsgelehrter des 15. Jahrhunderts*, Cologne, 1986.

Behne, A., 'Archivordnung und Staatsordnung im Mailand der Sforza-Zeit', *Nuovi Annali della Scuola speciale per archivisti e bibliotecari*, 2 (1988), 93–102.

Beloch, K. J., *Bevölkerungsgeschichte Italiens* (vol III), Berlin, 1961.

Belotti, B., 'Controversie sui confini di Zogno', *Bergomum*, 19/3 (1925), 151–63.

Belotti, B., 'La cacciata dei Brembillesi (1443)', *Bergomum*, 29/4 (1935), 211–32.

Beltrami, L., *Il castello di Milano sotto il dominio dei Visconti*, Milan, 1894.

Benigni, P. and C. Vivoli, 'Progetti politici e organizzazione d'archivi. Storia della documentazione dei Nove Conservatori della Giurisdizione e Dominio Fiorentino', *Rassegna degli Archivi di Stato*, 43 (1983), 32–82.

Benton, L. and R. J. Ross (eds.), *Legal Pluralism and Empires, 1500–1850*, New York, 2013.

Berend, N., 'Medievalists and the Notion of the Frontier', *Medieval History Journal*, 2/1 (1999), 55–72.

Berlioz, J. and O. Poncet (eds.), *Se donner à la France? Les rattachements pacifiques de territoires à la France (XIVe–XIXe siècle)*, Paris, 2013.

Bertoldi, A., 'Topografia del Veronese (secolo XV), *Archivio veneto*, 35/2 (1888), 455–73.

Bertoni, L., 'Strade e mercati. Itinerari commerciali e normativa daziaria nella Lombardia viscontea', in *Medioevo vissuto. Studi per Rinaldo Comba fra Piemonte e Lombardia*, ed. by B. Del Bo and P. Grillo, Rome, 2016, 121–47.

Bertoni, L., 'I regimi di popolo e la vigilanza annonaria sul territorio. L'esempio di Pavia', in *Tra polizie e controllo del territorio: alla ricerca delle discontinuità*, ed. by L. Antonielli and S. Levati, Soveria Mannelli, 2017, 125–44.

Bertuzzi, R., 'Le legazioni in Europa del cardinale Niccolò Albergati', in *La chiesa di Bologna e la cultura europea*, Bologna, 2002, 89–105.

Bianchi, R., 'Notizie del cartografo veneziano Antonio Leonardi. Con un'appendice su Daniele Emigli (o Emilei) e la sua laurea padovana', in *Filologia Umanistica. Per Gianvito Resta* (vol. I), ed. by V. Fera and G. Ferraù, Padua, 1997, 161–211.

Biggs, M., 'Putting the State on the Map: Cartography, Territory, and European State Formation', *Comparative Studies in Society and History*, 41/2 (1999), 374–405.

Billington, R. A., *American Frontier Thesis: Attack and Defense*, Washington DC, 1971.

Bishko, C. J., *Studies in Medieval Spanish Frontier History*, London, 1980.

BIBLIOGRAPHY 227

Black, J., 'The Limits of Ducal Authority: A Fifteenth-Century Treatise on the Visconti and their Subject Cities', in *Florence and Italy: Renaissance Studies in Honour of Nicolai Rubinstein*, ed. by P. Denley and C. Elam, London, 1988, 149–60.

Black, J., *Absolutism in Renaissance Milan: Plenitude of Power under the Visconti and the Sforza, 1329–1535*, Oxford, 2009.

Black, J., 'Double Duchy: The Sforza Dukes and the Other Lombard Title', in *Europa e Italia. Studi in onore di Giorgio Chittolini*, Florence, 2011, 15–27.

Black, J., 'The Emergence of the Duchy of Milan: Language and the Territorial State', *Reti medievali*, 14/1 (2013), 197–210.

Blair, A. M. and J. Milligan (eds.), *Toward a Cultural History of Archives*, special issue of *Archival Science*, 7/4 (2007).

Blanco, L., 'Confini e territori in età moderna. Spunti di riflessione', *Rivista storica italiana*, 121/1 (2009), 184–92.

Blickle, P., *Kommunalismus: Skizzen einer gesellschaftlichen Organisationsform* (vol. II), Munich, 2000.

Blockmans, W. P., 'Les origines des états modernes en Europe, XIIIe–XVIIIe siècles. État de la question et perspectives', in *Visions sur le développement des états européens. Théories et historiographies de l'état moderne*, ed. by Id. and J.-P. Genet, Rome, 1993, 1–14.

Blockmans, W. P., A. Holenstein, and J. Mathieu (eds.), *Empowering Interactions: Political Cultures and the Emergence of the State in Europe, 1300–1900*, London, 2009.

Bocchi, F., 'La città e l'organizzazione del territorio nell'Italia medievale', in *La città in Italia e in Germania nel Medioevo. Cultura, istituzioni, vita religiosa*, ed. by R. Elze and G. Fasoli, Bologna, 1981, 51–80.

Bognetti, G. P., 'Le miniere di Valtorta e i diritti degli arcivescovi di Milano, sec. XII–XIV', *Archivio storico lombardo*, 53/2–3 (1926), 281–308.

Bognetti, G. P., *Note per la storia del passaporto e del salvacondotto (a proposito di documenti genovesi del sec. XII)*, Pavia, 1933.

Boissellier, S. (ed.), *De l'espace aux territoires. La Territorialité des processus sociaux et culturels au Moyen Âge*, Turnhout, 2010.

Boissellier, S. and L. Malbos (eds.), *Frontières spatiales, frontières sociales au Moyen Âge*, Perpignan, 2020.

Bonaiti, F., 'Val San Martino. Una terra di mezzo', in *Naturalmente divisi. Storia e autonomia delle antiche comunità alpine*, ed. by L. Giarelli, Tricase, 2013, 189–204.

Bonfiglio Dosio, G., 'Condizioni socio-economiche di Brescia e del suo distretto', in *La signoria di Pandolfo III Malatesti a Brescia, Bergamo e Lecco*, ed. by Ead. and A. Falcioni, Rimini, 2000, 109–36.

Boone, M. and M. Howell (eds.), *The Power of Space in Late Medieval and Early Modern Europe: The Cities of Italy, Northern France and the Low Countries*, Turnhout, 2013.

Bordone, R, 'I confini della comunità. Incertezza territoriale e assetto insediativo tra medioevo ed età moderna in Piemonte', in *Città e territori nell'Italia del Medioevo: Studi in onore di Gabriella Rossetti*, ed. by G. Chittolini, G. Petti Balbi, and G. Vitolo, Naples, 2007, 53–74.

Borghi, A., 'Signorie di Valsassina. Il luogo strategico di Bajedo [*sic*] dai conti di Lecco a Simone Arrigoni', in *La rocca di Bajedo in Valsassina. Baluardo del Ducato di Milano*, Missaglia, 2007, 137–42.

228 BIBLIOGRAPHY

Borghi, A., 'La chiusa di Lecco e la *rocca dell'innominato* cerniera fra Adda e Lario', in *Fortificazioni nel bacino dell'Adda*, Sondrio, 2010, 125–38.

Bortolami, S., 'Frontiere politiche e frontiere religiose nell'Italia comunale. Il caso delle Venezie', in *Castrum* (vol. IV), ed. by J.-M. Poisson, Rome, 1992, 211–31.

Boucheron, P., 'Représenter l'espace féodal. Un défi à relever', *Espaces Temps*, 68–70 (1998), 59–66.

Bouloux, N., 'La céographie à la cour (Italie, XVe siècle)', *Micrologus*, 16 (2008), 171–88.

Bouloux, N., 'Trois cartes territoriales de Brescia. Première approche: leur contexte d'élaboration', *Cahiers de recherches médiévales et humanistes*, 21 (2011), 103–18.

Bourne, M., 'Francesco II Gonzaga and Maps as Palace Decoration in Renaissance Mantua', in *Imago Mundi*, 51 (1999), 51–82.

Boutier, J., S. Landi, and O. Rouchon (eds.), *Florence et la Toscane, XIVe–XIXe siècles. Les Dynamiques d'un état italien*, Rennes, 2004.

Boutier, J., S. Landi, and O. Rouchon (eds.), *Politique par correspondance. Les Usages politiques de la lettre en Italie (XIVe–XVIIIe siécle)*, Rennes, 2009.

Bowd, S. D., *Venice's Most Loyal City: Civic Identity in Renaissance Brescia*, Cambridge, MA, 2010.

Braddick, M., *State Formation in Early Modern England, c.1550–1700*, Cambridge, 2000.

Braddick, M., 'State Formation and Political Culture in Elizabethan and Stuart England: Micro-Histories and Macro-Historical Change', in *Staatsbildung als kultureller Prozess: Strukturwandel und Legitimation von Herrschaft in der Frühen Neuzeit*, ed. by R. G. Asch and D. Freist, Cologne, 2005, 69–90.

Branch, J., 'Mapping the Sovereign State: Technology, Authority, and Systemic Change', *International Organization*, 65/1 (2011), 1–36.

Branch, J., *The Cartographic State: Maps, Territory, and the Origins of Sovereignty*, Cambridge, 2013.

Bratchel, M. E., *Lucca, 1430–1494: The Reconstruction of an Italian City-Republic*, Oxford, 1995.

Brenner, N., 'Beyond State-Centrism? Space, Territoriality, and Geographical Scale in Globalisation Studies', *Theory and Society*, 28 (1999), 39–78.

Brenner, N. and S. Elden, 'Henri Lefebvre on State, Space, Territory', *International Political Sociology*, 3/4 (2009), 353–77.

Brett, A., 'The Space of Politics and the Space of War in Hugo Grotius's *De iure belli ac pacis*', *Global Intellectual History*, 1/1 (2016), 33–60.

Bueno de Mesquita, D. M., *Giangaleazzo Visconti, Duke of Milan (1351–1402): A Study in the Political Career of an Italian Despot*, Cambridge, 1941.

Bührer-Thierry, G., S. Patzold, and J. Schneider (eds.), *Genèse des espaces politiques (IXe–XIIe siècle). Autour de la question spatiale dans les royaumes francs et post-carolingiens*, Turnhout, 2018.

Buratti Mazzotta, A., 'Le fortificazioni nei documenti e nei disegni d'archivio', in *Le fortificazioni di Lecco. Origini di una città*, ed. by Ead. and G. L. Daccò, Milan, 2001, 37–56.

Burns, R. I., 'The *Guidaticum* Safe-Conduct in Medieval Arago-Catalonia: A Mini-Institution for Muslims, Christians and Jews', *Medieval Encounters*, 1/1 (1995), 51–112.

BIBLIOGRAPHY   229

Caggese, R., *Classi e comuni rurali nel Medioevo italiano. Saggio di storia economica e giuridica* (2 vols.), Florence, 1907–9.

Calzona A., and G. M. Cantarella (eds.), *Autocoscienza del territorio. Storie e miti dal monto antico all'età moderna*, Mantua, 2020.

Caniato, G., 'Mappa del territorio cremasco', in *A volo d'uccello. Jacopo De' Barbari e le rappresentazioni di città nell'Europa del Rinascimento*, ed. by S. Biandene and C. Tonini, Venice, 1999, 123–5.

Canning, J. P., 'The Corporation in the Political Thought of the Italian Jurists of the Thirteenth and Fourteenth Centuries', *History of Political Thought*, 1/1 (1980), 9–32.

Canning, J. P., 'Italian Juristic Thought and the Realities of Power in the Middle Ages', in *Politisches Denken und die Wirklichkeit der Macht im Mittelalter*, ed. by Id. and O. G. Oexle, Göttingen, 1998, 229–39.

Cappelli, G., *Maiestas. Politica e pensiero politico nella Napoli aragonese (1443–1503)*, Rome, 2016.

Cappellini, G., 'Confini fra Venezia e Milano in territorio bergamasco', *Atti dell'Ateneo di Scienze, Lettere ed Arti di Bergamo*, 44 (1984), 317–36.

Carpenter, C., 'The Duke of Clarence and the Midlands: A Study in the Interplay of Local and National Politics', *Midland History*, 11 (1986), 23–48.

Castagnetti, A., *L'organizzazione del territorio rurale nel medioevo. Circoscrizioni ecclesiastiche e civili nella* Longobardia *e nella* Romania. Bologna, 1982.

Castagnetti, A., *Le comunità rurali dalla soggezione signorile alla giurisdizione del comune cittadino*, Verona, 1983.

Casti, E., *Reality as Representation: The Semiotics of Cartography and the Generation of Meaning*, Bergamo, 2000.

Casti, E., 'State, Cartography, and Territory in Renaissance Veneto and Lombardy', in *The History of Cartography* (vol. III), ed. by D. Woodward, Chicago, 2007, 874–908.

Casti, E., 'Cartographic Semiosis: Reality as Representation', in *A Cartographic Turn: Mapping and the Spatial Challenge in Social Sciences*, ed. by J. Lévy, Lausanne, 2016, 135–65.

Cattaneo, A., *Fra Mauro's Mappa Mundi and Fifteenth-Century Venice*, Turnhout, 2011.

Cavalieri, P., 'L'Archivio della Camera dei Confini di Bergamo ed il confine occiden-tale della Repubblica di Venezia tra XVI e XVII secolo', in *Alle frontiere della Lombardia. Politica, guerra e religione nell'età moderna*, ed. by C. Donati, Milan, 2006, 289–317.

Cavalieri, P., *Qui sunt guelfi et partiales nostri. Comunità, patriziato e fazioni a Bergamo fra XV e XVI secolo*, Milan, 2009.

Cavallera, M., 'Questioni di dazi e di contrabbandi alla periferia dello Stato di Milano', in *Lungo le antiche strade. Vie d'acqua e di terra tra stati, giurisdizioni e confini nella cartografia dell'età moderna (Genova, Stati Sabaudi, Feudi Imperiali, Stati Farnesiani, Monferrato, Stato di Milano)*, ed. by Ead., Busto Arsizio, 2007, 167–220.

Cencetti, G., 'Il fondamento teorico della dottrina archivistica', *Archivi* 6 (1939), 7–13.

Cengarle, F., *Immagine di potere e prassi di governo. La politica feudale di Filippo Maria Visconti*, Rome, 2006.

230 BIBLIOGRAPHY

Cengarle, F., 'Le arenghe dei decreti viscontei (1330 ca.–1447). Alcune considerazioni', in *Linguaggi politici nell'Italia del Rinascimento*, ed. by A. Gamberini and G. Petralia, Rome, 2007, 55–87.

Cengarle, F., 'Vassalli et subditi. Una proposta d'indagine a partire dal caso lombardo (XV–XVI Secolo)', *Rechtsgeschichte*, 13 (2008), 117–32.

Cessi, R., 'Venezia alla pace di Ferrara del 1428', *Archivio veneto*, 31/2 (1916), 321–71.

Chabod, F., 'Y a-t-il un État de la Renaissance?', in *Actes du colloque sur la Renaissance*, Paris, 1958, 57–73.

Chiappa Mauri, L., 'Le merci di Lombardia. Le produzioni agricole e agroalimentari', in *Commercio in Lombardia* (vol. I), ed. by G. Taborelli, Milan, 1986, 119–45.

Chittolini, G., 'La crisi delle libertà comunali e le origini dello stato territoriale', *Rivista storica italiana*, 82 (1970), 99–120.

Chittolini, G., 'Stati padani, *stati del Rinascimento*. Problemi di ricerca', in *Persistenze feudali e autonomie comunitative in stati padani fra Cinque e Seicento*, ed. by G. Tocci, Bologna, 1988, 9–29.

Chittolini, G., 'Cities, *City-States*, and Regional States in North-Central Italy', *Theory and Society*, 18/5 (1989), 689–706.

Chittolini, G., 'Quasi-città. Borghi e territori in area lombarda nel tardo Medioevo', *Società e storia*, 47/1 (1990), 3–26.

Chittolini, G. (eds.), *Metamorfosi di un borgo. Vigevano in età visconteo-sforzesca*, Milan, 1992.

Chittolini, G., 'Organizzazione territoriale e distretti urbani nell'Italia del tardo Medioevo', in *L'organizzazione del territorio in Italia e Germania, secoli XIII–XIV*, ed. by Id. and D. Willoweit, Bologna, 1994, 7–26.

Chittolini, G., 'The *Private*, the *Public*, the State', *Journal of Modern History*, 67/ Supplement (1995), 34–61.

Chittolini, G., 'Alienazioni d'entrate e concessioni feudali nel ducato sforzesco', in *Città, comunità e feudi negli stati dell'Italia centro-settentrionale (secoli XIV–XVI)*, Bologna, 1996, 145–66.

Chittolini, G., 'Città e stati regionali', in *Città, comunità e feudi negli stati dell'Italia centro-settentrionale (secoli XIV–XVI)*, Milan, 1996, 19–37.

Chittolini, G., 'A Geography of the *Contadi* in Communal Italy', in *Portraits of Medieval and Renaissance Living: Essays in Honor of David Herlihy*, ed. by S. K. J. Cohn and S. A. Epstein, Ann Arbor, MI, 1996, 417–38.

Chittolini, G., 'Legislazione statutaria e autonomie nella pianura bergamasca', in *Città, comunità e feudi negli stati dell'Italia centro-settentrionale (secoli XIV–XVI)*, Milan, 1996, 105–25.

Chittolini, G., 'Principe e comunità alpine', in *Città, comunità e feudi negli stati dell'Italia centro-settentrionale (secoli XIV–XVI)*, Milan, 1996, 127–44.

Chittolini, G., 'Le terre separate nel ducato di Milano in età sforzesca', in *Città, comunità e feudi negli stati dell'Italia centro-settentrionale (secoli XIV–XVI)*, Milan, 1996, 61–83.

Chittolini, G., 'Poteri urbani e poteri feudali-signorili nelle campagne dell'Italia centro-settentrionale fra tardo medioevo e prima età moderna', *Società e storia*, 81 (1998), 473–510.

Chittolini, G., 'Tra Milano e Venezia', *Bergomum*, 95/1–2 (2000), 11–35.

BIBLIOGRAPHY 231

Chittolini, G., 'Fiscalité d'état et prérogatives urbaines dans le duché de Milan à la fin du Moyen Âge', in L'impôt au Moyen Âge. L'Impôt public et le prélèvement seigneurial, fin XIIe–début XVIe siècle (vol. I), ed. by P. Contamine, J. Kerhervé, and A. Rigaudière, Paris, 2002, 147–76.

Chittolini, G., 'Guerre, guerricciole e riassetti territoriali in una provincia lombarda di confine: Parma e il Parmense, agosto 1447–febbraio 1449', Società e storia, 108/2 (2005), 221–48.

Chittolini, G., 'Crisi e lunga durata delle istituzioni comunali in alcuni dibattiti recenti', in Penale, giustizia, potere: Per ricordare Mario Sbriccoli, ed. by L. Lacchè, Macerata 2007, 125–54.

Chittolini, G., 'Centri minori del territorio: terre separate, piccole città', in Storia di Cremona (vol. VI), ed. by Id., Azzano San Paolo, 2008, 64–79.

Chittolini, G., 'Models of Government from Below in Fifteenth-Century Lombardy. The Capitoli di Dedizione to Francesco Sforza, 1447–1450', in Empowering Interactions: Political Cultures and the Emergence of the State in Europe, 1300–1900, ed. by W. P. Blockmans, A. Holenstein, and J. Mathieu, London, 2009, 51–63.

Chittolini, G., 'Dominant Cities. Florence, Genoa, Venice, Milan, and their Territories in the Fifteenth Century', in The Medici: Citizens and Masters, ed. by R. Black and J. E. Law, Cambridge, MA, 2015, 13–26.

Chittolini, G., E. Conti, and M. N. Covini (eds.), Nell'età di Pandolfo Malatesta, signore a Bergamo, Brescia e Fano agli inizi del Quattrocento, Brescia, 2012.

Clayton, A. R. L. and F. J. Teute (eds.), Contact Points: American Frontiers from the Mohawk Valley to the Mississippi, 1780–1830, Chapel Hill, NC, 1998.

Cohen, A. P., 'Culture, Identity, and the Concept of Boundary', Revista de Antropología Social, 3/1 (1994), 49–61.

Coleman, E., 'The Italian Communes: Recent Work and Current Trends', Journal of Medieval History, 25/4 (1999), 384–90.

Comba, R., 'Il territorio come spazio vissuto. Ricerche geografiche e storiche nella genesi di un tema di storia sociale', Società e storia, 11/1 (1981), 1–27.

Concina, E., 'In vera pictura: Venezia, le città del dominio, il mondo. 1450 more veneto', in La vita nei libri. Edizioni illustrate a stampa del Quattro e Cinquecento dalla Fondazione Giorgio Cini, ed. by M. Zorzi, Venice, 2003, 151–5.

Connell, W. J. and A. Zorzi (eds.), Florentine Tuscany: Structures and Practices of Power, Cambridge, 2000.

Conzato, A., 'Sulle faccende da praticare occultamente. Il Consiglio dei Dieci, il Senato e la politica estera veneziana (1503–1509)', Studi veneziani, 55 (2008), 83–165.

Cook, T. and J. Schwarts (eds.), Archives, Records, and Powers, special issue of Archival Science, 2/1–4 (2002).

Corens, L., K. Peters, and A. Walsham (eds.), The Social History of the Archive: Record-Keeping in Early Modern Europe, special issue of Past & Present, 230/supplement 11 (2016).

Corrao, P., Governare un regno. Potere, società, istituzioni in Sicilia tra Trecento e Quattrocento, Naples, 1990.

Cosgrove, D., 'Cultural Cartography: Maps and Mapping in Cultural Geography', Annales de Géographie, 117/2 (2008), 159–78.

232 BIBLIOGRAPHY

Costa, P., Iurisdictio. *Semantica del potere politico nella pubblicistica medievale, 1100–1433*, Milan, 1969.

Costa, P., 'In alto e al centro: immagini dell'ordine e della sovranità fra medioevo ed età moderna', *Diritto pubblico*, 10/3 (2004), 815–49.

Costa, P., 'Uno spatial turn per la storia del diritto? Una rassegna tematica', *Max Planck Institute for European Legal History – Research Paper Series*, 7 (2013), 1–30.

Costantini, F., In tutto differente dalle altre città. *Mercato e contrabbando dei grani a Bergamo in età veneta*, Bergamo, 2016.

Costantini, F., 'La stagione dei trattati confinari tra Milano e Venezia. Controllo del territorio e criminalità di frontiera prima e dopo il biennio 1754–56', in *Tra polizie e controllo del territorio: alla ricerca delle discontinuità*, ed. by L. Antonielli and S. Levati, Soveria Mannelli, 2017, 197–223.

Costantini, F., 'Commercio e contrabbando di cereali in area lombarda tra Seicento e Settecento', in *Le vie del cibo. Italia settentrionale (secc. XVI–XX)*, ed. by M. Cavallera, S. Conca, and B. A. Raviola, Rome, 2019, 175–89.

Costantini, F., 'One City, Two Economic Areas: Wheat and Olive Oil Trade in Bergamo between Venice and Milan', in *Italian Victualling Systems in the Early Modern Age, 16th to 18th Century*, ed. by L. Clerici, London, 2021, 71–104.

Cotti, A., 'I santi all'assedio. Nascita e fortuna di una leggenda comunale tra XV e XVIII secolo', in *El patron di tanta alta ventura. Pietro Avogadro tra Pandolfo Malatesta e la dedizione di Brescia a Venezia*, Brescia, 2013, 121–43.

Covini, M. N., 'I castellani ducali all'epoca di Galeazzo Maria Sforza. Offici, carriere, stato sociale', *Nuova rivista storica*, 71 (1987), 531–86.

Covini, M. N., 'L'Amadeo e il collettivo degli ingegneri ducali al tempo degli Sforza', in *Giovanni Antonio Amadeo. Scultura e architettura del suo tempo*, ed. by J. Shell and L. Castelfranchi, Milan, 1993, 59–75.

Covini, M. N., 'Political and Military Bonds in the Italian State System, Thirteenth to Sixteenth Centuries', in *War and Competition between States*, ed. by P. Contamine, Oxford, 2000, 9–36.

Covini, M. N., 'Studiando el mappamondo. Trasferimenti di genti d'arme tra logiche statali e relazioni con le realtà locali', in *Viaggiare nel Medioevo*, ed. by S. Gensini, Pisa, 2000, 227–66.

Covini, M. N., 'Guerre e relazioni diplomatiche in Italia (secoli XIV–XV): la diplomazia dei condottieri', in *Guerra y diplomacia en la Europa occidental, 1280–1480*, Pamplona, 2005, 163–98.

Covini, M. N., La balanza drita. *Pratiche di governo, leggi e ordinamenti nel ducato sforzesco*, Milan, 2007.

Covini, M. N., 'Scrivere al principe. Il carteggio interno sforzesco e la storia documentaria delle istituzioni', *Reti medievali*, 9/1 (2008), 1–32.

Covini, M. N., 'Pétitions et suppliques pendant la domination des Visconti et des Sforza au Xve siècle. Exception, dérogation et forms simplifiées de justice', *L'Atelier du Centre de recherches historiques*, 13 (2015), 1–16.

Covini, M. N., *Potere, ricchezza e distinzione a Milano nel Quattrocento. Nuove ricerche su Cicco Simonetta*, Milan, 2018.

Covini, M. N., B. Figliuolo, I. Lazzarini, and F. Senatore, 'Pratiche e norme di comportamento nella diplomazia italiana. I carteggi di Napoli, Firenze, Milano,

BIBLIOGRAPHY   233

Mantova e Ferrara tra fine XIV e fine XV secolo', in *De l'ambassadeur. Les Écrits relatifs à l'ambassadeur et à l'art de négocier du Moyen Âge au début du XIXe siècle*, ed. by S. Andretta, S. Péquignot, and J.-C. Waquet, Rome, 2015, 113–62.

Cozzi, G., 'Politica e diritto in alcune controversie confinarie tra lo Stato di Milano e la Repubblica di Venezia (1564–1622)', *Archivio storico lombardo*, 78–79/3 (1952), 8–44.

Cozzi, G., 'La politica del diritto nella Repubblica di Venezia', in *Repubblica di Venezia e stati italiani. Politica e giustizia dal secolo XVI al secolo XVIII*, ed. by Id., Turin, 1982, 217–318.

Cozzi, G., 'Politica, società, istituzioni', in *Storia della Repubblica di Venezia. Dalla guerra di Chioggia alla riconquista della Terraferma*, ed. by Id. and M. Knapton, Turin, 1986, 3–271.

Crampton, J. W., 'Maps as Social Constructions', *Power, Communication and Visualization*, 25/2 (2001), 235–52.

Cursente, B. and M. Mousnier (eds.), *Les Territoires du médiéviste*, Rennes, 2005.

Dahlberg, L., *Spacing Law and Politics: The Constitution and Representation of the Juridical*, London, 2016.

Dameron, G., 'Feeding the Medieval Italian City-State: Grain, War, and Political Legitimacy in Tuscany, *c.*1150–*c.*1350', *Speculum*, 92/4 (2017), 976–1019.

Dauphant, L., *Le Royaume des Quatre Rivières. L'Espace politique français, 1380–1515*, Seyssel, 2012.

Dauphant, L., 'Entre la liste et le terrain. La Carte dans les négociations de paix au Xve siècle (Dauphiné et Savoie, France et Bourgogne)', *Cartes & Géomatique: revue du Comité français de cartographie*, 228 (2016), 11–21.

Davidson, N., '*As Much for its Culture as for its Arms*: The Cultural Relations of Venice and its Dependent Cities, 1400–1700', in *Mediterranean Urban Culture, 1400–1700*, ed. by A. Cowan, Exeter, 2000, 197–214.

De Certeau, M., *L'invention du quotidien* (vol. I), Paris, 1980.

De Craecker-Dussart, C., 'L'Évolution du sauf-conduit dans les principautés de la Basse Lotharingie, du VIIIe au XIVe siècle', *Le Moyen Âge*, 80 (1974), 185–243.

De Dainville, F., 'Cartes et contestations au Xve siècle', *Imago Mundi*, 24 (1970), 99–121.

Degrassi, D., 'Dai confini dei villaggi ai confini politici. L'area friulana nel tardo medioevo', *Reti medievali*, 7/1 (2006), 11–21.

Della Misericordia, M., 'Dividersi per governarsi. Fazioni, famiglie aristocratiche e comuni in Valtellina in età viscontea (1335–1447)', *Società e storia*, 22/3 (1999), 715–66.

Della Misericordia, M., '*Per non privarci de nostre raxone, li siamo stati desobidienti.* Patto, giustizia e resistenza nella cultura politica delle comunità alpine nello stato di Milano (XV secolo)', in *Forme della comunicazione politica in Europa nei secoli XV–XVIII. Suppliche, gravamina, lettere*, ed. by C. Nuvola and A. Würgler, Bologna, 2004, 147–215.

Della Misericordia, M., 'La comunità sovralocale. Università di valle, di lago e di pieve nell'organizzazione politica del territorio nella Lombardia dei secoli XIV–XVI', in *Lo spazio politico locale in età medievale, moderna e contemporanea*, ed. by R. Bordone, P. Guglielmotti, S. Lombardini, and A. Torre, Alessandria, 2006, 99–111.

234 BIBLIOGRAPHY

Della Misericordia, M., *Divenire comunità. Comuni rurali, poteri locali, identità sociali e territoriali in Valtellina e nella montagna lombarda nel tardo medioevo*, Milan, 2006.

Della Misericordia, M., 'Decidere e agire in comunità nel XV secolo' (un aspetto del dibattito politico nel dominio sforzesco)', in *Linguaggi politici nell'Italia del Rinascimento*, ed. by A. Gamberini and G. Petralia, Rome, 2007, 291–378.

Della Misericordia, M., *Figure di comunità. Documento notarile, forme della convivenza, riflessione locale sulla vita associata nella montagna lombarda e nella pianura comasca (secoli XIV–XVI)*, Morbegno, 2008.

Della Misericordia, M., 'Mappe di carte. Le scritture e gli archivi delle comunità rurali della montagna lombarda nel basso medioevo', in *Archivi e comunità tra medioevo ed età moderna*, ed. by A. Bartoli Langeli, A. Giorgi, and S. Moscadelli, Rome, 2009, 155–278.

Della Misericordia, M., 'Significare il confine. I simboli della delimitazione nelle testimonianze documentarie fra medioevo ed età moderna in Valtellina e nelle Alpi centrali', *Notiziario dell'Istituto archeologico valtellinese*, 9 (2011), 93–106.

Della Misericordia, M., 'I confini dell'economia. Dividere le risorse e delimitare il possesso nella montagna lombarda del tardo medioevo', in *Nell'età di Pandolfo Malatesta, signore a Bergamo, Brescia e Fano agli inizi del Quattrocento*, ed. by G. Chittolini, E. Conti, and M. N. Covini, Brescia, 2012, 241–324.

Della Misericordia, M., 'Essere di una giurisdizione. Istituzioni di giustizia e generazione dei luoghi nella montagna lombarda (secoli XIV–XVI)', *Quaderni storici*, 139/1 (2012), 77–124.

Della Misericordia, M., *I nodi della rete. Paesaggio, società e istituzioni a Dalegno e in Valcamonica nel tardo medioevo*, Morbegno, 2012.

Della Misericordia, M., 'Spazi politici e spazi economici. Territori, istituzioni comunitarie e mercati nella montagna lombarda del tardo medioevo', in *La costruzione del paesaggio agrario nell'età moderna*, ed. by G. Bonini, A. Brusa, and R. Cervi, Gattatico, 2012, 25–36.

Della Misericordia, M., *I confini dei mercati. Territori, istituzioni locali e spazi economici nella montagna lombarda del tardo medioevo*, Morbegno, 2013.

Della Misericordia, M., 'The rural communities', in *The Italian Renaissance State*, ed. by A. Gamberini and I. Lazzarini, Cambridge, 2013, 261–83.

Della Misericordia, M., 'Relazioni *interlocali* lungo una frontiera alpina. Fra Milano, Svizzera, Vallese e Grigioni nel XV secolo', in *Interlocal History from the Alps: From the Local to the Interlocal*, ed. by H. Sato, Kobe, 2016, 13–43.

Della Misericordia, M. 'Politiche della difesa e territorio tra Como e la frontiera alpina nel Quattrocento', in *Territorio 2020*, ed. by E. R. Laforgia and G. Gaspari, Varese, 2020, 127–195.

Della Misericordia, M., '*Nondimeno*. Una nota sul linguaggio della circostanza e dell'eccezione nel Carteggio sforzesco', in *Fiere vicende dell'età di mezzo. Studi per Gian Maria Varanini*, ed. by P. Guglielmotti and I. Lazzarini, Florence, 2021, 95–110.

Del Tredici, F., 'Loci, comuni, homines: il linguaggio degli atti notarili nella bassa pianura milanese (prima metà del Quattrocento)', in *Linguaggi politici nell'Italia del Rinascimento*, ed. by A. Gamberini and G. Petralia, Rome, 2007, 267–90.

BIBLIOGRAPHY 235

Del Tredici, F., 'La popolarità dei partiti. Fazioni, popolo e mobilità sociale in Lombardia', in *La mobilità sociale nel Medioevo italiano* (vol II), ed. by A. Gamberini, Rome, 2017, 305–34.

Demangeon, A. and L. Febvre, *Le Rhin. Problèmes d'histoire et d'èconomie*, Paris, 1935.

De Matteis, M. C. and B. Pio (eds.), *Sperimentazioni di governo nell'Italia centrosettentrionale nel processo storico dal primo comune alla signoria*, Bologna, 2011.

DeSilva, J. M., 'Taking Possession: Rituals, Space and Authority', *Royal Studies Journal*, 3/2 (2016), 1–17.

De Vergottini, G., 'Origini e sviluppo storico della comitatinanza', *Studi senesi*, 43 (1929), 347–484.

De Vincentiis, A., 'Memorie bruciate. Conflitti, documenti, oblio nelle città italiane del tardo medioevo', *Bullettino dell'Istituto storico italiano per il medio evo*, 106 (2004), 167–98.

De Vivo, F., 'Ordering the Archive in Early Modern Venice (1400–1650)', *Archival Science*, 10/3 (2010), 231–48.

De Vivo, F., 'Cœur de l'état, lieu de tension. Le Tournant archivistique vu de Venise (Xve–XVIIe siècle)', *Annales. Histoire, Sciences Sociales*, 68/3 (2013), 699–728.

De Vivo, F., *Archival Transformations in Early Modern European History*, special issue of *European History Quarterly*, 46/3 (2016).

De Vivo, F., 'Archives of Speech: Recording Diplomatic Negotiation in Late Medieval and Early Modern Italy', *European History Quarterly*, 46/3 (2016), 519–44.

De Vivo, F., A. Guidi, and A. Silvestri (eds.), *Archivi e archivisti in Italia tra medioevo ed età moderna*, Rome, 2015.

Diacciati, S., *Popolani e magnati. Società e politica nella Firenze del Duecento*, Spoleto, 2011.

Di Tullio, M., *The Wealth of Communities: War, Resources and Cooperation in Renaissance Lombardy*, Farnham, 2014.

Dodd, G. and M. Ormrod (eds.), *Medieval Petitions: Grace and Grievance*, Woodbridge, 2009.

Donattini, M., 'Confini contesi: Pellegrino Prisciani a Venezia (marzo 1485–gennaio 1486)', in *L'Italia dell'Inquisitore. Storia e geografia dell'Italia del Cinquecento nella Descrittione di Leandro Alberti*, ed. by Id., Bologna, 2007, 187–217.

Donnan, H. and T. M. Wilson, *Borders: Frontiers of Identity, Nation and State*, Oxford, 1999.

Dover, P., 'Deciphering the Diplomatic Archives of Fifteenth-Century Italy', *Archival Science*, 7/4 (2008), 297–316.

Dumasy-Rabineau, J., C. Serchuk, and E. Vagnon (eds.), *Pour une histoire des cartes locales en Europe au Moyen Âge et à la Renaissance*, Paris, 2022.

Durantiv L., 'The Archival Bond', *Archives and Museum Informatics*, 11/3 (1997), 213–18.

Durstelerv E. (ed.), *A Companion to Venetian History, 1400–1797*, Leiden, 2013.

Edney, M. H., *The Origins and Development of J. B. Harley's Cartographic Theories*, Toronto, 2005.

Edwards, K., *Families and Frontiers Re-Creating Communities and Boundaries in the Early Modern Burgundies*, Turnhout, 2002.

236 BIBLIOGRAPHY

Elden, S., 'There Is a Politics of Space because Space Is Political: Henri Lefebvre and the Production of Space', *Radical Philosophy Review*, 10/2 (2007), 101–16.

Elden, S., 'Thinking Territory Historically', *Geopolitics*, 15/4 (2010), 757–61.

Elden, S., *The Birth of Territory*, Chicago, 2013.

Ellebrecht, S., 'Qualities of Bordering Spaces: A Conceptual Experiment with Reference to Georg Simmel's Sociology of Space', in *Borders and Border Regions in Europe: Changes, Challenges and Chances*, ed. by A. Lechevalier and J. Wielgohs, Bielefeld, 2013, 45–67.

Ellis, S. G., 'The English State and its Frontiers in the British Isles, 1300–1600', in *Frontiers in Question: Eurasian Borderlands 700–1700*, ed. by D. Power and N. Standen, Basingstoke, 1999, 153–81.

Ellis, S. G., 'Defending English Ground: The Tudor Frontiers in History and Historiography', in *Frontiers and the Writing of History, 1500–1850*, ed. by Id. and R. Eßer, Hanover-Laatzen, 2006, 73–93.

Ellis, S. G. and L. Klusáková (eds.), *Frontiers and Identities: Exploring the Research Area*, Pisa, 2006.

Epstein, S. R., 'Town and Country: Economy and Institutions in Late Medieval Italy', *Economic History Review*, 46/3 (1993), 453–77.

Fara, A. (ed.), *Italia ed Europa centro-orientale tra medioevo ed età moderna. Economia, società, cultura*, Heidelberg, 2022.

Fasano Guarini, E., 'Gli stati dell'Italia centro-settentrionale tra quattro e cinquecento: continuità e trasformazioni', *Società e storia*, 21 (1983), 617–39.

Fasano Guarini, E., 'Center and Periphery', *The Journal of Modern History*, 67/ Supplement (1995), 74–96.

Fasano Guarini, E., 'Geographies of Power: The Territorial State in Early Modern Italy', in *The Renaissance: Italy and Abroad*, ed. by J. J. Martin, London, 2003, 88–103.

Faugeron, F., 'De la commune à la capitale du Stato di Terra: la politique annonaire et la constitution de l'État de Terraferme vénitien (1ère moitié du Xve siècle), in *Les villes capitales au Moyen Âge*, ed. by P. Boucheron, D. Menjot, and P. Monnet, Paris, 2006, 97–111.

Faugeron, F., *Nourrir la ville. Ravitaillement, marché et métiers de l'alimentation à Venise dans les derniers siècles du Moyen Âge*, Rome, 2014.

Favreau-Lilie, M.-L., 'Reichsherrschaft im spätmittelalterlichen Italien: Zur Handhabung des Reichsvikariates im 14./15. Jahrhundert', *Quellen und Forschungen aus italienischen Archiven und Bibliotheken*, 80 (2000), 53–116.

Ferente, S., *La sfortuna di Jacopo Piccinino. Storia dei bracceschi in Italia, 1423–1465*, Florence, 2005.

Ferente, S., 'Guelphs! Factions, Liberty and Sovereignty: Inquiries about the Quattrocento', *History of Political Thought*, 28/4 (2007), 571–98.

Ferente, S., *Gli ultimi guelfi. Linguaggi e identità politiche in Italia nella seconda metà del Quattrocento*, Rome, 2013.

Ferente, S., 'Stato, stato regionale e storia d'Italia', in *Italia come storia. Primato, decadenza, eccezione*, ed. by F. Benigno and I. Mineo, Rome, 2020, 85–104.

Fermon, P., *Le peintre et la carte. Origines et essor de la vue figurée entre Rhône et Alpes (XIVe-Xve siècle)*, Turnhout, 2018.

BIBLIOGRAPHY 237

Ferraglio, E., 'Aristocrazia, territorio e regime fiscale nel Libro dei privilegi di Brescia (ms. Queriniano H.V.5)', *Annali queriniani*, 1 (2000), 63–102.

Ferraglio, E., 'Il libro dei privilegi di Venezia per la nobiltà bresciana', in *Famiglie di Franciacorta nel Medioevo*, ed. by G. Archetti, Brescia, 2000, 61–82.

Ferraro, J. M., 'Proprietà terriera e potere nello Stato veneto: la nobiltà bresciana del '400–'500', in *Dentro lo Stado Italico. Venezia e la Terraferma fra Quattro e Seicento*, ed. by G. Cracco and M. Knapton, Trento, 1984, 159–82.

Filippi, F., 'Carta trecentesca del lago di Garda', in *Gli Scaligeri, 1377–1387*, ed. by G. M. Varanini, Milan, 1988, 324–5.

Folin, M., 'De l'usage pratico-politique des images de villes (Italie Xve–XVIe siècle)', in *Villes de Flandre et d'Italie (XIIIe–XVIe siècles). Les Enseignements d'une comparaison*, ed. by É. Crouzet-Pavan and É. Lecuppre-Desjardin, Leiden, 2008, 259–323.

Fossati, F., 'Francesco Sforza e la pace di Lodi', *Archivio veneto*, 95–96/1–2 (1957), 15–34.

Franceschini, G, 'Il confine fra Bergamasca e Valsassina dalla pace di Ferrara (1428) alla pace di Lodi (1454)', in *Atti e memorie del secondo congresso storico lombardo*, Milan, 1938, 95–106.

Francesconi, G., 'Il confine archiviato. Un frammento lucchese quattrocentesco del *Liber finium districtus Pistorii*', *Bullettino storico pistoiese*, 109 (2007), 155–74.

Francesconi, G., 'Scrivere il contado. I linguaggi della costruzione territoriale cittadina nell'Italia centrale', *Mélanges de l'École française de Rome (Moyen Âge)*, 123/2 (2011), 499–529.

Francesconi, G. and F. Salvestrini, 'Il *Liber finium districtus Pistorii*. Modelli e scritture del confine in età comunale', in *Il confine appenninico. Percezione e realtà dall'età antica ad oggi*, ed. F. Paola and R. Zagoni, Pistoia, 2001, 29–61.

Francesconi, G. and F. Salvestrini, 'La scrittura del confine nell'Italia comunale. Modelli e funzioni', in *Frontiers in the Middle Ages*, ed. by O. Merisalo, Louvain-la-Neuve, 2006, 197–221.

Fray, J., S. Gomis and S. Le Bras (eds.), *Flux réels versus flux immatériels. Contribution à la réflexion sur l'histoire des espaces*, special issue of *Siècles*, 46 (2019).

Fubini, R., 'Appunti sui rapporti diplomatici fra il dominio sforzesco e Firenze medicea. Modi e tecniche dell'ambasciata dalle trattative per la lega italica alla missione di Sacramoro da Rimini', in *Gli Sforza a Milano e in Lombardia e i loro rapporti con gli stati italiani ed europei (1450–1535)*, Milan, 1982, 291–334.

Fubini, R., *Italia quattrocentesca. Politica e diplomazia nell'età di Lorenzo il Magnifico*, Milan, 1994.

Fubini, R., 'The Italian League and the Policy of the Balance of Power at the Accession of Lorenzo de' Medici', *Journal of Modern History*, 67/Supplement (1995), 166–99.

Fubini, R., 'L'idea di Italia fra Quattro e Cinquecento. Politica, geografia storica, miti delle origini', *Geographia Antiqua*, 7 (1998), 53–66.

Fubini, R., '*Potenze grosse* e piccolo stato nell'Italia del Rinascimento. Consapevolezza della distinzione e dinamica dei poteri', in *Il piccolo stato. Politica, storia, diplomazia*, ed. by L. Barletta, F. Cardini, and G. Galasso, San Marino, 2003, 91–126.

Fuller, M. G. and M. Löw (eds.), *Spatial Sociology: Relational Space after the Turn*, special issue of *Current Sociology*, 65/4 (2017).

238 BIBLIOGRAPHY

Galantino, F., *Storia di Soncino con documenti* (vol I), Milan, 1869.

Gallo, R., 'Le mappe geografiche del palazzo ducale di Venezia', *Archivio Veneto*, 32/33 (1943), 3–162.

Gallo, R., 'A Fifteenth Century Military Map of the Venetian Territory of *Terraferma*', *Imago Mundi*, 12 (1955), 55–7.

Gamberini, A., 'Gian Galeazzo Visconti, duca di Milano', in *Dizionario biografico degli italiani* (vol. LIV), Rome, 2000, 383–91.

Gamberini, A., *La città assediata. Poteri e identità politiche a Reggio in età viscontea*, Rome, 2003.

Gamberini, A., 'Il contado di Milano nel Trecento. Aspetti politici e giurisdizionali', in *Contado e città in dialogo. Comuni urbani e comunità rurali nella Lombardia medievale*, ed. by L. Chiappa Mauri, Milan, 2003, 83–137.

Gamberini, A., 'La territorialità nel Basso Medioevo: un problema chiuso? Osservazioni a margine della vicenda di Reggio', in *Poteri signorili e feudali nelle campagne dell'Italia settentrionale fra Tre e Quattrocento: fondamenti di legittimità e forme di esercizio*, ed. by F. Cengarle, G. Chittolini, and G. M. Varanini, Florence, 2004, 47–72.

Gamberini, A., 'Istituzioni e scritture di governo nella formazione dello stato visconteo', in *Lo stato visconteo. Linguaggi politici e dinamiche istituzionali*, Milan, 2005, 35–68.

Gamberini, A., 'Linguaggi politici e territorio. Il Reggiano fra XIV e XV Secolo', in *Lo spazio politico locale in età medievale, moderna e contemporanea*, ed. by R. Bordone, P. Guglielmotti, S. Lombardini, and A. Torre, Alessandria, 2007, 89–97.

Gamberini, A., 'La memoria dei gentiluomini. I cartulari di lignaggio alla fine del medioevo', *Reti medievali*, 9 (2008), 1–15.

Gamberini, A., 'Principe, comunità e territori nel ducato di Milano. Spunti per una rilettura', *Quaderni storici*, 43/1 (2008), 243–65.

Gamberini, A., 'Rivendicazioni urbane, autonomie locali e interventi ducali: il Cremonese nel Quattrocento', in *Oltre le città. Assetti territoriali e culture aristocratiche nella Lombardia del tardo medioevo*, Rome, 2009, 53–81.

Gamberini, A., 'Processi di ricomposizione politica alla fine del medioevo e avvento degli stati regionali', in *Mundus*, 3/5–6 (2010), 120–7.

Gamberini, A., 'The Language of Politics and the Process of State-Building', in *The Italian Renaissance State*, ed. by Id. and I. Lazzarini, Cambridge, 2012, 406–24.

Gamberini, A. (ed.), *A Companion to Late Medieval and Early Modern Milan: The Distinctive Features of an Italian State*, Leiden, 2014.

Gamberini, A., *La legittimità contesa. Costruzione statale e culture politiche (Lombardia, secoli XII–XV)*, Rome, 2016.

Gamberini, A. and I. Lazzarini (eds.), *The Italian Renaissance State*, Cambridge, 2012.

Gardini, S., 'The Use and Reuse of Documents by Chancellors, Archivists and Government Members in an Early Modern Republican State: Genoa's *Giunta dei Confini* and its Archives', in *Engaging with Records and Archives: Histories and Theories*, ed. by F. Foscarini, H. Macneil, B. Mak, and G. Oliver, London, 2016, 107–26.

Gautier Dalché, P., 'De la liste à la carte: limite et frontière dans la géographie de l'Occident médiéval', in *Castrum* (vol. IV), ed. by J.-M. Poisson, Rome, 1992, 18–31.

BIBLIOGRAPHY 239

Gautier Dalché, P., 'Pour une histoire du regard géographique: conception et usage de la carte au xVe siècle', in *Micrologus*, 4 (1996), 77–103.

Genet, J.-P., L'historien et les langages de la société politique', in *The Languages of Political Society: Western Europe, 14th–17th Centuries*, ed. by A. Gamberini, J.-Ph. Genet, and A. Zorzi, Rome, 2011, 1–36.

Gentile, M., 'Leviatano regionale o forma-stato composita? Sugli usi possibili di idee vecchie e nuove', *Società e storia*, 89/3 (2000), 561–73.

Gentile, M., *Terra e poteri. Parma e il Parmense nel ducato visconteo all'inizio del Quattrocento*. Rome, 2001.

Gentile, M. (ed.), *Guelfi e ghibellini nell'Italia del Rinascimento*, Rome, 2005.

Gentile, M., 'Postquam malignitates temporum hec nobis dedere nomina....Fazioni, idiomi politici e pratiche di governo nella tarda età viscontea', in *Guelfi e ghibellini nell'Italia del Rinascimento*, ed. by Id., Rome, 2005, 249–74.

Gentile, M., 'Bartolo in pratica: appunti su identità politica e procedura giudiziaria nel ducato di Milano alla fine del Quattrocento', *Rivista internazionale di diritto comune*, 18 (2007), 231–51.

Gentile, M., 'Discorsi sulle fazioni, discorsi delle fazioni. *Parole e demonstratione partiale* nella Lombardia del secondo Quattrocento', in *Linguaggi politici nell'Italia del Rinascimento*, ed. by A. Gamberini and G. Petralia, Rome, 2007, 383–410.

Gentile, M., 'Aristocrazia signorile e costituzione del ducato visconteo-sforzesco. Appunti e problemi di ricerca', in *Noblesse et états princiers en Italie et en France au xVe siècle*, ed. by Id. and P. Savy, Rome, 2009, 125–55.

Gentile, M., 'Factions and Parties: Problems and Perspectives', in *The Italian Renaissance State*, ed. by A. Gamberini and I. Lazzarini, Cambridge, 2015, 313–21.

Gentile, M., 'La Lombardia complessa. Note sulla ricomposizione del ducato di Milano da parte di Filippo Maria Visconti (1412–1421)', in *Il ducato di Filippo Maria Visconti, 1412–1447. Economia, politica, cultura*, ed. by F. Cengarle and M. N. Covini, Florence, 2015, 5–26.

Gentile, M., 'Forms of Political Representation in Late Medieval Northern Italy: Utility and Shortcomings of the City-State Paradigm (14th–early 16th Century)', in *Political Representation: Communities, Ideas and Institutions in Europe (c.1200–c.1650)*, ed. by M. Damen, J. Haemers, and A. Mann, Leiden, 2018, 69–84.

Gentile, S., 'Umanesimo e cartografia: Tolomeo nel secolo XV', in *La cartografia europea tra primo rinascimento e fine dell'illuminismo*, ed. by D. Ramada Curto, A. Cattaneo, and A. Ferrand Almeida, Florence, 2003, 3–18.

Geselle, A., 'Domenica Saba Takes to the Road: Origins and Development of a Modern Passport System in Lombardy-Veneto', in *Documenting Individual Identity: The Development of State Practices in the Modern World*, ed. by J. Caplan and J. Torpey, Princeton, NJ 2001, 199–217.

Ginatempo, M. and L. Sandri,*L'Italia delle città. Il popolamento urbano tra Medioevo e Rinascimento*, Florence, 1990.

Giorgi, A. and S. Moscadelli, 'Cum acta sua sint. Aspetti della conservazione delle carte dei notai in età tardo-medievale e moderna (XV–XVIII sec.)', in *Archivi e archivisti in Italia tra medioevo ed età moderna*, ed. by F. de Vivo, A. Guidi, and A. Silvestri, Rome, 2015, 259–81.

240 BIBLIOGRAPHY

Giorgi, A. and K. Occhi (eds.), *Carteggi tra basso medioevo ed età moderna. Pratiche di redazione, trasmissione e conservazione*, Bologna, 2018.

Giraut, F., 'Conceptualiser le territoire', *Historiens et Géographes*, 403 (2008), 57–68.

Gomis, S. and V. Flauraud (eds.), *La cartographie ecclésiastique. Héritage patrimonial et innovation géomatique*, special issue of *Siècles*, 52 (2022).

Gommans, J., 'The Eurasian Frontier after the First Millennium A.D.: Reflections along the Fringe of Time and Space', *Medieval History Journal*, 1/1 (1998), 125–43.

Gottmann, J., *The Significance of Territory*, Charlottesville, VA, 1973.

Grendi, E., 'La pratica dei confini: Mioglia contro Sassello, 1715–1745', *Quaderni storici*, 63/3 (1986), 811–45.

Grendi, E., 'La pratica dei confini fra comunità e stati: il contesto politico della cartografia', in *Cartografia e istituzioni in età moderna*, Rome, 1987, 134–45.

Grewe, W. G., *The Epochs of International Law*, ed. by M. Byers, Berlin, 2000.

Grillo, P., 'La fenice comunale. Le città lombarde alla morte di Gian Galeazzo Visconti', *Storica*, 18/2 (2012), 39–62.

Grillo, P., *Milano guelfa, 1302–1310*, Rome, 2013.

Grillo, P., 'Il territorio conteso. Conflitti per il controllo del contado di Bergamo alla fine del Trecento', in *Controllare il territorio: norme, corpi e conflitti tra medioevo e prima guerra mondiale*, ed. by L. Antonielli and S. Levati, Soveria Mannelli, 2013, 237–52.

Groebner, V., 'Describing the Person, Reading the Signs in Late Medieval and Renaissance Europe: Identity Papers, Vested Figures, and the Limits of Identification, 1400–1600', in *Documenting Individual Identity: The Development of State Practices in the Modern World*, ed. by J. Caplan and J. Torpey, Princeton, NJ, 2001, 15–27.

Guenée, B., 'Les Limites de la France', in *La France et les Français*, ed. by M. François, Paris, 1972, 50–69.

Guenée, B., 'Des limites féodales aux frontières politique', in *Les lieux de mémoire* (vol. II), ed. by P. Nora, Paris, 1986, 11–33.

Guglielmotti, P., *Comunità e territorio. Villaggi del Piemonte medievale*, Rome, 2001.

Guglielmotti, P. (ed.), *Distinguere, separare, condividere. Confini nella campagne dell'Italia medievali*, special issue *Reti medievali*, 7/1 (2006).

Guglielmotti, P., 'Introduzione: Distinguere, separare, condividere. Confini nella campagne dell'Italia medievale', *Reti medievali*, 7/1 (2006), 35–46.

Guglielmotti, P., 'Linguaggi del territorio, linguaggi sul territorio. La Val Polcevera genovese (secoli X–XIII)', in *Linguaggi e pratiche del potere. Genova e il Regno di Napoli tra Medioevo ed Età Moderna*, ed. by G. Petti Balbi and G. Vitolo, Salerno, 2007, 241–68.

Guglielmotti, P., 'Confini e frontiere come problema storiografico: Visti dal medioevo', *Rivista storica italiana*, 121/1 (2009), 176–83.

Häkli, J., 'The Border in the Pocket: The Passport as a Boundary Object', in *Borderities and the Politics of Contemporary Mobile Borders*, ed. by F. Giraut and A.-L. Amilhat Szary, Basingstoke, 2015, 85–99.

Hale, J., 'Warfare and Cartography, ca. 1450 to ca. 1640', in *The History of Cartography* (vol. III), ed. by D. Woodward, Chicago, 2007, 719–37.

Harley, J. B., 'Maps, Knowledge, and Power', in *The Iconography of Landscape: Essays on the Symbolic Representation, Design and Use of Past Environments*, ed. by D. Cosgrove and S. Daniels, Cambridge, 1988, 277–312.

BIBLIOGRAPHY   241

Harley, J. B., *The New Nature of Maps: Essays in the History of Cartography*, ed. by P. Laxton, Baltimore, MD, 2002.

Harvey, M. M., 'Martin V and the English, 1422–1431', in *Religious Belief and Ecclesiastical Careers in Late Medieval England*, ed. by C. Harper-Bill, Woodbridge, 1989, 59–86.

Harvey, P. D. A., *The History of Topographical Maps: Symbols, Pictures and Surveys*, London, 1980.

Harvey, P. D. A., 'Local and Regional Cartography in Medieval Europe', in *The History of Cartography* (vol. II), ed. by J. B. Harley and D. Woodward, Chicago, 1987, 464–501.

Hattori, Y., 'Community, Communication, and Political Integration in the Late Medieval Alpine Regions: Survey from a Comparative Viewpoint', in *Communities and Conflicts in the Alps from the Late Middle Ages to Early Modernity*, ed. by M. Bellabarba, H. Obermair, and H. Sato, Bologna, 2015, 13–38.

Haubrichs, W. and R. Schneider (eds.), *Grenzen und Grenzregionen*, Saarbrücken, 1994.

Head, R., 'Knowing like a State: The Transformation of Political Knowledge in Swiss Archives, 1450–1770', *The Journal of Modern History*, 75/4 (2003), 749–51.

Head, R. (ed.), *Archival Knowledge Cultures in Europe, 1400–1900*, special issue of *Archival Science*, 10/3 (2010).

Herbers, K. and K. Wolf (eds.), *Southern Italy as Contact Area and Border Region during the Early Middle Ages*, Cologne, 2018.

Herzog, T., *Frontiers of Possession: Spain and Portugal in Europe and the Americas*, Cambridge, MA, 2015.

Hespanha, A. M., 'L'espace politique dans l'Ancien régime', *Boletim da Facultade de Direito Universitade de Coimbra*, 58 (1983), 455–510.

Hiatt, A., *Dislocations: Maps, Classical Tradition, and Spatial Play in the European Middle Ages*, Turnhout, 2020.

Higgs, E., 'Change and Continuity in the Techniques and Technologies of Identification over the Second Christian Millennium', *Identity in the Information Society*, 2/3 (2010), 345–54.

Hindle, S., 'Beating the Bounds of the Parish: Order, Memory and Identity in the English Local Community, c.1500–1700', in *Defining Community in Early Modern Europe*, ed. by M. J. Halvorson and K. E. Spierling, Aldershot, 2008, 205–27.

Holenstein, A., '*Rinviare ad Supplicandum*. Suppliche, dispense e legislazione di polizia nello Stato di antico regime', in *Forme della comunicazione politica in Europa nei secoli XV–XVIII. Suppliche, gravamina, lettere*, ed. by C. Nuvola and A. Würgler, Bologna, 2004, 177–226.

Holenstein, A., 'Introduction. Empowering Interactions: Looking at Statebuilding from Below', in *Empowering Interactions: Political Cultures and the Emergence of the State in Europe, 1300–1900*, ed. by Id., W. P. Blockmans, and J. Mathieu, London, 2009, 1–31.

Holland, L. A., *Janus and the Bridge*, Rome, 1961.

Hubert, E., 'Identificare per controllare. Lo stato e l'identificazione delle persone nell'Italia comunale e signorile', in *Tra polizie e controllo del territorio: alla ricerca delle discontinuità*, ed. by L. Antonelli and S. Levati, Soveria Mannelli, 2017, 273–90.

242 BIBLIOGRAPHY

Ilardi, V., 'The Banker-Statesman and the Condottiere-Prince: Cosimo de' Medici and Francesco Sforza (1450–1464)', in *Florence and Milan: Comparisons and Relations* (vol. II), ed. by C. H. Smyth and G. Garfagnini, Florence, 1989, 217–39.

Inglese, G., '*Italia* come spazio politico in Machiavelli', in *The Radical Machiavelli*, ed. by F. Del Lucchese, F. Frosini, and V. Morfino, Turnhout, 2015, 73–80.

Isaacs, A. K., 'Sui rapporti interstatali in Italia dal medioevo all'età moderna', in *Origini dello Stato. Processi di formazione statale in Italia fra medioevo ed età moderna*, ed. by G. Chittolini, A. Molho, and P. Schiera, Bologna, 1994, 113–32.

Ivetic, E., *Un confine nel Mediterraneo. L'Adriatico orientale tra Italia e Slavia (1300–1900)*, Rome, 2014.

Iwanczak, W., 'Borders and Borderlines in Medieval Cartography', in *Frontiers in the Middle Ages*, Louvain-la-Neuve, 2006, 661–72.

Janeczek, A., 'Frontiers and Borderlands in Medieval Europe: Introductory Remarks', *Quaestiones Medii Aevi Novae*, 16 (2011), 5–14.

Jones, P. J., *The Italian City-State: From Commune to Signoria*, Oxford, 1997.

Judde de Larivière, C., 'Du sceau au passeport. Genèse des pratiques médiévales de l'identification', in *L'Identification. Genèse d'un travail d'état*, ed. by G. Noiriel, Paris, 2007, 57–78.

Jütte, D., 'Entering a City: On a Lost Early Modern Practice', *Urban History*, 41/2 (2014), 204–27.

Kagan, R. L. and B. Schmidt, 'Maps and the Early Modern State: Official Cartography', in *The History of Cartography* (vol. III), ed. by D. Woodward, Chicago, 2007, 661–79.

Kampmann, C., *Arbiter und Friedensstiftung: Die Auseinandersetzung um den politischen Schiedsrichter im Europa der Frühen Neuzeit*, Paderborn, 2001.

Karp, H. J., *Grenzen in Ostmitteleuropa während des Mittelalters: Ein Beitrag zur Entstehungsgeschichte der Grenzlinie aus dem Grenzsaum*, Cologne, 1972.

Ketelaar, E., 'Archival Turns and Returns: Studies of the Archive', in *Research in the Archival Multiverse*, ed. by A. J. Gilliland, S. McKemmish, and A. J. Lau, Melbourne, 2016, 228–69.

King, M. L., *Venetian Humanism in an Age of Patrician Dominance*, Princeton, NJ, 1986.

Kingston, R., 'Mind over Matter? History and the Spatial Turn', *Cultural and Social History*, 7/1 (2010), 111–21.

Kintzinger, M., 'Cum salvo conductu: Geleit im westeuropäischen Spätmittelalter', in *Gesandtschafts- und Botenwesen im spätmittelalterlichen Europa*, ed. by R. C. Schwinges and K. Wriedt, Ostfildern, 2003, 313–63.

Klauser, F. R., 'Thinking through Territoriality: Introducing Claude Raffestin to Anglophone Sociospatial Theory', *Environment and Planning D: Society and Space*, 30/1 (2012), 106–20.

Knapton, M., 'Il Consiglio dei Dieci nel governo della terraferma. Un'ipotesi interpretativa per il secondo '400', in *Venezia e la Terraferma attraverso le relazioni dei Rettori*, ed. by A. Tagliaferri, Milan, 1981, 237–60.

Knapton, M., 'Il fisco nello stato veneziano di terraferma tra '300 e '500. La politica delle entrate', in *Il sistema fiscale veneto. Problemi e aspetti, XV–XVIII secolo*, ed. by G. Borelli, P. Lanaro, and F. Vecchiato, Verona, 1982, 15–57.

BIBLIOGRAPHY 243

Knapton, M., 'Le istituzioni centrali per l'amministrazione e il controllo della Terraferma', in *Venezia e le istituzioni di Terraferma*, ed. by G. Ortalli, Bergamo, 1988, 35–56.

Kosto, A. J., 'Ignorance about the Traveler: Documenting Safe Conduct in the European Middle Ages', in *The Dark Side of Knowledge: Histories of Ignorance, 1400 to 1800*, ed. by C. Zwierlein, Leiden, 2016, 269–95.

Kristof, L. K. D., 'The Nature of Frontiers and Boundaries', *Annals of the Association of American Geographers*, 49 (1959), 269–82.

Krocová, M. and M. Řezník, 'Boundaries and Identities in Academic Discourse', in *Crossing Frontiers, Resisting Identities*, ed. by L. Klusakova and I. M. Moll Jaroslav, Pisa, 2010, 5–32.

Kümin, B. (ed.), *Political Space in Pre-Industrial Europe*, Aldershot, 2008.

Kümin, B. and C. Usborne, 'At Home and in the Workplace: A Historical Introduction to the Spatial Turn', *History and Theory*, 52/3 (2013), 305–18.

Lacey, H., 'Protection and Immunity in Later Medieval England', in *Peace and Protection in the Middle Ages*, ed. by T. B. Lambert and D. Rollason, Toronto, 2009, 78–96.

Lamouroux, C., 'Frontières de France, vues de Chine', *Annales. Histoire, Sciences Sociales*, 58/5 (2003), 1029–39.

Lanaro, P., 'At the Centre of the Old World. Reinterpreting Venetian Economic History', in *At the Centre of the Old World: Trade and Manufacturing in Venice and the Venetian Mainland, 1400–1800*, ed. by Ead., Toronto, 2006, 19–69.

Lantschner, P., *The Logic of Political Conflict in Medieval Cities: Italy and the Southern Low Countries, 1370–1440*, Oxford, 2015.

Law, J. E., 'Verona and the Venetian State in the Fifteenth Century', *Bulletin of the Institute of Historical Research*, 52/125 (1979), 9–22.

Law, J. E., 'Relations between Venice and the Provinces of the Mainland', in *Componenti storico-artistiche e culturali a Venezia nei secoli XIII e XIV*, ed. by M. Muraro, Venice, 1981, 78–85.

Law, J. E., 'Un confronto fra due stati *rinascimentali*: Venezia e il domino sforzesco', in *Gli Sforza a Milano e in Lombardia e i loro rapporti con gli stati italiani ed europei (1450–1535)*, ed. by G. Chittolini, G. Peyronnet, and G. Airaldi, Milan, 1982, 397–414.

Lazzari, T., Campagne senza città e territori senza centro. Per un riesame dell'organizzazione del territorio della penisola italiana fra tardo-antico e alto medioevo (secoli VI–X), in *Città e campagna nei secoli altomedievali*, Spoleto, 2009, 622–51.

Lazzarini, I., 'L'informazione politico-diplomatica nell'età della pace di Lodi: raccolta, selezione, trasmissione. Spunti di ricerca dal carteggio Milano-Mantova nella prima età sforzesca (1450–1466)', *Nuova rivista storica*, 83/2 (1999), 247–80.

Lazzarini, I., 'La nomination des officiers dans les états italiens du bas Moyen Âge. Pour une histoire documentaire des institutions', *Bibliothèque de l'École des Chartes*, 159/2 (2001), 389–412.

Lazzarini, I., 'Transformations documentaires et analyses narratives au xVe siècle. Les Principautés de la plaine du Po sub specie scripturarum', *Mélanges de l'École française de Rome (Moyen Âge)*, 113 (2001), 699–721.

244 BIBLIOGRAPHY

Lazzarini, I., 'Materiali per una didattica delle scritture pubbliche di cancelleria nell'Italia del Quattrocento', *Scrineum–Rivista*, 2 (2004), 1–85.

Lazzarini, I., 'Ludovico III Gonzaga, marchese di Mantova', in *Dizionario biografico degli italiani* (vol. LXVI), Rome, 2006, 417–26.

Lazzarini, I., 'Introduzione: Scritture e potere. Pratiche documentarie e forme di governo nell'Italia tardomedievale (XIV–XV secolo)', in *Reti medievali*, 9 (2008), 1–10.

Lazzarini, I., *Il linguaggio del territorio fra principe e comunità. Il giuramento di fedeltà a Federico Gonzaga (Mantova 1479)*, Florence, 2009.

Lazzarini, I., 'La conquista di Pisa nel quadro del sistema territoriale italiano. La testimonianza delle cronache', in *Firenze e Pisa dopo il 1406. La creazione di un nuovo spazio regionale*, ed. by S. Tognetti, Florence, 2010, 65–83.

Lazzarini, I., 'Scritture dello spazio e linguaggi del territorio nell'Italia tre-quattrocentesca. Prime riflessioni sulle fonti pubbliche tardomedievali, *Bullettino dell'Istituto storico italiano per il medio evo*, 113 (2011), 137–207.

Lazzarini, I., 'Le pouvoir de l'écriture. Les chancelleries urbaines et la formation des états territoriaux en Italie (XIVe–xVe siècles)', *Histoire Urbaine*, 35/3 (2012), 31–49.

Lazzarini, I., *Communication and Conflict: Italian Diplomacy in the Early Renaissance, 1350–1520*, Oxford, 2015.

Lazzarini, I., 'De la *révolution scripturaire* du Duecento à la fin du Moyen Âge. Pratiques documentaires et analyses historiographiques en Italie', in *Le Moyen Âge dans le texte*, ed. by B. Grévin and A. Mairey, Paris, 2016, 72–101.

Lazzarini, I., 'Lettere, minute, registri. Pratiche della scrittura diplomatica nell'Italia tardomedievale fra storia e paleografia', *Quaderni storici*, 152/2 (2016), 449–70.

Lazzarini, I., 'Records, Politics and Diplomacy: Secretaries and Chanceries in Renaissance Italy (1350–c.1520)', in *Secretaries and Statecraft in the Early Modern World*, ed. by P. M. Dover, Edinburgh, 2016, 16–36.

Lazzarini, I., 'Culture politiche, governo, legittimità nell'Italia tardomedievale e umanistica. Qualche nota per una rilettura', in *Linguaggi e ideologie del Rinascimento monarchico aragonese (1442–1503)*, ed. by F. Delle Donne and A. Iacono, Naples, 2018, 268–79.

Lazzarini, I., 'I nomi dei gatti. Concetti, modelli e interpretazioni nella storiografia politica e istituzionale d'Italia (a proposito di tardo Medioevo e Rinascimento)', *Archivio storico italiano*, 176 (2018), 689–735.

Lazzarini, I., 'La memoria della città. Cronache, scritture e archivi urbani tra tardo medioevo e primo Rinascimento (esempi mantovani)', in *La Fabrique des sociétés médiévales méditerranéennes. Les Moyen Âge de François Menant*, ed. by D. Chamboduc de Saint Pulgent and M. Dejoux, Paris, 2019, 443–52.

Lazzarini, I., 'Registres princiers dans l'Italie septentrionale aux XIVe–xVe siècles. Une première enquête (Milan, Ferrare, Mantoue)', in *L'Art du registre en France, XIIIe–XVIe siècle* (vol. II), ed. by O. Guyotjeannin, Paris, 2019, 421–48.

Lazzarini, I., *A Cultural History of Peace in the Renaissance*, London, 2020.

Lazzarini, I., 'Y a-t-il un état de la Renaissance? Mito e realtà del Rinascimento politico (Italia, 1350–1520 ca.)', in *Al di là del Repubblicanesimo. Modernità politica e origini dello stato*, ed. by G. Cappelli, Naples, 2020, 29–54.

BIBLIOGRAPHY   245

Lazzarini, I., *L'ordine delle scritture. Il linguaggio documentario del potere nell'Italia tardomedievale*, Rome, 2021.

Lazzarini, V., 'Di una carta di Jacopo Dondi e di altre carte del Padovano nel Quattrocento', in *Scritti di paleografia e diplomatica*, ed. by P. Sambin, Padua, 1969, 117–22.

Lazzarini, V., 'I titoli dei Dogi di Venezia', in *Scritti di paleografia e diplomatica*, ed. by P. Sambin, Padua, 1969, 217–26.

Lee, D., *Popular Sovereignty in Early Modern Constitutional Thought*, Oxford, 2016.

Lefebvre, H., *La production de l'espace*, Paris, 1974.

Lesaffer, R., 'The Medieval Canon Law of Contract and Early Modern Treaty Law', *Journal of the History of International Law*, 2 (2002), 178–98.

Leverotti, F., *Diplomazia e governo dello stato. I famigli cavalcanti di Francesco Sforza*, Pisa, 1992.

Leverotti, F., 'Diligentia, obedentia, fides, taciturnitas... cum modestia. La cancelleria segreta nel ducato sforzesco', *Ricerche storiche*, 24/2 (1994), 305–36.

Leverotti, F., 'L'archivio dei Visconti signori di Milano', *Reti medievali*, 9/1 (2008), 1–22.

Leverotti, F., 'La cancelleria dei Visconti e degli Sforza signori di Milano', in *Chancelleries et chanceliers des princes à la fin du Moyen Âge*, ed. by G. Castelnuovo and O. Mattéoni, Chambéry, 2011, 39–52.

Levi, G., 'The Origins of the Modern State and the Microhistorical Perspective', in *Mikrogeschichte, Makrogeschichte: Komplementär oder inkommensurabel?*, ed. by J. Schlumbohm, Göttingen, 1998, 53–82.

Lewis, A. R., 'The Closing of the Mediaeval Frontier, 1250–1350', *Speculum*, 33/4 (1958), 475–83.

Linehan, P., 'Segovia: A Frontier Diocese in the Thirteenth Century', *English Historical Review*, 96 (1981), 481–508.

Longoni, V., *Fonti per la storia dell'alta Valle San Martino.* (vol II), Calolziocorte, 1988.

Lunari, M., 'I decreti visconteo-sforzeschi sul trasporto dei grani (dal codice 1230 della Biblioteca Trivulziana)', in *L'età dei Visconti.Il dominio di Milano fra XIII e XV secolo*, ed. by L. Chiappa Mauri, L. De Angelis Cappabianca, and P. Mainoni, Milan, 1993, 113–29.

Lunari, M., 'Forme di governo nella Milano sforzesca: L'ufficio di provvisione delle biade durante il ducato di Galeazzo Maria Sforza', *Società e storia*, 68/2 (1995), 245–66.

Luzzattov, G., 'L'economia veneziana nei secoli '400 e '500', *Bergomum*, 58/2 (1964), 59–71.

MacKay, A., *Spain in the Middle Ages: From Frontier to Empire 1000–1500*, London, 1977.

Magni, S. G., 'Politica degli approvvigionamenti e controllo del commercio dei cereali nell'Italia dei comuni nel XIII e XIV secolo: alcune questioni preliminari', *Mélanges de l'École française de Rome (Moyen Âge)*, 127/1 (2015).

Maier, C. S., *Once within Borders: Territories of Power, Wealth, and Belonging since 1500*, Cambridge, MA, 2016.

Mainoni, P., *Mercanti lombardi tra Barcellona e Valenza nel basso medioevo*, Bologna, 1982.

246 BIBLIOGRAPHY

Mainoni, P., *Le radici della discordia. Ricerche sulla fiscalità a Bergamo tra XIII e XV secolo*, Milan, 1997.

Mainoni, P., 'La fisionomia economica delle città lombarde dalla fine del Duecento alla prima metà del Trecento. Materiali per un confronto', in *Le città del Mediterraneo all'apogeo dello sviluppo medievale. Aspetti economici e sociali*, Rome, 2003, 387–404.

Mainoni, P., 'Fiscalità signorile e finanza pubblica nello stato visconteo-sforzesco', in *Estados y mercados financieros en el Occidente cristiano (siglos XIII–XVI)*, Pamplona, 2014, 105–55.

Mainoni, P., 'Una fonte per la storia dello stato visconteo-sforzesco: gli statuti dei dazi', in *Honos alit artes. Studi per il settantesimo compleanno di Mario Ascheri* (vol. II), ed. by P. Maffei and G. M. Varanini, Florence, 2014, 69–77.

Mainoni, P., 'The Economy of Renaissance Milan', in *A Companion to Late Medieval and Early Modern Milan: The Dinstinctive Features of an Italian State*, ed. by A. Gamberini, Leiden, 2015, 118–21.

Maire Vigueur, J.-C., 'Révolution documentaire et révolution scripturaire: Le Cas de l'Italie médiévale', *Bibliothèque de l'École de Chartes*, 153 (1995), 177–85.

Malanima, P., 'La formazione di una regione economica: la Toscana nei secoli XIII–XV', *Società e storia*, 6/2 (1983), 229–69.

Mallett, M., *Mercenaries and their Masters: Warfare in Renaissance Italy*, London, 1974.

Mannori, L., 'La nozione di territorio fra antico e nuovo regime. Qualche appunto per uno studio sui modelli tipologici', in *Organizzazione del potere e territorio. Contributi per una lettura storica della spazialità*, ed. by L. Blanco, Milan, 2008, 23–44.

Mantecón Movellás, T. A., 'Frontera(s) e historia(s) en los mundos ibéricos', *Manuscrits: Revista d'Història Moderna*, 32 (2014), 19–32.

Marchetti, P., *De iure finium. Diritto e confini tra tardo medioevo ed età moderna*, Milan, 2001.

Marchetti, P., 'Spazio politico e confini nella scienza giuridica del tardo medioevo', *Reti medievali*, 7/1 (2006), 131–46.

Marchetti, V. (ed.), *Confini dei comuni del territorio di Bergamo (1392–1395)*, Bergamo, 1996.

Margaroli, P., 'L'Italia come percezione di uno spazio politico unitario negli anni Cinquanta del Quattrocento', *Nuova rivista storica*, 74 (1990), 517–36.

Margaroli, P., *Diplomazia e stati rinascimentali. Le ambascerie sforzesche fino alla conclusione della Lega italica (1450–1455)*, Florence, 1992.

Marino, J., 'Administrative Mapping in the Italian States', in *Monarchs, Ministers and Maps: The Emergence of Cartography as a Tool of Government in Early Modern Europe*, ed. by D. Buisseret, Chicago, 1992, 5–25.

Martin, J. J., 'The Venetian Territorial State: Constructing Boundaries in the Shadow of Spain', in *Spain in Italy: Politics, Society, and Religion, 1500–1700*, ed. by T. J. Dandelet and J. A. Marino, Leiden, 2007, 227–48.

Martoccio, M., 'The Art of Mercato: Buying City-States in Renaissance Tuscany', *Past & Present*, 252/1 (2021), 53–99.

BIBLIOGRAPHY   247

Martone, L., *Arbiter/Arbitrator. Forme di giustizia privata nell'età del diritto comune*, Naples, 1984.

Mattingly, G., *Renaissance Diplomacy*, Boston, MA, 1955.

Mazzacane, A., 'Lo stato e il dominio nei giuristi veneti durante il secolo della Terraferma', in *Storia della cultura veneta* (vol. III), ed. by G. Arnaldi and M. Pastore Stocci, Vicenza, 1980, 577–650.

Mazzi, A., 'Zogno diviso tra guelfi e ghibellini', *Bollettino della Civica Biblioteca di Bergamo*, 11/1 (1917), 22–4.

Mazzi, A., 'I confini dei comuni del contado. Materiali per un atlante storico del Bergamasco', *Bergomum*, 16/1 (1922), 1–50.

Mazzi, G., 'Agli esordi della difesa. I primi interventi della Serenissima nei settori meridionali dello stato', *L'ambiente storico*, 10–11 (1987), 13–31.

Mazzi, G., 'La conoscenza per l'organizzazione delle difese', in *L'immagine del Veneto: Il territorio nella cartografia di ieri e oggi*, ed. by P. L. Fantelli, Padua, 1994, 117–23.

Mazzi, G., 'Governo del territorio e cartografia veneta tra Quattrocento e Cinquecento', in *Verona e il suo territorio nel Quattrocento. Studi sulla carta dell'Almagià*, ed. by S. Lodi and G. M. Varanini, Verona, 2014, 19–60.

Meccarelli, M., 'The Assumed Space: Pre-reflective Spatiality and Doctrinal Configurations in Juridical Experience', *Zeitschrift des Max-Planck-Instituts für europäische Rechtsgeschichte*, 23 (2015), 241–52.

Medin, A., 'Descrizione della città e terre bresciane nel 1493', *Archivio storico lombardo*, 13/3 (1886), 676–86.

Medolago, G., 'Abitati scomparsi nel basso medioevo presso l'Adda (Cremellina, Brivio Bergamasco, Lueno)', *Abelàse*, 1/1 (2006), 60–86.

Medolago, G., 'La comunità di Val Brembana Oltre la Goggia', in *Naturalmente divisi: Storia e autonomia delle antiche comunità alpine*, ed. by L. Giarelli, Tricase, 2013, 153–72.

Medolago, G., F. Oriani, and M. Sampietro, 'La Valsassina all'epoca della formulazione degli statuti', in *Gli statuti della Valsassina. Le norme della Comunità del 1388*, Lecco, 2008, 15–45.

Menant, F., *Campagnes lombardes au Moyen Âge. L'économie et la sociétéé rurales dans la région de Bergame, de Crémone et de Brescia du Xe au XIIIe siècle*, Rome, 1993.

Meron, T., 'The Authority to Make Treaties in the Late Middle Ages', *The American Journal of International Law*, 89/1 (1995), 1–20.

Meroni, E., 'Le parrocchie bergamasche di Valtorta, Valle Averara e Valtaleggio di rito ambrosiano già appartenenti alla Diocesi di Milano', *Memorie storiche della Diocesi di Milano*, 7 (1960), 93–116.

Meyer, A., 'Hereditary Laws and City Topography: On the Development of the Italian Notarial Archives in the Late Middle Ages', in *Urban Space in the Middle Ages and the Early Modern Age*, ed. by A. Classen and M. Sandidge, Berlin, 2009, 225–43.

Milanesi, M., 'La rappresentazione cartografica della regione. Dal medioevo al catasto teresiano', in *Commercio in Lombardia* (vol. I), ed. by G. Taborelli, Milan, 1986, 26–55.

248 BIBLIOGRAPHY

Milanesi, M., 'La cartografia italiana nel Medio Evo e nel Rinascimento', in *La cartografia italiana*, by Ead., V. Valerio, E. Casti, and L. Rombai, Barcelona 1993, 15–80.

Milanesi, M., 'Cartografia per un principe senza corte'. Venezia nel Quattrocento', *Micrologus*, 16 (2008), 189–216.

Milanesi, M., 'Nelle stanze di palazzo. Venezia, Firenze, Roma: qualche confronto', in *Cristoforo Sorte e il suo tempo*, ed. by S. Salgaro, Bologna, 2012, 97–117.

Milanesi, M., 'Introduzione', in *Verona e il suo territorio nel Quattrocento. Studi sulla carta dell'Almagià*, ed. by S. Lodi and G. M. Varanini, Verona, 2014, 7–15.

Milani, G., 'Lo sviluppo della giurisdizione nei comuni italiani del secolo XII', in *Praxis der Gerichtsbarkeit in europäischen Städten des Spätmittelalters*, ed. by F.-J. Arlinghaus, I. Baumgärtner, V. Colli, S. Lepsius, and T. Wetzstein, Frankfurt, 2006, 21–45.

Milani, G., 'Diritto e potere nel secolo XII. I giuristi, la *iurisdictio* e il fondamento ideologico dell'istituzione comunale in alcuni studi recenti', *Eadem Utraque Europa*, 7 (2008), 86–106.

Millet, H. (ed.), *Suppliques et requêtes. Le Gouvernement par la grâce en Occident (XIIe–XVe siècle)*, Rome, 2003.

Mineo, E. I., *Nobiltà di stato. Famiglie e identità aristocratiche nel tardo medioevo: La Sicilia*, Rome, 2001.

Mongiano, E., 'Delimitare e governare le frontiere. Le istituzioni per i confini nello stato sabaudo del secolo XVIII', in *Rappresentare uno stato. Carte e cartografi degli Stati sabaudi dal XVI al XVIII secolo*, ed. by R. Comba and P. Sereno, Turin, 2002, 165–78.

Montanari, D., *Quelle terre di là dal Mincio. Brescia e il contado in età veneta*, Brescia, 2005.

Montanari, D. (ed.), *Sommersi e sopravvissuti. Istituzioni nobiliari e potere nella Brescia veneta*, Brescia, 2017.

Morse, V., 'The Role of Maps in Later Medieval Society: Twelfth to Fourteenth Century', in *The History of Cartography* (vol. III), ed. by D. Woodward, Chicago, 2007, 25–52.

Müller, U., *Das Geleit im Deutschordensland Preußen*, Cologne, 1991.

Najemy, J. M., 'Stato, comune e *universitas*', *Annali dell'Istituto storico italo-germanico*, 20 (1994), 245–63.

Nardini, F., 'I signori della pianura. Potenza, proprietà, imprese dei Martinengo', in *Atlante della Bassa* (vol. I), Brescia, 1984, 85–100.

Nash, C., 'Performativity in Practice: Some Recent Work in Cultural Geography', *Progress in Human Geography*, 24/4 (2000), 653–64.

Newman, D., 'Territory, Compartments and Borders: Avoiding the Trap of the Territorial Trap', *Geopolitics*, 15/4 (2010), 773–8.

Nobili, P. G., 'Appartenenze e delimitazioni. Vincoli di vicinantia e definizioni dei confini del territorio bergamasco nel secondo terzo del Duecento', *Quaderni di Archivio bergamasco*, 3 (2010), 44–60.

Nobili, P. G., 'I contadi organizzati. Amministrazione e territorialità dei *comuni rurali* in quattro distretti lombardi (1210–1250 circa)', *Reti medievali*, 14/1 (2013), 81–130.

BIBLIOGRAPHY 249

Noiriel, G., 'Surveiller les déplacements ou identifier les personnes? Contribution à l'histoire du passeport en France de la Ie à la IIIe République', *Genèses*, 30 (1998), 77–100.

Nora, P. (ed.), *Les lieux de mémoire* (7 vols.), Paris, 1984–92.

Nora, P., 'Between Memory and History: *Les Lieux de Mémoire*', *Representations*, 26/2 (1989), 7–24.

Nordman, D., 'Frontiere e confini in Francia: evoluzione dei termini e dei concetti', in *La frontiera da stato a nazione: il caso Piemonte*, ed. by C. Ossola, C. Raffestin, and M. Ricciardi, Rome, 1987, 39–56.

Nordman, D., 'Sauf-conduits et passeports, en France, à la Renaissance', in *Voyager à la Renaissance*, ed. by J. Céard and J.-C. Margolin, Paris, 1987, 145–58.

Nordman, D., *Frontières de France. De l'espace au territoire, XVIe–XIXe siècle*, Paris, 1998.

Novak, P., 'The Flexible Territoriality of Borders', *Geopolitics*, 16/4 (2011), 741–67.

Nubola, C., 'Supplications between Politics and Justice: The Northern and Central Italian States in the Early Modern Age', *International Review of Social History*, 46/Supplement (2001), 35–56.

O'Connell, M., 'Voluntary Submission and the Ideology of Venetian Empire', *I Tatti Studies in the Italian Renaissance*, 20/1 (2017), 9–39.

Oscar, P. and O. Belotti (eds.), *Atlante storico del territorio bergamasco. Geografia delle circoscrizioni comunali e sovracomunali dalla fine del XIV secolo a oggi*, Bergamo, 2000.

O'Toole, J. M., 'The Symbolic Significance of Archives', *The American Archivist*, 56/2 (1993), 234–55.

Paasi, A., 'Boundaries as Social Processes: Territoriality in the World of Flows', *Geopolitics*, 3/1 (1998), 69–88.

Paasi, A., 'Fences and Neighbours in the Postmodern World: Boundary Narratives in Political Geography', *Progress in Human Geography*, 22/2 (1998), 186–207.

Paasi, A., 'Bounded Spaces in a *Borderless World*: Border Studies, Power and the Anatomy of Territory', *Journal of Power*, 2/2 (2009), 213–34.

Padrón, R., 'Charting Shores', in *Mapping Latin America: A Cartographic Reader*, ed. by J. Dym and K. Offen, Chicago, 2007, 33–7.

Pagani, L., 'Bergamo *Terra di San Marco*. Processi territoriali nei secoli XV–XVIII', in *Storia economica e sociale di Bergamo* (vol. III), ed. by A. De Maddalena, M. Cattini, and M. A. Romani, Bergamo, 1995, 10–57.

Paganini, C., 'Notule sulle vicende dei trasporti dei generi alimentari in Lombardia (secoli XIV–XVII)', in *Gli archivi per la storia dell'alimentazione* (vol. II), Rome, 1995, 1086–119.

Pagnoni, F., 'Notariato, fazione. Canali di mobilità sociale a Brescia tra XIV e XVI secolo', in *La mobilità sociale nel Medioevo italiano* (vol. II), ed. by A. Gamberini, Rome, 2017, 165–87.

Pal, M., *Jurisdictional Accumulation: An Early Modern History of Law, Empires, and Capital*, Cambridge, 2020.

Partner, P., *The Papal State under Martin V: The Administration and Government of the Temporal Power in the Early Fifteenth Century*, London, 1958.

250 BIBLIOGRAPHY

Parzani, D., 'Il territorio di Brescia intorno alla metà del Quattrocento', *Studi Bresciani*, 12 (1983), 49–74.

Parziale, L., *Nutrire la città. Produzione e commercio alimentare a Milano tra Cinque e Seicento*, Milan, 2009.

Pasero, C., 'Dati statistici e notizie intorno al movimento della popolazione bresciana durante il dominio veneto (1426–1797)', *Archivio storico lombardo*, 88 (1961), 71–97.

Pasero, C., 'Il dominio veneto fino all'incendio della Loggia', in *Storia di Brescia* (vol. II), Brescia, 1963, 3–79.

Paviot, J., 'Les cartes et leur utilisation à la fin du Moyen Âge. L'Exemple des principautés bourguignonnes et angevines', *Itineraria*, 2 (2003), 201–28.

Pavone, C., 'Ma poi è tanto pacifico che l'archivio rispecchi l'istituto?', *Rassegna degli archivi di Stato*, 30/1 (1970), 145–9.

Pederzani, I., *Venezia e lo Stado de Terraferma. Il governo delle Comunità nel Territorio Bergamasco (secc. XV–XVIII)*, Milan, 1992.

Pensa, P., 'Lecco e la Valsassina durante l'ultimo cinquantennio del ducato visconteo', *Periodico della Società storica comense*, 41 (1967), 75–101.

Péquignot, S. and P. Save, *Annexer? Les Déplacements de frontières à la fin du Moyen Âge*, Rennes, 2018.

Perrier Bruslé, L., 'The Border as a Marker of Territoriality: Multi-Scalar Perspectives and Multi-Agent Processes in a South American Borderland Region', *Geopolitics*, 18/3 (2013), 584–611.

Perrin, J. W., 'Azo, Roman Law, and Sovereign European States', *Studia Gratiana*, 15 (1972), 88–191.

Pesenti, G. and F. Carminati, *Valle Brembana antica terra di frontiera*, Bergamo, 1999.

Peters, E., 'Omnia permixta sunt: Where's the Border?', *Medieval History Journal*, 4/1 (2004), 109–27.

Petralia, G., 'Stato e *moderno* in Italia e nel Rinascimento', *Storica*, 8/3 (1997), 7–48.

Peyronel, G., 'Un fronte di guerra nel Rinascimento. Esercito sforzesco e comunità bresciane nella campagna del 1452–1453', *Nuova rivista storica*, 73/5–6 (1989), 537–608.

Peyronel, G., 'Un virtuose de la guerre et de la paix au quattrocento: François Sforza', *Fifteenth Century Studies*, 19/1 (1992), 191–208.

Peyronel, G., *Una finanza d'ancien régime. La repubblica veneta tra XV e XVIII secolo*, Naples, 2006.

Pezzolo, L., *Il fisco dei veneziani. Finanza pubblica ed economica tra XV e XVII secolo*, Verona, 2003.

Piccaluga, G., Terminus. *I segni di confine nella religione romana*, Rome, 1974.

Pichon, M., 'Espace vécu, perceptions, cartes mentales. L'Émergence d'un intérêt pour les représentations symboliques dans la géographie française (1966–1985)', *Bulletin de l'Association de géographes français*, 92/1 (2015), 95–110.

Piffanelli, L., 'Crossing Boundaries: A Problem of Territoriality in Renaissance Italy', *Viator*, 49/3 (2018), 245–75.

Piffanelli, L., *Politica e diplomazia nell'Italia del primo Rinascimento. Per uno studio della guerra* contra et adversus dominum ducem Mediolani, Rome, 2020.

BIBLIOGRAPHY 251

Pirillo, P., 'Fines, termini et limites. I confini nella formazione dello Stato fiorentino', *Reti medievali*, 7/1 (2006), 179–90.

Pirillo, P. and L. Tanzini (eds.) *Terre di confine tra Toscana, Romagna e Umbria. Dinamiche politiche, assetti amministrativi, società locali (secoli XII–XVI)*, Florence, 2020.

Pirovano, C., 'Carta militare della Lombardia', in *Segni e sogni della terra. Il disegno del mondo dal mito di Atlante alla geografia delle reti*, Milan, 2001, 174–8.

Pitteri, M., 'I confini della Repubblica di Venezia. Linee generali di politica confinaria (1554–1786)', in *Alle frontiere della Lombardia. Politica, guerra e religione nell'età moderna*, ed. by C. Donati, Milan, 2006, 259–88.

Portet, P., 'La mesure géométrique des champs au Moyen Âge (France, Catalogne, Italie, Angleterre). État des lieux et voies de recherche', in *Terriers et plans-terriers du XIIIe au XVIIIe siècle*, ed. by G. Brunel, O. Guyotjeannin, and J.-M Moriceau, Rennes and Paris, 2002, 243–66.

Povolo, C., 'Centro e periferia nella Repubblica di Venezia. Un profilo', in *Origini dello stato. Processi di formazione statale in Italia fra medioevo ed età moderna*, ed. by G. Chittolini, A. Molho, and P. Schiera, Bologna, 1994, 207–21.

Povolo, C., 'Un sistema giuridico repubblicano: Venezia e il suo stato territoriale (secoli XV–XVIII)', in *Il diritto patrio tra diritto comune e codificazione (secoli XVI–XIX)*, ed. by I. Birocchi and A. Mattone, Rome, 2006, 297–353.

Power, D. and N. Standen (eds.), *Frontiers in Question: Eurasian Borderlands, 700–1700*, Basingstoke, 1999.

Pozza, M., 'La Cancelleria', in *Storia di Venezia dalle origini alla caduta della Serenissima* (vol. III), ed. by G. Arnaldi, G. Cracco, and A. Tenenti, Rome, 1997, 365–87.

Provero, L., 'Una cultura dei confini. Liti, inchieste e testimonianze nel Piemonte del Duecento', *Reti medievali*, 7/1 (2006), 1–19.

Provero, L., *Le parole dei sudditi. Azioni e scritture della politica contadina nel Duecento*, Spoleto, 2012.

Pucci Donati, F., *Il mercato del pane. Politiche alimentari e consumi cerealicoli a Bologna fra Due e Trecento*, Bologna, 2014.

Pult Quaglia, A. M., 'Early Modern Tuscany: 'Regional' Borders and Internal Boundaries', in *Frontiers, Regions and Identities in Europe*, ed. by S. G. Ellis and R. Eβer, Pisa, 2009, 129–42.

Puppi, L., 'Appunti in margine all'immagine di Padova e il suo territorio secondo alcuni documenti della cartografia tra '400 e '500', in *Dopo Mantegna. Arte a Padova e nel territorio*, Milan, 1978, 163–5.

Purpura, G., '*Passaporti* Romani', *Aegyptus*, 82/1–2 (2002), 131–55.

Quaglioni, D., 'Das Publikum der Legisten im 14. Jahrhundert: Die *Leser* des Bartolus von Saxoferrato', in *Das Publikum politischer Theorie im 14. Jahrhundert*, ed. by J. Miethke, Munich, 1992, 93–110.

Quaglioni, D., 'Giurisdizione e territorio in una *quaestio* di Bartolo da Sassoferrato', *Archivio Scialoja-Bolla*, 2/1 (2004), 1–16.

Quantin, P. M., Universitas. *Expressions du mouvement communautaire dans le Moyen-Âge latin*, Paris, 1970.

252 BIBLIOGRAPHY

Radcliffe, S. A., 'Marking the Boundaries between the Community, the State and History in the Andes', *Journal of Latin American Studies*, 22 (1990), 575–94.

Raffestin, C., *Pour une géographie du pouvoir*, Paris, 1980.

Raggio, O., 'Visto dalla periferia. Formazioni politiche di antico regime e Stato moderno', in *Storia d'Europa* (vol. IV), ed. by M. Aymard, Turin, 1995, 483–527.

Raggio, O., 'Immagini e verità. Pratiche sociali, fatti giuridici e tecniche cartografiche', *Quaderni storici*, 36/3 (2001), 843–76.

Rao, R., 'Le inchieste patrimoniali nei comuni dell'Italia settentrionale (XII–XIV secolo)', in *Quand gouverner, c'est enquêter. Les Pratiques politiques de l'enquête princière (Occident, XIIIe–XIVe siècles)*, ed. by T. Pécout, Paris, 2010, 285–96.

Ratzel, F., *Anthropo-Geographie oder Grundzüge der Anwendung der Erdkunde auf die Geschichte*, Stuttgart, 1882.

Ratzel, F., *Politische Geographie*, Munich and Leipzig, 1897.

Raviola, B. A., 'Frontiere regionali, nazionali e storiografiche: bilancio di un progetto di ricerca e ipotesi di un suo sviluppo', *Rivista storica italiana*, 121/1 (2009), 193–202.

Redon, O., *Lo spazio di una città. Siena e la Toscana meridionale (secoli XIII–XIV)*, Rome, 1999.

Revel, J., 'Knowledge of the Territory', *Science in Context*, 4/1 (1991), 133–62.

Ricci, G., 'Cataloghi di città, stereotipi etnici e gerarchie urbane nell'Italia di antico regime', *Storia urbana*, 18 (1982), 3–33.

Rizzo, A., 'Travelling and Trading through Mamluk Territory: Chancery Documents Guaranteeing Mobility to Christian Merchants', in *History and Society during the Mamluk Period (1250–1517)*, ed. by B. J. Walker and A. Al Ghouz, Göttingen, 2021, 487–510.

Romano, D., *The Likeness of Venice: A Life of Doge Francesco Foscari, 1373–1457*, New Haven, CT, 2007.

Rombai, L., 'Cartografia e uso del territorio in Italia. La Toscana fiorentina e lucchese, realtà regionale rappresentativa dell'Italia centrale, in *La cartografia italiana*, ed. by Id., M. Milanesi, V. Valerio, and E. Casti Moreschi, Barcelona, 1993, 105–46.

Rombaldi, O., 'Carpineti nel medioevo', in *Carpineti medievale*, ed. by G. Badini, Reggio Emilia, 1976, 53–181.

Romiti, A., 'Riflessioni sul significato del vincolo nella definizione del concetto di archivio', in *Studi in onore di Arnaldo D'Addario*, ed. by L. Borgia, Lecce, 1995, 1–18.

Roncai, L. and E. Edallo, 'Un territorio in forma di città', *Insula Fulcheria*, 40/1 (2010), 102–19.

Roveda, E., 'Allevamento e transumanza nella pianura lombarda. I Bergamaschi nel Pavese tra '400 e '500', *Nuova rivista storica*, 71 (1985), 49–70.

Rovere, A., 'I *libri iurium* dell'Italia comunale', *Atti della Società ligure di storia patria*, 29/2 (1989), 157–99.

Rovere, A., Tipologie documentali nei *libri iurium* dell'Italia comunale, in *La Diplomatique urbaine en Europe au Moyen Âge*, ed. by W. Prevenier and T. de Hemptinne, Louvain and Apeldoorn, 2000, 417–36.

Rubinstein, N., 'Italian Reactions to Terraferma Expansion in the Ffteenth Century', in *Renaissance Venice*, ed. by J. R. Hale, London, 1973, 197–217.

BIBLIOGRAPHY 253

Ruggie, J. G., 'Territoriality and Beyond: Problematizing Modernity in International Relations', *International Organization*, 47/1, 1993, 139–74.

Ryan, M., 'Bartolus of Sassoferrato and Free Cities. The Alexander Prize Lecture', *Transactions of the Royal Historical Society*, 10 (2000), 65–89.

Sabbatini, R., *L'occhio dell'ambasciatore. L'Europa delle guerre di successione nell'autobiografia dell'inviato lucchese a Vienna*, Milan, 2006.

Sack, R., *Human Territoriality: Its Theory and History*, Cambridge, 1986.

Sahlins, P., *Boundaries: The Making of France and Spain in the Pyrenees*, Berkeley, CA, 1989.

Sahlins, P., 'Repensando Boundaries', in *Fronteras, naciones e identidades. La periferia como centro*, ed. by A. Grimson, Buenos Aires, 1999, 41–9.

Saletti, B., 'How Foreigners Entered Italian Cities in the Fifteenth Century: The Case of Bologna', in *Strangers at the Gate! Multidisciplinary Explorations of Communities, Borders, and Othering in Medieval Western Europe*, ed. by S. C. Thomson, Leiden, 2022, 78–97.

Salmini, C., 'Buildings, Furnishing, Access and Use: Examples from the Archive of the Venetian Chancery from Medieval to Modern Times', in *Archives and the Metropolis*, ed. by M. V. Roberts, London, 1998, 93–108.

Salter, M. B., *Rights of Passage: The Passport in International Relations*, Boulder, CO, 2003.

Salvemini, B., *Il territorio sghembo. Forme e dinamiche degli spazi umani in età moderna: Sondaggi e letture*, Bari, 2006.

Salvemini, G., *Magnati e popolani in Firenze dal 1280 al 1295*, Milan, 1899.

Salvi, S., *Tra privato e pubblico. Notai e professione notarile a Milano (secolo XVIII)*, Milan, 2012.

Sassen, S., 'When Territory Deborders Territoriality', *Territory, Politics, Governance*, 1/1 (2013), 21–45.

Sato, H., 'Fazioni e microfazioni: guelfi e ghibellini nella montagna bergamasca del Trecento', *Bergomum*, 104–5 (2010), 149–70.

Savy, P., 'Gli stati italiani del XV secolo: una proposta sulle tipologie', *Archivio storico italiano*, 163/4 (2005), 735–59.

Schaab, M., 'Gleit und Territorium in Südwestdeutschland', *Zeitschrift für Württembergische Landesgeschichte*, 40 (1981), 398–417.

Schauerte, T., 'Heraldische Fiktion als genealogisches Argument: Anmerkungen zur Wiener Neustädter Wappenwand Friedrichs III. und zu ihrer Nachwirkung bei Maximilian', in *Erzählen und Episteme: Literatur im 16. Jahrhundert*, ed. by B. Kellner, J.-D. Müller, and P. Strohschneider, Tübingen, 2011, 345–64.

Schieweck, S., 'Iberian Frontiers Revisited. Research Traditions and New Approaches', in *Ibero-Mediävistik: Grundlagen, Potentiale und Perspektiven eines internationalen Forschungsfeldes*, ed. by N. Jaspert, Münster, 2021, 237–70.

Schlesser, N. D., 'Frontiers in Medieval French History', *The International History Review*, 6/2 (1984), 159–73.

Schneider, C., 'Types of Peacemakers: Exploring the Authority and Self-Perception of the Early Modern Papacy', in *Cultures of Conflict Resolution in Early Modern Europe*, ed. by S. Cummins and L. Kounine, Farnham, 2015, 77–104.

254 BIBLIOGRAPHY

Scholz, L., *Borders and Freedom of Movement in the Holy Roman Empire*, Oxford, 2020.

Schulz, F., 'Cristoforo Sorte and the Ducal Palace of Venice', *Mitteilungen des Kunsthistorischen Institutes in Florenz*, 10/3 (1962), 193–208.

Schulz, F., 'New Maps and Landscape Drawings by Cristoforo Sorte', *Mitteilungen des Kunsthistorischen Institutes in Florenz*, 20/1 (1976), 107–26.

Schwarz, B., 'Die Organisation der päpstlichen Kurie und die aus dem Schisma herrührenden Probleme', in *Alle origini della nuova Roma*. *Martino V (1417–1431)*, ed. by M. Chiabò, G. D'Alessandro, and P. Piacentini, Rome, 1992, 329–45.

Scott, T., 'The Economic Policies of the Regional City-States of Renaissance Italy. Observations on a Neglected Theme', *Quaderni storici*, 145/1 (2014), 219–64.

Scotti, A., 'La cartografia lombarda: criteri di rappresentazione, uso e destinazione', in *Lombardia. Il territorio, l'ambiente, il paesaggio* (vol. III), ed. by C. Pirovano, Milan, 1983, 37–124.

Seccamani, R., 'Dati e rilievi sui resti della cappella di San Giorgio al Broletto dipinta da Gentile da Fabriano (1414–1419), in *Scritti in onore di Gaetano Panazza*, Brescia, 1994, 143–62.

Seed, P., *Ceremonies of Possession: Europe's Conquest of the New World, 1492–1640*, Cambridge, 1995.

Senatore, F., *Uno mundo de carta: Forme e strutture della diplomazia sforzesca*, Naples, 1999.

Senatore, F., 'Ai confini del *mundo de carta*. Origine e diffusione della lettera cancelleresca italiana (XIII–XVI secolo)', *Reti medievali*, 10 (2009), 48–50.

Sergi, G., 'La territorialità e l'assetto giurisdizionale e amministrativo dello spazio', in *Uomo e spazio nell'alto medioevo*, Spoleto, 2003, 479–501.

Settia, A. A., 'Il distretto pavese nell'età comunale: la creazione di un territorio', in *Storia di Pavia* (vol. III), Pavia, 1992, 117–71.

Settia, A. A., 'Tra Novara e Pavia: il problema dei confini nell'età comunale, in *Insediamenti medievali tra Sesia e Ticino. Problemi istituzionali e sociali (secoli XII–XV)*, ed. by G. Andenna, Novara, 1999, 17–30.

Sidney Woolf, C. N., *Bartolus of Sassoferrato: His Position in the History of Medieval Political Thought*, Cambridge, 1913.

Signaroli, S., 'Per una storia archivistica della cancelleria della Comunità di Valle Camonica', *Archivi*, 7/2 (2012), 69–80.

Silvestri, A., *L'amministrazione del regno di Sicilia. Cancelleria, apparati finanziari e strumenti di governo nel tardo medioevo*, Rome, 2018.

Simmel, G., *Soziologie: Untersuchungen über die Formen der Vergesellschaftung*, Berlin, 1908.

Simonetta M., *Rinascimento segreto. Il mondo del segretario da Petrarca a Machiavelli*, Milan, 2004.

Smail, D. L., 'The Linguistic Cartography of Property and Power in Late Medieval Marseille', in *Medieval Practices of Space*, ed. by B. A. Hanawalt and M. Kobialka, Minneapolis, MN, 2000, 37–63.

Smail, D. L., *Imaginary Cartographies: Possession and Identity in Late Medieval Marseille*, Ithaca, NY, 2000.

BIBLIOGRAPHY 255

Sohn, C., 'Navigating Borders' Multiplicity: The Critical Potential of Assemblage', *Area*, 148/2 (2015), 183–9.

Somaini, F., 'The Collapse of City-States and the Role of Urban Centres in the New Political Geography of Renaissance Italy', in *The Italian Renaissance State*, ed. by A. Gamberini and I. Lazzarini, Cambridge, 2012, 239–60.

Somaini, F., *Geografie politiche italiane tra Medio Evo e Rinascimento*, Milan, 2012.

Somaini, F., 'Territory, Territorialisation, Territoriality: Problems of Definition and Historical Interpretation', *Plurimondi*, 10/1 (2012), 19–47.

Somaini, F., 'Filippo Maria e la svolta del 1435', in *Il ducato di Filippo Maria Visconti, 1412–1447. Economia, politica, cultura*, ed. by F. Cengarle and M. N. Covini, Florence, 2015, 107–66.

Somaini, F. and F. Cengarle, '*Geografie motivazionali* nell'Italia del Quattrocento. Percezioni dello spazio politico peninsulare al tempo della Lega Italica (1454–1455)', *Semestrale di studi e ricerche di geografia*, 28/1 (2016), 43–60.

Star, S. and J. Griesemer, 'Institutional Ecology, *Translations* and Boundary Objects: Amateurs and Professionals in Berkeley's Museum of Vertebrate Zoology, 1907–39', *Social Studies of Science*, 19/3 (1989), 387–420.

Stock, O., 'History and the Uses of Space', in *The Uses of Space in Early Modern History*, ed. by Id., New York, 2015, 1–18.

Stopani, A., 'La memoria dei confini. Giurisdizione e diritti comunitari in Toscana (XVI–XVIII secolo)', *Quaderni storici*, 118/1 (2005), 73–96.

Stopani, A., 'Pratiche di mantenimento del possesso e conflitti intercomunitari. La Toscana di Antico Regime', in *Lo spazio politico locale in età medievale, moderna e contemporanea*, ed. by R. Bordone, P. Guglielmotti, S. Lombardini, and A. Torre, Alessandria, 2007, 135–44.

Storti, F., *El buen marinero. Psicologia politica e ideologia monarchica al tempo di Ferdinando I d'Aragona re di Napoli*, Rome, 2014.

Storti Storchi, C., *Diritto e istituzioni a Bergamo. Dal comune alla signoria*, Milan, 1984.

Storti Storchi, C. (ed.), *Lo statuto di Bergamo del 1331*, Milan, 1986.

Tabacco, G., 'L'allodialità del potere nel Medioevo', *Studi medievali*, 11 (1970), 565–615.

Taddei, G., 'Comuni rurali e centri minori dell'Italia centrale tra XII e XIV sec', *Mélanges de l'École française de Rome (Moyen Âge)*, 123/2 (2011), 319–34.

Taddei, G., 'L'organizzazione del territorio nella Toscana comunale (secc. XII–XIV)', in *Studi in onore di Sergio Gensini*, ed. by F. Ciappi and O. Muzzi, Florence, 2012, 105–36.

Tagliabue, M., 'Come si è costituita la *communitas* di Val S. Martino', in *Atti e memorie del secondo congresso* storico lombardo, Milan, 1938, 73–93.

Tanzini, L., *Dai comuni agli stati territoriali. L'Italia delle città tra XIII e XV secolo*, Noceto, 2010.

Taylor, P. J., 'Embedded Statism and the Social Sciences: Opening Up to New Spaces', *Environment and Planning A: Economy and Space*, 28/11 (1996), 1917–28.

TeBrake, W. H., *Medieval Frontier: Culture and Economy in Rijnland*, Houston, TX, 1985.

256 BIBLIOGRAPHY

Tenenti, A., 'Il potere dogale come rappresentazione', in *Stato: un'idea, una logica*. *Dal comune italiano all'assolutismo francese*, ed. by Id., Bologna, 1987, 193–216.

Thompson, J. W., 'Profitable Fields of Investigation in Medieval History', *American Historical Review*, 18/3 (1913), 490–504.

Tigrino, V., 'Castelli di carte. Giurisdizione e storia locale nel Settecento in una disputa fra Sanremo e Genova (1729–35)', *Quaderni storici*, 101/2 (1999), 475–506.

Tigrino, V., 'Azioni, trascrizioni, archiviazioni: a proposito di confini tra medioevo ed età moderna', *Quaderni storici*, 129/4 (2008), 755–67.

Titone, F., *Governments of the Universitates: Urban Communities of Sicily in the Fourteenth and Fifteenth Centuries*, Turnhout, 2009.

Toffolo, S., 'Cities Dominated by Lions: The Fifteenth-Century Venetian Mainland State Depicted by Inhabitants of the Subject Cities', *Viator*, 46/1 (2015), 305–25.

Toffolo, S., *Describing the City, Describing the State: Representations of Venice and the Venetian Terraferma in the Renaissance*, Leiden, 2020.

Torpey, J., 'Coming and Going: On the State Monopolisation of the Legitimate Means of Movement, *Sociological Theory*, 16/3 (1998), 239–59.

Torpey, J., *The Invention of the Passport: Surveillance, Citizenship and the State*, Cambridge, 2000.

Torre, A., 'La produzione storica dei luoghi', *Quaderni storici*, 37/2 (2002), 443–76.

Torre, A., *Luoghi. La produzione di località in età moderna e contemporanea*, Rome, 2011.

Torró, J., 'Viure del botí. La frontera medieval com a parany historiogràfic', *Recerques: història, economia, cultura*, 46 (2001), 5–52.

Toubert, P., 'Frontière et frontières: un objet historique', in *Castrum* (vol. IV), ed. by J.-M. Poisson, Rome, 1992, 9–17.

Turner, F. J., *The Frontier in American History*, New York, 1921.

Urban, W. L., 'The Frontier Thesis and the Baltic Crusade', in *Crusade and Conversion on the Baltic Frontier, 1150–1500*, ed. by A. V. Murrai, Aldershot, 2001, 45–71.

Vaccari, P., '*Utrum iurisdictio cohaeret territorio*: la dottrina di Bartolo', in *Bartolo da Sassoferrato. Studi e documenti per il VI centario* (vol. II), Milan, 1962, 737–53.

Vaccari, P., *La territorialità come base dell'ordinamento giuridico del contado nell'Italia medievale*, Milan, 1963.

Valerio, V., 'Cartography in the Kingdom of Naples during the Early Modern Period', in *The History of Cartography* (vol. III), ed. by D. Woodward, Chicago, 2007, 940–74.

Valetti Bonini, I., *Le comunità di valle in epoca signorile. L'evoluzione della Comunità di Valcamonica durante la dominazione viscontea (secc. XIV–XV)*, Milan, 1976.

Vallejo, J., 'Power Hierarchies in Medieval Juristic Thought', *Ius Commune* 19 (1992), 1–29.

Vallerani, M., 'Paradigmi dell'eccezione nel tardo medioevo', *Storia del pensiero politico*, 1/2 (2012), 185–211.

Valseriati, E. and A. Viggiano, 'Venezia in Lombardia: rapporti di potere e ideologie di parte (secc. XV–XVI)', in *Fortunato Martinengo. Un gentiluomo del Rinascimento fra arti, lettere e musica*, ed. by M. Bizzarini and E. Selmi, Brescia, 2018, 51–74.

Van Houtum, H., 'The Mask of the Border', in *The Ashgate Research Companion to Border Studies*, ed. by D. Wastl-Walter, Farnham, 2011, 49–61.

BIBLIOGRAPHY 257

Varanini, G. M., 'Ai confini dello stato regionale. Due documenti su castelli e fortificazioni di rifugio nel territorio veronese agli inizi del Quattrocento', in *Per Aldo Gorfer. Studi, profili artistici e bibliografia in occasione del settantesimo compleanno*, ed. by N. Vicenzi, Trento, 1992, 937–73.

Varanini, G. M., 'Il bilancio d'entrata delle Camere fiscali di Terraferma nel 1475–76', in *Comuni cittadini e stato regionale. Ricerche sulla terraferma veneta nel Quattrocento*, Verona, 1992, 73–123.

Varanini, G. M., *Comuni cittadini e stato regionale. Ricerche sulla terraferma veneta nel Quattrocento*, Verona, 1992.

Varanini, G. M., 'L'organizzazione del distretto cittadino nell'Italia padana dei secoli XIII–XIV (Marca Trevigiana, Lombardia, Emilia)', in *L'organizzazione del territorio in Italia e Germania, secoli XIII–XIV*, ed. by G. Chittolini and D. Willoweit, Bologna, 1994, 133–234.

Varanini, G. M., 'La tradizione statutaria della Valle Brembana nel Tre-Quattrocento e lo statuto della Valle Brembana superiore del 1468', in *Gli statuti della Valle Brembana superiore del 1468*, ed. by M. Cortesi, Bergamo, 1994, 13–62.

Varanini, G. M., 'Governi principeschi e modello cittadino di organizzazione del territorio nell'Italia del Quattrocento', in *Principi e città alla fine del medioevo*, ed. by S. Gensini, Pisa, 1996, 95–127.

Varanini, G. M., 'Gli ufficiali veneziani nella Terraferma veneta quattrocentesca', *Annali della classe di lettere e filosofia della Scuola normale superiore*, 4/1 (1997), 155–79.

Varanini, G. M., 'Archivi di famiglie aristocratiche nel Veneto del Trecento e Quattrocento. Appunti', in *Un archivio per la città. Le carte della famiglia Muzani dal recupero alla valorizzazione*, ed. by G. Marcadella, Vicenza, 1999, 24–38.

Varanini, G. M., 'L'organizzazione del territorio in Italia: aspetti e problemi', in *La società medievale*, ed. by S. Collodo and G. Pinto, Bologna, 1999, 133–76.

Varanini, G. M., 'L'invenzione dei confini. Falsificazioni documentarie e identità comunitaria nella montagna veneta alla fine del medioevo e agli inizi dell'età moderna', *Reti medievali*, 7/1 (2006), 1–26.

Varanini, G. M., 'I ghibellini di Belluno e la cancelleria gonzaghesca al momento della prima dedizione a Venezia (maggio 1404)', *Archivio storico di Belluno, Feltre e Cadore*, 78 (2007), 7–16.

Varanini, G. M., 'Considerazioni introduttive: Bergamo e la Montagna nel tardo medioevo. Il territorio orobico fra città e poteri locali', *Bergomum*, 105 (2010), 7–20.

Varanini, G. M., 'La terraferma veneta del Quattrocento e le tendenze recenti della storiografia', in *1509–2009. L'ombra di Agnadello: Venezia e la Terraferma*, ed. by G. Del Torre and A. Viggiano, Venice, 2011, 29–32.

Varanini, G. M., 'Per la storia agraria della pianura bresciana nel Quattrocento. Lo stato degli studi', in *Nell'età di Pandolfo Malatesta, signore a Bergamo, Brescia e Fano agli inizi del Quattrocento*, ed. by G. Chittolini, E. Conti, and M. N. Covini, Brescia, 2012, 83–108.

Varanini, G. M., 'Legittimità implicita dei poteri nell'Italia centro-settentrionale del tardo medioevo', in *La Légitimité implicite* (vol. I), ed. by J.-P. Genet, Rome, 2015, 223–39.

258 BIBLIOGRAPHY

Verga, C., *Crema città murata*, Rome, 1966.

Viggiano, A., *Governanti e governati. Legittimità del potere ed esercizio dell'autorità sovrana nello stato veneto della prima età moderna*, Conegliano, 1993.

Viggiano, A., 'Il Dominio da Terra: politica e istituzioni', in *Storia di Venezia dalle origini alla caduta della Serenissima* (vol. IV), ed. by A. Tenenti and U. Tucci, Rome, 1996, 529–75.

Viggiano, A., 'Le carte della repubblica. Archivi veneziani e governo della Terraferma (secoli XV–XVIII)', in *La documentazione degli organi giudiziari nell'Italia tardomedievale e moderna*, ed. by A. Giorgi, S. Moscadelli, and C. Zarrilli, Rome, 2012, 359–79.

Violante, C., 'La signoria *territoriale* come quadro delle strutture organizzative del contado nella Lombardia del XII secolo', in *Histoire comparée de l'administration* (IVe–XVIIIe siècles), ed. by W. Paravicini and K. F. Werner, Munich, 1980, 333–44.

Viroli, M., *From Politics to Reason of State: The Acquisition and Transformation of the Language of Politics, 1250–1600*, Cambridge, 1992.

Vitale, G., *Ritualità monarchica. Cerimonie e pratiche devozionali nella Napoli aragonese*, Salerno, 2006.

Vitolo, G., *L'Italia delle altre città. Un'immagine del Mezzogiorno medievale*, Naples, 2014.

Von Gierke, O., *Das Deutsche Genossenschaftsrecht*, Berlin, 1868.

Walther, H. G., 'Die Legitimität der Herrschaftsordnung bei Bartolus von Sassoferrato und Baldus de Ubaldis', in *Rechts-Staats-philosophie des Mittelalters*, ed. by E. Mook and G. Wieland, Frankfurt am Main, 1990, 115–39.

Watts, J., 'The Pressure of the Public on Later Medieval Politics', in *Political Culture in Late Medieval Britain*, ed. by L. Clark and C. Carpenter, Woodbridge, 2004, 159–80.

Watts, J., *The Making of Polities: Europe, 1300–1500*, Cambridge, 2009.

Webb, D., 'Italians and Others: Some Quattrocento Views of Nationality', *Studies in Church History*, 18 (1982), 243–60.

Wickham, C., 'Frontiere di villaggio in Toscana nel XII secolo', in *Castrum* (vol. IV), ed. by J.-M. Poisson, Rome, 1992, 239–51.

Wickham, C., *Community and Clientele in Twelfth-Century Tuscany: The Origins of the Rural Commune in the Plain of Lucca*, Oxford, 1998.

Wickham, C., *Courts and Conflict in Twelfth-Century Tuscany*, Oxford, 2003.

Wickham, C., *Sleepwalking into a New World: The Emergence of Italian City Communes in the Twelfth Century*, Princeton, NJ, 2015.

Wiederkehr, G. R., *Das freie Geleit und Seine Erscheinungsformen in der Eidgenossenschaft des Spätmittelalters: Ein Beitrag zu Theorie und Geschichte eines Rechtsbegriffs*, Zurich, 1977.

Wilson, T. M., 'Territoriality Matters in the Anthropology of Borders, Cities and Regions', *Cadernos do Centro de Memória do Oeste de Santa Catarina*, 25/2 (2012), 199–216.

Wolfthal, D. (ed.), *Peace and Negotiation: Strategies for Coexistence in the Middle Ages and the Renaissance*, Turnhout, 2000.

Wood, D., 'P.D.A Harvey and Medieval Mapmaking: An Essay Review', *Cartographica*, 31/3 (1994), 52–9.

BIBLIOGRAPHY 259

Woodward, D., 'Cartography and the Renaissance: Continuity and Change', in *The History of Cartography* (vol. III), ed. by Id., Chicago, 2007, 3–24.

Wurtzel, E., 'City Limits and State Formations: Territorial Jurisdiction in Late Medieval and Early Modern Lille', in *The Power of Space in Late Medieval and Early Modern Europe: The Cities of Italy, Northern France and the Low Countries*, ed. by M. Boone and M. Howell, Turnhout, 2013, 29–42.

Zalin, G., 'Il quadro economico dello stato veneziano tra Quattrocento e Cinquecento', in *L'Europa e la Serenissima: la svolta del 1509. Nel V centenario della battaglia di Agnadello*, ed. by G. Gullino, Venice, 2011, 35–73.

Zamperetti, S., *I piccoli principi. Signorie locali, feudi e comunità soggette nello stato regionale veneto dall'espansione territoriale ai primi decenni del Seicento*, Venice, 1991.

Zamperetti, S., 'Magistrature centrali, rettori e ceti locali nello stato regionale veneto in età moderna', in *Comunità e poteri centrali negli antichi stati italiani. Alle origini dei controlli amministrativi*, ed. by L. Mannori, Naples, 1997, 103–15.

Zamperetti, S., 'Dalla tutela cittadina all'identità politica territoriale. Il governo dei contadi nella Repubblica di Venezia in età moderna', in *Organizzazione del potere e territorio. Contributi per una lettura storica della spazialità*, ed. by L. Blanco, Milan, 2008, 45–56.

Zamperetti, S., 'Vicenza e il Vicentino nello stato veneziano. Una dedizione parentale?', *Studi veneziani*, 65 (2012), 613–24.

Zanichelli, G. Z., 'La committenza dei Rossi: immagini di potere fra sacro e profano', in *Le signorie dei Rossi di Parma tra XIV e XVI secolo*, ed. by L. Arcangeli and M. Gentile, Florence, 2007, 187–212.

Zenobi, L., 'Nascita di un territorio. La vicenda del monte di Brianza tra Trecento e Quattrocento', *Quaderni storici*, 144/3 (2013), 813–57.

Zenobi, L., 'Guerra, stato e poteri locali sul medio corso dell'Adda alla metà del Quattrocento. Organizzazione militare e difesa dei confini', *Società e storia*, 149/3 (2015), 469–91.

Zenobi, L., 'Itinerari di mobilità geografica e sociale nelle e dalle valli bergamasche a seguito dell'espansione veneziana', in *La mobilità sociale nel Medioevo italiano* (vol. II), ed. by A. Gamberini, Rome, 2017, 377–93.

Zenobi, L., 'Beyond the State: Community and Territory-Making in Late Medieval Italy', in *Constructing and Representing Territory in Late Medieval and Early Modern Europe*, ed. by M. Damen and K. Overlaet, Amsterdam, 2022, 53–79.

Ziegler, K.-H., 'The Influence of Medieval Roman Law on Peace Treaties', in *Peace Treaties and International Law in European History: From the Late Middle Ages to World War One*, ed. by R. Lesaffer, Cambridge, 2004, 147–61.

Zorzi, A., *La trasformazione di un quadro politico. Ricerche su politica e giustizia a Firenze dal comune allo Stato territoriale*, Florence, 2008.

4. Unpublished Theses

Carbonara, M., *Between Cartography and Representation: Borders and Maps of Early Modern Bologna and Modena*, doctoral thesis, University of East Anglia, 2016.

260 BIBLIOGRAPHY

Della Mea, E., *La sicurezza incerta del confine orientale. Venezia, Friuli e Istria dalle Guerre d'Italia al progetto di Palmanova*, doctoral thesis, Università degli Studi di Udine, 2016.

Palmer, R. J., *The Control of Plague in Venice and Northern Italy, 1348–1600*, doctoral thesis, University of Kent, 1978.

Parola, S., Per diffender le rexone de sua magnificentia. *I Martinengo di Brescia tra XIV e XVI secolo*, master's thesis, Università degli Studi di Milano, 2017.

Zenobi, L., 'Il rovescio della medaglia. Logistica e organizzazione del contrabbando ai confini', in *Guerra, stato e poteri locali sul medio corso dell'Adda alla metà del Quattrocento. Organizzazione militare e difesa dei confini*, master's thesis, Università degli Studi di Milano, 2014, 81–99.

General Index

For the benefit of digital users, indexed terms that span two pages (e.g., 52–53) may, on occasion, appear on only one of those pages.

Archives:
    Milanese 17–19, 71–2, 134–5, 164–5, 167–70
    Venetian 71–2, 115–16, 129
    Italian 102–3, 184–5
    historiography 159–62

Belonging: *See* Identity
Bridges 119–20, 137–8, 144, 173, 177–8, 204–6

Ceremonies:
    trading territories 61–7
    marking borders 100–9
Church squares 104–6
Customs:
    duties and tolls 127, 135–6, 139–47, 167, 173
    points and barriers 141–4, 146–7
    See also Taxation

Diplomacy: *See* Peace

Enclaves 78–9, 134–5, 137–8, 151, 172–3, 176–7, 207–9
Environment: *See* Natural resources

Feudalism 32–8
Food:
    regulation 141–5
    provision 142, 147–51
    circulation 145–7, 151
    smuggling 143–4, 146–7, 154
    See also Trade licences
Fortifications: *See* War

Gates, of a city 73–7, 142–4, 172–3:
    See also Customs
Geopolitics 8, 49–50, 56–61, 96–7, 108–9, 115–16, 155, 163–4, 167–9

Identity:
    civic 32–3, 189–90
    territorial 41, 65–6
    political 81–2, 87
    personal 127, 138
Information:
    about borders 69, 107, 117–18
    about movement 137–8, 146–7
    See also Knowledge
Infrastructures 78–9, 113, 141, 206–7, 212
International relations: *See* Geopolitics
Itineraries:
    of officials 62, 119–20, 128–9, 131, 134–5
    of exiles 85–6, 128–9, 134
    of notaries 104–6
    of traders 135–6, 139–57
    of troops 128–9, 137
    of the poor 134, 136
    of minorities 136
    of the clergy 137, 150–1
    See also Safe conducts

Justice:
    shaping territories 30, 40–1
    settling disputes 73–7, 139–40

Knowledge, of space 50–1, 62, 107–8, 118, 175–6, 178–9, 184–5, 187–9, 201–2

Landscape: *See* Topography

Maps 12–15, 89–94, 107, 151–5, 186–212:
    See also Records
Materiality:
    of border markers 105–7
    of luxury goods 135–6
    of banners 119–20, 192–3, 206–9
Memory 107–9, 162–76, 206–7

262 GENERAL INDEX

Natural resources:
 usage and exploitation 40–1, 81–2,
  100–2, 107–8
 wool 46–7, 81–2
 metals 46–7, 81–2, 129, 140–1
 lumber 81–2, 100–1, 140–1
 pastures 100–1, 106
 See also Water
Networks:
 of factional allegiance 79–87
 of food trade 139–57
 of borders and border
  markers 106, 139–40
 of roads and waterways 191–2, 207–9

Peace:
 arbitration 50–1, 56
 conflict resolution 120–1
 See also Treaties
Performance:
 marking borders 100–9
 mapping territories 186–200
 See also Memory
Propaganda 57–8, 66–7, 131–2

Records:
 books of borders 31, 103, 113, 171–2
 statutes 40–1, 47–8, 73–7, 114,
  177–8, 193
 letters 37–8, 63, 69–72, 126–7, 131, 135–8,
  145, 154, 165–7, 173, 201–2
 charters 30–1, 52, 86, 169–70, 189–90
 lists 30–1, 59–61, 131–2, 165, 200–1
 registers 31, 63, 116, 128–9, 131, 134,
  145–6, 163, 167–75
 decrees 34–5, 114–15, 142–4, 183–5
 mandates 63, 69–70, 77–8, 165–6
 deeds 87, 102–3, 105–6, 116–17,
  173–5, 214
 petitions 113, 129–31, 134–6, 154, 167
Representation: *See* Maps
Ritual: *See* Ceremonies
Rivers 177–9, 207–8, 209–10:
 See also Water

Roads 72–3, 78–9, 102, 144, 165–6, 173–4,
 178–9, 182–3, 191–2:
 See also Infrastructures

Safe conducts:
 granting 128–31
 revoking 132–3
 applying 134–6
State formation 12–17, 32, 45–6, 111–12,
 217–18

Taxation:
 state revenues 32–3, 36–7, 46–7, 142–3
 fiscal policies 33–40, 139–41
 privileges and exemptions 64–5, 71, 85–6,
  131–2, 140–1, 193–6
 shaping territories 100–1, 107–8, 113–15
 settling disputes 167, 177–8
Topography 6–7, 105–6, 108–9, 182–3,
 191–2, 210–11
Trade licences:
 recording 145–7
 issuing 149–51
 mapping 151–5
Travel: *See* Itineraries
Treaties:
 of Ferrara 50–6, 58–61, 79–80
 of Cremona 55–6, 58, 169–70
 of Lodi 56–61, 77–81, 124–5, 141, 145–6,
  167–70, 173

War:
 soldiers 86, 129, 131–3, 137, 147–50
 fortifications 72–3, 79, 86, 89–90,
  117–20, 177–8
Water:
 milling 119–20, 129
 fishing 119–20, 132–3, 167, 177–8
 sailing 134–5, 173
 routes 134–5, 177–8
 irrigation 167, 191–2
 damaging records 169–70, 209–10
 drawn on maps 183, 189, 204–6
Writing: *See* Records

Index of Names

For the benefit of digital users, indexed terms that span two pages (e.g., 52–53) may, on occasion, appear on only one of those pages.

Abulafia, David (historian) 2–3
Acquate, village near Lecco 72–3, 87–8
Adda, river:
    control 58–9, 64, 134–5
    bridges 119–20, 137, 177–8
    border disputes 117–20, 165–6, 177–8
Adriatic:
    frontier exchanges 4–5, 19–20
    Venetian territories 48–9, 73, 201–2
Agnadello, town of the Cremonese 59
Albergati, Niccolò (papal legate) 51–5, 59, 69–70
Alessandria 36–7
Almagià, Roberto (historian) 186–7, 190
American West 2
Appadurai, Arjun (anthropologist) 99, 107–8
Aragonese (family, kings of Naples) 46, 56–8, 201
Arrigoni (family of the Val Taleggio) 86, 93–5
Asti 186–7, 189–90

Baiedo, fortification in the Val Sassina 72–3, 90–3
Barbo, Paolo (Venetian patrician and diplomat) 63
Bellaviti (family of the Val Taleggio) 86, 93–5
Belluno 65–6
Benagli (family of the Bergamasco) 64–5, 118
Berend, Nora (historian) 2–3
Bergamo:
    Venetian expansion 33–6, 46–8, 50
    Milanese rule 35, 40–1
    territorial negotiations 52–6, 58–61, 63–4
    local nobility 64, 118
    border disputes 69–79
    political factions 79–87
    archival records 104, 113–17, 160–1, 177–9
    movement flows 23–4, 129, 131, 133

    itineraries to and from 134, 136–7
    food supply 149–55
    visual representation 202–3, 210–11
Bertoni, Laura (historian) 141
Bione, village near Lecco 72–3, 87–8
Bishko, Charles (historian) 2
Black, Jane (historian) 53–4
Blockmans, Wim (historian) 111
Bouloux, Natalie (historian) 187–9
Bowd, Stephen (historian) 193
Brescia:
    Venetian expansion 33–4, 46–8, 50
    Milanese rule 35, 40–1
    territorial negotiations 52, 55–6, 59–61, 63–5
    local nobility 64–5, 137–8, 173, 178–9
    political factions 81–2
    movement flows 129, 131, 133–4
    itineraries to and from 137–8, 147–51
    food supply 154–5
    border disputes 167
    visual representation 186–200
Brivio, fortification in the Milanese 178–9
Brumano, village between Bergamo and Lecco 87–95

Caggese, Romolo (historian) 100
Calolzio, village of the Val San Martino 64, 118
Canning, Joseph (historian) 24
Capralba, village near Crema 176–7
Caravaggio, town of the Geradadda 120–1, 150–1
Carmagnola, count of (condottiero) 46
Carraresi (family, lords of Padua) 46, 50–1, 201
Castelleone, village of the Cremonese 133
Casti, Manuela (historian) 183–4
Cattaneo (family of the Bergamasco) 118

264 INDEX OF NAMES

Cengarle, Federica (historian) 34–5
Chabod, Federico (historian) 15
Chittolini, Giorgio (historian) 9–10,
    15–16, 111–12
Como
  city 36–7
  lake 72–3, 115
  territory 104, 140–1
Corti, Giovanni (notary) 64
Costa, Paolo (legal scholar) 26
Covini, Maria Nadia (historian) 178–9
Crema:
  Venetian expansion 46–8, 56, 66–7
  autonomy from Cremona 40, 59
  archival records 172–3, 176–7
  border disputes 120–1
  itineraries to and from 133–8, 149–54
  visual representation 207–9
Cremona:
  territorial negotiations 58–61
  itineraries to and from 132–5, 140–1
  fertile lands 142, 147–51, 154–5
  border disputes 167, 173, 178–9
  visual representation 206

Da Vinci, Leonardo 72–3
De Ubaldis, Baldus (jurist and thinker) 27–8
De Vergottini, Giovanni (historian) 9–10
De Vivo, Filippo (historian) 170
Deleuze, Gilles (philosopher) 99
Della Misericordia, Massimo
  (historian) 102, 139–40, 173–4
Di Giorgio Martini, Francesco (architect and
  cartographer) 201
Dondi, Jacopo (painter and
  cartographer) 201

Elden, Stuart (political theorist) 24
England:
  borders 2, 103
  travel documents 126, 138
Este (family, lords of Ferrara) 50–1, 182–3

Fasano Guarini, Elena (historian) 111–12
Febre, Lucien (historian) 80–1
Federici (family of the Val Camonica) 52
Florence:
  borders 201–3
  dominion 19–20, 56, 58, 85–6
Foscari, Francesco (doge of Venice) 46

Foucault, Michel (philosopher) 99
France:
  borders 3–6
  travel documents 127
  Italian interests 202–3, 206–7
Friuli 46–8

Gambara (family of the Bresciano) 64–5,
  193–6
Gamberini, Andrea (historian) 16, 42
Garati, Martino (jurist and thinker) 42–3
Garda, lake 186–7, 191–2, 206–7
Genoa:
  republic 46, 50–1, 202–3
  doge 149–50
Geradadda:
  territorial negotiations 58–9
  local nobility 137–8
  archival records 176–7
  border disputes 120–1
  itineraries to and from 137
  food supply 150–4
  visual representation 201–2
Germany:
  borders 2
  travel documents 126–7
  traders from 135–6
Giappani, Giovanni (Milanese secretary and
  diplomat) 69–79
Gonzaga (family, lords then marquises of
  Mantua) 202–3, 206
Grendi, Edoardo (historian) 102–3, 112
Groebner, Valentin (historian) 127
Guenée, Bernard (historian) 3–4

Harvey, Paul (historian) 181, 183
Holenstein, André (historian) 111–12

Iseo, lake 191–2

Kosto, Adam (historian) 138

Lazzarini, Isabella (historian) 16, 50–1
Lecco:
  town of the Milanese 40, 53, 64
  strategic importance 72–3, 140–1
  jurisdiction 73–7, 87–8, 94–5
  border disputes 117–18, 172–3
  visual representation 90–3, 187–9,
    209–10

INDEX OF NAMES   265

Lee, Daniel (political scientist) 25–6
Lodi:
  city 36–7
  itineraries to and from 136–7, 151–4
Lord Smail, Daniel (historian) 107
Lucca 46, 202–3
Lunari, Marco (historian) 142–3

Machiavelli, Niccolò 19, 182–3
Mackay, Angus (historian) 2
Maggi, Annibale (architect and
  cartographer) 189–90
Malatesta, Pandolfo (condottiere then lord of
  Bergamo, Brescia, and
  Lecco) 41, 187–9
Mallet, Michael (historian) 58
Mantua:
  marquis 36–7, 149–50, 202–3
  city 184–5, 204–6
Marseilles 107
Martin V (pope) 51
Martinenghi (family of the Bresciano) 64–5,
  137–8, 193–6
Martinengo, town of the Bergamasco 53–6
Mathieu, Jon (historian) 111
Mattingly, Garrett (historian) 45–6
Medici (family, lords of Florence) 56–8
Mincio, river 155, 184–5, 191–2
Monferrato:
  marquis 36–7
  territory 149–54
Monza, town of the Milanese 40
Morosini, Paolo (Venetian patrician and
  humanist) 33–4, 134–5
Morterone, village between Bergamo and
  Lecco 87–95
Mozzanica, village of the Cremonese 59

Naples:
  king 36–7, 46
  kingdom 19–20, 56, 58
  borders 201, 203–4
Nordman, Daniel (historian) 127
Novara 36–7

Of Bologna, Azo (jurist and thinker)
  25–6
Of Sassoferrato, Bartolus (jurist and
  thinker) 26–8, 209–10
Oglio, river 64–5, 167, 173, 191–2

Padua 182–3, 186–7, 189–90
Pandino, town of the Cremonese 59
Parma:
  city 36–7
  fiefs 41–2
  itineraries to and from 154–5
  map 186–7
Pavia:
  city 30–1, 40
  itineraries to and from 150–5
Perledo, village of the Valsassina 115
Piacenza:
  city 36–7
  fiefs 41–2
  itineraries to and from 140–1, 151–5
Pianchello, fortification in the Val
  Taleggio 72–7, 79–87, 93–5
Piccinino, Jacopo (condottiere) 131–3, 137
Piedmont 99, 186–7
Pisato, Giovanni (painter and
  cartographer) 204–7
Pizzino, fortification in the Val Taleggio
  72–7, 79–87, 93–5
Po:
  river and delta 134–5, 201, 204–6
  valley 144–5, 149–55
Pontano, Giovanni (Neapolitan diplomat and
  humanist) 201
Power, Daniel (historian) 4

Raffestin, Claude (geographer) 99
Ravenna 135–6
Reggio:
  territory 16
  fiefs 41–2
  map 197–8
Revel, Jacques (historian) 107
Rivolta, town of the Geradadda 137, 150–1
Romagna 46, 182–3
Rome 58, 201
Rota (family of the Bergamasco) 64, 118
Rovigo 182–3

Sack, Robert (geographer) 7–8
Sahlins, Peter (historian) 4
Salvioni (family of the Val Taleggio)
  86, 93–5
Salzana, river 87–93
Sanudo, Marino (Venetian patrician and
  diarist) 206–7

266 INDEX OF NAMES

Savoy:
  duke of 36–7, 46–7, 50–2
  Bona, duchess of Milan 202–3
Scholz, Luca (historian) 127
Scott, Tom (historian) 155
Sforza (family, condottieri then dukes
  of Milan):
  Francesco
    rising to power 46, 56
    establishing his authority 37–8,
      56–8, 77–8
    dealing with border disputes 59–61,
      64–5, 73, 179
    dealing with movement
      flows 131–2, 137
    dealing with information
      management 164–5, 167–9
  Galeazzo Maria 36–7, 145–6, 168–9,
    202–3
Sicily 4–5
Simonetta, Cicco (first secretary to the
  Sforza) 33–4, 135–6, 164–5,
  167–8, 202–3
Somaini, Francesco (historian) 9–10
Soncino, fortification in the Cremonese 173
Sorte, Cristoforo (engineer and
  cartographer) 185
Sottochiesa, village of the Val Taleggio 79,
  83, 89–95
Spain:
  borders 2, 4–5
  traders from 135–6
  travel documents 126, 138
  Italian interests 160–2
Standen, Naomi (historian) 4

Torre, Angelo (historian) 99, 112
Tortona 36–7
Trentino 47–8
Trevigiano 47–8
Treviglio, town of the Geradadda 150–4
Treviso 206–7
Trezzo, fortification in the Milanese 119–20
Turner, Frederick Jackson (historian) 2
Tuscany:
  war with Milan 46
  political factions 82–3
  rural communities 100
  border disputes 202–3

Vailate, village of the Geradadda 176–7
Val Averara, valley between Bergamo
  and Lecco:
  border disputes 73–9, 87–95
  political factions 83, 86
Val Brembana, valley between Bergamo
  and Lecco:
  border disputes 73, 90–3
  political factions 83, 87
Val Brembilla, valley between Bergamo
  and Lecco:
  border disputes 90–3
  political factions 83
Val Camonica, valley once subject to Brescia:
  separation from the city 52–3
  territorial negotiations 55–6
  social organisation 104
  notaries of the federation 174–5
  visual representation 196–7
Val San Martino, valley between Bergamo
  and Lecco:
  territorial negotiations 53–6, 81–3
  interactions with the locals 117–19
Val Sassina, valley near Lecco:
  local fortifications 72–3
  territorial negotiations 73–7
  political factions 86–8
  social organisation 104
  archival records 115
Val Taleggio, valley between Bergamo
  and Lecco:
  local fortifications 72–7
  territorial negotiations 79–97
  visual representation 209–11
Val Tellina, valley once subject to Como:
  political factions 81–2
  social organisation 104
Val Torta, valley between Bergamo and Lecco:
  border disputes 73–9, 87–95
  political factions 83, 86
  archival records 115
Van Houtum, Henk (geographer) 124
Varanini, Gian Maria (historian) 4–5,
  47–8, 65–6
Varese, town of the Milanese 40
Vedeseta, village of the Val Taleggio
  83–6, 89–95
Vercurago, village of the Val San
  Martino 72–7, 117–18, 172–3

INDEX OF NAMES 267

Verona
  territory 47–8
  borders 185–6
  map 186–7
Vicenza 65–6
Vigevano 40, 147–9
Vimercate, town of the Milanese 40
Violante, Cinzio (historian) 9–10
Visconti (family, lords then dukes of Milan):
  territorial policies 40–2, 52–3, 70–1, 150–1
  economic policies 140–5
  banners 206–9
  Gian Galeazzo
    claims over Lombardy 34–5

consequences of his death 46, 187–9
ruling the Bergamasco 81–3, 114–15
Filippo Maria
  feudal policies 41–2
  waging war 46–7
  making peace 50–1, 53–5
Voghera 40

Wickham, Chris (historian) 100, 102–3
Wood, Daniel (historian) 200–1

Zamperetti, Sergio (historian) 65–6
Zogno, village of the Val Brembana 82–3
Zona (family of the Bergamasco) 118